THE LAW IN PHILOSOPHICAL PERSPECTIVES

THE LAW IN PHILOSOPHICAL PERSPECTIVES

My Philosophy of Law

Edited by

LUC J. WINTGENS

European Academy of Legal Theory
and
the Centre of Legal Theory,
University of Brussels,
Belgium

KLUWER ACADEMIC PUBLISHERS
DORDRECHT / BOSTON / LONDON

A C.I.P. Catalogue record for this book is available from the Library of Congress.

ISBN 0-7923-5796-5

Published by Kluwer Academic Publishers,
P.O. Box 17, 3300 AA Dordrecht, The Netherlands.

Sold and distributed in North, Central and South America
by Kluwer Academic Publishers,
101 Philip Drive, Norwell, MA 02061, U.S.A.

In all other countries, sold and distributed
by Kluwer Academic Publishers,
P.O. Box 322, 3300 AH Dordrecht, The Netherlands.

Printed on acid-free paper

Printed in the Netherlands.

To G.V.
1909 – 1999
for the unconditionality

Table of Contents

Editor's Preface

In the age of collections that is ours, many volumes of collections are published. They contain contributions of several well known authors, and their aim is to present a selective overview of a relevant field of study.

This book has the same purpose. Its aim is to introduce students, scholars and all those interested in current problems of legal theory and legal philosophy to the work of the leading scholars in this field. The large number of publications, both books and articles, that have been produced over the last decades makes it however quite difficult for those who make their first steps in this domain to find firm guidelines.

The book is then new in its genre because of its method. The choice was made not to reprint an example of contributors' earlier basic articles or a part of one of their books. This would only give a partial view of the rich texture of their work. Rather, the authors were asked to make an original synthesis of their own contributions to the field of legal theory and legal philosophy. Brought together in this volume, they constitute a truly *author*-ised view on their work.

This book is also new in that each essay is complemented with bibliographical information in order to encourage further research on the author's work, as it was selected by himself. This will help the reader to make quick progress in familiarising himself with the whole of the published work of the contributors.

The main criterion for selection, as follows from the foregoing, is pedagogical in nature. According to this criterion, the essays should be suitable for assignment and discussion in seminars and courses in law faculties and philosophy and social sciences departments. The authors were asked to formulate the general line of their thought, referring for the development of their argumentation, to their own original publications. Where possible, they have marked important evolutions in their thought as they have noticed these themselves, as well as further developments in their field of research.

Furthermore, the authors were brought together in light of the fact that no important overview of their work is available thus giving them the opportunity to summarise their work in an original contribution. This is the pedagogical purpose of this volume.

Apart from the pedagogical criterion, and apart from the academic achievements and the reputation of the contributors, this volume also provides an extensive range of well known representatives of legal theory from different countries, including Austria, Belgium, Finland, Germany, Great-Britain, Sweden and the United States.

The editor wants to cordially thank all the contributors for their willingness to collaborate on this volume and for their advice and encouragement in putting this volume together. Their work in this project will make it a valuable instrument for all those for whom it is intended.

INTRODUCTION: THE LAW IN PHILOSOPHICAL PERSPECTIVES.

MY PHILOSOPHY OF LAW

LUC J. WINTGENS

UNIVERSITY OF BRUSSELS

Whoever studies or teaches law, whatever branch it might be, will sooner or later face the question "what is law?". When searching for the roots of Modern law, the answer one expects to hear from a civil lawyer is found in article 6 of the Universal Declaration of the Rights of Man and Citizen of August 26 1789: law is the expression of the general will. It is considered to be one of the first steps towards the Modern concept of law. As such, this answer can be considered to be the standard reflex response of lawyers since the start of the Modern age and it is still prevalent in the minds of many among them. It suggests both that law is man-made and the idea that it requires democratic legitimation. It contains the belief in rights that have been consecrated world-wide in constitutions lying at the heart of modern legal orders.

The need for a democratic foundation of the law and the respect of fundamental rights as one of the most deeply rooted convictions of mankind today, has in this century survived the atrocities inflicted by inhuman political regimes. It serves as a paradigm beyond which no political act can ever deserve the term "law".

A further question that comes to the lawyer's mind is no less important than the question dealing with the law's origin. It concerns the question of how to study the law. One way to do so includes studying the authoritative texts containing the rules and judicial decisions that organise social life. This study aims to describe and systemise valid law, which can be considered a current definition of what lawyers call legal science. Legal science, at least in civil law systems, counts as an "authoritative" supplementary source of law, though not an official one.

The crumbling of natural law thinking, in its classical and its rational versions, raised the need in the field of law creation and legal reasoning for new reflection on the foundation and application of law.

If the decision of the majority as the expression of the general will were to be the sole justification for the law's existence, the organisation of society would soon suffer the tyranny of the majority. And seen from that perspective, judicial decisions would seem to be fully justified as deductive applications of established rules.

This *prima facie* satisfactory approach to law in legal practice, however, hides certain deeper complexities regarding a phenomenon of which Kant himself said that those occupied with it were still looking for an satisfactory definition. The approach sketched above reflects a current answer to the question "*Quid sit iuris*", *i.e.* an answer that serves well the needs of legal practice. But is it also an answer to the question "*Quid ius?*". The Kantian answer to this question alludes to the existence of a particular universal standard, serving as a touchstone for the correctness of the law's content. This type of answer, anyhow, seems to be rather problematic nowadays.

How complex the concept of law actually is, becomes apparent once we realise that the search for the law's rational character is not merely a matter of theoretical reason, a situation in which practical philosophy had ran aground since the beginning of Modern times. Above all, law is a matter of practical reasoning, about why and how things ought to be done. The reduction of philosophical matters to objects of theoretical thought – which can be termed "rationalism" – has been felt to be unsatisfactory, at least in the last half of this century. The limits of this approach became clear in the mind after the collapse of the Third Reich, after which a new attempt was made to redefine "law" in terms of the opposition between positivism and jusnaturalism. As it turned out, this oppositional frame for explaining the law's existence and meaning had had its best days.

The breakdown of the jusnaturalistic legitimation of law together with the insight that law, although man-made, cannot have any content as was claimed by Kelsen, presented lawyers with the considerable challenge and responsibility of re-considering the nature of law and legal thought.

This challenge brought philosophical thought to the heart of the problem. As far as law is concerned, the insight gained ground that purely deductive legal thinking was not the only, and certainly not the most satisfactory account of legal (mostly *judicial*) thinking. In this respect, many serious efforts were made to outline new approaches to legal reasoning, with the purpose of prying the locks of legalism.

While freeing legal thought from the chains of legalism – to which the late Judith Shklar contributed decisively in the early 1960s – there was a growing awareness that law needed new justification more ever.

Although during the 1960s and 1970s some parts of society were still charmed by the attractiveness of ideologies – with Marxism in first place – the sudden disappearance of its last symbol – the Berlin wall – was the clearest expression of the weakness of ideologies: the fact that they cannot be penetrated by reason.

The idea that ideologies cannot make the world a better place and that only reason has the ability to do so, strengthens my conviction that, with all the failures this century has experienced, there is good reason to believe that we can enter the next millennium with head erect.

It is from the cradle of this conviction that the idea for this book was born.

Whereas in the preface to his *Rechtslehre* Kant expressed the belief that there are different ways to philosophise but that there is only one path of pure reason and that it was necessary for many attempts to be made in order to arrive at the one true rational system that was his own, this idea has become less acceptable today. The search for a unique concept of law would again condemn practical philosophy, the domain to which law undoubtedly belongs, to the shackles of theoretical thinking.

Instead of a unique, and hence universal, concept of law, valid for all times and places, we nowadays face a plethora of ideas, each corresponding to an acceptable way of organising society. Although this pluralism might fail to satisfy a hard-core Kantian, it does, however, confirm our experience that law is not a science. If law is not a science (like "nature" itself is not a science, but an *object* of science), this does not exclude, however, that a science of law is possible. In civil law systems, this science is commonly labelled "legal dogmatics".

According to Kant's device, to be truly critical, the attitude of the lawyer towards his own activity must include a reflection on its possibility conditions. A science of law, in order to be scientific, requires an inquiry of its theoretical underpinnings. Legal science therefore is not a fortuitous collection of authoritative opinions on the law, being itself an expression of the general will, but is instead a scientifically organised activity, whose epistemological foundations are equally scrutinised by rational inquiry. Legal science, consequently, is a matter of reason.

What about law itself? Since it is not a science, one can ask what its relation with rationality is. The disconnection between theoretical and practical reason in Modern philosophy might lead us to believe that any reflection on the rational nature of law would be merely speculative, since the realm of reason is filled merely with theoretical matters, not with practical affairs.

This is based on a reduction of the nature of reason that is out of place. The suggestion made here, is that law is a practice, subject to the requirements of rational justification. Again, it could be argued that justification is a matter of persuasion, and in a certain sense it is, but that is not all.

It is clear that *rational* argumentation is more demanding since it aims to articulate the reasonable, hence acceptable nature of normative propositions. While using arguments that are open to criticism a proponent shows his readiness to convince his audience, not merely to persuade them.

The idea on which this collection of articles relies is that no single unique theory of law exists, one that by means of rational proof might turn out to be the only acceptable one. Why would it be qualified "acceptable" if it is "proven" to be the only *correct* one?

The life of law, according to a much quoted phrase by O. W. Holmes, has not been logic: it has been experience. This corresponds to my view of law as justification. Holmes' view, however attractive it might seem, must not make us forget that experience as part of our understanding of the law is more than dealing with "just facts". If facts are unmistakably part of the experience, they are also always pre-structured by our way of looking at them, be it in terms of their *relevance* for the outcome of an individual case or as moulded by the rules that make them relevant for the future from the perspective of a new rule. And further, it can be said that there are not pure facts to be found at large in the real world. In the realm of law, they call for legal shape and form, hence for conceptualisation.

Concepts like sovereignty, democracy, justice, rules, property, contract, tort and the like – to mention only the most general ones – are not of a purely legal nature, since it is not so easy to grasp the pure essence of the law, at least not in our own age of legal pluralism. The concepts mentioned here are themselves related to theories, and consequently these theories are, at least implicitly, included in our way of dealing with law. In this sense it can be said that law is theory-dependent.

Social relations are permeated with theories. The law, as it seems to me, relies on theories, *i.e.* coherent sets of propositions aiming to justify the use of power. These theories, including theories of sovereignty, democracy, justice, rights, rules, principles, etc. form part of the law, and the more justified they are, the more they support the legal orders we live by.

Again, these theories are not of the sort that allow for deductive conclusions about what law is viz. ought to be, nor do they permit restructuring the law on the basis of one specific criterion (legal validity, effectiveness/ efficiency/efficacy, justice, etc.). Pure theories of law, just like purely sociological, economic or moral theories, to mention just a few, reduce unduly the phenomenon to only one of the aspects of its richer texture and cannot give an accurate account of the whole idea of law as a practice.

It is an understatement that society is growing more and more complex, that everything is changing at an ever quickening pace, up to the point that even change is changing. So awareness of the complexity of law can then be considered an indication that law is increasingly being understood in relation to its social context.

From this it follows that the current idea of law has become multi-facetted and its study includes – in my opinion – a number of theories. Consequently, the study of the law in jurisprudence is best achieved by considering as many theoretical perspectives as possible. Again, this is not intended to locate object and method of study as parts of two different realms, with law "simply being there" to be studied by the jurisprudential scholar. With a view to its multi-facetted character, it is obvious that the study of law needs a multi-layered methodological approach that includes perspectives gleamed from many and different disciplines, such as sociology, ethics, epistemology, etc.

This new form of studying law is a useful completion to legal science or legal dogmatics. The latter is more oriented towards legal practice, as an adequate description and systematisation of law is one of the prime needs in adjudication.

In addition, legal theory aims at broadening the scope of legal research, and the contributions to this volume confirm the rich potential of this relatively new approach.

The title of this volume, *The Law in Philosophical Perspectives* reflects the idea that law can be studied from a range of different philosophical perspectives and viewpoints, resulting in a multitude of theories.

The subtitle *My Philosophy of Law* then refers to a collection of articles published in 1941 as the proceedings of a symposium of important American philosophers of those days. This volume includes contributions by Walter Wheeler Cook, John Dewey, Lon Fuller, Leon Green, Karl Llewellyn, Roscoe Pound and Max Radin, among many others. Some of the contributors to the present volume have preferred to write with reference to that title, and its inclusion in the title of the present volume honours that preference. It counts as a tribute to these thinkers, though not necessarily as an agreement with all their ideas.

This book reflects the need to combine and compare new approaches to the philosophy and theory of law, in order to obtain a more comprehensive understanding of present law at the beginning of a new millennium.

THE SYSTEMATISATION AND INTERPRETATION OF STATUTES. SOME THOUGHTS ON THEORETICAL AND PRACTICAL LEGAL SCIENCE

AULIS AARNIO

UNIVERSITY OF TAMPERE, FINLAND

1. As an Introduction

I will begin by specifying the three concepts required to understand the topic. These are the concept of method, the characterisation of what should be understood by legal science (namely, legal dogmatics or "*Rechtsdogmatik*") and thirdly, the perspective on the method of discourse adopted in this presentation.

1.1. Some Basic Concepts

In connection with, for example, the natural sciences, the word "method" refers to a group of concepts, inferences and norms, with which it is possible to collect data, process it, form determining hypotheses, test them and write out the obtained results. Roughly put, it could be said that in this sense method is an "institution of calculus" which guarantees the result when the appropriate facts are fed into the system.

The method of legal science is not and cannot be such. As my teacher Aatos Alanen said, legal thinking is not mathematics. By emphasising this point, Alanen wanted to focus attention on the fact that legal thinking, such as the interpretation of regulations or the application of norms to practice, is not a mechanical process that follows unambiguous rules. Literally, it is a matter of weighing and balancing.

If this remark is taken at face value, as it should be in my opinion, the method of legal science is shown to be more a point of view of justice, rather than a mere system of calculus. The extent to which this point of view can be specified will become apparent later. For now it is enough to reiterate the basic claim: the so-called method of legal thinking is not the same as the methods of the natural sciences or technical research.

Philosophically speaking, this difference is centred on the much debated problem of "two cultures". Lord Charles Percy Snow made a remark in 1959 about how the "scientific cultures of the humanities and the natural sciences have become so estranged from one another that a chasm of understanding is growing between the two"[1]. With his comment, Snow challenged scholars to deliberate upon whether such a gap exists, and if so, what it could be.

---

[1] E. Saarenheimo, (ed.), *Aikamme kaksi kulttuuria. Humanistisen ja luonnontieteellisen*

I believe that this difference can be made somewhat in the way that Georg-Henrik von Wright has formulated it in his work[2]. Here von Wright makes a methodological division between the natural sciences and the humanistic sciences, "*Naturwissenschaften*" and "*Geisteswissenschaften*", on the basis that the natural sciences explain phenomena while the humanistic sciences interpret and understand deeds and events. Thus the humanities can, quite rightly, be called "human sciences"[3]. Let me reveal my methodological cards at this point. I expressly link legal science to the family of the humanities in the following way: legal science does not explain but interprets, and thus has links to, for example, historical and literary research. Simultaneously, legal science is at its deepest level a social science, though its point of contact with the empirical social sciences is problematic[4]. But I will leave these family connections with social science to rest for now and return to legal science.

1.2. Regarding Legal Science

The concept of legal science is ambiguous. It covers several specialised fields which are partly independent and partly interdependent, namely those of legal dogmatics, the sociology of law, comparative jurisprudence and legal history. Additionally, legal theory is often spoken of as being a field of study in its own right. Therefore, it is probably the most appropriate to talk about the legal sciences in the plural[5].

The oldest of these, and probably the most significant in relation to practice in continental Europe, is legal dogmatics. Traditionally, its task has been defined as (1) the interpretation of the content of statutes and (2) the systematisation of legal norms. The former can also be called the practical emphasise, while the latter can be termed the theoretical dimension of legal science. For reasons I will return to later, I speak of practical and theoretical legal science. They each have their own methods but are, nonetheless, in an interactive relationship with one another[6].

---

kulttuurin välistä rajankäyntiä (Two cultures of our time. Defining interdisciplinary boundaries between humanistic and natural scientist cultures), Porvoo, 1967, 5 and 138 ff.

[2] G.-H. von Wright, *Explanation and Understanding*, New York, 1971,

[3] M. Juntunen and L. Mehtonen, *Ihmistieteiden filosofiset perusteet* (The philosophical foundations of human sciences), Jyväskylä, 1977, passim.

[4] More closely see A. Aarnio, "Onko oikeustiede yhteiskuntatiede?" (Is legal science a social science?), *Lakimies*, 1993, p. 492 ff.; id., "Yksilö ja yhteiskunta. Oikeusfilosofin näkökulma" (An individual and the society. A legal philosopher's perspective) in *Mutta missä on yhteiskunta?* (But where is the society?) *Festschrift for Kauko Pietilä*, S. Hakala, K. Sondermann and T. Uusitupa (eds.), Tampere, 1996, 109 ff.

[5] Id., *Laintulkinnan teoria* (Theory of legal interpretation), Helsinki, 1989, 47 ff.

[6] Id., *ibid.*, 302 ff.

Considering the history of law, it is obvious that the practical and theoretical emphases in legal science vary due to the demands of the circumstances of each society. This has certainly been the situation in Finland, whose socio-legal history is reflected in my own methodical choices in the following sections.

The characteristic features of Finnish legal thinking from the latter part of the period of autonomy, namely from approximately 1880 through the Second World War, were on the one hand legalism and on the other hand, the construction of thinking connected to legalism. By the former I mean an attitude that leans on the law and the significance of the legislator as a primary source of jurisdiction, emphasises a literary interpretation of law, and thus is reluctant to accept the flexible application of law. Constructivism, on the other hand, emphasises the significance of concepts in legal thinking. It was embodied in the German notion of conceptual legal dogmatics ("*Begriffsjurisprudenz*") that was first brought to Finland in 1880s by Robert Montgomery, but which was still a notable part of Finnish civil, criminal, and procedural law, as late as the 1930s, although by this point its influence was in decline[7].

1.3. A Point of View

In outlining the points of departure for the way of thinking I represent, two further matters should be mentioned.

I received my basic legal education within the general discipline of civil law, but already in the early stages my teachers Matti Ylöstalo and Simo Zitting directed my interest towards the law of inheritance and, concomitantly, the law of marital property. This orientation could not but have an impact on my way of attempting to understand – at a later stage – the fundamental questions of legal thinking.

For its part, the Finnish law of inheritance, similar to the law of property and the law of obligations, was in the strong grip of conceptual legal dogmatics practically all the way to the 1950s. The framing of questions in Finnish inheritance law[8] was defined by the classical disputes of the German law of inheritance, such as whether the estate of a defunct is an independent juristic person, whether the inheritor's right of joint ownership is divisible or indivisible, and whether an inheritor's share of the estate is movable or immovable.

---

[7] Id., "Suomalaisen oikeusteorian kehityspiirteitä" (Developmental features of Finnish legal theory), *Lakimies*, 1973, 339 ff. More generally about the arrival of conceptual legal dogmatics in Finland, see H.T. Klami, *Oikeustaistelijat* (The legalists), Porvoo, 1977, 66 ff., particularly 77 ff.

[8] A. Aarnio, *Perillisen oikeusasemasta* (About the legal status of an heir), Porvoo, 1967, 23 ff. and 88 ff.

On the other hand, after the Second World War Finland rapidly began to change from an agrarian society towards a modern industrial one, and, later, to a post-industrial society. The change was so speedy that in the 1950s and 1960s Finland was among the most rapidly changing countries in the world. This dynamic could not but have an impact on legal thinking and was posing problems in legal dogmatics.

The change in civil law was augured already between 1920 and 1930 by certain Finnish Swedish-speaking legal scholars, such as Eric af Hällström. However, the transitional stage proper did not take place until the turn of decade in the 1940s and 1950s[9]. At that time, Jorma Vuorio in labour law, Osvi Lahtinen and Matti Ylöstalo on the general questions of the civil law and Simo Zitting in the law of property transferred the focus from conceptual legal dogmatics to so-called analytical jurisprudence. Naturally, the forerunners were the representatives of the Uppsala School, such as Karl Olivecrona and Alf Ross, but also included people like Östen Undén[10].

However, Finnish legal thinking was also directly influenced by the Anglo-Saxon world. This was due to the rise of analytical philosophy which grew into a dominant position after the Second World War. Key figures in this were Eino Kaila, and later, Georg-Henrik von Wright. The latter had a close relationship to the leading Finnish theoreticians[11].

It thus became clear that legal science had to separate from the ballast of conceptual legal dogmatics and to formulate a way of thinking which could meet the demands of a dynamic, ever more complex society of ownership that openly recognised conflicting interests.

In Finland, Simo Zitting's analysis of the concept of proprietary rights offered a certain kind of a paradigmatic model for the new way of thinking. Zitting based his work on the well known analysis of Hohfeld and Alf Ross, but he applied these exemplary models to the needs of the Finnish legal system and society in an original and creative way[12].

---

[9] About change particularly, see M. Helin, *Lainoppi ja metafysiikka. Tutkimus skandinaavisen oikeusrealismin tieteenkuvasta ja sen vaikutuksesta Suomen siviilioikeuden tutkimuksessa vuosina 1920-1960* (Legal dogmatics and metaphysics. A treatise on the paradigm of legal realism and its impact on Finnish civil law research during 1920-1960), Helsinki, 1988, 276 ff.

[10] Id., *ibid.*, 199 ff.

[11] von Wright was a member of the Theoria Iuris – circle lead by Otto Brusiin.

[12] See particularly S. Zitting, "Omistajan oikeuksista ja velvolli-suuksista I-II" (About rights and obligations of the owner I-II), *Lakimies*, 1952, 387 ff. and 640 ff.; id., "Omistu-soikeudesta systemaattisena käsitteenä" (About ownership as a systematic concept), *ibid.*, 1953, 590 ff.; id., "Kysymys omistusoikeuden siirtymähetken määräämisestä" (The question about the definition of the transitional moment of ownership), *ibid.*, 1955, 640 ff.

I surfaced in this world as a student of legal science at the end of the 1950s, and inspired by Simo Zitting, I started studying Alf Ross' legal theory in 1959. This choice defined my methodical choices for the years to come. As a matter of fact, my entire career as a legal scholar ever since has been (with all due respect) distancing myself from Alf Ross, whom I still regard as the most significant legal theorist ever having an influence on the Nordic countries.

Finally, I would like to make a certain precision. My view of questions of method has been characterised by the differentiation between the *discussion* of method and the *usage* of method. Among other things, legal theory examines the method of legal science and legal thinking in general. The object of differentiation is method. For his part, a practitioner of legal science uses ("applies") a certain method, whether he recognises that this is what he is doing or not.

My interest in the theory of legal thinking, theoretical as well as practical legal science, has its roots primarily in the needs of the legal scholarship I practice, and secondly in inadequate self-understanding. I have been occupied with the question of what I am doing when I say I am systematising or interpreting statutes (legal norms). What is the theoretical nature of the activity called legal science – my own work?

I have thus arrived in the field of legal theory, having started from legal science. This has been a significant factor in defining the way I have posed, and will pose, my questions. This journey has also led me to understand the Nordic tradition of theoretical questions as always having a practical emphasis on them. The name of the discipline, general jurisprudence, was not born by a whim of chance.

This is connected to the fact that each and every significant Nordic theoretician of jurisprudence has been a lawyer by education. The list is impressive: Alf Ross, Karl Olivecrona, Vilhelm Lundstedt, Per-Olof Ekelöf, Stig Jørgensen, Torstein Eckhoff, Aleksander Peczenik, Stig Strömholm, Otto Brusiin, Kaarle Makkonen, etc.

I would not exclude the point of view that a person who does not have experience in legal research cannot talk about the method of actual legal science. What is basically involved is the so-called knowledge of the doer, the reconstruction of the researcher's experience through theoretical concepts. In any case, it is apparent that to be able to talk about the method of legal science to those who make and utilise the results of that research (judges, lawyers, administrators) one must be able to talk about issues familiar to them and to do so using a language which is not totally foreign to them.

Just as it is impossible to make rye bread using a recipe for a sponge cake, it is also impossible to offer the methodical instructions of some other science to a producer of legal knowledge. This is the message I received from my teachers, and which for the past thirty years, to the best of my knowledge, I have striven - by trial and error – to bring forward.

2. Theoretical Jurisprudence, in Other Words, the Systematisation of the Rule of Law

2.1. The Point of Departure

What has been presented above, albeit in an abridged form, shows that I began my career in *theoretical legal science*. Given the prevailing situation at the beginning of the 1960s, the only way to get away from the stagnant framing of a question in the law of inheritance was to break the tradition of the German-based conceptual legal dogmatics. Instead of honing the existing problematic to be sharper and clearer, the questions were turned topsy turvy. Why? The answer is simple.

The structure of the legal norm (rule) is the same everywhere: to a description of certain sets of circumstances (F) descriptions of legal consequences (S) are joined. It is the basic task of practical legal science to clarify these relations between facts and circumstances/legal consequences (F→S). However, to be able to grasp the nucleus of various juridical phenomena, for example, proprietary rights, authorisation, compensation for damage, or invalidity, legal science must have a corpus of concepts adequate enough to differentiate between them. Concepts that are too abstract or ambiguous prohibit the recognition of the fact-consequence relationship characteristic to the phenomenon. Law becomes opaque, so to speak. This was the question posed in the methodological turn that followed the Second World War. I will present one solitary example.

2.2. A Crisis in Thought Concerning Inheritance Rights

Classic German legal science had wasted plenty of energy in discussing whether inheritance is transferred to an heir at the actual moment of death, or whether transfer occurred afterwards at some future point of time. The point of departure was that the transfer takes place at a certain moment, and thus it is the definition of precisely that moment that presents the problem. Analytical study abandoned this whole problem and replaced it with another: what does the transfer of an inheritance actually mean?

When the problem is defined this way, there are several possible answers available to define the actual moment of the transfer. The core of the problem is that there is not one specific moment, but that the transfer of the inheritance, as also the right of ownership in general, is a course of consecutive events that are legally significant. According to this way of phasal thinking, there are some effects connected with the death of the decedent and some others connected with the reception of the inheritance, just as there àre to the distribution of the estate.

It is a question of expediency ("a matter of taste") whether the inheritance is declared to be transferred from the decedent to the heir at the moment of death or at a later point. The decisive factor is what is precisely meant by the term "transfer", that is, which legal consequences are connected with which composition of facts and circumstances. Within the chronological dimension we can talk about a multi-staged transfer[13].

Even analytical legal science has not been able to get rid of legal concepts. From this particular point of view, it was never in opposition to conceptual legal dogmatics. Analytical legal science only challenged the notion of conceptual legal dogmatics according to which legal consequences can be derived from legal concepts. The thesis ran thus: the content of the legal norm cannot be concluded from concepts.

According to analytical legal science, concepts are instruments to obtain a more exact hold on the legal system. As my teacher Simo Zitting said, there must be the capacity to formulate the demands of modern law and society more precisely than before. Thus, the novelty was in reformulating the questions, not in the denial of concepts or in their self-assertive meditation[14].

At the time, this insight had a decisive effect on my own work. I found the need to position the problematic shaped by German conceptual legal dogmatics in a new way. The point was to create a new, more fine-textured body of concepts, which would enable the analysis of the fact-consequence relationship significant to inheritance law. A richer body of concepts gives – I thought – richer answers. Only then can justice begin to reflect on the preconditions of the particular society to which it belongs. And if it is anything, this is essential, since legal concepts must correspond at all times to the respective conditions of the society.

With the concepts of the 1930s and their concomitant questions, it was not possible to master the Nordic post-war reality of the 1960s. It was, and is, essential to pose one's questions on the preconditions of the present time, and if this skill is mastered, legal science is able to reply to the challenges arising from contemporary society. This was the theoretical basis on which Finnish analytical civil law research was constructed from approximately the end of 1940s. It also characterised my theoretical interest until the beginning of the 1970s. Besides the fundamental questions of inheritance law, my attention was drawn to the form and formalities in legal thinking. It is precisely the questions of form that make an interesting object for the analytical research approach. As an example, perhaps

---

[13] A. Aarnio, *Perillisen oikeusasemasta* (About the legal status of an heir), 63 ff.

[14] See, *e.g.*, S. Zitting, "Kysymys omistusoikeuden siirtymähetken määräämisestä" (The question about the definition of the transitional moment of ownership), 664 ff. and id., *Omistajanvaihdoksesta silmälläpitäen erityisesti lainhuudatuksen vaikutuksia* (About change of ownership with particular attention to the impact of registration of the estate), Helsinki, 1951, 11 ff., particularly the footnote.

I may mention a summary of my thinking at the beginning of the 1970s, which has been published under the title "Formal Incorrectness and the Invalidity of a Legal Transaction"[15].

2.3. Attention to the Reformulation of Questions

As I have pointed out, at the beginning of my career my method was clearly weighed on the reformulation of *basic conceptual questions*. As the popular phrase, influenced by Ludwig Wittgenstein, went at that time: the world is full of answers, one only has to find the right questions. The infamous fly-on-the-glass-pane metaphor by Wittgenstein signified the same thing. Instead of bouncing of the glass walls, we should find our way out of the trap.

The above-mentioned could be restated as the notion that the state of the Finnish civil law, on the one hand, and the transformation of Finnish society, on the other, naturally lead the researcher of the 1960s to the general doctrine of the law. The revaluation of thinking appeared to be a certain necessity of practice, a little like twenty years later when it was thought to be important to take the social dimension of law into consideration.

The particular issue of interest to me at the beginning of the 1960s was the transfer of the share in the estate, or the inheritance portion. At that time, the topic was closely connected with the dispute of German origin about whether the right of joint ownership was divisible or indivisible. If it was thought to be indivisible, the share of an estate of an individual inheritor would be most closely comparable to a share in a partnership. By nature, it is movable and assignable in the way the share is. The proprietary right to the share is transferred at the very moment of the assignment and the assignee replaces the assignor as a joint-owner of the estate. The transfer of a share in an estate causes the transfer of all contractual rights and responsibilities.

The theory of a divisible, that is, a fractional co-ownership presented the issue in such a way that each one of the co-owners had a share of each individual object included in the estate. Thus, the transfer of a share in an estate equals the transfer of the share of each individual object in the estate and the form of the transfer is defined according to whether the object is movable or immovable.

A closer examination proved that the controversy between these two theories was partially presumable, even though they differed in the required form of the transfer. Independent of the details of the controversy, the whole problem can be eliminated by reformulating the question. It is not essential to argue about the divisibility or indivisibility of the co-ownership, but to analyse:

[15] A. Aarnio, "Formal Incorrectness and the Invalidity of a Legal Transaction", *Scandinavian Studies in Law*, 1971.

- how the joint possession of the parties is organised after the death and before the distribution;
- how to initiate the estate distribution;
- who may participate in the distribution;
- how to contest the distribution, etc.

Each one of the parties has a specific position during the time of both the joint possession and the distribution of the estate. These fact-consequence relationships can be examined directly in the light of the statutes of the Act on Inheritance, but only if the problem of co-ownership which disturbs this examination and is in fact unnecessary can first be eliminated[16].

The question of whether the estate can be considered a juristic person is closely connected with the analysis of the inheritor's legal position. As Osvi Lahtinen demonstrated, this question is also wrongly positioned[17]. Rather than deliberating over the juristic nature of the death estate, the problem of how to exactly identify the individual joint-owners (inheritors, beneficiaries of general legacy, and the surviving spouse, up to the time of distribution) can be resolved by recourse to official certificates and other legal documents, and the question what kind of relationships prevail between the joint-owners should be considered. Thus, for example, the dispute about whether it is possible to register title of property to a death estate becomes a secondary matter.

It is also not possible to clarify the position of a party to an estate if one does not take a stand on the concepts of right, duty, responsibility, competence, liability, and freedom. If one does not have a stand on causality, adequacy, fault, and other basic concepts of the law of compensation, it is impossible to make an appropriate examination of compensation in situations of joint administration of an estate.

Theoretical legal science, according to my understanding of it in the work I have done during the 1960s and later, is the analysis of these concepts and the ones related to them. Theoretical legal science analyses conceptual entities, reclassifies concepts, formulates theories that assist in getting a grip on the interpretations of the legal rule without any disturbing theoretical ballast. To simplify: theoretical legal science systematises the rule of law.

---

[16] See in more detail id., *Perillisen oikeusasemasta* (About the legal status of an heir), 104 ff.

[17] See particularly O. Lahtinen, "Till läran on juridiska personer", (On the theory of the legal person), *Tidskrift for Rettsvitenskap*, 1949, 47 ff.; id., "Kuolinpesä-konstruktiosta" (About death estate construction), *Lakimies*, 1955, 112 ff.

3. Practical Legal Science as the Clarification of the Content of the Legal System

3.1. Eliminating the Obstacles for Interpretation

From this, it is only a short step to the idea which has long dominated my writings in the theory of legal thinking and observations concerning the method of legal research.

Analytical legal science used to attempt to divide the traditional concepts into sub-concepts for two reasons:

(1) to prevent deduction from concepts

and

(2) to make it possible to interpret the legal rule in such a way that each respective circumstance in society is taken into consideration.

To my own way of thinking, the latter point was decisive. A high-level theoretical legal science (conceptual analysis, formulation of legal theory, systematisation) makes the practical legal science of high qualitative demands on the lines laid down by Simo Zitting possible. It is not hard to find reasons for this.

Concepts are like a lens through which we observe "legal reality". The lens is not allowed to distort the image, it may not be obscure or cloudy. To use another figure of speech: through concepts we can "grab" the legal rule. If the body of concepts is underdeveloped, law becomes opaque and not even legal research can "grab" it. This is exactly why only an exact body of concepts free from conflict enables a reliable interpretation of the legal rule that will satisfy even controversial legal interests.

This idea, perhaps modest from a contemporary point of view, was the beginning for the interpretative theory which I have been outlining in my fields, partly in co-operation with Robert Alexy and Aleksander Peczenik[18].

3.2. Why is an Argumentative Theory Needed?

Before I get into the details of the question, I would like to remind you of two essential factors in the method of discussion.

Theoretical concepts, or more generally, the general discipline of law, belong to the toolbox of every lawyer. Even the most practical lawyer has to utilise the basic concepts of law in their work. Nobody can resolve a problem of damages without utilising the concepts of causality or adequacy. Thus, if one evicts theoretical concepts via the front door, then in no time they sneak back in through the kitchen entrance. Jurisdiction without theory does not exist.

This is why every generation of lawyers in the Roman law tradition must put some of their mental capital into maintaining a certain level of theoretical

---

[18] See, *e.g.*, A. Aarnio, R. Alexy and A. Peczenik, "The Foundation of Legal Reasoning", *Rechtstheorie*, 1981, 133 ff., 357 ff. and 423 ff.

legal dogmatics (legal doctrines) as a general discipline. In this way, and only this way, is it possible to transfer the tradition of legal thinking to another generation. This will not be transferred by learning individual cases, or random interpretations of them, by heart. If the grip on general legal doctrines loosens, the understanding of the essential characteristics of law is also lost – and, even worse, the feeling of what is right and wrong in human (legal) relationships is lost.

Yet, the interest that has been ignited throughout Europe in legal argumentation is not an invention of legal philosophers. The question is not about some kind of a decision or an agreement among the hobbyists of theory to discuss for a few the interpretation and argumentation of particular judgements in particular. The real reasons run deeper. These reasons have been illuminated – better than by anybody else, I think – by Gunnar Bergholtz in his excellent research *Ratio & Auctoritas*. To put Bergholtz's main idea in a nutshell: a clear correlation prevails between the level of democratic development and the demands made on legal decision making. Demand from citizens for properly reasoned judgements does not come out of a void. Faith in authority has crumbled, the level of understanding has risen, people's consciousness about their own rights has grown, and interaction between human beings has increased. Citizens frequently ask: "Why was the case resolved in this way, why not in that way?" Such questions pose a natural challenge to the users of legal power[19].

Thus, the interest in arguing for juridical decisions has been born in society, not among theoreticians. This is not a fashion but a fact dictated by societal development. Thus interpreted, the theory of legal argumentation has just been an attempt to meet the challenge of societal development[20].

My own career has included all of these interesting experiences. I have had the opportunity to live through two different periods of challenge. The first, taking place in the 1960s, made traditional theoretical legal science controversial. The second, starting in the 1970s, contested the formal-juridical tradition of the interpretation of legal rules.

Both of these periods have raised sharp controversy in Finland. On the one hand, analytical legal science positioned itself in opposition to the conceptual legal dogmatics derived from German legal thinking. On the other hand, modern argumentative theory was opposed by the legalistic tradition of interpretation.

If one wants to see anything common in these two fronts, it is very probably the controversy of stability and elasticity – form and content. The

---

[19] See G. Bergholtz, *Ratio & auctoritas. Ett komparativ-rättsligt bidrag till frågan om domsmotiveringens betydelse främst i tvistemål*, Lund, 1987, 97 ff. and 359 ff.

[20] About this, see, *e.g.*, A. Aarnio, *Laintulkinnan teoria* (Theory on legal interpretation), 184 ff. and id., *Reason and Authority. A Treatise on the Dynamic Paradigm of Legal Dogmatics*, Aldershot, 1997, 44 ff.

traditional way of thinking grew from the needs of a static, formal, agrarian society. Modern thinking – theoretical as well as practical – is attached to a dynamic, complex society shattering within its problematic. There, the legal remedy of the individual forms part of the integrity of society, content overrules form, or at the very least, models concepts of the form's role. All of this is closely connected with that development towards the welfare state. The forms of justice are still essential, they are also central values in the Nordic welfare state, but material law has become increasingly important next to form. It is precisely this fact that forces us to re-evaluate our ways of thinking, it creates the need to develop legal argumentation.

These new arrangements have been the soil from which the new theory of argumentation has sprouted, in Finland at least. Without repeating what has been written on the subject during the past twenty years, I will attempt to outline a viewpoint that is very important to me.

3.3. Three Images of Jurisdiction

From the Middle Ages on, legal theorists have attempted to establish the status of legal science. First, it was a matter of defining science as such. Then, to examine what kind of legal research fulfils the qualifications of science. This has been the procedure of the classic, as well as the rational, law of nature. Indeed, this has been the way that the great German classics and the leading theorists of the century have worked[21]. These attempts I will divide into two main groups, probably wronging many fine-textured theories by doing so. Nevertheless, the first I will call formalism and the second, realism.

According to a *formalistic legal theory*, legal science must be cleansed of values and assessments. Its task is simply to present alternative interpretations of legal regulations and analyse possibilities of interpretation, but not to make a choice between them. However, legal science may describe the intention of the legislator, but that description may not lead into placing one of the descriptions in front of the others. As a self-assertive representative of formalism, Hans Kelsen may be mentioned[22].

The bearer of the name of Scandinavian realism has been Alf Ross[23]. The philosophical points of departure for the later stages of his thinking had their

---

[21] See id., *Laintulkinnan teoria* (Theory on legal interpretation), 101 ff.

[22] H. Kelsen, *Puhdas oikeusoppi* (Pure theory of law), Porvoo, 1968, 363 ff., partic. 370 ff. and more generally about Kelsen's theory S. Laakso, "Puhtaan oikeusopin problematiikkaa" (Problematics of pure legal dogmatics) in *Oikeustiede – Jurisprudentia* (Legal science – Jurisprudence), 1980, 95 ff. and id., *Oikeuden systeemiyhteys puhtaassa oikeusopissa. Tampereen yliopiston hallinto-oikeuden laitoksen julkaisuja 1/1981*, (The systematic link in pure legal dogmatics. A publication of the Tampere University department of administrative law 1/1981), passim.

[23] See A. Ross, *Om ret og retfaerdighed* (On law and justice), Copenhagen, 1953, passim,

roots in logical positivism. The basic idea of Ross is that every meaningful scientific sentence can be traced to an experience (sentences of perception). Thus, scientific theory can only include three kinds of sentences: logical deductions, perceptive sentences, or sentences logically derived from them. Namely, logic and positivism.

On this basis, Ross formulated one of the most brilliant theories of legal science ever developed. He started off from a generally accepted basic thesis: the research aim of legal dogmatics is the jurisdiction in force. However, the answer he provided radically differed from the answer of formalism, and most significantly, from so-called American realism. Here we come to the fundamental thesis of Ross' legal philosophy.

According to this theory, a legal norm is valid when it is spontaneously applied in an authoritative use. As an authority himself, Ross was particularly observant of the courts of law. Based on this, Ross' answer could be written in the form: a legal norm is valid if it is included in the prevailing judge's ideology.

It follows from this that the research task of legal science must be the investigation of the practices of the courts of law. Even the premises of scientific legal thinking must return to the empirical. They must be based on experience. Hence, court practice becomes the natural empirical reality to be examined by legal science.

Since mere practical description is not an adequate measure for the needs of science, Ross developed his famous prognostic theory: the task of practical legal science is to anticipate the behaviour of the courts of law, that is to say, whether a certain norm is included in the prevailing ideology of judges. Small wonder that even Ross himself named his way of thinking behaviouristic idealism[24]. It is a mix of behavioural research and examination of prevailing normative ideology.

The objective of this presentation is not to examine whether Ross' program of "scientification" can be consistently followed through[25]. Together with some other theorists I am sceptical of that, and I rather suspect that Ross' theory is strongly coloured by hermeneutics and by distancing itself from both logical positivism and the various currents of realism[26].

---

and M. Helin, *Lainoppi ja metafysiikka* (Legal dogmatics and metaphysics), 139 ff., 217 ff. and 238 ff.; M. I. Niemi, *Päämäärien valta-kunta. Konventionalistinen analyysi lainopillisen tiedon edellytyksistä ja oikeusjärjestelmän perusteista* (The realm of goals. A conventional analysis of the preconditions of knowledge in legal dogmatics and basis of legal system), Helsinki, 1996, 68 ff. and A. Aarnio, *Reason and Authority*, 112 ff.

[24] A. Ross, *Om ret og retfaerdighed* (On law and justice), 85 ff.

[25] See, *e.g.*, M. I. Niemi, *Päämäärien valtakunta* (The realm of goals), 59 ff.

[26] Markku Helin has emphasised this feature, see M. Helin, *Lainoppi ja metafysiikka* (Legal dogmatics and metaphysics), 169 ff., partic. 176 ff. and A. Aarnio, *Reason and Authority*, 120 ff.

Independent of how Alf Ross' ideas are finally to be interpreted, I see problems in the processes of turning both formalism and realism into science.

My own suggested answer could well be called neo-realism, to utilise a term adopted by Aleksander Peczenik[27]. The term in itself is not necessarily entirely successful in describing my theory, but the choice of a name is not essential in the matter. Once again, what is important is the redesign of the basic question.

Instead of asking whether legal science is scientific or not, it should be asked what legal science actually means in everyday research practice. It cannot be denied that legal science is – at least in every western democracy – understood as a practical field of research. In the societal division of labour the task of systematising legal rules and of clarifying the content of the legal system, that is, to interpret legal norms has fallen to legal science[28]. The interest of knowing is targeted both in the system and its content. Knowledge of both the system and the content is sought.

In various situations, the legal community thus presupposes normal recommendations from legal science. In reality this has meant that legal science has not been satisfied, or could have been satisfied by simply describing the possible alternatives of interpretations, or to predict the practices of the authorities. Neither of these solutions would help, let us say, the work of courts of law.

Judges are not merely interested in the alternatives of interpretation, neither do they care to know the prognosis of how they themselves are going to act. A judge would turn to legal science for assistance to clarify how to decide in a present case. Which rule applies to which case and what is the exact content of a certain regulation applied? To fulfil the realistic expectations of the legal community, legal science must in this situation make interpretative choices: within the prevailing fact and circumstances X the legal consequence Y should be carried out.

If this mundane point of departure is accepted and legal science is taken as simply as it is offered – as is common in Nordic countries – the primary theoretical question also changes. It is not so very useful to contemplate whether legal science is science or not, since the answer is decidedly dependent on how science is seen in general. This is something that does not interest a judge, lawyer, or layman who expects to hear practical answers[29]. Questions about the

---

[27] See A. Peczenik, *Juridikens metodproblem* (The problem of legal method), Stockholm, 1974, 26.

[28] On the structure of norms see A. Aarnio, *Laintulkinnan teoria*, (Theory on legal interpretation), 65 ff.

[29] A. Aarnio, *Oikeussäännösten tulkinnasta* (On interpreting the statutes of law), Helsinki, 1982, 197.

scientific nature of legal science are useless when the societal task of legal science is concerned.

What is essential is the readiness of legal science at any given time to answer the questions presented in a legal community, or, in wider terms, in a civil community: "Why should we do it like this?" To answer this question, legal science must produce well-founded arguments about the content of the legal system. This is the only way in which a legal community can get answers for its why-questions, since this is the only means to control whether the stand taken by legal science is just an attitude, or a random whim adopted from a random source.

From this point of view there is equally little interest in knowing whether the standpoints of legal science are the only ones that are correct. What is most essential is to be able to assess if these standpoints are argued in the best possible way that is, taking all aspects into account[30].

This is something that places legal theory face to face with a new challenge, that of legal argumentation. Besides systematisation, argumentation has been the other cornerstone of my methodological interest. My objective has been to develop such rules of play that by following them, it would be possible to realise the ideal of reasoning in the legal community[31].

Since legal theory is not an empirical science, it will not be satisfied by simply describing ways of interpretation in the field of legal dogmatics. It strives to construct a model of good argumentation. Argumentation is the nucleus of all theory, in theory of legal science as well as within theoretical physics or in the social sciences.

This model – or an outline of it – has gradually evolved over the last three decades. To briefly summarise the birth and contents of this model, I would like to divide it into four characteristic parts.

(1) The model of deduction represented by legalism is formalistic. According to this, a legal decision is a syllogism in which the conclusion is derived from two premises[32]. On the one hand, as I have noted above, it is characteristic of legalism to have limited sources of law. The law and its literary interpretation are the points of departure, as well as the literal interpretation of statutes, and the purpose of the legislator is to provide complementary

---

[30] In a broader sense, see A. Peczenik, *Vad är rätt? Om demokrati, rättssäkerhet, etik och juridisk argumentation* (What is law? On democracy, legal certainty, ethics and legal argumentation), Stockholm, 1995, 676 ff.

[31] See A. Aarnio, "One Right Answer and the Majority Principle", *A.R.S.P.*, 1994, 36 ff.

[32] About syllogism, see R. Alexy, *Theorie der juristischen Argumentation*, Frankfort-on-Main, 1978, 273 ff. and E. Backman, "Oikeudellisen ajattelun loogisista perusteista" (Concerning a logical basis for legal thinking), *Lakimies*, 1970, 1037 ff. See also A. Aarnio, *Laki, teko ja tavoite* (Law, act and objective), Forssa, 1975, 123 ff.

knowledge. But, on the other hand, the attitude toward court decisions is irresolute.

Reflecting on this background, the new rhetorics outlined by Theodor Viehweg and later developed into a proper theory by Chaïm Perelman, provided a new opening to the Finnish theory of legal argumentation in the 1960s[33]. The ideas of Stephen Toulmin, which were first brought into the Finnish discourse by Lars D. Erikson, had an influence in the same direction[34].

If we take into consideration the effect this had on Finnish thinking, we find two elements at the core of the new rhetorics. First of all, the traditional division between deduction and induction was broken. Argumentation, next to logical deduction and inductive generalisation, equalled valid thinking. Here both Viehweg and Perelman paid homage to Aristotle's ancient notion of the practical syllogism and topology.

Perelman stated the other central point of the new rhetorics by noting that in legal and moral argumentation the question is not one of persuasion, but of convincing. Argumentation means that reason is allowed to speak[35]. The gate for the development of a theory of argumentation opened up.

(2) About the same time, Ludwig Wittgenstein's late linguistic philosophy was assuming its full force in Finland. The main novelty of this theory was perhaps the transference of the focal point from the picture theory of language towards the use of language. The concept of language as a game, as a form of action, became central.

It seemed to be apparent that Wittgensteinian linguistic philosophy could form a *philosophical* base for the pragmatics of legal language. It was possible to see questions about the confirmation of legal clauses, preconditions of certainty, and the social degree of language in a new light[36].

(3) The *doctrine of the sources of law* began to be discussed more in Nordic legal theory. Aleksander Peczenik's work, *Juridikens metodproblem*[37] had

---

[33] About new rhetorics see C. Perelman, *Retoriikan valtakunta* (The realm of rhetorics), Tampere, 1996, passim. Concerning legal thinking, see, *e.g.*, A. Aarnio, *Oikeussäännösten tulkinnasta* (On interpreting the statutes of law), 190 ff.

[34] L. D. Eriksson, "Rättslig argumentering och den dialektiska logiken" (Legal argumentation and dialectical logic), *Tidskrift utgiven av Juridiska föreningen i Finland*, 1996, 445 ff. See also S. Toulmin, *The Uses of Argument,* Cambridge, 1958; S. Toulmin, R. Rieke and A. Janik, *An Introduction to Reasoning*, New York, 1979.

[35] See C. Perelman, Chaïm, *Retoriikan valtakunta* (The realm of rhetorics), 16 ff., partic. 24 ff. and A. Aarnio, *Reason and Authority*, 214 ff.

[36] See A. Aarnio, "Oikeuskielen tulkinta ja ymmärtäminen. Näkökulma Wittgensteinin myöhäisfilosofiaan" (Interpreting and understanding legal language. A perspective on the late philosophy of Wittgenstein) in *Oikeus, kieli ja kritiikki* (Law, language and critique), A. Hirvonen and K. Kaarlo (eds.), Helsinki, 1990, 99 ff.

[37] A. Peczenik, *Juridikens metodproblem* (The problem of legal method), partic. 48 ff.

more than a minor impact in this discussion. However, the criticism by Kaarle Makkonen directed at the justifications of the court judgements must also be remembered when Finland is considered[38]. Makkonen was the first to pay attention to the lack of justifications. In his dissertation, he analysed various ways of justifying court judgements and thus created a basis for the theory of legal argumentation in Finland[39].

(4) The latest phase in this development has been an idea constructed on Jürgen Habermas' communicative theory of *procedural* argumentation[40]. Among other issues, Habermas has emphasised the nature of argumentation as a process. Based on this, Robert Alexy has outlined his well known theory of juridical argumentation[41].

If the four elements described above are compressed into a description of the foundation pillars of modern argumentation theory, we might end up with something like the following.

Legal argumentation is a process that utilises certain bases (sources of law) and which is directed to convince the opposite side (audience) about the justification of the decision or interpretation. On the basis of this, I have formed a regulative principle: argue your claim in such a way that as many members of the legal community as possible, who deliberate the matter in a rational way, taking all possible aspects of the matter into consideration, can accept your claim[42].

Thus, the objective of argumentation is its rational acceptability. The task of argumentation theory, for its part, is to specify the process of reasoning in such a way that compliance with the regulative principle is possible.

It is apparent that the regulative principle and the argumentation model behind it are only ideals. They are models, as the Paris Meter is a model for every meter in the world. The problem with the argumentation model is not that it is only an ideal or a model. Even with its limitations and abstraction it has a *directive* significance. It demonstrates approximately what would be a good argument in the society, or, in other words, an argument which produces believable (legitimate) results.

A model directs attention to the rationality of reasoning, to the fact that it is a consideration which presents arguments pro and contra (discourse) and not

---

[38] See K. Makkonen, "Ajatuksia juridisen kielen loogisesta analyysistä" (Thoughts about the logical analysis of legal language), *Lakimies*, 1959, 49 ff.

[39] Id., *Zur Problematik der juristischen Entscheidung*, Turku, 1965, partic. 122 ff. and 218 ff. See also id., *Luentoja yleisestä oikeustieteestä* (Lectures on general legal science), Helsinki, 1981, 154 ff.

[40] See R. Alexy, *Theorie der juristischen Argumentation*, 134 ff. and K. Tuori, "Modernin oikeuden ytimessä" (In the nucleus of modern justice), *Oikeus*, 1993, 2 ff.; M. Kusch, *Ymmärtämisen haaste* (The challenge of understanding), Oulu, 1986, 197 ff.

[41] R. Alexy, *Theorie der juristischen Argumentation*, 259 ff.

[42] A. Aarnio, *Laintulkinnan teoria* (Theory of interpreting law), 285 ff.

syllogistic deduction. However, a model also emphasises the fact that the credibility of a claim is dependent on material factors. The result must also be materially acceptable.

Argumentation that meets these preconditions leads them to reinforce each other. And the "best possible" argumentation is the one that takes all aspects into consideration and forms a coherent entity of them[43]. Contrary to popular thinking, rational acceptability is not a "purely" ideal concept although the rationality of reasoning does set certain ideal demands (standards) on the discretionary process. This is the nucleus of the demand for rationality. Arbitrary and random activity do not meet our expectations of what is law and legal decision making. The other side of the regulative principle refers to the arguments used, the source of law. It is a question of the rational use of this source in legal argumentation. Through a legal source, a model is linked to legal reality. Hence, it cannot be claimed that the regulative principle is "purely" ideal.

If understood in this way, legal argumentation may be compared with solving a jigsaw puzzle. The principles of legal interpretation and rational discretion are the rules of the game and legal sources its pieces. The bigger and more unified the game, the more credible the argumentation.

However, compared to an ordinary jigsaw puzzle the legal puzzle has one additional specific quality. In the legal puzzle, the final image of the game can not be recognised beforehand. The image to be constructed is unknown. It will become apparent during the course of the game. This is exactly what makes legal interpretation and decision making so difficult. No one can say in advance what is a credible argument.

The decisive factor in solving a legal puzzle is the *coherence* of the resolution. Legal sources must form a homogeneous entity, but our concept of law is constructed in such a way that we are not willing to accept arbitrary coherence (such as, by drawing lots) as being solid. It may be so in some individual case, but the concept of justice presupposes rational argumentation, not arbitrariness. This is why solving the puzzle combines the rationality of reasoning and the coherence of resolution.

Even a well argued interpretative statement or court decision remains just a kind of an experimental ball which is thrown to the legal community for evaluation. If it passes, it is accepted and the argumentation has been convincing (enough). Otherwise the interpretation or the decision will not achieve legitimacy in the legal community.

The fact that the identifying marks of credibility cannot be unequivocally defined, does not have fatal consequences for legal deliberation. Following the regulative principle guides the scholar and the judge in making the most

---

[43] On coherence, see A. Peczenik, *Vad är rätt?* (What is law?), 571 ff.

appropriate decisions. That is the maximum that can be demanded from legal dogmatics and decision making.

It must be humbly admitted that law is made by man, researched by man, and realised by man. Law is written down with man-made language and the results of its investigation, as well as the judgements given, are given in the form of that language. The scholar and the judge are prisoners of language. Neither one of them is an almighty Hercules the Researcher, Hercules the Judge. We live in the realm of human beings and we only have human capacities with which to realise law. This and only this is the message of the regulative principle.

3.4. To Conclude

The answer to the question concealed by the title is two-fold. My method is organised around two supporting pillars, theoretical and practical legal science.

The method of the former is the analysis of concepts. The richer the corpus of legal concepts, the more versatile the ways in which we can pose questions become. And, when questions become more versatile, the image of the content of the legal system also gets richer.

Thus theoretical legal science attempts to open conceptual possibilities for the questions that practical legal science must face. These are questions about legal facts and circumstances/legal consequences. To simplify, questions of the interpretation and of the application of law. That is why the method of practical legal science is argumentative.

The more credible legal science is in convincing members of the legal community about the justification of its interpretative statements, the stronger the legitimacy it holds as a discipline both in the legal community and in society will be. Any legal science that fumbles along by using opaque concepts, leaning on authority, and lacking discourse, will quickly reach the end of its path.

It is on this understanding of legal thinking that my method is constructed – complete with its limitations and strengths.

Bibliographical Information

I. Monographs

1. *Perillisen oikeusasemasta* (On the legal status of an heir), Porvoo, 1967 (including *Zusammenfassung*).
2. *Kysymyksiä testamenttioikeuden alalta* (Questions on the law of inheritance), Vammala, 1969 (including *Zusammenfassung*).
3. *Luentoja perintöoikeudesta I* (Lectures on the law of inheritance I), Vammala, 1970.
4. *Oikeudellisen ajattelun perusteista* (On the bases of legal thinking), Vammala, 1971.
5. *Luentoja perintöoikeudesta II* (Lectures on inheritance law II), Vammala, 1971.
6. *Jälkisäädökset* (Last will and testament), Vammala, 1972.
7. *Perintöoikeus* (Law of inheritance), Vammala, 1974.
8. *Laki, teko ja tavoite* (Law, act and goal), Forssa, 1975.
9. *Jälkisäädökset* (Last will and testament), Vammala, 1975[2].
10. *On Legal Reasoning*, Loimaa, 1976.
11. *Aviovarallisuusjärjestelmät* (Community property systems), Helsinki, 1978.
12. *Mitä lainoppi on?* (What is jurisprudence?), Helsinki, 1978.
13. *Denkweisen der Rechtswissenschaft*, Vienna, 1979.
14. *Oikeussäännösten tulkinnasta* (On the interpretation of statutes), Helsinki, 1982.
15. (with Sami Mahkonen) *Suomen avioliittoikeus* (Finnish matrimonial law), Jyväskylä, 1983.
16. (with Ahti Saarenpää and Pekka Santala) *Maatilan sukupolvenvaihdos* (The transfer of a farm to a descendent), Jyväskylä, 1983.
17. (with Urpo Kangas)) *Suomen jäämistöoikeus I* (Finnish law of inheritance I), Jyväskylä, 1983[3].
18. *Suomen jäämistöoikeus II* (Finnish law of inheritance II), Jyväskylä, 1991[2].
19. (with Markku Helin) *Suomen avioliittooikeus* (Finnish matrimonial law), Jyväskylä, 1992[3].
20. *The Rational as Reasonable*, Dordrecht, 1987.
21. *Lo racional como razonable*, E. Garzón Valdés (transl.), Madrid, 1991.
22. *Le rationnel comme raisonnable*, G. Warland (transl.), Brussels/Paris, 1992.
23. (with Markku Helin) *Avioliittolain muutetut säännökset* (The revised statutes of marriage act), Tampere, 1988.
24. *Laintulkinnan teoria* (The theory of legal interpretation), Juva, 1989.
25. (with Urpo Kangas and Pertti Puronen) *Perunkirjoitusopas* (A guide to the inventory of the deceased's estate), Jyväskylä, 1996[4].
26. (with A. Peczenik and G. Bergholtz) *Juridisk argumentation* (Legal argumentation), Stockholm, 1990.

27. (with Urpo Kangas) *Avioliitto, perintö ja testamentti* (Marriage, inheritance and last will and testament), Jyväskylä, 1994.
28. Swedish edition *Äktenskap, arv och testamente*, Jyväskylä, 1995.
29. *Derecho, racionalidad y comunicación social. Ensayos sobre filosofía del derecho*, Mexico D.F., 1995.
30. *Reason and Authority. A Treatise on the Dynamic Paradigm of Legal Dogmatics*, Aldershot, 1997.

II. Essays and collections of articles

1. *Legal Point of View*, Helsinki, 1978.
2. *Philosophical Perspectives in Jurisprudence*, Helsinki, 1983.
3. *Murusia matkan varrelta* (Bits and pieces along the way), Tampere, 1985.
4. *Sankarit vailla siipiä* (Heroes without wings), Tampere, 1985.
5. *Lain ja kohtuuden tähden* (For law and reasonableness), Juva/Porvoo, 1986.
6. *Wegen zu Recht und Billigkeit. Vorträge und Aufsätze*, Berlin, 1988.
7. *Hämärässä laulaa punakylkirastas* (Redwing sings in the twilight), Tampere, 1987.
8. *Silmäyksiä* (Glances), Tampere, 1989.
9. *Järki ja auktoriteetti. Puhuttua ja kirjoitettua vuosilta 1988–1994* (Reason and authority. Words and thoughts from 1988–94), Tampere, 1994.
10. *Kohtaamisia. Lehtikirjoituksia vuosilta 1994–95* (Encounters. Newspaper articles from 1994–95), Tampere, 1995.
11. *Sirpaleita* (Fragments), Tampere, 1997.
12. *Ajatuksia Johannes Richterin varjossa.* (Thoughts in the shadow of Johannes Richter), Tampere, 1998.

MY PHILOSOPHY OF LAW: THE INSTITUTIONALISATION OF REASON*

ROBERT ALEXY

UNIVERSITY OF KIEL/GERMANY

Every philosophy of law is implicitly or explicitly an expression of a concept of law. All concepts of law derive from the interpretation and weighing of three elements: (1) due enactment, (2) social efficacy, and (3) substantial correctness[1]. Somebody who solely concentrates on due enactment and social efficacy, not giving any weight to substantial correctness in a definition of law advocates a positivist concept of law. Hans Kelsen's theory is an example for such a concept. His famous sentence "Therefore, any content whatever can be law"[2] expresses this clearly. The most extreme antipode to legal positivism is held by those who define the law exclusively by its substantial correctness. Such a pure notion of natural law is not interesting for somebody who wants to recognise, follow, interpret, and apply the valid law. The decisive question concerning the adequacy of a concept of law is therefore not whether substantial correctness rather than due enactment and social efficacy should define the law, but instead whether substantial correctness should do so in addition.

Enactment and efficacy form the real or institutional side of the law whereas correctness forms its ideal or discursive dimension. My thesis is that an adequate concept of law can only derive from a nexus of the two. This connection can only be achieved in a comprehensive theory of the legal system. The discourse theory of the democratic constitutional state provides such a theory. I will try to develop this theory in four steps. The first step deals with the foundation underlying the whole, the claim to correctness. It will be shown that this claim is necessarily connected with law. Succeeding so, the germ is found which is to burst the positivist concept of law. Yet, the content of the claim to correctness is still left open at this stage. A first specification is made in a second step which deals with discourse theory as a theory of practical correctness. This will show not only the possibilities but also the limits of discursive rationality. The latter will lead us to the third step: the necessity of law. The necessity of law

---

* The authors thanks are due to Kirsten Bock for translating this article into English.

[1] Cf. R. Alexy, "A Definition of Law" in *Prescriptive Formality and Normative Rationality* in *Modern Legal Systems. Festschrift for Robert S. Summers*, W. Krawietz, N. MacCormick and G.-H. von Wright (eds.), Berlin, 1994, 101 ff.

[2] H. Kelsen, *Reine Rechtslehre*, Vienna, 1960², 201.

does not imply the dismissal of discursive rationality. This is to be explained in the fourth step which is about the nexus of the real or institutional and the ideal or discursive on the different levels of the legal system.

1. The Claim to Correctness

My theory stands and falls with the thesis that the law necessarily raises a claim to correctness. This thesis is formulated very generally. If one wants to specify it, three questions need to be answered: (1) what does it mean that the law raises a claim? (2) what is to be understood by the necessity of this claim? (3) what is the substance of the claim, what is correctness?

1.1. To Raise a Claim

In a strict sense, claims can only be raised by subjects having the capacity to speak and to act. The fact that the law raises a claim to correctness can therefore only mean that it is raised by those who work in and for the law creating, interpreting, applying, and enforcing it. Paradigmatic cases are the legislator and the judge. Raising this claim means firstly that their institutional acts hence statutory enactments and judgements by the courts, are connected with the non-institutional act of *assertion* of correctness of the legal act in substance and in procedure. Correctness implies justifiability. The claim to correctness therefore secondly comprises a *guarantee* for justifiability. The assertion and the guarantee are thirdly attached to the *expectation* that anyone who takes the point of view of the respective legal system and is reasonable accepts the legal act as correct. The raising of the claim to correctness therefore consists in the trias of (1) assertion of correctness, (2) guarantee for justifiability, and (3) expectation of acceptance[3]. This trias is not only connected with institutional acts such as enactments and judicial judgements. Everybody who brings forward arguments as a participant in a legal system, for instance as a lawyer before a court or as a citizen in a public debate, for or against specific matters of the legal system raises the claim being composed of the assertion of correctness, the guarantee for justifiability, and the expectation of acceptance.

1.2. The Necessity

The claim to correctness is only of interest for the concept of law if it is necessarily connected with the law. If the law could raise this claim as well as not, it would only be one of numerous contingent features of the law without any

---

[3] For further details cf. R. Alexy, "Recht und Richtigkeit" in *Festschrift for Aulis Aarnio*, W. Krawietz, R. S. Summers, O. Weinberger and G.-H. von Wright (eds.), Berlin, 1997 (in print).

importance for the definition of law. The necessity can be demonstrated and explicated by two examples.

1.2.1. An Absurd Constitutional Article

The first example is about the prime article of a new constitution of the state *X* in which the minority suppresses the majority. The minority wants to continue savouring the advantages of oppression but also wants to be honest. The constitutional convention therefore resolves on the following sentence as first article of the constitution:

(1) *X* is a sovereign, federal, and unjust republic.

This constitutional article is faulty in a way. The question is to determine what is wrong. Without doubt it infringes the conventions about constitutional wordings, but this alone does not explain the flaw. A basic rights catalogue of a hundred pages would, for example, also be most unusual or unconventional, but in spite of its unusualness and its inexpediency, it does not have the downright non-sensicality of the injustice clause. The same is true for the moral fault. From the moral point of view there would be no difference if the injustice clause were removed and replaced by an article which explicitly deprives the suppressed majority of rights but there is, from the viewpoint of faultiness. The injustice clause is not only immoral but also somehow mad. It is said, that the injustice clause is only a political mistake because it is "politically inexpedient"[4]. This is indeed so, but it does not fully explain the defect. Much might be politically inexpedient in a constitution and in this sense technically defective without seeming to be so strange as our first article[5]. Neither the conventional nor the moral, nor the technical defectiveness explains the absurdity of the injustice clause. This results, as often in the case of the absurd, from a contradiction. Such a contradiction emerges because the act of giving a constitution encloses a claim to correctness which is mainly a claim to justice in this case. Claims comprise – as mentioned – assertions. In the case of the claim to justice raised here, it is the assertion that the constituted republic is just. This assertion implicit in the act of giving a constitution contradicts the explicit content of the constituent act, the injustice clause.

---

[4] E. Bulygin, "Alexy und das Richtigkeitsargument" in *Rechtsnorm und Rechtswirklichkeit. Festschrift for Werner Krawietz,* A. Aarnio, S. L. Paulson, O. Weinberger, G.-H. von Wright and D. Wyduckel (eds.), Berlin, 1993, 23 ff.

[5] Cf. R. Alexy, *Begriff und Geltung des Rechts*, Freiburg/Munich, 1994², 66.

1.2.2. An Absurd Decision

The second example is about a judge who announces the following verdict:

(4) The defendant is (wrongly, because the valid law was interpreted incorrectly) sentenced to life imprisonment.

This judgement provokes a bundle of questions that will not be followed up here[6]. In the context at issue, it is only of importance that the assumption of a conventional, moral, or technical fault as well as of an offence against the positive law[7] is insufficient here too, to comprehend the peculiar character of the fault. The absurdity in this sentence explains itself again only from a contradiction. The claim to a correct application of the law is always raised in a judicial decision however poor this claim may be accomplished. The claim to correctness which is raised with the institutional act of sentence contradicts its classifying itself as wrong. Raising a claim to correctness means, among other things, the implicit assertion that the jugdement is correct. This implicit assertion contradicts the explicit and public assertion connected with the judgement that it is wrong. This contradiction between the implicit and the explicit explains the absurdity.

1.2.3. The Alternative

It could be argued that all this does not yet show the necessity of the claim to correctness. Absurdity may be avoided in both cases. It would only take a radical change in the present practice and in what the law stands for at present. If constitutions would be understood solely as means of power, will, and force, and judicial decisions as mixtures of emotion, fiat, and commands, the claim to correctness will disappear and with it the contradiction and absurdity in our examples. The claim to correctness would be replaced by something like a power claim.

The consequence of this objection will become obvious if it is enlarged and generalised. Claims to correctness do not only exist in law. They are also raised in connection with moral value and obligation judgements and their most general form is linked with the speech act of assertion. Moral statements that do not raise this claim are not moral judgements but only the expression of emotions,

---

[6] Cf. on this U. Neumann, *Juristische Argumentationslehre*, Darmstadt 1986, 87 ff.; E. Bulygin, "Alexy und das Richtigkeitsargument", 23, on the one side and R. Alexy, *Begriff und Geltung des Rechts*, 69 ff.; id., "Bulygins Kritik des Richtigkeitsarguments" in *Normative Systems in Legal and Moral Theory. Festschrift for Carlos E. Alchourron and Eugenio Bulygin*, W. Krawietz e.a. (eds.), Berlin, 1997, p. 247 ff., on the other side.

[7] Cf. id., *Begriff und Geltung des Rechts*, 69.

suggestions to feel similar, or reports about feelings and attitudes[8]. Whoever drops the claim to correctness generally looses the possibility to state assertions of any kind because only such speech acts which raise a claim to truth or correctness are assertions[9]. The elimination of the possibility to assert something would change our language and the way we understand ourselves and thus our lives completely. Instead of judgements and assertions only feelings and opinions would be left, justification would become persuasion, and manipulation and strong beliefs would take over the place of correctness and truth. Everything would be subjective, nothing objective.

This clarifies the sense in which the claim to correctness is necessary. It is necessary relative to a practice that is essentially defined by the distinction of true or correct and wrong[10]. Yet, this practice is a practice of a special kind. We can indeed try to dismiss the categories of truth, correctness, and objectivity. But if this should succeed, our talking and acting will be quite different as it is now. The price would not only be high. To a certain degree it would consist in ourselves.

1.3. The Substance

The thesis that a claim to correctness is raised does not imply anything about its substance. This is rather an advantage than a disadvantage because else this claim could not be raised in all fields. The criteria of correctness depend on the context. For a constitutional convention there are therefore different criteria as are valid in the daily work of the parliamentary legislator and again others for judicial decisions. Yet, one thing marks the claim to correctness in all contexts: it comprises a claim to justifiability[11]. In the field of law this always means, directly

---

[8] Cf. id., *A Theory of Legal Argumentation*, Oxford, 1989, 39 ff.

[9] For further detail see id., "Discourse Theory and Human Rights", *Ratio Juris*, 1996, 214 ff.

[10] The relativity of the necessity of the claim to correctness to a specific practice coincides in its structure with the thesis by Grice and Strawson saying that it be one thing to admit that there is no absolute necessity to adopt or use any conceptual scheme or system whatever and quite another thing to say that there are no necessities within any conceptual scheme or system we adopt or use. The latter does not follow from the first (H.P. Grice and P.F. Strawson, "In Defense of a Dogma" in 65 *Philosophical Review*, 157 ff. (1956). The necessity within a specific conceptual scheme or system and also within a specific practice is in opposition to the necessity of a specific conceptual scheme or system as such or a specific practice as such quite consistent with Quine's thesis saying that no sentence and no rule is immune from revision (W.V.O. Quine, "Two Dogmas of Empiricism" in id., *From a Logical Point of View*, Cambridge (Mass.), 1961^2, 43).

[11] R. Alexy, "Discourse Theory and Human Rights", 215.

or indirectly, justifying general or individual[12] norms. It concerns normative or practical questions. In order to explain to which contents the claim of correctness leads in the different institutional contexts of the law, I will begin with the question of how the justification of norms in general, hence independent from law, is possible. The answer is given by the theory of general practical discourse.

2. Discourse Theory

2.1. The Basic Ideas of Discourse Theory

Discourse theory is a procedural theory of practical correctness. The following definition underlies procedural theories of practical correctness: a norm *N* is correct, if and only if *N* can be the result of the procedure *P*[13].

The procedure of discourse is one of argumentation. This makes a fundamental difference between discourse theory and procedural theories of the Hobbesian tradition relying on negotiation and decision making procedures[14].

The procedure *P* in discourse theory can be defined by a system of discourse rules[15] that express the conditions of rational practical argumentation. Some of these rules word general requirements of rationality being also valid independent of discourse theory. These include freedom from contradiction, universalisability in the sense of a consistent use of applied predicates, linguistic and conceptual clarity, empirical truth, consideration of consequences, balancing, exchange of roles or role reversal, and the analysis of the genesis of moral views. All these rules are valid in monologues, too. This already makes it clear that discourse theory in no way, as was held against it[16], replaces justification by merely producing consensus. It fully encloses the rules of rational argumentation applicable to monological justification. Its distinctive feature exclusively consists in adding a second level to this one, namely that of the rules referring to the procedure of discourse. These rules have a non-monological character. They aim at the impartiality of the discourse. This aim is to be achieved by securing the freedom and equality of the argumentation. The most important of these rules are as follows:

---

[12] The most important example for an individual norm is the judicial decision. Cf. H. Kelsen, *Reine Rechtslehre*, 20.

[13] R. Alexy, "Problems of Discourse Theory", 20 *Critica*, 44 (1988).

[14] Cf. *e.g.*, J. M. Buchanan, *The Limits of Liberty*, Chicago/London, 1975, 6 ff. and 26 ff.; D. Gauthier, *Morals by Agreement*, Oxford, 1986, 113 ff.

[15] For an attempt to build such a system with the help of 28 rules of discourse cf. R. Alexy, *A Theory of Legal Argumentation*, 188 ff.

[16] Cf. O. Weinberger, "Grundlagenprobleme des institutionalistischen Rechtspositivismus und der Gerechtigkeitstheorie", *Rechtstheorie*, 1994, 258 ff.

1. Everyone who can speak may take part in discourse.
2. (a) Everyone may question any assertion.
   (b) Everyone may introduce any assertion into the discourse.
   (c) Everyone may express his or her attitudes, wishes, and needs.
3. No speaker may be prevented from exercising the rights laid down in (1) and (2) by any kind of coercion internal or external to the discourse[17].

These rules express the ideas of universal freedom and equality on the level of argumentation. If they are valid that is, if everyone can decide freely and equally about what she is willing to accept, the following condition of universal agreement is necessarily valid: a norm can only find universal agreement in a discourse if the consequences of its general observance for the satisfaction of the interests of everybody are acceptable to everyone.

It is a central assumption of discourse theory that the acceptance in discourse may firstly be dependant on arguments and that secondly, there is a necessary relation between universal agreement or consent under ideal conditions and the concepts of correctness and moral validity. This relation can be put in the following wording:

Correct and therefore valid are exactly those norms that, in an ideal discourse, would be judged correct by everyone.

Weakening this statement, it becomes Habermas' abstract discourse principle: "Just those action norms are valid to which all possibly affected persons could agree as participants in rational discourses"[18].

This corresponds at least in its basic intention to Kant's principle of legislative authority: "Therefore only the concurring and united will of all, insofar as each decides the same thing for all and all for each, and so only the general united will of the people, can be legislative"[19].

This shows that discourse theory stands in the Kantian tradition.

2.2. The Limits of Discourse Theory

Discourse theory leads to numerous problems. Three of them are of special importance. The first one is concerned with discourse theory as a theory of practical correctness. It could also be called the "*problem of status*". The status problem refers to the question whether there actually is, as discourse theory asserts, a necessary relation between discourses and practical correctness[20]. The second problem relates to the justification of rules of discourse. The *problem of*

---

[17] R. Alexy, *A Theory of Legal Argumentation*, 193.

[18] J. Habermas, *Between Facts and Norms. Contributions to a Discourse Theory of Law and Democracy*, Cambridge (Mass.), 1996, 107.

[19] I. Kant, *The Metaphysics of Morals*, M. Gregor (transl.), Cambridge, 1991, 125.

[20] Cf. on this R. Alexy, "Problems of Discourse Theory", 54 ff.

justification can be resolved if it is possible to show that firstly those who participate in the practice of asserting, asking, and arguing necessarily presuppose these rules, and that secondly the participation in such a practice is necessary for everyone in some way or other. I have tried to explain elsewhere that the former as well as the latter are true[21]. Here, I will let the third problem come to the fore. It is the *problem of applicability* of discourse theory.

2.2.1. Real and Ideal Discourses

Under the aspect of applicability the main weakness of discourse theory consists in its system of rules not supplying a procedure that allows for a finite number of operations to always reach exactly one result. This is due to three reasons. Rules of discourse enclose firstly no provision concerning the starting points of the procedure. Starting points are the normative convictions and interpretations of interests of the participants, just as they appear. Secondly, the rules of discourse do not lay down all steps in argumentation. Thirdly, some of the rules of discourse are of ideal character and can therefore only be approximately fulfilled.

The latter leads to a fundamental distinction in discourse theory: that between ideal and real discourses. The throughout ideal practical discourse is defined by the search for an answer to a practical question under conditions of unlimited time, unlimited participation, and complete absence of coercion in producing complete linguistic and conceptual clarity, complete empirical information, complete ability and willingness to change roles, and complete freedom from prejudice. The concept of ideal discourse causes a number of problems[22] and is subject to strong criticism[23]. Never has a human being participated in an in every respect ideal discourse and no mortal will ever do so. It will always be speculative and never be absolutely certain what could be the result of an ideal discourse. It is not even certain whether the throughout ideal discourse would lead to a consensus for every practical question or whether there are such discourse resistant differences between people that would exclude unanimity in all practical questions even under ideal conditions.

And yet, all of this does not lead to devaluate the concept of ideal discourse. The concept of ideal discourse is always present in real discourse as a regulative idea[24]. As a regulative idea it expresses the aim or final point of

---

[21] Id., "Discourse Theory and Human Rights", 212 ff.

[22] Cf. id., "Problems of Discourse Theory", 48 ff.

[23] Cf. O. Weinberger, "Grundlagenprobleme des institutionalistischen Rechtspositivismus und der Gerechtigkeitstheorie", 259 ff.

[24] For the concept of the regulative idea cf. I. Kant, *Critique of Pure Reason*, W. S. Pluhar (transl.), Indianapolis, 1996, 518 and 619.

discourses. Real practical discourses are defined by the search for an answer to a practical question under the conditions of limited time, limited participation, and limited coercivelessness under limited linguistic and conceptual clarity, limited empirical information, limited ability to change roles, and limited freedom from prejudice. Regardless of these limitations, the real discourse is necessarily connected with the ideal discourse. Whoever tries to convince an opponent by reason presupposes that he would agree under ideal conditions. In this way, the ideal discourse as a regulative idea and the claim to correctness are the two sides of a coin.

In opposition to this could be said that the ideal discourse is senseless as a regulative idea. This would be so indeed if an approximation to it would be either impossible or irrelevant concerning correctness. Yet, it is easy to see that an approximation of real to ideal discourses is possible. So there are limited and open, vague and clear, know-all and critical discourses, and all of these and even more exist in various degrees. The question, therefore, can only be whether there is an internal nexus between approximation to ideal discourses and practical correctness. It is a central assumption of discourse theory that this is the case. Practical discourses not only deal with the assessment of common interests but essentially also with the correct solution of conflicts of interests. A correct solution of a conflict of interests is in its core a matter of correctly fixing the relative weight of the interests at play. Let us assume that the norm N_1 solves a conflict of interests meeting unanimous approval after a discourse from which all opponents unwilling to consent had been excluded and in which one group had been dominant, emotional rhetoric had been ruling the field, wrong facts had been treated as truth until the end, and the winners had solely pursued their own interest and were unwilling to notice others. Compare this scenario to a solution of the same conflict of interests using the norm N_2 which meets with unanimous approval after a discourse from which nobody had been excluded and in which nobody had been dominant, discussion had been clear and precise, only true or probable assumptions about the facts had been made, and everybody had been trying as much as possible to consider the situation of others and had been discussing with them the interpretation of their interests. The second case is without doubt closer to the ideal discourse than the first and therefore, at least *ceteris paribus*, N_2 is closer to correctness than N_1. This is sufficient for our purpose: approximation of the real towards the ideal discourse is not irrelevant concerning correctness.

2.2.2. The Discursive Modalities

The nexus of the real with the ideal discourse can only clear up the indetermination of the result to a rather limited extend. There is some that is unsuitable as a result of a sufficient and in general practically possible approach towards an ideal discourse. Slavery is an example. It can be said to be discursively impossible[25]. Other results can be found with sufficient certainty as results of discourse and are therefore to be called "discursively necessary". Democracy is an example[26]. Nevertheless, there is a broad space besides the discursively impossible and the discursively necessary enclosing the discursively merely possible in which different results can be found in a rational manner. Here, discourse theory reaches a boarder that it cannot cross by itself.

3. The Necessity of Law

Discourse theory does not offer a procedure which always secures exactly one outcome by means of a finite number of operations. This causes a broad space of the discursively merely possible and can be called "problem of knowledge". The problem of knowledge leads to the necessity of legally regulated procedures that guarantee a decision. Voting in parliament is the most important example. If this is projected on to the three elements of the concept of law, due enactment, social efficacy, and substantial correctness, it can be said that the weight is shifted from substantial correctness to due enactment by the problem of knowledge.

The problem of knowledge is not the only problem that leads the way from pure discourse theory to law. Two more must be added: the problem of enforcement and the problem of organisation. The problem of enforcement takes its rise from the difference between the insight to correctness or legitimacy of a norm and its observance. The unanimous agreement reached in a discourse about a norm as just and therefore correct is not necessarily followed by its observance by everyone. But if some are able to violate a norm without any further ado, its observance cannot be demanded from anyone. The fact that insights do not always correspond with the respective action supplies a second reason for the necessity of law, namely, a reason for law as a system of rules backed by force[27]. This gives fundamental weight to social efficacy enclosing organised coercion[28] in defining law. Finally, the problem of organisation results from numerous moral demands and desirable aims that cannot be sufficiently achieved or reached by individual action and spontaneous cooperation alone. Just think of unemployment benefit or support of countries in need. Necessary organisation requires law. This is also true for the administration of law itself. Law needs to be organised by law.

---

[25] Cf. R. Alexy, *A Theory of Legal Argumentation*, 207; id., "Discourse Theory and Human Rights", 224.

[26] Cf. id., "Discourse Theory and Human Rights", 233.

[27] The knowledge and the enforcement problem mainly correspond to Kant's argument of transition from the state of nature to the civil state. Cf. I. Kant, *The Metaphysics of Morals*, 124.

[28] Cf. R. Alexy, *Begriff und Geltung des Rechts*, 139 ff.

Regarding the concept of law, this implies an intensification of weight of due enactment as well as social efficacy to the debit of substantial correctness.

4. Institution and Ideal

One could think that in view of the weight that the knowledge, the enforcement, and the organisation problem put on due enactment and social efficacy substantial correctness might be ousted from the concept of law. Due to this, discourse theory seems to dismiss itself and leave everything to legal positivism grounded in the classical argument to evade anarchy and civil war and to prepare effective co-operation, in short, in legal certainty[29].

However, this argumentation misses two points. Firstly, it is not recognised that the relatively big weight of legal certainty looses the more the heavier justice and thus substantial correctness are ousted. This creates the possibility of a point in which priority shifts. Secondly, it is left out of consideration that there is not only a relation of alternative between due enactment together with social efficacy, hence positivity, on the one hand and substantial correctness on the other hand but also one of supplementation, permeation, and reinforcement. This supplementation, permeation, and reinforcement is the condition of the legitimacy of law.

4.1. The Threshold of Extreme Injustice

If it were true that the better arguments are in favour of a strict priority of due enactment and social efficacy over substantial correctness, Kelsen's famous sentence "Therefore, any content whatever can be law"[30] would be correct in every respect. After 1945 Gustav Radbruch objected that the conflict between justice, that is substantial correctness, and legal certainty is to be generally solved in favour of legal certainty but this must not be absolute. The priority of the enacted and efficacious over justice comes to a limit whenever a positive law contradicts justice to an "unbearable degree" *("unerträgliches Mass")*[31]. This can be reduced to the formula: extreme injustice is no law[32].

The particular of this formula is its not demanding a complete congruence of law and morality. It leaves the enacted and efficacious law untouched even if it is unjust. It only installs an utmost limit in law.

---

[29] In this way C. Braun, "Diskurstheorethische Normenbegründung in der Rechtswissenschaft", *Rechtstheorie*, 1988, 259 ff.

[30] H. Kelsen, *Reine Rechtslehre*, 201.

[31] G. Radbruch, "Gesetzliches Unrecht und übergesetzliches Recht" (1946) in *Gesamtausgabe*, III, A. Kaufmann (ed.), Heidelberg, 1990, 89.

[32] R. Alexy, *Mauerschützen*, Hamburg 1993, 4.

The German jurisdiction after 1945 applied Radbruch's formula to National Socialist injustice[33] and after 1989 to norms of the German Democratic Republic justifying homicide on the German-German boarder[34]. All of this is highly disputed and cannot be discussed further here[35]. But notice that the plausibility of this formula can be viewed differently according to the perspectives of a participant or an observer[36]. There is much in favour to regarding it from the perspective of an observer as wrong, whereas from the perspective of a participant as right. Ultimately, a balancing of normative reasons will decide. In this weighing the claim to correctness being always connected with the law, even with such of extreme injustice, plays a major part. Having this in mind, the better reasons are, taken the perspective of a participant, on the side of Radbruch's formula[37]. In doing so it is, *e.g.*, excluded that after 1945 somebody could claim an institutional fact such as the loss of citizenship of a deceased person that was due to a norm of racial legislation created during National Socialism[38]. Substantial correctness is therefore of defining consequence for the concept of law even though only by fixing an utmost limit. In this way, it has an independent weight as against due enactment and social efficacy[39]. This is already sufficient to classify the concept of law as "non-positivistic".

---

[33] BGHZ (Decisions of the Federal Court of Justice in Civil Cases) 3, 94 (107); BGHSt (Decisions of the Federal Court of Justice in Criminal Cases) 2, 173 (177); 2, 234 (237 ff.); 3, 357 (362 f.); BVerfGE (Decisions of the Federal Constitutional Court) 3, 58 (119); 3, 225 (232); 6, 132 (198); 6, 389 (414); 23, 98 (106); 54, 53 (68).

[34] BGHSt 39, 1 (16); 40, 218 (232); 40, 241 (244); 41, 101 (106 ff.). Cf. on this R. Alexy, *Mauerschützen*, 7 ff.

[35] Instead of many, I will only name the most prominent antipode of Radbruch which is H. L. A. Hart, "Positivism and the Separation of Law and Morals" 71 *Harvard Law Review,* 615 ff. (1957-58).

[36] Cf. R. Alexy, *Begriff und Geltung des Rechts*, 51 ff. and 70 ff.

[37] For a substantiation on the basis of an analysis of eight arguments for and against cf. id., *ibid.*, 72 ff.

[38] Cf. BVerfGE 23, 98 (100 f. 106).

[39] Radbruch's formula causes the greatest problems in the field of criminal law. At stake is especially the question whether the elimination of norms of legal justification of an unjust regime violates the principle "*Nullum crimen, nulla poena sine lege*" which is part of the constitutions of most states. But this is not a problem that affects Radbruch's formula as such. It only affects its applicability within criminal law. Cf. on this R. Alexy, *Der Beschluss des Bundesverfassungsgerichts zu den Tötungen an der innerdeutschen Grenze vom 24. Oktober 1996*, Hamburg, 1997.

4.2. The Democratic Constitutional State

Radbruch's formula is only effective in an exceptional situation: in the case of an extremely unjust law. Such exceptional situations mark a national disaster. In a normal situation it is not the dramatic alternative between positivity and correctness that forms the problem but their supplementation, permeation, and reinforcement. Discourse needs the law to gain reality, and the law needs discourse to gain legitimacy. In Radbruch's formula the institutional is only confined by the ideal. Now, their internal connection is to be unfolded which till now most perfectly manifests itself in the democratic constitutional state.

Discourse theory leads to the democratic constitutional state because it makes two fundamental requirements regarding the substance and structure of the legal system: basic rights[40] and democracy.

4.2.1. Basic Rights

In discourse theory freedom and equality underlie discourse. The rules of discourse express this clearly. This suggests to infer freedom and equality in all aspects of action from freedom and equality in discourse. However, such a direct conclusion from rules of speech to legal rules is not possible. It needs further premises. To substantiate legal freedom one needs to add the premise that somebody who enters a discourse with an interest to solve political problems through discursively generated and controlled consensus has to accept the freedom of others outside of discourses as well[41]. Whoever takes part in a discourse without this motivation has at least to pretend such interests if she wants to achieve legitimacy through argument. This leads to a discourse-theoretical tyrant-dilemma: on the one hand, terror disguised by arguments is cheaper and more stable than naked force, on the other hand, argumentation provokes criticism and lying unmasking[42].

The interest in a discursive solution of political problems finds its most important impact on the side of the substantiation of freedom. Hypothetical consensus in an ideal discourse plays a respective part on the side of the substantiation of equality. The outcome of ideal discourse is, in principle, purely

---

[40] Basic rights are rights that are of such importance that their guarantee or non-guarantee cannot be left to a simple parliamentary majority (cf. R. Alexy, *Theorie der Grundrechte*, Frankfort-on-Main, 1994, 406). As constitutional rights they limit the competence of parliament. Human rights are rights that all humans are entitled to independent of their recognition by positive law. All human rights should be catalogued as basic rights in every constitution. Constitutions may besides human rights enclose additional rights as basic rights.

[41] Cf. R. Alexy, “Discourse Theory and Human Rights”, 223 ff.

[42] Id., *ibid.*, 226.

speculative. Yet, in some elemental cases there is sufficient certainty about what is discursively necessary or impossible. Equality of human rights is one of these elemental cases. Unequal human or basic rights cannot be justified in an ideal discourse because in an argumentation governed by freedom, equality, and rationality arguments for unequal distribution of human rights will not last[43].

The rights to freedom and equality form the core of basic rights. All other basic rights are either special cases of these two rights or necessary means of achieving and securing a sufficient degree of freedom and equality. The latter is true, *e.g.*, in the case of the right to the basic means of living[44].

To use freedom is autonomy. In a theory of the democratic constitutional state it is of fundamental importance that basic rights protect private as well as public autonomy. This is done by a broad spectrum of rights reaching from freedom of expression to freedom of assembly and to freedom of the press and latterly to the right to general, free, equal, and secret elections. This is the way in which a necessary connection between basic rights and democracy is constituted[45].

---

[43] In detail on this id., *ibid.*, 227 ff.

[44] Id., *ibid.*, 227; id., *Theorie der Grundrechte*, 458 ff.

[45] The fact that basic rights are discourse-theoretically justifiable implies that a constitutional convention is not free to choose whether the constitution shall guarantee basic rights or not. A constitution does only meet the claim to correctness and is therefore only legitimate if guaranteeing those rights as basic rights as demanded by discourse theory. Starting with a decisionistic concept of sovereignty of the people according to which a people is sovereign if it is able to decide whatever it wishes, discursive necessity of basic rights is a limitation of the sovereignty of the people from the outside. Using, on the other hand, a deliberative or discursive concept of sovereignty of the people according to which a people is sovereign if it forms its will in a free discourse, the basic rights are necessarily, at least under ideal conditions, part of its will. The basic rights cannot restrict an ideal procedure of constituting a constitution because they are already part of its definition. This is different though in a real procedure of constituting a constitution. Real discourses can miss what is correct and can therefore fail to guarantee basic rights. The basic rights do limit the real procedure in this case but limitation is different from that connected with a decisionistic concept of the sovereignty of the people. Basic rights do not alienate the sovereignty of the people understood in discursive terms but formulate what the people represented in the constitutional convention wanted as their very own under ideal conditions. Projected onto the concept of law it can be said that using the decisionistic conception of the sovereignty of the people, due enactment and social efficacy are limited by something quite different, namely substantial correctness, whereas using a discursive conception, the duly enacted and socially efficacious is in the ideal case always also substantially correct and in the real case at least aiming or trying to be so, thereby causing an internal nexus between the institutional and the ideal side corresponding to the necessary connection between law and the claim to correctness.

4.2.2. Democracy

Most variant ideas of democracy exist. The principle of discourse demands a deliberative democracy. Deliberative democracy is more than a procedure to produce an optimal arrangement of interest beneath the threshold of dictatorship or civil war. In deliberative democracy the level of interest and power is superposed by a level of argument on which all participants try for the correct political outcome. In this way, the possibility of discursive rationality is a prerequisite. If the idea of discursive rationality would be a mirage, deliberative democracy will be an illusion. If this were right, a sentence such as formed by the German Federal Constitutional Court that "the free discussion is the essential foundation of the free and democratic society"[46] could be no more than an expression of a plain ideology.

It is one thing that deliberative democracy is feasible only if there is something like rational practical discourse. The other is that the idea of discourse can only be realised to such an extent as it is realisable by an institutionalisation of deliberative democracy. Whoever wants correctness must want discourse. Whoever wants discourse must want democracy.

The organisation of the democratic institutions is to be done by democratic procedures. Democracy is insofar reflexive. But some basic lines may be already traced down on the basis of discourse theory. There is, to introduce two examples, the free play of arguments in the electronic media to be protected that ought not to be distorted or suppressed by money or power, and the financing of the political parties is to be regulated in such a way that the rebinding of the political process to reason and responsibility of the citizens is safeguarded and preserved[47].

4.2.3. Constitutional Adjudication

If the process of political will-formation succeeds, the majority in parliament is to bring the requirements of deliberative democracy, just as in our two examples above, into the form of statutes. The statutes are also to respect and concretise the basic rights. But what happens if statutes are enacted that violate basic rights or destroy deliberative democracy? This happening, one may trust in the self-healing abilities of democracy or one may prescribe the medicine of constitutional review. In favour of the latter is that otherwise chronic deficiencies might loom up and crises may lead to a deadly end even though it could have been prevented. Majorities tend to secure privileges and beloved habits even if

---

[46] BVerfGE 90, 1 (20 ff.).

[47] Cf. R. Alexy, "Grundgesetz und Diskurstheorie" in *Legitimation des Grundgesetzes aus der Sicht von Rechtsphilosophie und Gesellschaftstheorie*, W. Brugger (ed.), Baden-Baden, 1996, 355 ff.

they violate rights of minorities and it can never be bared that some force may win a majority that wants to stop deliberative democracy. Constitutional adjudication is however not a cure-all. If there are not enough people left who want democracy, nobody can save it. Moreover, constitutional adjudication can also exhibit negative effects. Every constitutional review bears the danger of paternalism[48]. This can only be banished firstly if constitutional adjudication is as an argumentative representation of the people much closer to discursive ideals than the political process leading to the repealed statute and secondly if the decision of the constitutional court is acknowledged by the people in the following political process as their own being subject of critical discussion and reflection[49].

4.3. Legal Argumentation

No legislator can build a system of norms that is perfect to such a degree that any case can be solved in simply subsuming the facts under a rule. This is due to several reasons. Of special importance are vagueness of the legal language, the possibility of contradicting norms, missing of norms on which the decision could be based, and the possibility to decide against the wording of a norm in special cases[50]. Insofar there is a necessary openness of the law[51].

Within the range of openness of the positive law there is, by definition, no possibility to decide on the grounds of the positive law because if this were possible, one's location would not be within the range of openness. Positivists like Kelsen and Hart are therefore only consequent in empowering a judge, similar to the legislator, to decide on other reasons than legal standards within the range of openness[52]. The claim to correctness on the other hand leads to a non-positivistic interpretation. It can be unfolded in two ways: (1) using the argument of principle and (2) the special case thesis.

4.3.1. The Argument of Principle

The argument of principle builds on the distinction of rules and principles. Rules are norms that make something definitely obligatory, prohibited, or permitted, or definitely empower to something. They enclose a definite ought. If the conditions are met, the legal consequences are necessary. Being not agreeable, the alternatives are either to declare the rule invalid and exempt it from

---

[48] Cf. J. Habermas, *Between Facts and Norms*, 266.

[49] Cf. R. Alexy, "Basic Rights and Democracy in Jürgen Habermas' Procedural Paradigm of the Law", *Ratio Juris*, 1994, 234 ff.

[50] Cf. id., *A Theory of Legal Argumentation*, 1 ff.

[51] Cf. H. L. A. Hart, *The Concept of Law*, Oxford, 1994^2, 128.

[52] H. Kelsen, *Reine Rechtslehre*, 350; H. L. A. Hart, *The Concept of Law*, 126, 135 and 204 ff.

the legal order or to introduce an exemption into the rule and thereby create a new rule. Subsuming is the form how to apply rules. Principles, in opposition, enclose an ideal ought[53]. They are precepts to be optimised. As such they do not comprise a definite but only a *prima facie* ought. They require to realise something to the highest degree possible relative to the factual and legal possibilities[54]. In a quite short though somehow vague[55] manner principles can be named "optimisation precepts". Principles as ideal precepts demand more than what is really possible. They collide with other principles. Their typical form of application is weighing and balancing. Only weighing and balancing leads from the ideal *prima facie* ought to the real and definite ought.

The starting point of the argument of principle is the claim to correctness requiring a balancing every time it is possible. The only possible objects of balancing are principles. The claim to correctness necessarily belonging to the law implies that balancing as required by it also necessarily belongs to the law. But if weighing and balancing belong to the law, their objects necessarily do too. The claim to correctness leads to an incorporation of principles, which present the reasons underlying the old as well as new rules, into the concept of law. This is how ideal reasons for what is definitely required become part of the law.

---

[53] R. Alexy, *Recht, Vernunft, Diskurs*, Frankfort-on-Main, 1995, 203 ff.

[54] Id., "Individual Rights and Collective Goods" in *Rights*, C. Nino (ed.), Aldershot, 1992, 166.

[55] Vagueness results from a mingle of two levels: an object and a meta-level. On the object level principles are ideal precepts and therefore precepts to be optimised. As such they can be realised to different degrees while rules can only be either fulfilled or not fulfilled (R. Alexy, *Recht, Vernunft, Diskurs*, 202 ff.). Principles being ideal precepts are the subjects of balancing. Opposing this, optimisation precepts are located on a meta-level determining what is to be done with whatever is on the object level. Optimisation precepts require that their subjects, the precepts that are to be optimised, are realised as far as possible. Still, optimisation precepts as such cannot be optimised but only either be fulfilled or not. Therefore, they, as has often and aptly been remarked, have the structure of rules (Cf. A. Aarnio, "Taking Rules Seriously", *A.R.S.P.*,1990, 187; J.-R. Sieckmann, *Regelmodelle und Prinzipienmodelle des Rechtssystems*, Baden-Baden, 1990, 63 ff.). Anyhow, talking about optimisation precepts still make sense. This concept expresses what is the core of principles in a notably simple way. Moreover, there is a necessary relation between the ideal ought, hence the very principle, and the optimisation precept as a rule: The ideal ought implies the optimisation precept and vice versa. These are the two sides of one thing. The question raised by Aleksander Peczenik whether the optimisation precept is sited in or out of the meaning of the principle which it is necessarily accompanying (A. Peczenik, *On Law and Reason*, Dordrecht/Boston/London, 1989, 77 ff.) is thus to be answered that it is covered by the meaning of a principle because its demolition would cause the respective principle to loose its character as a principle.

The ideal reasons for what is definitely required by the law do always enclose moral principles. Connecting this to the claim to correctness, two consequences arise. The claim to correctness firstly requires that the moral principles to be acknowledged in the law are correct. Legal correctness thus implies elements of moral correctness. It is substantial correctness of moral principles which makes them legally considerable and nothing else. This concerns the substance of moral principles brought into the law by the claim to correctness. The second consequence deals with the application of moral principles, hence their balancing against other moral principles and against specific legal principles such as principles affecting legal certainty, procedure, and effectiveness of law. Participation of moral principles in balancing signifies moral arguments taking part in justification of decisions resulting from balancing. If the claim to correctness is to be fulfilled, it needs a rational moral argumentation. Here, we return to the idea of discourse.

It could be opposed to the latter that the theory of principle brings up quite a different idea superseding discourse: namely, coherence. This is partly right and partly wrong. It is right in so far as the theory of principle encloses the idea of coherence. Balancing is one of the most important operations to bring about and secure coherence and therefore unity of the legal system. The importance of coherence for the correctness of law cannot be overestimated[56].

It would be wrong though to place coherence as the highest or one and only criteria for correctness of an interpretation of the law for which certain tendencies can be detected with some authors[57]. The idea of coherence cannot substitute the idea of discourse but only supplement and strengthen it. Its sole mastery would lead to legal holism according to which all premises are already part of or hidden in the legal system and need only to be discovered. Yet, norms regardless of whether being rules or principles cannot by themselves form a system and a system of norms cannot by itself establish and secure coherence. This can only be done by person and procedure. This is the point at which the special case thesis comes into play.

---

[56] Cf. R. Alexy and A. Peczenik, "The Concept of Coherence and Its Significance for Discursive Rationality", *Ratio Juris*, 1990, 130 ff.

[57] The historically most important example is Friedrich Carl von Savigny's theory of the "organic whole" and of "internal interdependence or relation which connect the single legal concepts and rules to one big unity" (F. C. von Savigny, *System des heutigen römischen Rechts*, I, Berlin, 1840, XXXVI ff.). More recently, there is Ronald Dworkin's theory of integrity to be noticed being identical with the idea of coherence under methodological aspects: "Law as integrity, then, requires a judge to test his interpretation of any part of the great network of political structures and decisions of his community by asking whether it could form part of a coherent theory justifying the network as a whole" (R. Dworkin, *Law's Empire*, Cambridge (Mass.)/London, 1986, 245).

4.3.2. The Special Case Thesis

The special case thesis states that legal discourse is a special case of general practical discourse[58]. In the end, legal discussion, like general practical argumentation, is concerned with what is obligatory, prohibited, or permitted, hence practical questions. A claim to correctness is raised in general practical discourse as well as in legal discourse. It is a matter of a special case because the claim to correctness in legal discourse is distinct from that in general practical discourse for it is not concerned with what is absolutely correct but about what is correct within the scope of a specific legal system. What is correct in a legal system essentially depends on what is authoritatively or institutionally fixed and what fits into the system. Expressing this in a short formula, it can be said that legal argumentation is bound to statutes and to precedent and has to observe the system of law elaborated by legal dogmatics[59]. Having statutes, precedent, or dogmatics determine a decision clearly and leaving no doubts under the aspect of correctness, a case is decided solely by the authoritative and institutional. If statutes, precedent, or dogmatics do not determine the answer to a legal question[60], as hard cases are characterised, additional evaluation is required that cannot be solely derived from the authoritative material given. If the claim to correctness shall be satisfied, these additional premises need to be justified. But this can only be achieved in general practical argumentation if the authoritative or the institutional alone does not give a sufficient answer. Within this scope considerations of practicality and views about what is good for the community have their legitimate place. But it still does not alter the fact that the guiding question of judicial decision making in the range of openness is a question about correct balance and correct distribution. Questions concerning correct balance and correct distribution are questions of justice. Yet, questions about justice are moral questions.

---

[58] R. Alexy, *A Theory of Legal Argumentation*, 212 ff.

[59] These requirements are expressed in the specific rules and forms of legal discourse. Cf. id., *ibid.*, 221 ff. and 300 ff.

[60] Here, I will not discuss the case of thorough doubts about an outcome being peremptorily required by the authoritative raising the problem of a decision against the wording of a statute or an overruling of a precedent. Cf. on this R. Alexy and R. Dreier, "Statutory Interpretation in the Federal Republic of Germany" in *Interpreting Statutes. A Comparative Study*, N. MacCormick and R. S. Summers (eds.), Aldershot, 1991, 95 ff.

This is the way in which the claim to correctness establishes a necessary connection between law and morality on the level of application of law[61].

[61] The special case thesis has been subject to numerous objections. Habermas, *e.g.*, put forward that the legal discourse should not be understood as a special case of the *moral* discourse because in law next to moral reasons there are also ethical and pragmatic reasons to play a legitimate part (J. Habermas, *Between Facts and Norms*, 230 ff.). According to Habermas moral arguments aim at what is equally good for all human beings. To him, this embodies the question of justice (id., *ibid.*, 153 ff. and 282). Ethical-political discourses are at stake whenever questions of "collective self-understanding" arise on the agenda enclosing a discussion about common traditions and forms of life (id., *ibid.*,108) as well as about collective goals and goods (id., *ibid.*, 154). The pragmatic usage of practical reason is finally to be required if "balancing of interests" are the matter (id. *ibid.*) to be achieved by "negotiating compromises" under the observance of fair bargaining conditions (id., *ibid.*, 108). Taking this as a basis, Habermas is indeed right in his thesis about the legal discourse not being a special case of moral discourse because the legal discourse is not only open to moral but also to ethical and pragmatic reasons (id., *ibid.* 283). But this does not affect the special case thesis. A "general practical discourse" is to be understood as a practical discourse in which moral, ethical, and pragmatic questions and reasons are connected with one another. The formation of such a concept of practical discourse makes sense and is necessary because there is not only a relation of supplementation between those three kinds of reason but also one of permeation. Presuming this concept of general practical discourse, the special case thesis holds true (R. Alexy, "Jürgen Habermas' Theory of Legal Discourse" 17 *Cardozo Law Review*, 1033 ff. (1996)). It has been objected by Klaus Günther that the special case thesis misunderstands that legal discourse is not a discourse of justification but a discourse of application (K. Günther, "Critical Remarks on Robert Alexy's 'Special-Case Thesis'", *Ratio Juris*, 1993, 143 ff.). It is to be advanced against this that the jurisdiction needs to develop a system of precedential rules to meet the postulates of equality and legal certainty. But these rules are justifiable as well as they need to be justified (R. Alexy, "Justification and Application of Norms", *Ratio Juris*, 1993, 157 ff.). Other critics of the special case thesis are A. Kaufmann, *Grundprobleme der Rechtsphilosophie*, Munich, 1994, 79, and U. Neumann, *Juristische Argumentationslehre*, 86 ff. For a detailed discussion in defense of the special case thesis cf. I. Dwars, "Application Discourse and Special-Case Thesis", *Ratio Juris*, 1992, 67 ff.

Bibliographical Information

I. Books

1. *Theorie der juristischen Argumentation*, Frankfort-on-Main, 1996[3].

A Theory of Legal Argumentation, R. Adler and N. MacCormick (transl.), Oxford, 1989.

Teoría de la argumentación jurídica, M. Atienza and I. Espejo (transl.), Madrid, 1989.

Theoria dell' argomentazione giuridica, M. La Torre (transl.), Milan, 1998.

2. *Theorie der Grundrechte*, Frankfort-on-Main, 1994[2].

Teoría de los derechos fundamentales, E. Garzón Valdés (transl.), Madrid, 1993.

3. *Begriff und Geltung des Rechts*, Freiburg and Munich, 1994[2].

El concepto y la validez del derecho, J. M. Seña (transl.), Barcelona, 1994.

Concetto e validità del diritto, F. Fiore (transl.), Turin, 1997.

4. *Derecho y razón práctica*, Mexico, 1993.

5. *Recht, Vernunft, Diskurs. Studien zur Rechtsphilosophie*, Frankfort-on-Main, 1995.

6. *Theoría del discurso y derechos humanos*, Bogota, 1995.

II. Articles

1. "Idee einer prozeduralen Theorie der juristischen Argumentation", *Rechtstheorie*, 1981, 177-188 and in R. Alexy, *Recht, Vernunft, Diskurs. Studien zur Rechtsphilosophie*, Frankfort-on-Main, 1995, 94-108.

"La idea de una theoría procesal de la argumentación jurídica" in *Derecho y filosofía*, E. Garzón Valdés (ed.), Barcelona/Caracas, 1985, 43-57 and in R. Alexy, *Derecho y razón práctica*, Mexico, 1993, 59-73.

2. (with A. Aarnio and A. Peczenik) "The Foundation of Legal Reasoning", *Rechtstheorie*, 1981, 133-158, 257-279 and 423-448 and in *Legal Reasoning*, I, A. Aarnio and N. MacCormick (eds.), Aldershot, 1992, 15-40 and 233-281.

"Grundlagen der juristischen Argumentation" in *Metatheorie juristischer Argumentation*, W. Krawietz and R. Alexy (eds.), Berlin, 1983, 9-87.

"I fondamenti del ragionamento giuridico" in *L'analisi del ragionamento giuridico*, P. Comanducci and R. Guastini (eds.), Turin, 1987, 121-187.

3. "Idée et structure d'un système du droit rationnel", *Archives de philosophie du droit*, 1988, 22-38.

"Idee und Struktur eines vernünftigen Rechtssystems" in *Rechts- und Sozialphilosophie in Deutschland heute*, *A.R.S.P.*, 1991, 30-44.

4. "Probleme der Diskurstheorie", *Zeitschrift für philosophische Forschung*, 1989, 81-93 and in R. Alexy, *Recht, Vernunft, Diskurs. Studien zur Rechtsphilosophie*, Frankfort-on-Main, 1995, 109-126.

"Problems of Discourse Theory", 20 *Crítica*, 45-65 (1988).

"Problemas de la teoría del discurso" in *Congreso Internacional Extraordinario de Filosofia*, I, University of Cordoba (ed.), Cordoba, 1987, 59-70.

"Problemas da Teoria do Discurso", *Anuário do Mestrado em Direito*, 1992, 87-105.

5. "Individuelle Rechte und kollektive Güter" in *Internationales Jahrbuch für Rechtsphilosophie und Gesetzgebung*, I, O. Weinberger (ed.), 1989, 49-70 and in R. Alexy, *Recht, Verunft, Diskurs. Studien zur Rechtsphilosophie*, Frankfort-on-Main, 1995, 232-261.

"Individual Rights and Collective Goods" in *Rights*, C. Nino (ed.), Aldershot, 1992, 163-181.

"Derechos individuales y bienes colectivos" in R. Alexy, *El concepto y la validez del derecho*, Barcelona, 1994, 179-208.

6. "Zur Kritik des Rechtspositivismus", *A.R.S.P.*, 1990, 9-26.

"On Necessary Relations Between Law and Morality", *Ratio Juris*, 1989, 167-183.

"Sobre las relaciones necesarias entre el derecho y la moral" in R. Alexy, *Derecho y razón práctica*, Mexico,1993, 37-58.

7. (with R. Dreier) "The Concept of Jurisprudence", *Ratio Juris*, 1990, 1-13 and *Indian Socio-Legal Journal*, 1992, 1-10.

8. (with A. Peczenik) "The Concept of Coherence and Its Significance for Discursive Rationality", *Ratio Juris*, 1990, 130-147.

9. (with R. Dreier) "Statutory Interpretation in the Federal Republic of Germany" in *Interpreting Statutes. A Comparative Study*, N. MacCormick and R. S. Summers (eds.), Aldershot, 1991, 73-121.

10. "Rights, Legal Reasoning and Rational Discourse", *Ratio Juris*, 1992, 143-152.

"Derechos, razonamiento jurídico y discurso racional" in R. Alexy, *Derecho y razón práctica*, Mexico, 1993, 23-35 and *Isonomía*, 1994, 37-49.

11. "Eine diskurstheoretische Konzeption der praktischen Vernunft", *A.R.S.P.*, 1993, 11-29.

"A Discourse-Theoretical Conception of Practical Reason", *Ratio Juris*, 1992, 231-251.

"Una concepción teórico-discursiva de la razón práctica" in R. Alexy, *El concepto y la validez del derecho*, Barcelona, 1994, 131-157.

12. "Normenbegründung und Normanwendung" in *Rechtsnorm und Rechtswirklichkeit. Festschrift für Werner Krawietz*, A. Aarnio, e.a. (eds.), Berlin, 1993, 3-17 and in R. Alexy, *Recht, Vernunft, Diskurs. Studien zur Rechtsphilosophie*, Frankfort-on-Main, 1995, 52-70.

"Justification and Application of Norms", *Ratio Juris*, 1993, 157-170.

13. "Legal Argumentation as Rational Discourse", *Rivista internazionale di filosofia del diritto*, 1993, 165-178.

"L'argomentazione giuridica come discorso razionale", *Informatica e diritto*, 1994, 5-20.

"Interpretación jurídica y discurso racional" in R. Alexy, *Teoría del discurso y derechos humanos*, Bogota, 1995, 35-61.

"Die juristische Argumentation als rationaler Diskurs" in *Facetten der Wahrheit. Festschrift for Meinolf Wewel*, E. Garzón Valdés and R. Zimmerling (eds.), Freiburg/Munich, 1995, 361-378.

14. "A Definition of Law" in *Prescriptive Formality and Normative Rationality in Modern Legal Systems. Festschrift for Robert S. Summers*, W. Krawietz, e.a. (eds.), Berlin, 1994, 101-107.

15. "Basic Rights and Democracy in Jürgen Habermas' Procedural Paradigm of the Law", *Ratio Juris*, 1994, 227-238.

"Grundrechte und Demokratie in Jürgen Habermas' prozeduralem Rechtsparadigma" in *Gerechtigkeit und Geschichte. Beiträge eines Symposions zum 65. Geburtstag von Malte Dießelhorst*, O. Behrends and R. Dreier (eds.), Göttingen, 1996, 78-89.

16. "Juristische Interpretation" in R. Alexy, *Recht, Vernunft, Diskurs. Studien zur Rechtsphilosophie*, Frankfort-on-Main, 1995, 71-92.

"Interpretazione giuridica" in *Enciclopedia delle scienze sociali*, V, Istituto della enciclopedia italiana (ed.), Rome, 1996, 64-71.

17. "Diskurstheorie und Menschenrechte" in R. Alexy, *Recht, Vernunft, Diskurs. Studien zur Rechtsphilosophie*, Frankfort-on-Main,1995, 127-164.

"Teoría del discurso y derechos humanos" in R. Alexy, *Teoría del discurso y derechos humanos*, Bogota, 1995, 63-136.

"Discourse Theory and Human Rights", *Ratio Juris*, 1996, 209-235 and *A.R.S.P.*, 1997, 81-104.

18. "Jürgen Habermas' Theorie des juristischen Diskurses" in R. Alexy, *Recht, Vernunft, Diskurs. Studien zur Rechtsphilosophie*, Frankfort-on-Main, 1995, 165-174.

"Jürgen Habermas' Theory of Legal Discourse", 17 *Cardozo Law Review*, 1027-1034 (1996).

19. "Law, Discourse, and Time", *A.R.S.P.*, 1995, 101-110.

20. (with R. Dreier) "Precedent in the Federal Republic of Germany" in *Interpreting Precedents. A Comparative Study*, N. MacCormick and R. S. Summers (eds.), Aldershot, 1997, 17-64.

MY PHILOSOPHY OF LAW

MARTIN P. GOLDING

DUKE UNIVERSITY, DURHAM

NORTH CAROLINA, USA

1. An Approach to Legal Philosophy

My approach to the philosophy of law is similar to that of most American (U.S.) philosophers. The philosophy of law, like many other branches of philosophy, is comprised of two sorts of issues, conceptual (analysis of legal concepts) and normative (matters of values and ideals). And like most American legal philosophers, as I believe the case to be, I have not been concerned with whether, and how, the philosophy of law should be distinguished from jurisprudence, legal theory, and legal dogmatics (a term that is virtually unknown among American writers), which is a problem that Continental thinkers are so worried about. I have been, and I believe most American legal philosophers have been, governed more by the interest of a topic than by such systemic considerations. American legal philosophy, at least, may therefore seem somewhat parochial, driven, as it often is, by questions deriving from U.S. constitutional law and the common law.

The reason why the above mentioned distinctions are not stressed in American legal thought is, I suspect, that the notion that law is a "science" or that legal analysis or theory is a "science" is rarely to be found among American writers. This does not mean that the concerns of Continental theoreticians never occur. Legal scholars, when they try to systematise a branch of the law and when they do doctrinal study, might be doing legal dogmatics without knowing it.

So the question of the epistemological status of their statements does arise: are they empirical statements about the law, or are they some other sort of statement? As far back as the non-judicial writings of Justice Oliver Wendell Holmes in the 1880s and 90s, we find the idea that statements of law are generalised predictions of the decisions of courts. In its most plausible interpretation, Holmes seems to be talking about what lawyers are doing when they respond to their clients' questions on the matters of law of interest to them. As far as systematic statements of the law are concerned, the cases are different.

No one would doubt that the American Law Institute's *Model Penal Code* is a set of proposals about the criminal law, and not a set of predictions. On the other hand, the

Institute's older *Restatements of the Law* (of Torts, Contracts) do sometimes appear to be statements about what the law really *is*, and if so, they are normative propositions of a particular sort. But few writers seem to have worried about the status of such propositions in the way that someone like the Danish theorist Alf Ross might have been[1].

To be sure, there have been scholars who have stressed the need for empirical research about the law, particularly the legal realists of the 1920s and 30s and many others. No one, I think, denies that such research could be important and useful in many ways, especially when it bears on proposals for legal reform. And the conclusions of such research do enter into philosophical discussions (*e.g.*, discussions of capital punishment and prohibitions on the use of drugs). Yet, legal philosophers have no difficulty in distinguishing between the empirical elements, on the one side, and the analytical and normative issues, on the other.

Now, the above account may suggest that American legal philosophy is a kind of "particular jurisprudence", as John Austin might have called it. For the topics are sometimes local in nature, or generated by local interests. However, the characterisation as particular would be inaccurate. American legal philosophers have been interested in the criteria of validity in American law, which is not an easy question. And from that question it is a quick step to more general problems about the nature of legal validity. It is true that practicing lawyers hardly take notice of these general problems, but American legal philosophers are as occupied with them as their Continental counterparts.

Sometimes conceptual and normative issues come together, though in too many ways to detail here. Normative issues obviously invoke controversy, but so can the conceptual. Conceptual analysis aims at clarifying ideas, formulating them in perspicuous terms: "What can *X* reasonably mean?", is asked. There are, then, criteria of adequacy that have to be satisfied for a given analysis to be acceptable. Legal philosophers might disagree over what these criteria are, in any given case. In effect, they would be disagreeing over how a concept should be "rationally reconstructed", and normative considerations may enter into the controversy.

---

[1] The exception is Felix S. Cohen, the most philosophical member of the American legal realist movement. Cohen thought that such propositions were ethical claims for which the authors of the Restatements had failed to supply adequate justification. For a critical discussion, see my article, "Realism and Functionalism in the Legal Thought of Felix S. Cohen", 66 *Cornell Law Review*, 1032-1057 (1981). For Ross, see his *On Law and Justice*, London, 1958, a translation of a 1953 Danish work. Cf. A. Aarnio and A. Peczenik, "Beyond the Reality. A Criticism of Alf Ross' Reconstruction of Legal Dogmatics" in *Meaning, Interpretation and the Law*, A. Peczenik (ed.), Tampere, 1986, 10-29. According to the authors, "legal dogmatics in the Continental sense is almost unknown in the Anglo-Saxon countries" (id., *ibid.*, 25).

Perhaps the foremost topic in conceptual analysis is the concept of law, itself. What does it mean to say that a legal system exists in a society? Legal theorists are divided on this question. The basic point in contention is whether the conditions for the existence of a legal system can be specified entirely in morally neutral terms[2]. Legal positivists maintain that it can, while philosophers associated with the natural law tradition maintain that it cannot.

I lean toward the second position. In my opinion the answer to the question, "what does it mean to say that a legal system exists in a society?" involves a normative element, namely, the *ideal* of the rule of law. More about this later, however. Before I go into this subject and other matters that have occupied me, I want to give some background on how my views have developed over the years, beginning with a bit of autobiography. After doing that, I shall organise my exposition in terms of a very few writers (*e.g.*, Holmes) with whose views I might have differences or agreements, in order to make it accessible. In so doing, I am aware that I am putting aside many important legal theorists and important topics.

2. The Development of My Thought

I began teaching the philosophy of law in the late 1950s at Columbia University. At the time, my courses focused on theories of the nature of law: legal positivism (principally John Austin and Hans Kelsen), natural law (principally Aquinas), and American legal realism. I cannot say that I then had a position of my own, and my courses largely were critical examinations of the various writers I assigned. I was somewhat opposed to natural law theory because I was suspicious of the idea of natural rights which, I wrongly thought, seemed to be entailed in a natural law theory[3].

It is probably strange for an American to be suspicious of natural rights, because they are part of our founding tradition, but this skepticism (though now mitigated) has always remained with me. I found legal positivism to be attractive: as a matter of general theory, its separation (or more accurately its distinction) of law and morality seemed right. Yet I found Austin and Kelsen to be too full of difficulties to swallow positivism

---

[2] This question is distinct from the related issue of whether the conditions for the existence, validity, or obligation of a particular law can be specified entirely in morally neutral terms. As discussed later, the quality of the citizen's obligation to obey a bad or unjust law is affected by whether it is an element of a system that by and large conforms to rule of law.

[3] Natural rights theories are in the natural law tradition, but the tradition was highly developed before such theories arose. For an attempt to generate natural rights out of Thomistic natural law, see J. Finnis, *Natural Law and Natural Rights*, Oxford, 1980.

whole. On the other hand, Kelsen had convinced me that legal realism was the wrong approach.

At that time, then, my thinking was unsettled and naive, and I needed different versions of positivism and natural law if I was to achieve any clarity. These came when I encountered the work of H. L. A. Hart[4] and (later) Lon L. Fuller[5]. Hart supplied a better version of positivism than either Austin and Kelsen, and Fuller supplied the procedural, rule of law emphasis that was missing in Hart. Over the years, I also began to achieve a greater appreciation both for the thought of St. Thomas Aquinas and the insights of American legal realism.

Because all of these influences are so varied and at times incompatible with each other, my philosophy of law remained (and still remains, though less so) somewhat unsettled, but I hope not naive. All of these sources (legal positivism, natural law, and legal realism) have influenced my thinking on two fundamental topics in legal philosophy, the normativity of law and legal reasoning. But there were other influences of significance.

Here I should interpose a few words on my philosophical education. As an undergraduate, my training was largely in the British analytical tradition (G. E. Moore, Bertrand Russell, and – still my favorite – C. D. Broad) and logical positivism (Rudolph Carnap and Hans Reichenbach, who was one of my teachers, and who preferred to be called a logical empiricist)[6]. I still maintain a great respect for all of these men, but I never swallowed logical positivism (not to be confused with legal positivism) whole, either. This was partly due to my study of the history of philosophy, in which I read many then out-of-fashion writers, *e.g.*, mediaeval thinkers and the British idealists.

I also studied American pragmatism (C. S. Peirce, G. H. Mead, and John Dewey), my knowledge of which was deepened as a graduate student. Toward the end of my graduate education I began to teach what may be called the philosophy of social science and, aside from studying some classical economic theory, I read works by

---

[4] H. L. A. Hart, *The Concept of Law*, Oxford, 1961.

[5] L. L. Fuller, *The Law in Quest of Itself*, Chicago, 1940. This early book has never thrilled me. And though I was initially antagonistic to his *The Morality of Law*, New Haven, 1969[2], I subsequently was more or less convinced by it. I think that his *Anatomy of the Law*, New York, 1968, which I came to later, is first-rate, and shows serious deficiencies in legal positivism. And the collection of essays, *The Principles of Social Order*, K. Winston (ed.), Durham (N. C.), 1981, has fine pieces.

[6] Deserving of special mention is my teacher Robert M. Yost, professor emeritus of philosophy at the University of California, Los Angeles. Although his philosophical interests were far different from those I later acquired, he trained me in the analytic tradition and set the standard of critical thinking I have tried to achieve.

philosophically-minded historians, anthropologists, and sociologists (Henry Sumner Maine, Ferdinand Toennies, Max Weber, and others). During this period and in the 1960s I diligently attended courses at Columbia Law School, including Roman law, a subject not much studied in the United States.

All of these sources shaped my thinking in the philosophy of law. It was my early training in the analytic tradition that sustained my interest in conceptual issues generally. And my later study convinced me that legal philosophy should always keep closely in touch with empirical realities. But the primary reason why I did not swallow logical positivism was that I have always been a religiously committed Jew. Yet this commitment, I believe, has not influenced the bulk of my work in the philosophy of law.

My first work substantial work in legal philosophy, however, was in the Jewish area, a doctoral dissertation, *Community, Covenant, and Reason: a Study in Jewish Legal Thougt*", submitted to Columbia University in New York in 1959. Jewish law (Halakhah) is a full legal system that covers almost all that is contained in a secular, modern system and much more of a religious nature.

Drawing on jurisprudential writing, most of it in Hebrew, that stretches over 2,000 years, I attempted to describe the concept of community presupposed by Jewish law (Halakhah) generally; I attempted to formulate the theory of legal authority underlying the power of particular Jewish communities to enact further legislation; and I attempted to formulate a theory of legal reasoning that accounts for the pluralism (opposed opinions) found in the juristic elaboration of the Halakhah. In the course of my exposition, I made reference to theorists outside of the Jewish legal tradition: for instance, Thomas Hobbes, John Austin and Roscoe Pound.

Except for two sections culled from it, the dissertation remains unpublished, and I find it interesting that it anticipates the work of later scholars on Jewish legal theory[7]. Though I did nothing further in the field until fairly recently, looking back on it now I find it pleasantly surprising how continuous with the dissertation my subsequent work in legal philosophy has been. For instance, it is a noteworthy feature of the classical Jewish legal materials, particularly the Talmud (from the third to the sixth centuries of the common era, but based on earlier sources) that the law is expounded basically without any terms that are translatable by the word "rights." Modern expositors

[7] M. P. Golding, "The Juridical Basis of Communal Associations in Mediaeval Rabbinic Legal Thought", 28 *Jewish Social Studies*, 67-78 (1966); id. "Reasoning and the Authoritative Expansion of the Law" in *Studies in Jewish Philosophy*, N. M. Samuelson (ed.), Lanham, 1987, 421-462. See also my edited book (with an Introduction), *Jewish Law and Legal Theory*, New York, 1994. This work contains a number of pieces that discuss whether Jewish law is best described in terms of a positivist theory or a natural law theory.

inevitably do use the word, while the classical materials tend to use more concrete terminology.

Nor do the latter materials seem to have any term that corresponds to the idea of moral or natural rights. (There are of course many other normative notions in play.) This fact later led me to examine the history of the concept of rights, how the concept developed in Western moral and legal thinking. It also fed my skepticism about rights, though I have begun to accommodate myself to the idea. I admit that one can no longer avoid rights-talk if one wants to engage in current moral discussion. Although I cannot go into the subject here, I maintain that rights-discourse presupposes a concept of community, because of its essentially pragmatic function[8].

And, as I shall very briefly explain later, I think that the concept of community enters even into the analysis of legal reasoning, as well. Because the system I dealt with in the dissertation is characterised by disagreement in the juristic elaboration of the law, I was in effect concerned with the "right answer" problem that Ronald Dworkin in *Taking Rights Seriously* made so notorious, though I didn't then have the technical equipment to formulate it adequately. Instead, when I began to focus on U.S. constitutional law and common law, I was concerned with what distinguishes the judicial function from the legislative, law making function. But my early work on Jewish law has always served as a point of comparison with other systems, although not explicitly.

3. Anti-Reductionism

With autobiography out of the way, I now want to turn back to conceptual analysis. In order that the exposition not be too abstract it will be useful to begin with examples drawn from a specific branch of law. Many of them are found in the area of

---

[8] My work on rights may be found in the following articles: "Towards a Theory of Human Rights", 52 *The Monist*, 512-49 (1968); "The Concept of Rights: A Historical Sketch" in *Bioethics and Human Rights*, E. and B. Bandman (eds.), Boston, 1978, 44-50; "Obligations to Future Generations", 56 *The Monist*, 85-99 (1972); "Justice and Rights: A Study in Relationship" in *Justice and Health Care*, E. Shelp (ed.), Dordrecht, 1981, 23-36; "From Prudence to Rights: A Critique" in *Human Rights*, J. R. Pennock and J. W. Chapman (eds.), New York, 1981, 165-74; "The Primacy of Welfare Rights", 1 *Social Philosophy and Policy*, 119-136 (1984); "Community and Rights", 9 *Bulletin of the Australian Society of Legal Philosophy*, 185-96 (1985); "The Presuppositions of Rights Discourse", *A.R.S.P.*, 1988, 135-39; "The Significance of Rights Language", 18 *Philosophical Topics*, 53-64 (1990); "Aristotelian Ethics and Natural Rights: a Critique", 18 *Reason Papers*, 71-77 (1993).

responsibility, a subject I have taught for many years, though I have only recently begun to write for publication in the area[9].

What are the conditions under which someone may be held criminally liable for committing an offence? American law usually (but not always) requires that the accused shall have committed an "act", sometimes an "intentional" act, that there be a "causal" connection between the act and a "harm", and so on. Further, sometimes a crime can be committed "negligently". The law also allows for "justifications" and "excuses" as defenses against a criminal charge. All of these terms are grist for the philosophers mill: what do they mean? There is of course a long jurisprudential tradition on these topics, beginning with the third book of Aristotle's *Nicomachean Ethics*.

My views on this last question have been largely influenced by the essays of H. L. A. Hart, in his collection *Punishment and Responsibility*. For instance, his criticism of John Austin's analysis of an act as a willed (or desired) muscular movement seems to me to be devastating. But I do not completely agree with Hart's inclination to view the notion of a voluntary act as a negative concept, that a voluntary act is one that is not involuntary, a position that he attributes to Aristotle. Hart questions the possibility of characterizing voluntary acts in positive terms. This inclination, however, does not fit Aristotle's *prohaireta*, actions chosen after deliberation. In fact, given Hart's emphasis, for the criminal law, on the moral importance of choice, that man is a choosing being, I find it surprising that he downplays this aspect of Aristotle[10].

This last consideration leads to normative questions about responsibility and shows how conceptual and normative issues are sometimes connected. What should the criteria of culpability be? And to what extent should the criminal law track our common moral ideas? It is clear, I believe, that our interest in the conceptual issues derives from these normative questions. Moreover, answers to conceptual questions may affect answers to normative questions, and vice versa.

Conceptual analysis is, in one respect, "reductionist". When the concept *C* is analysed in terms of concepts *X*, *Y*, and *Z*, *C* is thereby reduced to these other concepts. But this is reductionism in a trivial sense. We shall take an example of a more substantive type of reductionism, again from the criminal law, in which a writer is

---

[9] For a revised edition of a book published some years ago, see my *Philosophy of Law*, Prentice-Hall N. J., 1975.

[10] Hart offers the suggestion that the general rules of law constitute a "*choosing* system, in which individuals can find out, in general terms at least, the costs they have to pay if they act in certain ways." See H. L. A. Hart, *Punishment and Responsibility*, Oxford, 1969, 44. In this way, a rationale for excuses is provided, still keeping to a negative notion of voluntary acts. Yet Hart's respect for man as a choosing being is much deeper.

engaged in the more general project of reducing the moral components in the analysis of legal concepts and of overcoming what he regards as the confusion of law and morality.

The writer I have in mind is Justice Oliver Wendell Holmes, whose work I want to use as a foil for presenting some of my own views. Holmes maintains that the *meaning* of psychological terms in the criminal law (*e.g.*, the term "malice") is different from their meaning in everyday moral discourse. (Traditionally, murder is causing death with malice aforethought.) His argument fundamentally appeals to normative considerations. This kind of reductionism is bound to be controversial.

In the United States, perhaps the single most influential book on culpability is Holmes' work *The Common Law* published in 1881, written before he became a judge, a book I will have occasion to mention in another context[11]. As part of the more general project of reducing the moral components in the law, the project of reducing law to supposed "hard fact", Holmes there argues in favor of "external" (objective, behavioral) standards of criminal liability over internal or subjective standards. (I am putting aside Holmes' treatment of civil liability.) Holmes readily concedes that the moral discourse of everyday life uses subjective standards; that is, it takes the (internal) state of mind of the agent as crucial to the moral judgement that we pass on him. Even a dog, says Holmes, knows the difference between being stumbled over and being kicked. Thus, we judge a person differently if he has accidently injured us than we would if he deliberately did so.

But the law, he maintains, properly uses external standards of blame. All that is required for criminal liability is that the agent acted in a way that would be regarded as reprehensible for the "average member" of the community to so act. (This is Holmes' concession to morality.) Thus, the usual *mens rea* requirements are unnecessary. (Perhaps it would be more accurate to say "almost all that is required", for Holmes does add that the agent should have knowledge of circumstances. But he is rather confusing on this point, and it is not clear how far it moderates the position.) In effect, then, Holmes' thesis is the "reasonable man" standard so familiar to the common law.

Holmes offers three arguments for it. The first is an appeal to the history of law. "[W]hile the terminology of morals is still retained, and while the law does still and always, in a certain sense, measure legal liability by moral standards", he asserts, "it nevertheless, by the very necessity of its nature, is continually transmuting those moral

[11] I discuss Holmes in two places: "Holmes' Jurisprudence: Aspects of its Development and Continuity", 5 *Social Theory and Practice*, 183-207 (1979); "Jurisprudence and Legal Philosophy in 20th Century America: Major Themes and Developments", 36 *Journal of Legal Education*, 441-480 (1986).

standards into external and objective ones, from which the actual guilt of the party concerned is wholly eliminated"[12]. Secondly, he believes that law has shown a movement from primitive crudity to a more realistic sophistication, in which certain moral preconceptions are overcome, preconceptions such as human dignity and the Kantian idea that human beings should not be treated as mere means for society's ends.

"No society", says Holmes, "has ever admitted that it could not sacrifice individual welfare to its own existence. If conscripts are necessary for its army, it seizes them, with bayonets in their rear, to death. It runs highways and railroads through old family places in spite of the owner's protest (...)"[13]. Hence, there can be no objection to the elimination of actual, personal guilt. Finally, he claims, that just as the tests of criminal liability are external (*i.e.*, behavioral), so are the standards of culpability external or objective.

None of these arguments is entirely satisfactory. The historical claim is dubious and the second argument is a crude kind of utilitarianism. I agree that no society has ever admitted that it could not sacrifice individual welfare to its own existence. But this hardly shows that social aims shouldn't be pursued in ways that are fair to the individual. And finally, the last argument is a plain *non sequitur*: the fact that the tests of liability are objective does not show that the standards of culpability are external. I am of course not suggesting that the "reasonable man" standard should be entirely abandoned. It has a legitimate place in the law and it may be supported by a variety of arguments. The reasonable man standard is used whenever criminal negligence is at issue. And here I agree with Hart (against Jerome Hall, who seems to think that to punish negligence is to punish mere inadvertence) that a main consideration should be whether the accused reasonably could have avoided committing the wrong.

Holmes' argument, if pushed, would extend the scope of strict liability in the criminal law, and it would restrict, if not eliminate, excuses against a charge. Of course, there are problematic excuses; for instance, the "abuse" excuses, where the accused pleads for exemption or mitigation on grounds of having been a victim of abuse (child abuse, spousal abuse, bad upbringing). Nevertheless, it is through the admission of justifications and excuses, and by the distinction between justification and excuse, that the law tracks our ordinary moral judgements. This tracking is important if the criminal law is to retain its moral force, which I think is vital.

---

[12] O.W. Holmes, *The Common Law*, M. De Wolfe Howe (ed.), Boston, 1963, 33. Here Holmes seems to be influenced by Sir Henry Sumner Maine's thesis that the movement of "progressive" societies is from status to contract. By the "necessity" of its nature, Holmes means that the law sets patterns of conduct to which individuals must conform regardless of their motives and intentions.

[13] Id., *ibid.*, 37.

The reason why I went into the above topic was not merely to express some of my views about the criminal law but also to present one example of how conceptual and normative issues are intertwined. In so doing, I have also revealed the anti-reductionist tendency of my thought. Another instance of this tendency concerns legal rights, for which Holmes again makes a good starting point.

4. Rights and Interests

I mentioned above Holmes' idea that statements of law are generalised predictions of the decisions of courts and what I take to be its most plausible interpretation. In fact, however, Holmes seems to take the prediction theory quite literally and to apply it to the idea of legal rights. A right, he says, is the "hypostasis of a prophecy"[14]. What he means is as follows. Traditionally, the law contains two kinds of rights: primary and secondary (or remedial). Thus, I have a right that you should not trespass on my property, and this is a primary right. If you threaten to trespass, I have a secondary right to prevent you from doing so, by activating the agency of the law. In other words, I have a remedy I can bring to bear against you. The secondary, remedial right is the only kind of right Holmes recognises. And this latter right is a prediction, a prophecy, about what the courts will do. We think it is something more, because we hypostatise the prediction, regard it as something concrete.

But is Holmes correct in eliminating primary legal rights or reducing them to remedial rights? Holmes thinks that these latter rights are the *real content* of the law. Now, remedial rights are important of course, but I don't think primary rights, *or some comparable normative notion*, can be eliminated from judicial thinking. For a judge will grant someone a remedy because he deems it that a primary right is being threatened, or if not a primary right that is being threatened, at least some interest that is deserving of protection. It might not be obvious that this is the case when the judge's instant situation falls under an already recognised rule. But it is shown in the judge's justification for granting the remedy when the situation is a new one. In the common law (and in constitutional law, too) this sort of process is quite frequent. Judges' appeals to some normative ground for the granting of remedies are inescapable[15].

But need that normative ground be a right? Not necessarily, I believe. It is true that the language of rights (and duties) is pervasive in the exposition of the contents of legal systems, to the point that some theorists have thought that they are, in a way, what law is about. Stated differently, the notions of rights and duties are part of the "minimum

---

[14] The phrase occurs in a 1921 letter to Sir Frederic Pollock and again in a 1932 letter. See *Holmes-Pollock Letters*, II, Cambridge (Mass.), 1961, 64 and 307.

[15] On judicial justification generally, see my elementary book, *Legal Reasoning*, New York, 1984.

vocabulary" necessary for describing any legal system. Of course, I don't deny there are legal rights. In my view, however, interests are more fundamental than rights: rights derive from interests[16]. Litigations (although usually formulated in terms of rights) can be seen as conflicts between interests, and judicial justifications, therefore, can be analysed in terms of the interests that courts determine to be worthiest of legal protection in the given circumstances. But, in any event, there must be some normative ground submitted in justification for granting a new remedy, be that ground a right, rightness reasons, an interest, or something else.

American judges often speak in terms of balancing (weighing) interests, and sometimes in terms of balancing interests against rights. A good example is a case currently before the U.S. Supreme Court, *Clinton v. Jones*[17]. This case concerns the question whether the President may be required to defend himself in civil lawsuit for alleged actions before he became President or whether the lawsuit should be postponed until his term is over. (Paula Jones claims in the civil suit that Mr. Clinton sexually harassed her when he was Governor of Arkansas, thereby violating her constitutional right to equal protection of the law.) It is argued on one side that the President is not above the law[18], and on the other that no President should be taken away from his constitutional duties. (Suppose he has to attend a NATO meeting.)

Many issues are raised involving separation of powers, supremacy of Federal law, varieties of official immunities under English common law, and factual questions. In *Nixon v. Fitzgerald* (1982) the Court ruled that the President has complete immunity from a private civil damage suit for any action within the "outer perimeter" of his official duties. But it has never decided how to handle a suit because of allegations that date

---

[16] One way to begin thinking about this matter is to ask, Suppose we were to make up a legal system, a code of law, for example, from whence would we start, from rights or from interests? I would start with the latter. My approach differs from natural rights theorists and from Ronald Dworkin, who maintains that we start with a political theory that assigns moral rights to individuals. But the matter is admittedly complex, since liberty-interests often are equated with a certain kind of right. Human rights, I believe, presuppose a view of the human good. See R. Dworkin, *Taking Rights Seriously*, Cambridge (Mass.), 1977. See my article, "Towards a Theory of Human Rights", 512 ff.

[17] 117 S. Ct. 1636.

[18] "[L]et a day be solemnly set apart for proclaiming the charter; let it be brought forth ... [so] the world may know, that so far we approve of monarchy, that in America *the law is king*. For as in absolute governments the king is law, so in free countries the law *ought* to be king; and there ought to be no other." T. Paine, *Common Sense* in *Common Sense and Other Political Writings*, N. F. Adkins (ed.), Indianapolis (Indiana),1953, 32. *Common Sense* (January 1776) was one of the first public appeals for American independence from the British crown.

from before President's inauguration, or because it involves purely personal matters. In sum, there is an absence of directly applicable law or precedent.

What, then, is the Court to do? This question is asked regarding the process of decision, not the outcome. (This case probably will be decided by the time this article is published, but I won't hazard a guess as to its outcome)[19]. And the answer is given by the remarks of Justice Kennedy in the oral argument. The Court has to balance the rights of plaintiff and the needs of the Presidency, or as he more aptly puts it, it has to balance interests[20]. It is more apt because when X is weighed against Y, they have to be the same sort of thing. Of course, the Court will also take into account any values mandated by the Constitution and any already established rights.

5. Principled Judicial Decision Making

The above case has another interesting aspect, which illustrates the relations between the judicial function and the legislative, law making function. Although the case concerns a constitutional question, Holmes' *Common Law* may again be used as a point of departure.

It is one of the principal themes of this book, reiterated on virtually every page, that the growth of the common law is *legislative* and rests upon judges' views of public policy, considerations of what is expedient for the community concerned. In other words, (appellate) judges whose decisions serve as precedents will seek to lay down the best rules for the given situations. Of course, judicial justifications are presented in a logical form, as if the decision were being deduced from pre-existent law. "Behind the logical form", however, says Holmes, "lies a judgement as to the relative worth and importance of competing legislative grounds, often an inarticulate and unconscious judgement, it is true, and yet the very root and nerve of the whole proceeding"[21].

---

[19] On May 27, 1997, the U.S. Supreme Court rendered its decision in this case. In a unanimous decision the Court held that a sitting President can be sued for actions outside the scope of his official duties. The Court ruled that neither the Constitution nor public policy justified giving the President a delay until after he has left office. The decision does allow the trial court to accommodate the President's schedule as much as possible.

[20] Reported in *The New York Times*, January 14, 1997, A1, B6. Interest analysis was significantly influenced by the work of Roscoe Pound. Early on he connected it with a theory of social engineering. For his latest statement, see R. Pound, "A Survey of Social Interests", 57 *Harvard Law Rev.*, 1 (1943).

[21] O. W. Holmes, *Collected Legal Papers*, New York, 1921, 181. Holmes never explains how "relative worth" is to be determined, but he does suggest that economics and statistics should be employed.

Judges, then, do make law, and very much so in the fashion of legislatures. This proposition, however, should be understood with a significant qualification. Holmes confines his position to "important litigations", that is, cases that raise a new issue, one not completely covered by the prior law[22]. What, then, distinguishes the judicial function, in this area, from the legislative, law making function?

This is a very large topic, on which there is a large literature, and which cannot be fully treated here. Holmes says nothing on this question in *The Common Law*. That Holmes holds the law can "run out", thus allowing for an exercise of discretion from the judge, is clear. The important point of distinction between the judicial function and a legislature's law making function, however, is that judges are required to be objective, restrained (as Holmes was as a constitutional law judge), and principled in a way that legislatures are not required. Legislatures, which respond to the exigencies of the moment, may enact law *ad hoc*; judges, in their occasional exercise of discretion, may not.

The notion of principled decision is expounded by Professor Herbert Wechsler of Columbia University as follows: "A principled decision (...) is one that rests on reasons with respect to all the issues in the case, reasons that in their generality and their neutrality transcend any immediate result that is involved"[23]. I substantially agree with Wechsler, though I think it is easier to explain what a principled judge is than what a neutral principle is[24].

Basically, what is required is (1) that reasons (often, applicable statutes and precedents) be given for a decision; and (2) that these reasons be general or neutral, *i.e.*, transcend the case at hand. In the latter respect judicial reasons are like explanations in the natural sciences, which also should not be *ad hoc*[25]. Thus, a reason for deciding a case in a given way is also a reason for deciding like cases in that way; moreover, the

---

[22] In his theoretical writings Holmes does not say very much about statute law and constitutional law. One has to glean his views from his judicial opinions. Holmes, the self-restrained constitutional law judge, is a rather different character from Holmes the legal historian and theorist. See my article, "Holmes' Jurisprudence: Aspects of its Development and Continuity", 183-207. I believe that in the statutory and constitutional areas American judges often behave like common-law judges. On common law method, see my paper, "Substantive Interpretation and Common Law Elaboration", *A.R.S.P.*, 1994, 23-35. For a comparative discussion, see P. S. Atiyah and R. S. Summers, *Form and Substance in Anglo-American Law*, Oxford, 1987.

[23] H. Wechsler, "Toward Neutral Principles of Constitutional Law", 73 *Harvard Law Rev.* 1, 19 (1959).

[24] See my article "Principled Decision Making and the Supreme Court", 63 *Columbia Law Review*, 35-58 (1963).

[25] See my paper "Principled Judicial Decision Making", 73 *Ethics*, 247-54 (1963).

judge is thereby making a commitment regarding decisions in future cases. If cases are to be distinguished, this also must be done on the basis of reasons that in their generality go beyond the instant cases.

It is this last feature – in effect, the drawing of lines – which frequently poses great difficulties for judges. Many examples of this sort of problem could be supplied, but *Clinton v. Jones* is perhaps enough. This case will pose such a difficulty if the Supreme Court should decide that the President is subject to some private lawsuits while still in office but has absolute immunity from others. The Court will have to draw a line in a way that is not arbitrary or *ad hoc*.

In any event, the notion of principled decision explains why the *reductio ad absurdum* is a standard form of argument in judicial reasoning. A reason that would lead the judge to an unacceptable decision in the case at hand, and the class of cases to which it belongs, should be rejected. A decision is unacceptable if it frustrates certain given values or is contrary to applicable statutes and precedents. And if the values are in competition, a reasoned balance between them should be struck.

Principled decision making allows for discretion on the part of judges, but it calls for the principled exercise of discretion. It is discretion exercised under the constraint of reasons, and the reasons contained in a judicial opinion should determine the meaning of any precedent that is set for the particular judge committed to those reasons. Legislatures, too, may enact law in a non-arbitrary fashion, under the constraint of reasons, but they are not committed to them in the same way as principled courts. Moreover, the reasons embodied in the legislative history of an enactment do not necessarily determine its subsequent application. However, we do not have the space to develop this topic here.

A dispute-settling mechanism, the distinctively judicial function, that has the above design has a social justification: it satisfies a society's need for peaceful methods of dispute resolution that are relatively stable and predictable in their results and that promote the society's values (whatever they are)[26]. The last point is important. For a decision to be acceptable, it must have some foothold in values that are widely accepted in the community. Judicial opinions, which are addressed to the losing litigant, the legal profession, and the community at large, must contain reasons that appeal to these audiences. In this way, decisions can be accepted as reasonable, if not correct[27].

---

[26] Adjudication, of course, is not the only possible method of dispute settlement. See my book, *Philosophy of Law*, Chapter 6.

[27] See my paper, "A Note on Discovery and Justification in Science and Law" in *Justification*, J. R. Pennock and J. Chapman (eds.), New York, 1986, 124-140.

The idea mentioned above, that the law "runs out", has been associated with legal positivism by Ronald Dworkin, and he rejects it[28]. In his initial attack Dworkin argued that in addition to rules, the law contains (moral) principles, which judges regard as binding on them, for deciding cases. These principles are of such an amplitude that no strong discretion is ever required or allowed, even when there is no applicable rule. Put in other words, judges are never free to decide cases in any way they please. Now, I agree with this statement to the extent, and it is a large extent, that judges are required to be principled. In fact, in his early writing Dworkin seems to grant that articulate consistency (which involves rationality, fairness, and effectiveness) is a viable, discretion-limiting, alternative to his own approach[29]. I would spell out this alternative in terms of principled decision making.

It would be impossible to discuss Dworkin's work in a way that does justice to it. It has gone through many transformations and elaborations. I shall say only a few words about it. The reason why Dworkin found principled decision to be inadequate as a normative theory of judicial decision is that it did not allow saying that a litigant was entitled to a particular decision, despite the fact that judges are required to do the best they can in reaching a principled result. To bolster his position, Dworkin later argued that the law rests on a set of individual moral rights, which judges have a duty to enforce[30].

Even in "hard cases" there will (almost) always be a uniquely "right answer" to questions of law. Now, if what is meant by the "right answer" is the answer that is supported by the best argument, I would generally agree. But I don't think there is any way of showing that it will be a uniquely right answer. Dworkin's invention of a superhuman, omniscient judge Hercules, whose judgement determines what the best argument is, does not help his position, because he doesn't show the impossibility of another such judge, Hercules II, who might come to a different result. Two human, principled judges may well come to divergent answers, each based on pretty good arguments.

Dworkin's more recent work, *Law's Empire*, puts forward the conception of law as "integrity", which presupposes a full-blown political theory. It is much too complex for discussion here. Suffice it to say that Dworkin is no longer entitled to hold the right-

---

[28] The focus of Dworkin's initial attack is H. L. A. Hart's *The Concept of Law*. See R. Dworkin, "The Model of Rules I" in *Taking Rights Seriously*, 14-45. See also his discussion of the "semantic sting" in *Laws Empire*, Cambridge (Mass.), 1986, 45 ff..

[29] See id., "A Model of Rules I", 33. Dworkin is not satisfied with articulate consistency because it does not allow us to say that a litigant is pre-entitled to a given result.

[30] See id., "Hard Cases" in *Taking Rights Seriously*, 81-130.

answer thesis, in my opinion. Moreover, in the light of at least some of his examples[31] he is no longer (he never was) entitled to a sharp distinction between principle (in his sense, based on moral rights) and policy (based on interests) which is vital to his approach.

6. The Rule of Law

Near the outset of this article I noted that the concept of law is perhaps the foremost topic in conceptual analysis. What does it mean to say that a legal system exists in a society? Can the conditions for the existence of a legal system can be specified entirely in morally neutral terms? I think these conditions involve a normative element, the *ideal* of the rule of law. Moreover, it is a legal system's adherence to the rule of law that accounts for the normativity, the "oughtness", of its laws.

I have always found positivist accounts of law's normativity to be puzzling. According to John Austin, laws (in a given society) are the commands of the political superior; they impose duties, and are backed up by sanctions. But Austin's command theory of duty seems wrong. The commands of the chief of a concentration camp are backed by sanctions, but do the inmates take them as imposing duties? Kelsen regards laws as sanction-stipulating statements, and he places the "ought" in the legal norm itself, wherein it is stipulated that the sanction ought to be applied. Because he is anxious to avoid any kind of natural law theory, Kelsen maintains that there is a special legal kind of normativity, distinct from a moral ought and ultimately deriving from the Basic Norm, but he is unclear as to what that could be. Moreover, since legal norms govern only the officials of the given system, Kelsen fails to explain the normativity of law for the ordinary citizen.

Morė recent writers, to skip over important figures, hold that laws provide reasons for actions, and in that way have their normative hold on those persons subject to the laws. And the laws do this because the laws are accepted as guides to conduct. (Who accepts them? If it is only the acceptance of officials that counts, as H. L. A. Hart seems to maintain[32], we have the same failure mentioned above.) Now, this approach seems promising to me, but I think that the authority of law presupposes at least a minimal, even if indirect, connection with morality. In this way, I lean toward a natural law position.

I start with the legal system as a whole rather than individual laws, and I agree with Lon Fuller's idea that the existence of a legal system is a matter of *degree*. "It is truly astounding", says Fuller, "to what extent there runs through modern thinking in

---

[31] Id., *Law's Empire*, 240 ff.

[32] See H. L. A. Hart, *The Concept of Law* and id., *Essays on Bentham*, Oxford, 1982, 243-68.

legal philosophy the assumption that law is like a piece of inert matter – it is there or not there"[33]. Law making is the purposive enterprise of subjecting human conduct to the governance of rules and, like other enterprises, it can be accomplished well or badly. The degree to which a legal system exists is determined, not by its production of rules, but rather by the degree to which it adheres to the *rule of law*. Further, the quality of the citizen's obligation to obey the law is affected by that degree. Where violations of the rule of law are pervasive, the obligation of particular laws, the normativity of the laws, is lessened and perhaps nonexistent.

The rule of law (also called "legality") is explicated by Fuller in terms of *implicit* laws of law making, which constitute "the internal morality of law", "the morality that makes law possible". The eight canons of this morality are summarised as follows: (1) there must be general rules, (2) the rules must be promulgated, (3) the rules must typically be prospective, not retroactive, (4) the rules must be clear, (5) the rules must not require contradictory actions, (6) the rules must not require actions that are impossible to perform, (7) the rules must remain relatively constant over time, and (8) there must be a congruence between declared rules and the acts of administrators[34].

Fuller argues in some detail that any attempt to rescue made law (positive law) from dependence on implicit or inherent laws of law making must fail. The positivist slogan, "All law is positive law", is therefore to be rejected, insofar as it implies that we can understand the existence of legal systems solely by reference to positive, made law. Even if these canons were written into a constitution, interpretation of the document would have to respect not only its words but also the implicit ideals of orderly and decent government that the words attempted to express. The rule of law is not self-enforcing. It requires a commitment on the part of the officials of the system.

The thought that underlies the inner morality of law is that law making and governance must themselves be subject to rules that are not legal rules, to rules internal to the very idea of governing by rules. Governing by rules is not managerial control. Law is not a one-way projection of authority. Law depends for its existence on a *reciprocity of expectations* between the governed and the governors, expectations that survive only when there is adherence to the rule of law. The quality of the citizen's obligation to obey the law is much affected by whether officials have adhered to the inner morality of law, even before we come to the question of whether some particular law is a good law. And the official's expectation that citizens normally will obey the law depends on the official's commitment to act only on the basis of his own declared rules.

---

[33] L. L. Fuller, *The Morality of Law*,123.

[34] Id., *The Principles of Social Order*, 158 (summary by the editor).

Failure to adhere to any of the canons of legal morality is a symptom of *legal pathology*, a way in which a system can go wrong and fail to achieve the status of law, which happens when its failures are persistent regarding any one of the eight canons or relatively pervasive regarding a few. When the authorities exercise power against the citizenry in ways that are not congruent with declared law, it is violence that is being exercised against them, not law. Because of problems in implementing the conditions of the rule of law, every legal system suffers from some degree of legal pathology[35]. (For instance, the rules must remain relatively constant over time, but won't there be a need for changes, even dramatic changes, in the law?) Still, the differences in degree are morally significant.

The reason why these problems are of concern at all, however, is not just the theoretical interest in when a legal system exists, but, more importantly, their bearing on the reasonable expectations of the members of the community, which it is the function of the rule of law to protect. Legal pathology (always a matter of degree) undermines social co-operation, co-ordination of conduct, and the obligations of law, because it undermines planning, predictability, and reasonable expectations.

Adherence to the rule of law does not of course guarantee that the laws that are enacted will be good laws. The approach to the question of the normativity of law is "holistic". The power of law to bind us and to serve as a guide to conduct presupposes the minimal, even if indirect, connection with morality described above. It does not settle the question of whether there is an obligation to obey a particular law that happens to be unjust. Nevertheless, it makes a difference whether or not an unjust or bad law is an element of a system that by and large conforms to rule of law. I think there are many affinities between the internal morality of law and justice and between it and more traditional natural law theories (*e.g.*, Thomistic). These affinities, however, cannot be spelled out here.

The rule of law is currently beset by a fascinating and disturbing irony. While many countries around the world are fervently trying to institute or restore the rule of law and are looking to Western nations as models, some American legal academics have launched severe attacks on the idea. The assaults generally come from left-leaning law teachers, especially those associated with the Critical Legal Studies movement, who tend to see law as alienating and who identify the rule of law as an ideology of capitalist

---

[35] For a discussion, see my article "Retroactive Legislation and Restoration of the Rule of Law", *Jahrbuch für Recht und Ethik*, 1993, 169-192.

domination[36]. While I cannot go into a critical discussion in this article, let me say that legal pathology, to which all legal systems are subject, will explain many of the faults found in the law. And I would again emphasise that legal pathology is a matter of degree. When the rule of law fails we get Nazi law and other perversions that unfortunately have been so prevalent in this century. The choice between upholding the ideal of the rule of law and such other regimes seems to me to be an easy one[37].

---

[36] For an early statement, see Horwitz, "The Rule of Law: An Unqualified Human Good?", 86 *Yale L. J.*, 561 (1977). Horwitz's statement is less radical than many later ones. For other critical discussions, see *The Rule of Law*, A. Hutchinson and T. Monahan (eds.), Toronto, 1987.
[37] See my article "Transitional Regimes and the Rule of Law", *Ratio Juris*, 1996, 387-395.

Bibliographical information

I. Books

1. *Philosophy of Law*, Prentice-Hall N.J., 1975 (Japanese translation, Tokyo, 1985; Chinese translation, Beijing, 1988).
2. *Legal Reasoning*, New York, 1984.
3. *Jewish Law and Legal Theory*, New York, 1994 (editor).
4. *Free Speech on Campus* (editor) forthcoming.

II. Articles

1. "Kelsen and the Concept of 'Legal System'", *A.R.S.P.*,1961, 355–86.
2. "Principled Decision Making and the Supreme Court", 63 *Columbia Law Review*, 35–58 (1963).
3. "Principled Judicial Decision Making", 73 *Ethics*, 247–54 (1963).
4. "The Juridical Basis of Communal Associations in Mediaeval Rabbinic Legal Thought", 28 *Jewish Social Studies*, 67–78 (1966).
5. "Towards a Theory of Human Rights", 52 *The Monist*, 512–49 (1968).
6. "Preliminaries to the Study of Procedural Justice" in *Law, Reason, and Justice*, G. Hughes (ed.), New York, 1969, 71–100.
7. "Obligations to Future Generations", 56 *The Monist*, 85–99 (1972).
8. "Aquinas and Some Contemporary Natural Law Theories", 48 *Proc. of the American Catholic Philosophical Association*, 238–47 (1974).
9. "On the Adversary System and Justice" in *Philosophical Law*, R. Bronaugh (ed.), Westport (Conn.), 1978, 98–121.
10. "The Concept of Rights: A Historical Sketch" in *Bioethics and Human Rights*, E. and B. Bandman (eds.), Boston, 1978, 44–50.
11. "The Nature of Compromise: a Preliminary Inquiry" in *Compromise in Ethics, Law, and Politics*, J. R. Pennock and J. Chapman (eds.), New York, 1979, 3–25.
12. "Holmes' Jurisprudence: Aspects of its Development and Continuity", 5 *Social Theory and Practice*, 183–207 (1979).
13. "Justice and Rights: A Study in Relationship" in *Justice and Health Care*, E. Shelp (ed.), Dordrecht, 1981, 23–36.
14. "From Prudence to Rights: A Critique" in *Human Rights*, J. R. Pennock and J. W. Chapman (eds.), New York, 1981, 165–174.
15. "Realism and Functionalism in the Legal Thought of Felix S. Cohen", 66 *Cornell Law Review*, 1032–1057 (1981).
16. "Discovery and Justification in Science and Law" in *Theory of Legal Science*, A. Peczenik, L. Lindahl and B. van Roermund (eds.), Dordrecht, 1984, 295–305.

17. "The Primacy of Welfare Rights", 1 *Social Philosophy and Policy*, 119-136 (1984).
18. "Aesthetics and Legal Reasoning: A Strand in American Legal Thought", *Rechtstheorie*, 1985, 31–37.
19. "Community and Rights", 9 *Bulletin of the Australian Society of Legal Philosophy*, 185-196 (1985).
20. "Note on Discovery and Justification in Science and Law" in *Justification*, J. R. Pennock and J. Chapman (eds.), New York, 1986, 124-140.
21. "Jurisprudence and Legal Philosophy in 20th Century America: Major Themes and Developments", 36 *Journal of Legal Education*, 441-480 (1986).
22. "Theory of Juristic Reasoning" in *Maimonides as Codifier of Jewish Law*, N. Rakover (ed.), Jerusalem, 1987, 51-60.
23. "Reasoning and the Authoritative Expansion of the Law" in *Studies in Jewish Philosophy*, N. M. Samuelson (ed.), Lanham, 1987, 421-462.
24. "The Logical Force of Arguments by Analogy in Common Law Reasoning" in *Reason in Law*, III, C. Faralli and E. Pattaro (eds.), Milan, 1988, 273-279.
25. "The Presuppositions of Rights Discourse", *A.R.S.P.*, 1988, 135-139.
26. "Liberty, Equality and the Freedom of Association: a Preliminary Essay", 13 *Bulletin of the Australian Society of Legal Philosophy*, 107-121 (1989).
27. "The Significance of Rights Language", 18 *Philosophical Topics*, 53-64 (1990).
28. "Communities and the Liberal Community: Some Comments and Questions" in *Democratic Community*, J. W. Chapman and I. Shapiro (eds.), New York, 1993, 115-125.
29. "Aristotelian Ethics and Natural Rights: a Critique", 18 *Reason Papers*, 71-77 (1993).
30. "Retroactive Legislation and Restoration of the Rule of Law", *Jahrbuch für Recht und Ethik*, 1993, 169-192
31. "Substantive Interpretation and Common Law Elaboration", *A.R.S.P.*, 1994, 23-35.
32. "Transitional Regimes and the Rule of Law", *Ratio Juris*, 1996, 387-395.
33. "Liberal Theory and Jewish Politics" in *Tikkun Olam: Jewish Responsibilities to Society*, D. Shatz (ed.), New York, 1997, 201-214.

LEGAL COMMUNICATION IN MODERN LAW AND LEGAL SYSTEMS. A MULTI-LEVEL APPROACH TO THE THEORY AND PHILOSOPHY OF LAW

WERNER KRAWIETZ

UNIVERSITY OF MÜNSTER/GERMANY

1. Is There a New Approach Within the Current Varieties of Jurisprudential Thinking?

Selecting an appropriate starting-point appears to me to be the most important step in the process of developing any theory, be it a legal or/and a social theory of law. The development of a legal theory is a project which does not occupy the same field as orthodox jurisprudence; their tasks and agendas differ from each other in some important aspects. Almost exactly three decades ago – in 1968 – when I took the decision together with two colleagues to found a new journal which covering mainly the current problems of basic legal research I realised that this could not be a specialist journal in the usual sense either in the field of law or in that of philosophy. Law is far too important a matter to be left to moral philosophers who draw on natural law or law of reason. For their cognitive interests the empirical research into the functions and structure of the modern communication systems of law is, after all, not a central concern. In view of the need to comprehend the foundations of law and legal systems it seemed vital to me, therefore, above all (i) to stake out an independent position for basic legal research and (ii) to strengthen and increase Cupertino between jurists, philosophers and social scientists, in particular sociologists – irrespective of the hermeneutic tasks of legal dogmatics. It was obvious also that a project of this kind would have to take direct account of the analytical and logical demands involved in the construction of a theory of norms, particularly of a theory of law and legal action in order to lead to a greater clarification and deeper understanding of the relationship between norms and action in the legal system. When the new periodical appeared for the first time in 1970 under the title *Rechtstheorie*, published by Duncker & Humblot in Berlin and edited by Karl Engisch, Hans Kelsen and Ulrich Klug as well as H. L. A. Hart and Sir Karl R. Popper, philosophy was not central to its program. Described as *Journal for Logic, Methodology, Cybernetics and Sociology of Law* in its subtitle it has stood for decades now not only for a modern form of analytical jurisprudence but also for a rationally based theory and a sociology of law as well as of the social sciences in as far as they are concerned with theories of norms and action, but without excluding philosophy (in the broadest possible sense).

Do I see any new developments evolving in the field of the contemporary theory and philosophy of law and how do I evaluate them? This is the question directed by the editor of this volume to me and to all of its contributors. It is not as difficult to answer this question as may appear at first sight as many alleged innovations of the second half of the century have turned out not to be new at all at closer inspection. This applies particularly to the *New Topic*, *New Rhetorics* and *New Dialectics* which have occupied the theory of practical legal argumentation to a large extent since the 1950s. This re-orientation of legal thinking was – in terms of the history of philosophy – closely connected with the language of law, especially the language of the courts and the techniques developed already in antiquity in topic and rhetoric and used in the treatment of legal concepts (*topoi, loci*), legal texts and of problems posed by legal decisions. What is often overlooked is the fact that the new approaches in the modern theory of legal argumentation have a common root in the philosophical dialectics and philosophy of language of antiquity which in modern legal thinking go back to Aristotle. It was by these that the conventional self-conception of jurisprudence and of legal logic (*logica iuridica*) practised and cultivated by it has been questioned and qualified.

Genuinely new, by contrast, has been the development of formal logic and modern philosophy of language which has led to the construction of a normative and structural theory of law largely dominated by logic. Logic of norms, especially legal logic, is concerned with the formal use of the normative terminology of legal language – regardless of the respective meaning of its content[1]. The applicability of formal logic to law and jurisprudence makes it plausible, in my opinion, to demand that modern (formal, mathematical) logic should be utilised not only for legal science but also for legal philosophy. Indeed, modern legal thinking has already been extensively transformed by the ever increasing demands of legal linguistics, legal logic and legal information science for a restructuring of modern legal language which has become essential over the last decades as a result of the growing computerisation of all activities connected with law. It has been pointed out with good reason, however, on the part of the philosophy of language that the scientific clarification of conceptual structures with the means of formal logic does raise the question, (i) whether logic is still to be regarded as a part of philosophy in this respect and (ii) whether the insights gained in this way can still be considered as "philosophical". On the other hand, it appears, that not even analytical hermeneutics which make use of formal logic in the service of law can entirely dispense with language- and communication-theoretical considerations in legal argumentation. In Weinberger's opinion the

[1] Cf. in this volume O. Weinberger, "Neo-Institutionalism: My Views on the Philosophy of Law", 245-264 and others who have made a contribution to this field with their own original research.

problem of hermeneutic understanding is always a part of the information- and communication process in law and jurisprudence[2]. For this theory of practical legal argumentation for which he uses the term "analytical hermeneutics" "language-theoretical, communication-theoretical and hermeneutic considerations are of defining importance" and the interpretation of law is never "a mere application of logic".

Formal logic can be placed into the service of law as the current developments in legal information science and legal logic demonstrate. It is an indispensable tool for the theory and philosophy of law. Judged in the light of a sceptical and critical assessment both of norms and facts it does not, however, create the possibility of comprehending and justifying the rightness of law purely *cognitively*, that is, only with the analytical means of formal logic – without volitive and evaluative assessments, value judgements and decisions. While analytical jurisprudence and philosophy of language in conjunction with formal logic have brought about a new form of legal thinking, this is by no means sufficient, however, to describe and explain in a socially adequate manner the interplay between the setting of rules and the following of rules.

What kind of problems did I respond to when I conceived my theory and philosophy of law? From the outset it was not the substance of law that stimulated and focussed my legal thinking but its social functions[3]. As the most recent research undertaken in the context of speech-act theory and in the field of new ontology and deontology of law have shown communication in the realm of law can be understood satisfactorily only if a non-linguistic conception of the norm, in particular, of the legal norm is adopted. This, as I shall demonstrate in the course of the following, does not preclude a theory for the justification of norms based on the analysis and philosophy of language but includes it.

What led me to return to the problems inherent in the relations between law and institutions and to seek a new justification of institutionalism and of the communication theory of law[4] was, above all, the critical (re-)examination of three aspects of legal thought which had dominated my legal thinking in the 1950s and 1960s. These were: a critique (i) of the metaphysical-speculative approaches in philosophy, in particular, a critical assessment of the idealistic legal and social philosophy from Kant to Hegel which entailed an increased

---

[2] O. Weinberger, "Grundlagenprobleme des Institutionalistischen Rechtspositivismus", *Rechtstheorie*, 1994, 191 ff., 215 ff.

[3] Cf. W. Krawietz, *Das positive Recht und seine Funktion. Kategoriale und methodologische Überlegungen zu einer funktionalen Rechtstheorie*, Berlin, 1967.

[4] W. Krawietz, "Begründung des Rechts – anthropologisch betrachtet. Zur Institutionentheorie von Weinberger und Schelsky" in *Theorie der Normen*, W. Krawietz, H. Schelsky, G. Winkler e.a. (eds.), Berlin, 1984, 541–556; id. "Ansätze zu einem Neuen Institutionalismus in der modernen Rechtstheorie der Gegenwart", *Juristenzeitung*, 1985, 706–714.

clarification of the historical and social basis underlying the formation of all law, (ii) of the ensuing phase of increased idealistic-philosophical activities and achievements (natural law, law of reason) which in the theory and philosophy of law, at least, ended in a long overdue leave-taking from the philosophy of German idealism with both aspects – in terms of law – leading to a stronger and more immediate orientation on the problems of legal practice, practical jurisprudence and practical philosophy, and, finally, (iii) of the all but inevitably resulting move toward an empirical philosophy which promised to open up the social phenomena of the reality of law[5].

In respect of the possibilities of a Cupertino between empirical philosophy and social sciences (of action) among which jurisprudence, too, was counted as an empirical legal science and as a science of observation ("*Beobachtungs-wissenschaft*") this means that the standpoint of the individual specialist sciences had to be presupposed by the theory and philosophy of law, in other words, the work of jurisprudence as well as sociology had to have been done already, it had to exist and to have been carried out before a theory and philosophy could set about tackling its transcendental view of man[6] and his social world by crossing the boarders of the individual specialist sciences involved. This happened particularly in the philosophical anthropology which – understood as philosophy of the institutions – increasingly turned to the historically and socially conditioned systems of social guidance and forms of action determined and shaped by the manifold institutionalisations of social behaviour.

Institutionalist legal theories both of the old and of the new provenance are so much in vogue again today because basic legal research has in the last two decades more clearly than previously exposed the secret deficiencies by which the merely analytical approaches in modern legal theory have always been afflicted and which they are still suffering from to this day, namely (i) the positivist constriction of its norm theory and (ii) their shortcomings in legal and social theory. In continental Europe this applies, for instance, to the various types of pure theories of law which probably constitute the purest embodiment – albeit each to a different extent – of analytical jurisprudence in its present form. It is quite obvious today, however, that the exaggerated positivism of these schools supported and strengthened by the postulate for purity which they advocate has hitherto prevented these approaches of analytical jurisprudence from ascertaining additionally and to a sufficient degree the presuppositions and foundations of

---

[5] Id., "Die Normentheorie Helmut Schelsky's als Form eines neuen Institutionalismus im Rechtsdenken der Gegenwart" in *Helmut Schelsky – ein Soziologe in der Bundesrepublik,* H. Baier (ed.), Stuttgart, 1986, 114–148.

[6] Id., "Über die Fachgrenzen der Soziologie hinaus: Helmut Schelsky's 'tranzendentale' Theorie von Recht und Gesellschaft" in *Helmut Schelsky als Soziologe und politische Denker*, W. Krawietz and O. Weinberger (eds.), Stuttgart, 1985, 17–20.

their norm theory which are provided by social theory. The renewal of institutionalist forms of jurisprudence taking place at present, described lately by Weinberger as neo-institutionalism does, on the other hand, appear to provide a suitable way of compensating the deficiencies in the hermeneutic-analytical legal theories which the basic research in legal and social theory has diagnosed. My own impression that more questions are raised than are answered in the context of modern institutional theories of law, too, has been expressed very aptly by MacCormick and Weinberger when they say: "Neither pure normativism nor legal realism, nor the various sociological theories of law provide satisfactory explanations of the nature and existence of law"[7].

Who are those who, in my opinion formulate different answers to current problems, I was asked by the editor of this volume. And how do I evaluate these answers in terms of my own theory and philosophy of law? In my conception of legal and social theory I have never fallen into the individualistic misunderstanding that society exists basically only of individuals or of groups of individuals.

Against this view of legal and moral individualism, according to which all law is simply a result of the properties and decisions of individuals, that is, it results from the expressed and unified will of the assembly of such individuals or of their formations in groups, and in this way serves as a universal means for bringing about a binding order I am putting forward a version of legal thinking that is informed and shaped by history and society. According to my view, all law – with reference to all members of a legal community who are included in its normative system – is always found at a higher socio-structural level than are all actual individuals or their formations in groups whose behaviour is regulated on the basis of and in accordance with the standards of this legal system.

One cannot, therefore, determine, describe, or explain the law as a normative, emergent social structure – not even by means of merely analytical-theoretical tools – by taking principally the unbound individuals as one's point of departure without having already determined the emergent properties and characteristics of the legal system itself. The legal system as a whole is and remains a subsystem of society. Law gives effect to, mirrors or is otherwise expressive of the prevailing social relations. This precisely is the central insight of my legal theory which I share with the representatives of German legal realism, sociological jurisprudence, the sociological institutional theory of law and systems theory. I shall return to this point below.

Thus it is simply not the case that all law can be understood as a subsequently imposed limitation and restriction, as it were, on individuals and formations of groups affected by law who are *a priori* not limited but are

---

[7] N. MacCormick and O. Weinberger, *Grundlagen des Institutionalistischen Rechtspositivismus*, Berlin, 1985, 5.

absolutely "free". As a result I was never able to share the love that both analytical philosophy and Anglo-American idealism have had for socio-philosophical individualism, and an individualistic theory of action, which seeks to trace all human action to the properties of the individual, the acting individual, that is, to trace them to *a priori* life essences informed by reason. These approaches do not manifest an interest in the concrete social forms of life and interaction between human beings, nor an interest in the organised social relations accessible through experience and observational methods of analysis in the social sciences, let alone an interest in the social reality of the law.

2. Technological Imperatives and Law in the Modern Information Society

As a result of technological inventions we are today in the position of communicating with each other very fast and efficiently via e-mail, telephone, telefax, personal computer and internet, *i.e.* with the help of computerisation and electronic data processing. One aspect of this development is the easy communication of legal prescriptions, principles and legal concepts which are formally valid within the framework of a legal order and which achieve effectivity, *i.e.* gain *social* validity, as normative rules through their influence on human experiences and actions. This allows them to make a real impact both nationally, that is, in the respective state legal systems, and also internationally. One example for the way law is already involved in the new media is to be found in the normative possibilities of *on-line shopping* in the virtual shopping malls of Europe, another in the trade, distribution and cashless money transfers conducted via the internet, in short, all those transactions we are already witnessing as *electronic commerce*.

The resulting legal informations and the rules of legal communication are being dealt with by a fast growing number of statutory prescriptions which as information-, telecommunication- and media-law have gained their own independent status. Clearly, the new technological possibilities have also changed the practical possibilities of legal actions carried out by individuals. But not only they have been affected by these changes. With them the social reality of law has also changed. Unfortunately, research, in particular, the vital basic research in the legal sciences, has not kept up in all areas with the changing possibilities of practical legal action.

Despite a variety of criticism that is being levelled against its traditional conception there is at present a prevailing tendency in dogmatic legal science (in the continental European usage of this category and conception) to continue to adhere – in practical legal argumentation, judicial decisions as well as in legal thinking – to the merely conventional orthodoxy and understanding of the relations and nature of legal practice and practical (dogmatic) legal science[8]. It

[8] In contrast to this T. Hoeren, "Vom praktischen Nutzen der Rechtswissenschaft",

appears that traditional legal doctrine, and particular legal method as well as general jurisprudence of norms and principles which is concerned with both of these have not yet fully caught up with the modern possibilities of practical legal communication. I am not only referring here to the failure to tie the technological development (computer science, legal expert systems, legal information technology) into the law. What is missing, above all, is a new and innovative intellectual penetration by dogmatic legal science of the structures and processes inherent in modern legal communication in the widest sense whereas empirical legal research and legal theory have contributed a great deal to their clarification in the course of the last two decades. This situation has, in my view, also changed the position of philosophy in relation to the specialist sciences which deal, in whatever way, with the law in their basic research. Legal theory thus leads, as we shall see later, a double life: one in the law, and one in philosophy.

It is precisely from this point that my reflections concerning the theory and philosophy of law take their cue. It is my intention to show in the following that (1) not only the practice of law has changed and is continuing to change but also the legal thinking connected with it. This development can (2) be gauged clearly from the fundamental concepts used by the various approaches in the theory and philosophy of law and their interpretation of the problems. Further I shall demonstrate that (3) the theory and philosophy of law are also substantially involved in the much needed reorientation. The existing, anything but satisfactory state of affairs can only be overcome, however, if, and only if, the traditional philosophy of law abandons its purely conceptual, idealistic orientation and self-reflection. Instead, the theory and philosophy of law has to get used to orientating itself on the institutional fact that all law has to be regarded as a normative social phenomenon.

Law is above all and first and foremost a social structure or the normative structure of society, *i.e.* legal order in its structure is always an integral part of the social order. It is my goal, therefore, to construct and develop a structural theory of law which deals not only with the linguistic structure but with the social structure of norms, especially legal norms, and with the societal deep structure of the legal order which underlies all social and legal systems. For this reason, I am abandoning in the following, for the purposes of this study the usual conceptual distinction and dichotomy between legal norm and legal reality (in the usage of the technical terms in German: "*Rechtsnorm/Rechtswirklichkeit*") which normally serves the practice of law, practical (dogmatic) jurisprudence and legal method as a means of orientation in the interpretation and application of valid law[9]. With a

---

Zeitschrift für Rechtspolitik, 1996, 284–287, esp. 285 ff.

[9] See already W. Krawietz, "Juristische Methodik und ihre rechtstheoretischen Implikationen", *Jahrbuch für Rechtssoziologie und Rechtstheorie*, 1972, 12–42, esp. 35-38.

view to the specific cognitive interests of the theory and philosophy of law I am replacing it with a differentiation using three technical terms. These distinguish – following René König – between (i) legal norm, (ii) legal reality and (iii) social reality of law, *i.e.* the societal infrastructure of legal regulations and the legal order ("*soziale Wirklichkeit des Rechts*")[10]. This distinction which I consider to be of great importance has, in fact, always determined my own access to law and legal theory[11].

Those of us who today understand law as a normative social communication are faced with the task of trying to formulate and develop appropriate basic concepts and a juridical *theory* of communication. However, as Blankenburg has rightly emphasised in view of the demands to be made on any present day theory of law it has to be such that the hypotheses derived (or, at least, derivable) from it have to be capable of (i) being operationalised and (ii) of being tested against the reality of legal activities[12]. This is the only way of ensuring that the theory of law is saved from the suspicion of having metaphysical or ideological leanings. From this arises the need to clarify the connection between the only statistically identifiable and identified regularities of human behaviour, social norms and individual legal acts. Law is something we may speak of if in a living society and its constitution there exist normatively coded expectations of behaviour concerning the possibility of distinguishing between right or wrong, lawful or unlawful which can demand compliance, *i.e.* which have social validity. The normative coding is that which gives communication within the legal system its legal meaning; it excludes other meanings from the legal system. The mere fact that such demands are made is not enough, in other words. The rules of law consist of rules which are valid by virtue of emanating from particular legal sources. Of social or legal norms we can only speak if – in institutional terms – such possibilities and regularities of legal behaviour actually have a chance of being observed.

Ultra posse nemo obligatur, that means in the above context – in law *ought to* presupposes *to be able to*. It is pointless to demand of a crashing aeroplane that it should keep to the speed limit. The social validity of norms, especially legal norms, therefore, implies that the subject of the act can actually take his/her orientation from the legal order and adhere to it. The fact that – apart from other motives – this order has to be regarded as *binding*, *i.e.* to be treated as a pattern of correct behaviour which has to be obeyed, at the same time increases

[10] Cf. R. König, "Das Recht im Zusammenhang der sozialen Normensysteme" in *Abweichendes Verhalten*, K. Lüderssen and F. Sack (eds.), Frankfort-on-Main, 1982, 186-207.

[11] W. Krawietz, *Das positive Recht und seine Funktion*, 22–24 and 27.

[12] For a detailed account see E. Blankenburg, "Diskurs oder Autopoiesis: Lassen sich Rechtstheorien operationalisieren?", *Zeitschrift für Rechtssoziologie*, 1994, 115–125.

the chance that others will also take the orientation for their actions from it. Normative communication in the framework of valid law makes this possible in practice and strengthens this regulation by constant repetition.

To provide an answer to the questions, which concept of law and which conception of a theory of law today's socially adequate theory and philosophy of law should be based on, will be a much harder task. To both questions Erhard Blankenburg has recently contributed important insights. With reference to the first problem he has in his study of "the use and limits of a gradual concept of law" (where he distinguishes in the intercultural comparison between different stages in which human behaviour gradually submits to the law) rightly drawn attention to the fact that a comparison of different legal cultures and social forms of life and of the growing distance between "lived" law and state law is able to show the extent to which "criteria of truth and rightness" in jurisprudence and the other social sciences "are interwoven with each other"[13]. It does, indeed, appear imperative that *normative behaviour*, too, should be made observable and recognisable with reference to valid law and the "regularities of behaviour" underlying it by using the methods of the social sciences[14]. When dealing with the contemporary "theory debate" (see below: fig. 1 and 3), particularly with the *discourse theory of law* (Habermas, Alexy) and critical *reflexive jurisprudence* (Teubner) Blankenburg has rightly pointed out that these authors have placed their theories "into the service of the law-internal need to construct patterns of argumentation for the justification of these theories"[15]. In doing so they do more to "determine the theory of law (as the theory which is integral to the legal system of thought)", he believes, "than law (as that which becomes effective in social action)"[16]. Here Blankenburg, indeed, places his finger on an open wound. His assessment may well be essentially correct. Theory and philosophy of law are today in danger of "missing the object (of law as the reality of action)" and of forgetting or even ignoring its requirement of "empirical description"[17]. In my view the theory of law ought to be called upon to provide a system of categories and concepts that would facilitate the scientific description of any legal order whatsoever.

3. Legal Hermeneutics as Method and Theory in the Basic Legal Research

It is one of the most important tasks of contemporary theory and philosophy of law to develop a theory of norms and action which takes account

---

[13] Id., "Nutzen und Grenzen eines graduellen Rechtsbegriffs" in *Theodor Geiger*, S. Bachmann (ed.), Berlin, 1995, 147–157.

[14] Id., *ibid.*, 151.

[15] Id., "Diskurs oder Autopoiesis", 115 ff.

[16] Id., *ibid.*, 116.

[17] Id., *ibid.*, 118.

of the demands of our modern information society. We can only *understand* the relationship between legal norms and action sufficiently well in socially adequate terms if, and only if, we are in the position of *observing, describing and explaining* the procedures of information processing by which all legal communication and legal action takes place, for we can only effectively understand what we can also explain. On the other hand, we can only *explain* what we have already understood in legal terms – no matter which or how[18]. From the methodological and theoretical point of view this is not an approach through legal hermeneutics in the traditional sense but a new form of *empirical-analytical hermeneutics of law* and the basis of an information- and communication theory which operates on the institutional level of an empirical differentiation *and* an analytical-conceptual dichotomisation and correlation of norms and action. The theorisation of this problem here takes place, as we explained at the beginning, on the level of legal and social theory on the basis of the respective, already established legal practice and in accordance with the empirical-analytical distinction between the three conceptual steps and technical terms, proposed by René König: (i) legal norm, (ii) legal reality and (iii) the social reality of law[19].

In contrast to this approach conventional theories of normative action are usually based on the behaviour of individuals and on the law as prescribed by the norm-sentences of the respective valid law from which it takes its orientation. From the purely analytical-conceptual point of view their approach is usually based on a bipartite division, *i.e.* a dichotomy of norms and facts[20]. On this basis these legal theories examine whether and to what extent a legal action by individuals which is understood as a causal event also corresponds to certain intentions of the agents (both of the law-giver and of the addressee of the law)[21].

---

[18] See already W. Krawietz, *Das positive Recht und seine Funktion*, 7 and 110-117; id., "Sprachphilosophie in der Jurisprudenz" in *Philosophy of Language. An International Handbook of Contemporary Research*, I, M. Dascal, D. Gerhardus, K. Lorenz and G. Meggle (eds.), Berlin/New York, 1996, 1482–1486.

[19] See for a detailed account see K. Veddeler, *Rechtsnorm und Rechtssystem in René Königs Normen- und Kulturtheorie*, Berlin, 1998.

[20] Cf. W. Krawietz, "Zur Korrelation vond Rechtsfrage und Tatfrage in der Rechtsanwendung" in *Rechtsprechungslehre*, N. Achterberg (ed.), Cologne, 1986, 526-528 and 552 ff.

[21] Critical towards the conventional understanding is G.-H. von Wright, *Handlung, Norm und Intention*, Berlin/New York, 1977; id., "Das Verstehen von Handlungen", *Rechtstheorie*, 1989, 3–34; id., *Normen, Werte, Handlungen*, Frankfort-on-Main, 1994. On the function of human intentionality (in the wider sense of the goals and intentions of an acting person) in linguistic action now see also J. Nuyts, "Intentionalität und Sprachfunktionen" in *Intentionalität – Bedeutung – Kommunikation. Kognitive und handlungstheoretische Grundlagen in der Sprachtheorie*, G. Preyer (ed.), Opladen, 1997, 51–71.

Actions are seen as the intentional behaviour of a certain agent or subject of an action, in other words, by a "human being", a "person", an individual or legal subject, and legal actions appear as acts or expressions of a will (so-called "will" theory)[22] as declared by a legal subject (subject theory). From the point of view of legal dogmatics, I would suggest, we can now also use the term *deliberate normative intentionalism*. A fully developed intentionalist conception and theory of norms and action taking its orientation from the goals, purposes and values which human beings have set for themselves[23] is to be found for the first time in the theory of law underlying Rudolf von Ihering's *The Purpose in Law* and in his accompanying legal methodology and sociological jurisprudence[24]. All legal action understood as information processing and communication of law, is today always intentional behaviour steered by information. By this I do not mean that legal theory does not offer causal explanations, so much is obvious. It is self-evident that a normative intentionalism which from the outset regards the continual production and reproduction of law by way of deliberate action as intended and willed does not *exclude* causalism from law but *presupposes* it, as I have previously demonstrated.

Legal practice and legal science do, undoubtedly, require normative standardisations and patterns of social behaviour for the orientation of individual action. They also need, however, socially adequate theories, more than anything else, which make it possible to impute individual (concrete) acts of behaviour to certain persons. It is one of the tasks of a theory and philosophy of law to register, observe and reconstruct these processes of attributing responsibilities (rights and duties) analytically and conceptually in order to be able to describe, interpret and explain them. From the point of view of the practice and the theory of law legal communication nowadays appears in this process as the fundamental operation which, as we know, serves to produce a normative information and to communicate it in such a way that it can be understood. The distinction between communication and action makes possible the continued development and elaboration of normative systems of meaning, especially those of law. The communicative structure of legally patterned facts and the concrete legal action and juridical decision which occur in the normatively structured communication in accordance with the norms and rules of law have to be clearly distinguished from each other, however. Rather than being inescapably determined by this structuralisation it leaves room for spontaneity in the production and reproduction of law within the legal system, that is, for *spontaneous law*.

---

[22] Fundamental for the classical *will* theory of norms is G.-H. von Wright, *Norm und Handlung*, Königstein/Ts., 1979, 124 ff.

[23] See already W. Krawietz, *Das positive Recht und seine Funktion*, 66–68 and 72–75.

[24] Particularly A. Gromitsaris, *Theorie der Rechtsnormen bei Rudolph von Ihering*, Berlin, 1989, 247 ff., 266–268 and 275.

All this also applies to the contemporary analytical-hermeneutic problem posed by the process of understanding normative meaning, in particular the systems of meaning in law. So far legal hermeneutics have not, however, been developed and understood as a normative communication theory. Since Dilthey and Schleiermacher, as well as later following Gadamer it has been regarded in jurisprudence as a method and theory used primarily in the humanities for interpreting and understanding all human artefacts (including legal texts)[25]. Hermeneutical legal understanding has not been examined, however, in terms of its social conditions and presuppositions, let alone interpreted, as an institutionally determined and systemically steered, genuine social operation (compare fig. 1).

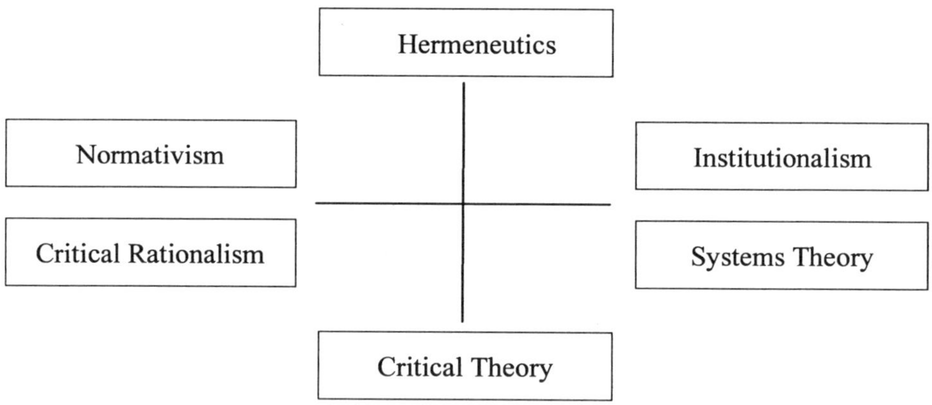

Fig. 1

A further deficiency in the basic research of today's legal sciences is to be found in the fact that approaches to a theory of norms and action which are narrowly individualistically focussed tend to ignore more complex, more or less organised, genuinely social "collective subjects".

The legal and social existence of collective subjects is seriously debated to this day in contemporary theories of law and state. Again and again we find the assertion that only "human beings", "individuals", "persons" or legal subjects exist in reality while the existence and reality of social, collective subjects is denied.

Collective subjects like, for instance, *the* school, *the* local authority, *the* regional government or *the* state, do, in fact, exert a significant and determining influence on human behaviour/action, as will be shown in the following, and can,

[25] With particular reference to law, also with an epistemological intention, see: H. G. Gadamer, "Hermeneutik als theoretische und praktische Aufgabe", *Rechtstheorie*, 1978, 257–274.

at the very least, be seen as social agents. These include, in the formulation of legal and social theory, all institutions, organisations and social systems wherein a communal communicative way of life finds expression. We are talking here about a *transindividual* normative attribution of responsibility to collective subjects (*the* local authority, *the* state, *the* church!). The legal attribution and imputation of collective rights and duties has been largely missing from the point of view represented by legal dogmatics and, precisely for this reason, requires a thorough analysis from the standpoint of legal theory[26]. An information- and communication theory of law which seeks to include *organised social action* must, therefore, attempt to balance and compensate potential deficits of an entirely agent- and subject-based, individualistic theory of action.

4. New Basic Concepts, Levels and Stages of Theorising in Contemporary Legal Thinking

In basic legal research it is not uncommon to find that terms like *general* legal theory (in contrast to the *particular* legal theories or legal doctrines within dogmatic legal science), legal theory and legal philosophy are used as if they all had the same meaning. This applies particularly to the Anglo-American areas of law although here the term *jurisprudence* tends to appear more frequently than general theory of law. In view of this it might be tempting to use the terms jurisprudence, legal theory, and legal philosophy simply as synonyms (although I do not share this view). In continental European usage, on the other hand, the term and concept of *jurisprudence* (*iuris prudentia*) is employed mainly to denote legal practice and practical (dogmatic) legal science including the legal method of practical legal argumentation in the latter. As a result we find that a distinction is made nowadays between these concepts, on the one hand, and legal theory and legal philosophy, on the other. The relationship of these two remains, however, controversial to this day. What, we may ask, is the nature of the relationship and the connection between (i) law as an, at least partially – theorised object and (ii) legal theory and legal philosophy?

The problems and difficulties we encounter in the theory and philosophy of law at present arise, as I see it, from the simple fact that legal theory does not relate to its object, law or legal systems, in the same way as a natural science relates to its object, nature. In other words, legal theory deals with an object that is *already* theorised in everyday life.

A legal system consists of a complex body of practices, particularly *practices of reasoning and justification*. The intellectual, theorised aspect of the legal order is embodied in legal doctrine: the corpus of norm-sentences, norms

[26] W. Krawietz, "Theorie der Verantwortung – neu oder alt? Zur normativen Verantwortungsattribution mit Mitteln des Rechts" in *Verantwortung*, K. Bayertz (ed.), Darmstadt, 1995, 204 and 206–207.

and rules, principles, doctrines and concepts used as basis for legal reasoning and justification. It includes elaborate conceptual structures of principles and doctrines, explicit and sophisticated forms of reflection and criticism. It is only when we have understood the nature of legal doctrine that we can comprehend the workings of courts, lawyers and even legislatures.

Anyone inquiring today into the nature of the relationship between theory and philosophy of law is, therefore, confronted with the problem that the meaning of the word and concept "theory" is ambiguous in its use. On the one hand, it refers to legal science, on the other, to legal philosophy, *i.e.* a branch of philosophy that is concerned with law and the legal systems. This means, we have to ask ourselves the following basic questions: (i) How is legal theory related to legal science and (ii) how is legal theory related to the philosophy of law?

In almost all spheres of life we have seen for some time now a progressive rationalisation and an increasing expansion of science and its influences. As for the possibilities of an increasing rationality in our dealings with valid law it has to be said that we are faced with a number of differing standards and a variety of rival concepts of rationality. What kind of practical and theoretical possibilities of a rational orientation in respect of the law exist in the sciences and in philosophy appears to depend on (i) what we mean by law, (ii) what we mean by legal science and (iii) how we determine the relationship of legal science to legal practice and to the other scientific disciplines which are – each in its own way – concerned with human action. This applies above all to the relationship to the social sciences and to philosophy, in particular to moral philosophy or ethics.

As for my own attitude to the theory and philosophy of law it has always been based on the *primacy of legal practice*. This means that all theory of law rests on legal practice. Consequently it is not the practice that follows the theory but the theory arises from the practice. This holds true not only for practical dogmatic legal science but also for practical philosophy of law both of which owe their names to their orientation on the practical experience of law in the everyday life of society.

The fact that legal science serves practical purposes would suggest that these might in turn be used for guidance in the search for a general conceptual viewpoint in law. One might assume that a specific practical point of view like that of a citizen seeking advice on his legal affairs could point the way to dividing up, conceptualising and classifying the legal material used in fulfilling his practical needs. It is unlikely, however, that a neutral set of general (or generalisable) concepts applicable to any legal order could be found by such a process. If practical needs rather than the abstract aspirations of "universal" legal science are to be served by the concepts of legal theory then these cannot be expected to be either general or neutral in different cultures and political systems.

In jurisprudence (in the continental European usage of *iuris prudentia*) the *distinction between theory and practice* – however plausible and obvious it may appear nowadays – is by no means self-evident and, therefore requires an explanation. It is a differentiation made from an empirical and analytical-conceptual point of view which only gradually took root in modern legal life and legal thinking. The reason for this is to be found in the special circumstances which very gradually led to the eventual founding of jurisprudence as a separate branch of legal science. In Germany, at least, the development of a *general* theory of law (in the sense of the German usage of "*Allgemeine Rechtslehre*") occurred already in the course of the nineteenth century. Space does not permit a more detailed account of the genesis and development of modern legal theory as it appears to me but I have commented on it repeatedly on previous occasions. Today all legal practice in the state legal systems of modern society – but not only here – in each case already assumes the existence of a theory of law of whatever kind, be it implicit or explicit! This raises the question whether it will be possible in future, too, to conceive of such a theory of law and of legal science as a separate branch of science which is no more than a *general* form of jurisprudence comprising the theory and practice of civil law, criminal and public law or whether it ought not now to cross the borders of law and legal science and enter the realms of legal and social theory, sociology and philosophy of law.

Due to the limitations of space I cannot offer here a reconstruction and full defence of my own approach to legal theory. In the following I shall be dealing only with some insights which appear important to me and some guidelines I can offer for future work in legal theory. We are experiencing at the moment a period of transition and transformation in modern legal thinking, as I shall explain more closely. A significant feature of this situation is the fact that legal theory is finding itself in an emancipatory phase, that is, it is turning more and more into an independent discipline following its own internal demands. The theory and philosophy of law are setting themselves increasingly apart from the traditional philosophico-juridical or philosophico-moral theories of norms and principles and the like. They are, as I shall be showing below, trying to find a new basis for modern legal theory. This can only be done, however, if legal theory distances itself consciously in its method and its systematic access to law from all of these predecessors.

My own theory of law, however, also dissociates itself quite consciously from connections to earlier forms of classical legal philosophy from Aristotle down to Kant and Hegel. This is true, above all, in the case of philosophical idealism, especially idealistic legal and social philosophy, but also applies to the older approaches based on the concept of natural law and their metaphysical assumptions and implications which do not stand up to the critique of epistemology and the philosophy of science. The fact that its mode of proceeding and the thought processes involved are also based on philosophical implications and presuppositions does not escape my notice; it belongs, however, to a different chapter of the inquiry into the structure and functions of law as will be shown below. My theory and philosophy of law has, above all, nothing in common with either the philosophers of natural law or with the philosophers of reason of the seventeenth and eighteenth centuries or with their current successors[27]. These thinkers accepted "nature" and pure "reason" as guides, and with the help of these guides they believed they could recognise the "natural laws", as it were, inherent in the legal life of human beings, *i.e.* laws or cognisable principles arising without human intervention and serving a putatively natural, or, at any rate "reasonable" process of rendering perfect the societal life of mankind. The frequently expressed hopes that natural law and its successor, the law of reason, might be in the position to answer today's difficult political, legal and moral questions, both great and small, or, at least, to provide an analytical-conceptual framework for dealing with them with the help of the received theory and philosophy of law have not, as far as I can see, been fulfilled hitherto.

Considering what has been said so far, we are (i) in respect of the *rational orientation of law* and (ii) of the science of law, clearly, faced today with a number of different *theories* of a law of reason, some of an older, some of a newer kind, not to mention the current, even internationally active, return to efforts aimed at continuing and further developing legal thinking based on traditional natural law and law of reason. Within the field of conventional general theory of law and principles there are a number of authors who never tire of advocating a "renaissance of natural law or the law of reason"[28]. So, for instance, Ralf Dreier who to this day wants to fall back on "the tradition of the law of reason" in his search for a suitable legal theory and legal philosophy[29]. I am unable to share this wish for reasons connected with my entirely different approach to law. It would appear to me – for reasons to be discussed below – to be ill-advised to go down this road in legal theory. Law that is already coded, conditioned and determined by society and history as well as constitutionally and legally is *not*, in my opinion, something that could or ought to be subjected *ad libitum* to a moral-ethical or reasonable disposition by a theory and moral philosophy. Trying to give a certain gloss to the postulates of a natural law or a law of reason by draping the word and concept *law* around them appears, therefore, a highly problematical thing to do. The use of this term must not blind us to the fact that this is an *inadmissible equivocation* since "natural *law*" and

[27] Id., W. Krawietz, "Normativismus und Skeptizismus? Zum Verhältnis von Regelsetzung und Regelbefolgung in der kritischen Rechtstheorie Kants" in *Formalismus und Phänomenologie im Rechtsdenken der Gegenwart*, W. Krawietz and W. Ott (eds.), Berlin, 1987, 334–335.

[28] R. Dreier, "Neues Naturrecht oder Rechtspositivismus", *Rechtstheorie*, 1987, 368–385.

[29] Id., *ibid.*, 370 ff.

"*law* of reason" are not law in the sense of the positivity of all law (including customary practice). At best we are dealing here with legal-political demands inspired by moral or ethical considerations. Only an empirically *and* analytically clean conceptual distinction and a rational orientation are capable of establishing clarity in this situation. The same applies to the relations between *law* and *scientific reason*. Just like the relationship between law and morality the relation between law and reason requires a clear analytical and conceptual separation which also attempts to do justice to the *societal* complexities of its subject. It appears thoroughly misguided to me, therefore, to speak of a law of reason if the intention is to pass off as valid laws what are, in fact, merely moralising, perhaps even "reasonable" normative demands not covered by democratic, political-legal decisions. All such postulates – despite being camouflaged as reasonable truths – are by no means legally binding and represent no more than moral appeals with, at best, legal-political intentions. The key question here is, whether and to what extent it is possible at all to perceive right law or the rightness of law and the legal order, in other words, to substantiate legal norms and their application on the basis of their content – and without any volitive/evaluative contribution and additional input! – in a purely cognitive way. As far as the perception of the validity and the binding nature of law, or of the right content of norms and actions in law and morality, is concerned, it must be said that the sciences and philosophy are extremely sceptical about the practical possibility of substantiating norms and values in a purely *cognitive* way, *i.e.* without any volitive and evaluative practical input!

Clearly, in everyday life and in the day-to-day application of law as well as in the scientifically guided and supported ways of mastering both there is nowadays a consistent demand, be it *expressis verbis* or, at least, implicitly, for *all* interpersonal orientations to be conducted *rationally* whenever possible. This demand also applies to human experiences and actions in the realm of law which, after all, covers and regulates all areas of social behaviour and action. However, *knowing who* those are who are orientating themselves rationally, or, at least, ought to do so, makes a difference when we are dealing with the *rationality of law*. Is it all of us, meaning human beings, citizens or legal subjects living in *legal communities*, each group bound by the laws of its community, reflecting rationally – which always means critically – the respective *valid* law which they have to comply with? Do we mean those who are active in the bureaucratically ordered *organisation of the state* and operate, guided and steered by the rules of law, at every tier and on all levels of the legal order with its clearly differentiated division of responsibilities (rights and duties) and its hierarchical structure? Or are we talking of the scientists and the *sciences* in the sense of those disciplines which are connected with the norms and with social actions including *philosophy*, especially, *practical philosophy*, all of which require a rational orientation – perhaps even an entirely *new* orientation? If we reject the pretensions to the universality of law (in the sense of "natural law" and/or "law of nature") on which much legal theory appears to be built, how can we continue to uphold the claim of modern theories that they contribute to our *understanding and explanation of law and legal systems* in a way that goes beyond the limited horizons of dogmatic (doctrinal) legal science? It may not be going too far to suggest, what we are seeing here are two contrasting types of rationality. In the following I shall concentrate on examining the normative rationality of those orientations which human actions receive from valid law.

I wish to differentiate right away (as I have always done in earlier publications) between "reason" and "rationality" in respect of law and the fundamental research concerned with it. One particular (typically German) school of thought represented in the general theory of law and principles, albeit not part of the mainstream of modern theory and philosophy of law, frequently uses the terms "reason" and "rationality" as synonyms[30]. In my view, this option for a concept of reason, for rational as reasonable principles and rational as merely reasonable rules, is too one-dimensional. It underestimates the practical and theoretical possibilities of a separate *juridical rationality* which is already being applied and firmly established in modern legal systems and in the behavioural sciences, including legal science, with their foundations in experience and observation and their concern with *both* norms and action.

My starting-point being the *primacy of legal practice* as a fundamental aspect to be taken into account by any rational understanding and explanation of law and the basic research dealing with it, I am not merely concerned with the above distinction but want to go beyond it and attempt to establish and research more closely the *rationality potential* of practical life experience and of the social sciences in their relationship with law (under the influence of legal science) and philosophy. In examining the nature of legal practice and legal science (including legal theory) we are studying actual social phenomena. The social reality that forms the subject matter of any theory and philosophy of law is, however, already theorised. The social reality of law consists, as I have previously pointed out, not of brute facts and data presented to scientific investigations but of normative-institutional legal facts, legal actions and practices, especially legal communications. I am following in my approach Georg-Henrik von Wright who in his *Science and Reason* – published in German in 1988 – distinguishes between (1) *judgements on reasonableness* and (2) *judgements on rationality*. In von Wright's view the first are "value-orientated" because they are concerned with "the right way of life", namely, "with that which is considered good or bad for man". *Judgements on rationality*, on the other hand, are – similar to Max Weber's

---

[30] Explicitly so in R. Alexy, "Idee und Struktur eines vernünftigen Rechtssystems" in *Rechts- und Sozialphilosophie in Deutschland heute*, R. Alexy, R. Dreier and U. Neumann (eds.), Stuttgart, 1991, 30–44.

view – first and foremost "purpose-oriented"[31]. The concept of a purpose-oriented rationality of norms and action which was developed by von Wright has proved particularly suitable for the new conception of a theory of norms and action and also points the way ahead to the continuing development of a modern theory of law. Those acting in accordance with the prescriptions of the respective valid law act not only legally but also in a formal sense rationally.

The classical idea of legal science as it appears today in the perspective of some theories appertaining to the law of reason seems far closer to the Kantian notion of reason which has lost much ground in contemporary legal thinking. According to this point of view, actions should be subsumed under wider general moral principles or maxims which are consistent with one's standing as a moral being and with the like standing of others. My approach to legal science as well as to the theory and philosophy of law rests on a different view. My conscious decision to opt for the primacy of legal practice precludes *ab extra*, as it were, the possibility of wanting to develop a legal theory in one's head by way of reasonable thought processes only to superimpose it at all cost on the social reality of law. Theories reflect and are reflected in our social relationships. The gulf between theory and practice rests, above all, on a failure to appreciate the extent to which man's social relations with his fellow men are steered and guided by social forms of life. This also applies, and particularly so, to legal communication. Space does not permit me to provide a thorough and detailed examination of the *judicial rationality* as I see it, nor to show how the latter is currently presented on the various levels of abstraction and reflection practised in modern legal thinking. Below I shall attempt to outline the different levels of practical and theoretical argumentation in the diverse social systems of modern society (see fig. 2). Drawing on this background I shall make a distinction between various steps in legal communication, that is, in the production and reproduction of legal norms and rules in modern legal systems. Further, I want to identify and differentiate, as I have done on previous occasions, various forms of social formation of law as well as different levels of legal thinking and, finally, I shall provide a brief sketch and characterisation of these levels which, in my opinion, make possible a more differentiated approach to law and a more profound understanding of its nature. The structural levels differ from each other in the degree of abstraction and in the distance from the respective contextual problems of the practical uses of law without, however, losing the standing orientation to these reference points.

---

[31] Cf. G.-H. von Wright, *Wissenschaft und Vernunft*, Münster, 1988, 29 ff., who rightly regards the contemporary "discussion about rationality" as "one of the key topics in philosophy, sociology and cultural anthropology".

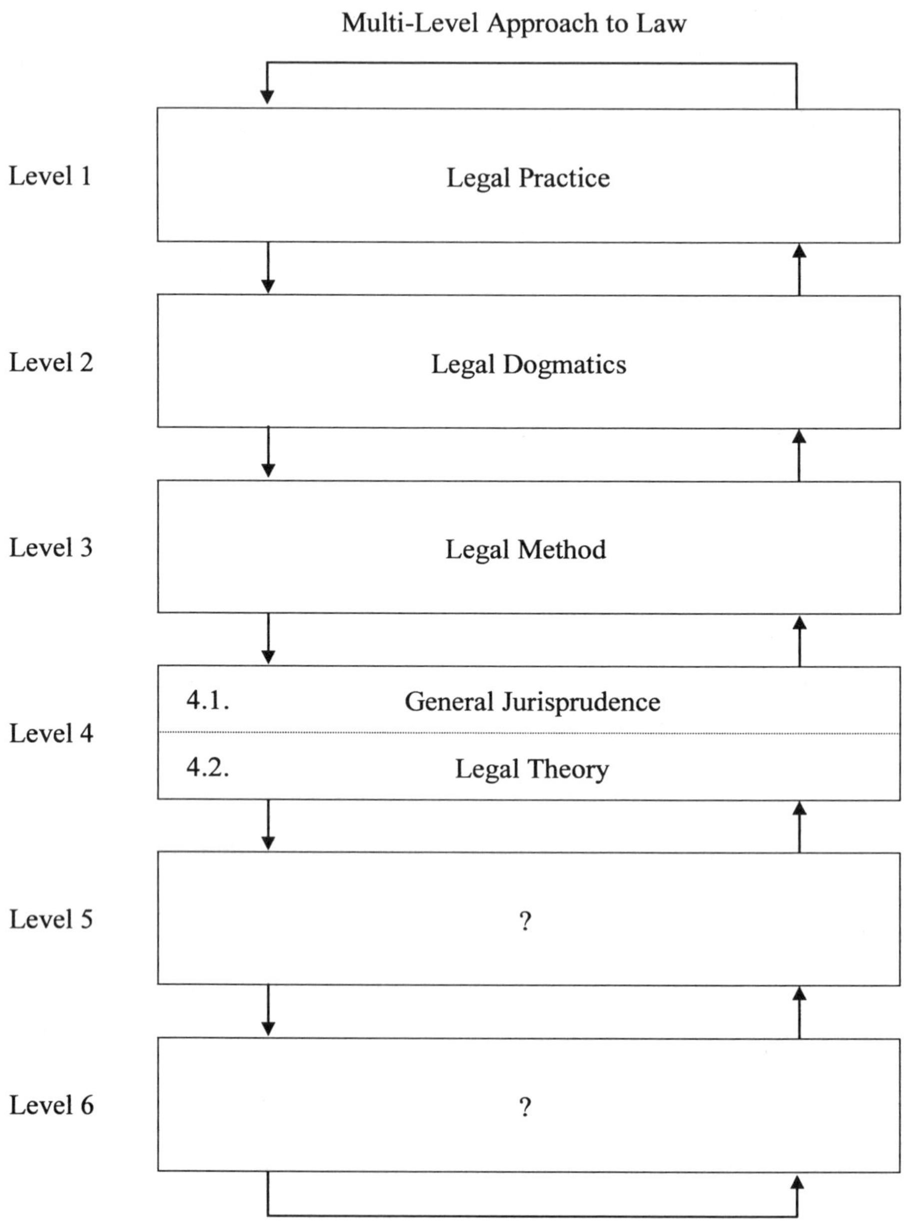
Multi-Level Approach to Law
Level 1
Legal Practice
Level 2
Legal Dogmatics
Level 3
Legal Method
Level 4
4.1.
General Jurisprudence
4.2.
Legal Theory
Level 5
?
Level 6
?

Fig. 2

On *level 1* we are dealing with the different forms of legal action and rational conduct practised in everyday life as well as in state and non-state legal systems. Everybody involved in law and in legal behaviour is familiar with the individuality and independence of the juridical rationality that can be achieved in all applications of the law, especially in individual cases and decisions taken by judges. *Level 2* is the level of the practical (dogmatic) science since – with regard to established legal practice and the respective valid law – it is commonly practised within the framework offered by the *legal dogmatics* (of civil law, criminal law and public law).

Here, too, we find a certain rationality of juridical argumentation, action and decision making in the process of following the legal norms, rules and principles. This rationality is evident particularly where the standard tasks of dogmatic legal science are undertaken. The latter being intent on presenting all valid law as much as possible in a comprehensive system of concepts, norm sentences and norm propositions. The level of rationality achieved – or, at least, achievable – can be gauged from certain typical operations and their results. I am thinking here in particular (i) of the identification of the norms of valid law ("legal sources"), (ii) of the expounding and interpreting thereof to the point of preparing and applying legal rules in individual cases as well as (iii) of the formation of legal and/or juristic concepts and systems. By contrast, *level 3*, that of legal method, seen as *hermeneutica iuris*, has always stood fully in the service of practical legal dogmatics, but to this day it is, unfortunately, nowhere near fully utilising the *potential* of rationality that nowadays is available to the methodology of the legal *sciences* as it is to all normative disciplines. Quite apart from the fact that the special nature of social norms and legal rules has always been controversial even traditional jurisprudence has become aware of a comprehensive and genuinely scientific specialisation in the perception of the law determined and shaped by different areas of cognitive interest in law.

It is only at *level 4*, that is, at a relatively high degree of desistance, abstraction and generality of the hypotheses put forward and of the legal experiences acquired and examined with their help, that a *general* theory of law – or, more appropriately – a *legal theory* based on new foundations emerges. In the following I shall be dealing with *level 4* alone although there is no doubt that legal theory in a fully developed form would also have a feedback and produce significant effects on *levels 1-3*. Following the abandonment of the traditional concept of juridical rationality a profound *change in legal thinking* occurred throughout Europe in the 1950s, that is, at the same time as juridical logic (*logica iuridica*; legal logic) in a new sense was founded and the (formal) logic of norms in the service of law and jurisprudence entered a new stage. Due to the fact that this change took place slowly and appeared at first to be limited to the theory and philosophy of law it initially remained largely unnoticed by the practice of law and by the practical (dogmatic) science of law[32]. Admittedly (i) a *general* jurisprudence (in relation to all *specialised*, genuinely dogmatic legal theories orientating themselves on specific areas of the law) and (ii) the distinction between *jurisprudence* and a legal *theory* seeking to identify, substantiate and perceive the law scientifically had already developed in the course of the 19th century. It was not until very much later, mainly in the 1960s and increasingly in the 1970s, that the notion became established which acknowledges that the development of theories, especially *legal theories*, is a scientific activity (work, reflection, etc.) entirely in its own right and with its own rationality and the aim to interpret *and* explicate legal experiences and actions. In the course of the last decades a growing differentiation between different approaches has taken place in modern legal thinking on *level 4*, in other words, in the realm of *general jurisprudence* (level 4.1) and *legal theory* (level 4.2) respectively. Taking this development into account we have to ask ourselves today, above all, whether those dealing with the law – not so much the practioners of the law as the legal scientists! – always and constantly have to be *bound as strictly* by the law in their work as is naturally the case on *levels 1-3*. The question is, therefore, whether legal theory (or the legal theorist engaged in its pursuit) itself or himself has to assume the position of *expressing* (or *prescribing*) norms.

In line with the *multi-level approach* which I have expounded here I am making an analytical and conceptual distinction between the diverse aspects of the problems and attempting to treat each of them separately. What is at issue here from the point of view of the theory of norms and action – also in respect of *levels 1-3* – is the problem of the *possibility of a practical and theoretical perception of the law*. This is a crucial problem for every *normative* discipline and, especially so, for the *science* of law. The key question to be asked in this context is whether and to what extent it is possible at all to perceive right law or the rightness of law and legal systems, in other words, to substantiate legal norms and their application on the basis of their content – and without any volitive/evaluative contribution and additional input! – in a purely *cognitive* way. One theory concept that, by contrast, appears rather narrow and not very promising – seen from the point of view of the approach to the problem taken here – is the one advocated by Alexy and Dreier. Being still wholly caught up in the long-since obsolete theory concept of general jurisprudence which they still practise under the concept of a *theory of principles* they continue to regard legal dogmatics as the "juridical research interest *par excellence*". It is for this reason also that they want to define legal theory as a "general *juridical* theory of law and

[32] Comprehensively treated in W. Krawietz, "Ulrich Klugs Theorie und Philosophie des Rechts im Umriß" in *Ulrich Klug (1913–1993) zum Gedächtnis*, Verein zur Förderung der Rechtswissenschaft (ed.), Cologne, 1995, 11–28, esp. 21 ff.

of jurisprudence" and its research interest "by its reference to dogmatics"[33]. Surprising as it seems that this kind of "theory" of law sees its *opus proprium* in legal dogmatics and their increasing theorisation, it is, of course, welcome to pursue such a course if it particularly wants to compete with conventional legal dogmatics! As for its relationship with the philosophy and sociology of law their theory wants to exclude these specialisms to a large extent although they are indispensable, in my opinion, for the fundamental research in modern legal theory. It regards them as "extra-juridical disciplines" and dispensable in so far as they are "not taught and practised in law by and for those involved in law but by and for philosophers and/or by and for sociologists"[34]. The reason for erecting such antiquated barriers between different professional groups in legal thinking is, according to the authors, to be found in the fact that in matters of norm and theory, and especially, legal theory, philosophers and sociologists only pursue a "research interest which is objectively philosophical or sociological" rather than juridical. In my own conception it is precisely *not* a *theory of legal dogmatics* standing in the service of a dogmatic jurisprudence and limited by its specific cognitive interests that I am putting forward here for a *theory of norms*, and especially *not* for a *theory of law*[35]. The creation of a theory of the kind Alexy and Dreier aim to produce may have a relative justification, if any at all, on *levels 1-3* in practical juridical argumentation. It is hardly suitable, though, for evolving a truly *general* legal theory which in this day and age has to be developed on the basis of comparative law and of a comparative jurisprudence[36]. This is why I am concerned to construct a theory of norms and action, that is, a legal theory which is – for the time being, at least – relieved of the burden of being bound by legal dogmatics with a normative content. It has little in common with the traditional, longstanding orthodoxy of the concept of *general* jurisprudence which has seen itself as a mere theory of principles for far too long. I shall for the moment leave open the question on which level of the multi-level approach pursued here, or rather in what sequence (on level 5 or level 6) legal sociology and legal philosophy are to be introduced into co-operation with legal theory. It would appear appropriate for me to begin by examining *levels 1-4* in the theory and re-

[33] See R. Alexy and R. Dreier, "The Concept of Jurisprudence", *Ratio Juris*, 1990, 1–13; R. Dreier, *Recht-Staat-Vernunft. Studien zur Rechtstheorie*, Frankfort-on-Main, 1991, 213 ff.

[34] In particular id., *ibid.*, 218 ff. See also R. Alexy and R. Dreier, "The Concept of Jurisprudence", 3 ff. and 9 ff. For a more differentiating point of view within the framework of my own *multi-level-approach* see W. Krawietz, "Recht ohne Staat? Spielregeln des Rechts und Rechtssystem in normen- und systemtheoretischer Perspektive", *Rechtstheorie*, 1993, 81–133, esp. 104 ff. and 111 ff.

[35] See W. Krawietz, *Recht als Regelsystem*, 97 ff., 162 ff. and 195.

[36] Further to this new line of research in the *comparative theory of law* see R. Narits, "Interpretation of Law in the Estonian Legal System", *Juridica International*, 1996, 11-15.

construction of legal systems from the point of view of sociological theory, especially the theory and sociology of law (*level 5*) and only then to progress to dealing with the philosophical problems (*level 6*) occurring on *every* level of reflection. I am aware, however – and I am taking this into account – that the sequence in the integration of research interests as it is currently practised tends to be the reverse.

It is important to recognise that the development of a legal theory from the very beginning involves the integration of a norm-*descriptive* point of view with the norm-*prescriptive* theory of law, by way of complementing each other, as it were. If done thoroughly and consistently this could also have repercussions for *levels 1-3* of legal thinking. This appears, at least, to be the only way of clarifying also the relationship between legal theory and philosophy and the theory and sociology of law. A theory may offer a justification for law or a critique showing that it is unjustified (unjust), as Alexy and Dreier want to do. Alternatively a theory may offer a framework for legal thinking explaining what the structure and functions of law are and how they relate to legal communication, that is, to norms and action, or both. It is not uncommon today for a single legal theory to attempt both to evaluate and to explain.

The nature of the turning-point in legal thinking which I have here outlined and which I want to describe as a *shift of paradigms in legal theory* is as follows: since Rudolf von Ihering's breakthrough to a theory and sociology of law, at least a *general legal theory* which is increasingly gaining independence can and must be understood (i) as a historical-societal theory of law, and (ii) as a discipline based on experience and observation in dealing with the respective valid law and of the way it is followed, in other words, as an empirical science. Consequently jurisprudence cannot simply limit itself to providing no more than a hermeneutic characterisation of norm sentences and their meaning. Instead, it must always also – from a *normative-realistic point of view* – refer to law in the form it is actually complied with, namely, as rule. Otherwise it would not be able either to conduct its business as hermeneutic legal science in a socially adequate manner.

It is *not* my intention, however, (and I have no wish to suggest it should be anybody else's) to opt for a *particular* level or even for *one single level* (for instance, in the sense that one might be expected, or even had to decide exclusively for legal dogmatics *without* tolerating other cognitive interests with reference to valid law). Also, it would be trivial to emphasise the different nature of the questions arising on the different levels – which is not something that will be missed by anyone involved in law (although these differences are not always taken into account in the construction of theories!). What I do want to stress, on the other hand, is the need for such an *integrated approach to law* and the advantage to be gained from it, because it alone enables us to use the newly found insights of linguistics, sociology, philosophy and similar disciplines and make them well and truly our own in the course of constructing a modern legal theory.

The real achievement of the multi-level approach – apart from the primacy of practice which has to be adhered to on *every* level – lies, in my opinion, (i) in the distancing – which increases from level to level – from the respective content-related problems in the application of law; (ii) in the degree of abstraction from the structural problems of specific contents which also increases with every level, and (iii) in the reconstruction of the social functions of law (made possible by these other two) which with the help of suitable normative-structural tools can be usefully employed and channelled. All this happens thanks to the fact that (iv) it is not the individual levels of legal thinking that convey (each on its own) needed insights into law. Only the *entirety of the various levels* interactively provides a more differentiated access to law and a deeper insight into its characteristics. The latter also comes about, and particularly so, because (v) the juridical work done on each individual level – at least, in the reflection accompanying all orientations on valid law – can but does not have to utilise – the insights of the subsequent level-specific theorisations of legal science. We must be clear, however, that (vi) legal linguistics and legal sociology (level 5) – despite being highly relevant for the creation of a legal theory can *not* simply *ab extra* provide some *models* for future proceedings on levels 1-4. Instead, the reverse is true: *which* linguistic and/or sociological insights relating to law are needed and suitable for constructing a modern theory of law and must, therefore, become part of a general legal theory, this question has to be examined first and foremost from the perspective of legal theory. The same must hold true for philosophy and its sub-disciplines (*level 6*) if their insights are to find a use *in the service of law*. The first thing to be done, above all, would be to explore and clarify – in the multi-level approach on *level 5* – the preceding levels of the theory construction from the point of view of *a theory and sociology of law* and only then to deal, on *level 6*, with the *philosophical* (*i.e.* anthropological, ontological/ deontological, logical, epistemological and other) *problems* occurring on all levels of abstraction. In the contact with neighbouring disciplines of legal science, too, and particularly here, the suggested multi-level approach appears a suitable means, (vii) to render possible the *co-operation between legal science and associated disciplines* founded on the inter- and multi-disciplinary teamwork established by legal science and permitted by *level 4* with a view to the respective *valid* law (*levels 1-3*). It goes without saying that all this must also be taken into consideration in the course of researching legal communication. There is, of course, no reason why further levels in the approach to law should not be introduced and integrated into the existing scheme.

5. My Theory of Law as Theory of Legal Communication

From the point of view of a juridical communications- and systems theory the normative communication of law consists of a *tripartite selection process*. In social-structural and dynamic-functional terms this process binds together (i) information, (ii) utterance and (iii) understanding in a single *emergent legal unit*. Separately these components have – deontically or deontologically – no independent existence. It is only when and if the selectivity of the three operations has a social congruence in the realm of law, *i.e.* if they coincide with each other, as it were, that a normative communication actually takes place. The following may serve as an *example*: the legislator (1) passes a law by setting down the normative informations required for it in form of an *if-then* regulation, (2) he publishes the law in the usual form by addressing it and communicating it to those whom it concerns, so that (3) the addressees of the law who have to comply with it, (a) the citizens and legal subjects and (b) the legal staff of the state, have knowledge of it, so that they can understand it. Whether this communication of law is transmitted technologically or takes place in the conventional way (publication of the law in a law gazette, official records etc.) can here be left open.

In the following we have to identify (i) the elements and components that constitute the individual normative *communication of law* and (ii) to clarify which *institutional and systemic requirements* have to be fulfilled for an information to be conveyed successfully and a legal communication to be considered socially adequate. In any case, what matters is that the legal communication actually reaches the respective addressee and is, therefore, able to direct him to adhere to the behaviour intended and prescribed by the law, *i.e.* that it becomes socially effective, it has a social impact.

The factual/normative *information* – whichever way it is *produced* – does not only have to be *uttered* but also needs to be *understood* because a legal communication is only possible on the basis of understanding. From the normative-realistic point of view the *understanding* on the part of the recipient has to be regarded as a *partial aspect of selecting normative meaning*. It is both empirically and analytically distinct from information and utterance and always has a degree of independence. Among the conditions for the positivity of all law there is, therefore, *no* such thing as *automatic production of law*[37]. The success of a normative communication is not measured by the fact that something has been conveyed correctly or wrongly but by the fact that a normative information has been *produced, uttered* and *understood* which can and may but does not have to provide a link for further juridical communication to issue from it. It only has to

[37] The fact that the production of law is act-dependent and organisation-bound is also emphasised by A. Gromitsaris, *Normativität und sozialer Geltungsgrund des Rechts*, Berlin, 1992, 18 ff., 211 ff.

be *possible* in practical terms to react to the communicated legal text (law, contract etc.) by *acceptance/rejection* which presupposes in any case that is has been understood. The juridical rationality which finds expression in the legal communication can, consequently, be seen as a *normative structural coupling*, *i.e.* a rationality of linkage ("*Anschlußrationalität*").

Legal communication is, then, successful if the addressee and recipient has understood the factual/normative utterance directed to him by the lawgiver and has thereby been put into the position of finding his own orientation by conforming with or deviating from the norm. The ensuing behaviour which expresses the acceptance/rejection is, however, already to be regarded as the *beginning of a further, new communication*. It produces a new (factual and normative) information which may be followed by further communications and actions – be they conforming or rejecting.

The most fundamental unit in social interactions and transactions spanning a variety of organised social systems is, therefore, *not the human being, the individual, the person or the subject* as the voluntarist agent of human action but the normative-socially structured *juridical communication* which interlinks with other juridical communications and thereby invests the social order of law with a concrete content, binding character and normative stability. This is the only way to answer the question we are faced with at every turn, the basal question posed by all legal practice and occupying all theory and the philosophy of law: the first question we ask when we begin to study law and that arises at every level of legal thinking: "What *ought* we to do?"

Previously law was not understood and interpreted as the content of a normative communication, either in legal practice (*level 1*) or in legal dogmatics (*level 2*), either in legal method (*level 3*) or in general jurisprudence (*level 4*). And in the critically reflected legal thinking informed largely by an idealistic and mainly analytical philosophy (informed by the law of reason, principles etc.) an approach to the law and its application which was shaped by technology was on the whole alien. It was certainly not common practice to regard dealing with law – objectivated in juridical processes of decision making – as processing legal information and acts of normative communication. Nowadays, on the other hand, the entire production and reproduction of law and legal systems appears to us to be conditioned and determined by technological, as well as political, cultural, economic and other social factors, not to mention existing structures of authority and power. At present all law is, therefore, regarded – particularly in the juridical institutions- and systems theory – as a normative communication structure of socio-legal communities. It determines the legal actions of human beings but does not rob them of their spontaneity and freedom.

What we regard as *normative communication* generally in the realm of law nowadays was on the whole until recently treated hermeneutically, *i.e.* in the sense of the traditional humanities and the *hermeneutica iuris* cultivated by them.

However, the hermeneutic method and the understanding of legal texts generally only referred to the interpretation and application of legal *prescriptions* rather than to the actually effective legal *acts or actions* and their scientific analysis. They in turn require description, interpretation and explanation.

As for the relationship between *norms and action* the hermeneutic understanding in law remained limited to the *text* and its normative meaning. This normally did not extend to the social *context* and the insights and findings of the social sciences which study all law and its application in the context of its social impact[38]. What was largely ignored was the fact that we cannot begin to grasp, understand and explain the normative meaning and social significance of interpersonal communications which are structured and steered by the means of law unless we also study the nature of the social impact of law. Our everyday knowledge does not seem to be sufficient to understand properly how exactly the law affects our lives.

Supported by anthropological, ethological, linguistic, cultural and other research in the social sciences[39] there is now a growing insight that the law and its impact on human behaviour requires more detailed basic research both in law and the social sciences. At present the areas where it must start and on which it must focus are, if I am not mistaken, the theory of law and state, social theory, and, above all, the theory and sociology of law. The relevance of these areas will become much clearer in the future. The fact that today's great legal and social *framework*-theories like those of Habermas and Luhmann are also conceived as communication theories in their entire research design and strategy should give us food for thought. What is still missing at the moment, however, is a sufficiently developed communication theory of law which – entirely in the sense of the Blankenburg's demand for operationability – permits us to put forward or deduce from it empirically testable hypotheses and partial theories which can be empirically tested. My own efforts are intended to remedy this deficiency.

It was not until the 1970s that theories of normative communication made their entrance into the realm of law – if only hesitantly to begin with and in a narrow form, focussed, above all, on the application of law as pronounced by judges. It found expression in the drastically condensed slogan which was common currency in the theory and practice of law: *Law is a communication addressed to judges*!

---

[38] See the report by G. Schmidt-Eichstaedt, "Wirkungsforschung im Recht. Unter welchen Voraussetzungen erfüllen Gesetze ihren Zweck?", *Deutsches Verwaltungsblatt*, 1998, 322–326.

[39] Cf. the profound work by H. Hof, *Rechtsethologie. Recht im Kontext von Verhalten und außerrechtlicher Verhaltensregelung*, Heidelberg, 1996. He demands – for reasons I cannot here discuss in detail – "an ethological re-orientation of law and legal science".

What this condensed version does from the point of view of communication theories, is to ignore almost entirely the *primary system* or *subject system of law* in the terms Alchourrón and Bulygin have very fittingly used to describe the contexts of everyday social interaction, in other words, the *system of norms* "which regulates the behaviour of legal subjects"[40]. As the above formula demonstrates this approach which sees the law essentially as a normative communication addressed to judges referred *mainly* to the *secondary* system or – even more narrowly – to the *judges'* system[41] and was confined to this limited area. However, this legal positivism practised by judges ("*Richterrechts-positivismus*" – as it was labelled by Andrés Olléro on one occasion so convincingly[42]) proved too narrow from the start. This is, by the way, precisely the weak point – both from the point of view of legal practice and legal theory – at the heart of the Anglo-American legal systems with their exaggerated emphasis on the relevance of the law as pronounced by judges[43]. A scientific approach to law or rather to conceptions of law which has been restricted to such narrow confines may appear justifiable if the analysis of law is also territorially limited. In the context of a truly general and global theory of law with a view even to a global society (general theory of law, comparative jurisprudence), such an approach appears, however, far too one-sided.

Hence not only the definition of the concepts of the legal norm, the legal order and the legal system, or legal systems but also the application of rules of law to individual cases took place largely in the light of hermeneutics. Evolving institutions, organisations and other social systems, too, were first and foremost regarded as *artefacts* (ideal legal order, ideal theory of law etc.) to be interpreted hermeneutically in the sense of the humanities instead of being recognised as *normative-institutional facts* which are to be examined first and foremost with the means of the social sciences, that is, as social structures and procedures which for their part are organisationally and systemically steered and influenced.

The scientific system, too, on the various levels of self-abstraction and critical self-reflection in legal thinking, in the context, that is, of (i) legal dogmatics (*level 2*), (ii) legal method (*level 3*) and (iii) general jurisprudence (*level 4*), was initially dominated by approaches outside the communication theory.

---

[40] C. E. Alchourrón and E. Bulygin, *Normative Systeme*, Freiburg, 1994, 245.

[41] Id., *ibid.*, 249 ff.

[42] A. Ollero, "Zum Verhältnis von Positivität und Geschichtlichkeit im Recht" in *Formalismus und Phänomenologie im Rechtsdenken der Gegenwart*, W. Krawietz and W. Ott (eds.), Berlin, 1987, 135–140.

[43] This impression is sustained by *Interpreting Statutes: A Comparative Study*, N. MacCormick and R. S. Summers (eds.), Aldershot, 1991 and *Interpreting Precedents: A Comparative Study*, N. MacCormick and R. S. Summers (eds.), Aldershot, 1997.

An information- and communication theory dealing with the relationship between norms and action is not a finished product. To construct and develop it is a highly demanding task which remains as yet largely unaccomplished. In pursuing this purpose a very broad concept of communication in the context of the modern institutions- and systems theories of law has to be used as a basis. This concept takes its orientation from the dichotomisation into institutional facts and norms customary in the language of law. Starting-points are practical linguistic informations and normative communications – or, at least, those that can be formulated linguistically – with a social relationship to the law without this being necessarily provided by the state! Law is a specific form of social relation but not all law is formalised. There is, as I have pointed out on an other occasion, not only a formal law but also an informal one. All forms of social behaviour which serve to establish, concretise and change legal norms, be they general or individual ones, are to be counted as legal communications. In accordance with a social differentiation established in German law as early as in the nineteenth century, we shall, however, in the following make a distinction, both from a structural and from a functional point of view, between primary and secondary systems in our analysis of law[44]. In legal communication we regard the day-to-day legal actions in everyday life undertaken by citizens and legal subjects who derive the orientation for their behaviour from already socially established legal expectations as part of the *primary system* of law while all decision taking activities by the highly organised and bureaucratised legal staff of the state, *i.e.* legislative, executive and judiciary, belong to the *secondary system* of law.

No longer is law to be interpreted narrowly and reduced to no more than a static legal order comprising all valid norms, rules and regulations and based only on the hermeneutic access to legal texts. Instead the entire legal order is to be understood as a dynamic, and in its entirety socially established network of all legal acts, communications and actions which together constitute the legal system. Communications and legal acts occurring in a particular field always follow on from preceding communications and legal acts. In this way they contribute – by way of normative structural coupling, that is, a kind of juridical rationality of linkage – to the continual production and reproduction of the legal system. It follows that the information- and communication system of law is a vast network made institutionally permanent and composed of systemic operations consisting of directives and norms and made up of any number of legal communications. These are created, interlinked and thereby further developed in the everyday practice of law. This network is capable of growing in any direction thematically and of being enlarged at will. All social areas of human activity can be comprised within it and practically the entire world encompassed by it. The juridical argumentation which we deal with in everyday

---

[44] W. Krawietz, *Recht als Regelsystem*, 110 ff. and 153 ff.; id., *Recht ohne Staat*, 121 ff.

legal life as well as in the other legal practice which is normally organised by the state, *i.e.* in the secondary system of law, becomes accessible to a deeper understanding only if we distinguish both empirically and analytically between the different levels at which law is produced and analysed as is shown in my conception of the *multi-level approach.* In addition it seems imperative to consider it also both in its interdependence and in the context of its impact[45]. This is shown by the arrows in fig. 2. Changes taking place on a certain level of the creation or observation of law cause reactions on the levels above (preceding) as well as setting in train consequences and repercussions on the levels below (following).

Following the distinction between directives and norms advanced by the contemporary analytical-normative theory of law of Scandinavian legal realism[46], especially of Danish and Swedish, as well as Polish provenance[47] or by German legal realism and sociological jurisprudence[48] it can be said that the legal system procreates itself by *self-referentially* linking new legal directives and legal norms to previously validated ones. Legal validity is a product of the legal system and is worked out from moment to moment. In this way further starting-points for further directives and legal norms are formed and these at the same time produce and reproduce the *legal system.* In form and content it presents itself as an *internally consistent, normative whole formed by the primary and secondary systems of the law.* We are, consequently, dealing not only with a system of norm sentences but – and this should be taken note of – with a social system consisting of the entirety of all relevant juridical communications as well as – from the dynamic-functional point of view – embracing the constant flow of new communications and legal actions.

One might say, therefore, that the legal system gains its social identity as a result of its self-generated, (deliberate) legal-normative acts. The directives and norms proceeding from them are not issued in accordance with a preconceived master-plan but pragmatically and in each case according to requirement, and at certain points, as it were, *ad hoc.* Directives and norms emanate from previous directives and norms which in turn give rise to new directives and norms and so on.

---

45 On the latter cf. id., *ibid.*, 106 ff. and 113 ff. See also id., "Reasonableness versus Rationality of Law? On the Evolution of Theories in Jurisprudence" in *Justice, Morality and Society. A Tribute to Aleksander Peczenik*, A. Aarnio e. a. (eds.), Lund, 1997, 221-245, esp. 237 ff.

46 For a detailed account see A. G. G. de Groot, *Der skandinavische Realismus und seine Bedeutung für die rechtliche Grundlagenforschung*, Amsterdam, 1997.

47 K. Opalek, *Theorie der Direktiven und der Normen*, Vienna/New York, 1986.

48 See H. Weber-Grellet, *Rechtsphilosophie*, Münster, 1997, 89 ff.

What distinguishes legal communication structurally and functionally from other forms of normative communication in the realms of religion, ethics etc. is, above all, the fact that it always occurs with reference to already valid and effectively operative legal *norms* (or to norm *sentences* in the symbolising form of the legal language, respectively) which are used in an assumed, already established, normatively binding legal practice (vested with binding normative powers) in a particular regional society. In our society moral discourse is excluded from legal communication by the binary code of the legal system. The binary code which qualifies the different operations as *law/non-law*, *legally valid/legally invalid, legal/illegal*, *lawful/unlawful*, *right/wrong*, screens out other kinds of discourse. Its aim is, therefore, the production (which always also means reproduction) of legal decisions in a self-referential *legal system of directives and norms* which by way of linking communications differentiates itself increasingly through further directives and norms. Whether these are laws, administrative or judicial decisions, contracts or other directives in their normative form makes no difference from the point of view of the *theory* of norms and action.

In view of the traditional, conventionally applied or implicitly pre-supposed concept of legal action which is commonly used in legal practice (*level 1*) and legal dogmatics (*level 2*) those examining the communication of law from the perspective of the theory of norms and action have to be prepared to see some overdue corrections and necessary re-arrangements in the design of the theory. The latter now seems imperative although the legal concept of action had hitherto appeared entirely secure. Appearances can be deceptive. In contrast to the traditional individualistic concept of action the following reflections take their cue from the realisation that all communication of law and all legal action in the everyday life of communities has essentially always been guided and steered by normative institutions, organisations and social systems. These normative-institutional facts have not been taken into account sufficiently, in my opinion, either by constitutional juridical positivism, or by contemporary statutory and legal positivism which today is advocated in the context of the normativism of pure legal science (Kelsen, Robert Walter) as well as that of "institutional legal positivism" (MacCormick, Weinberger)[49]. Although these approaches include the actions of collective subjects[50] in their theories of norms and institutions they tend to continue to adhere to an essentially individualistic subject orientation and methodological individualism in their theory of action.

---

[49] A good survey over the development of contemporary British and Austrian institutionalism is offered by N. MacCormick and O. Weinberger, *Grundlagen des Institutionalistischen Rechtspositivismus*, whose contributions to this volume were, however, produced independently from each other.

[50] Most recently in O. Weinberger, *Alternative Handlungstheorie*, Vienna, 1996, 234 ff. and 255 ff.

The concept of normative communication employed in the following reflections covers – both empirically and in terms of legal norm sentences – the entire field of legal communication, in other words, (1) the level of national (state) law, (2) the level of the European communities and the law of the European Union and (3) the level of international law of nations and communities. It comprises within it, therefore, the entirety of *directives and norms* which are *self-referentially* produced in the legal system of modern society, that is, with continual logical and social *reference of the respective legal system to itself*, to its constitution, previously passed laws, etc. The concept of legal communication extends to all forms of legal action and all kinds of normative attributions of responsibility, in particular to the attribution and imputation of rights and duties as we know them today in the realms of civil law, criminal law and public law. Such a communicative system is conceived to be self-referential, self-maintaining, and self-reproducing.

A concept of law based solely on the state and concerned exclusively with *formal* state law without taking account of the manifold *informal* social conditions and prerequisites for the production of law seems, by contrast, far too narrow. By normative self-reference I mean the institutional legal fact that self-organisation and self-production of the legal system and of the required laws take place in the legal systems of modern society, *i.e.* the communicative system is conceived as self-referential, self-maintaining and self-reproducing. There is a continual self-reproduction of the legal system in the sense that it continually refers back to itself in all its factual/normative operations, *i.e.* it takes into account other operations and actions it has previously undertaken.

Law does not, however, only come into existence in specific bodies set up by the state or in highly bureaucratised states with their legal staffs. The state has neither a monopoly nor a prerogative for the creation of law. From the point of view of the theory of law and of the systems theory law comes into existence in *all social institutions and systems*, namely in interaction systems, organisations and in the *variety-pool* of society, be it a *regional* society or – on a higher level of abstraction – *global* society as a whole[51]. What I mean by global society is not – as in Luhmann's approach – world society in its differentiation into independent functional subsystems of society but the social reality of law in its interaction and organisation systems *as well as* in state legal systems. My systems-theoretical approach to law differs from Luhmann's – apart from the fact that he does not mention *state* legal systems – above all, because the concept of law and society used by me here rests on the differentiation between *regional*

[51] For a detailed discussion see W. Krawietz, "Staatliches oder gesellschaftliches Recht? Systemabhängigkeiten normativer Strukturbildung im Funktionssystem Recht" in *Kritik der Theorie sozialer Systeme. Auseinandersetzungen mit Luhmanns Hauptwerk*, W. Krawietz and M. Welker (eds.), Frankfort-on-Main, 1992, 247–301, esp. 274 ff.

society and *global* society, that is, society *as a whole*. This distinction appears to me to be of vital importance as a guiding principle for the social observation of law. It is only by adhering to it that the theory of law can avoid the danger of missing the access to the "social reality of law" in its observations and of getting lost in speculations about the world society of law. Unless I am wholly mistaken the turn to the social reality of law is now not only possible but indispensable!

This is why – with a view to the requirements to be met by a theory of normative communication – an attempt is here being made to sketch the outlines of a socially adequate framework theory of legal communication which rejects as a matter of principle the narrow limitations imposed on legal thinking by individualistic actor- and subject-centred theoretical approaches.

The basis for my approach is the *positivity* of all law which – in accordance with the genuinely normative theory of social institutions and systems advocated by me – will be understood as *selectivity* of law in the following. Whatever is selected to become law, endowed with legal validity and established institutionally, is always a selection from other existing possibilities – neither more nor less. Every actually made ruling, therefore, proves contingent, considering that it might have turned out to be different. This does not, however, mean that the law is arbitrary since new rulings in the legal system normally – self-referentially – follow on from previously made rulings (of the constitution, laws, legal rulings and so on). It is precisely the *way the legal system regulates and processes itself* that constitutes genuine juridical rationality as I have demonstrated on another occasion. It also dominates all practical legal argumentation and all legal action.

This selectivity continues on the different levels of law production in the secondary system of law, *i.e.* in the legislative, executive and the judiciary. From the point of view of legal dogmatics it appears in the law production, on the one hand, as a means of concretising and strengthening itself as well as securing its structures, and, on the other hand, as self-hierarchisation of the legal system[52]. The communication concept which is commonly used in the *general* theory of social institutions and systems[53] may here assist us in finding our bearings. This

---

[52] See already W. Krawietz, *Recht als Regelsystem*, 22 and 133 ff. for the basic concept of the structural theory of law which was formulated by me to replace the conventional metaphor of the "stepped" structure of the legal order.

[53] Cf. id., "Neue Sequenzierung der Theoriebildung und Kritik der allgemeinen Theorie sozialer Systeme" in *Kritik der Theorie sozialer Systeme. Auseinandersetzungen mit Luhmanns Hauptwerk*, 14–42, esp. 16 ff. and 27 ff. It is, by no means, my intention here to introduce a certain opposition to Luhmanns' theory-conception but to remove a deficit in the information- and communication-based approach to operations which are relevant to the relations between norms and action. Fundamental as ever remains N. Luhmann, "Was ist Kommunikation?" in *Soziologische Aufklärung*, Opladen, 1995, 113–124. And there is no intention – neither here, nor anywhere else – to diminish its original achievements. On

concept of communication which I have discussed above can also be employed to substantiate the legal theory of norms and action.

From the point of view of a *theory* of norms and action the legal systems of modern society as a whole in their form, structure and functions can – virtually, at least, – be regarded as *one* single information- and communication system although this possibility has not been fulfilled completely in reality as yet. Society everywhere is served in its orientation and in the way it steers human actions by the normative networks of the legal systems which are formulated and fixed by the language of law, in other words, in respect of the complexities of the circumstances of life all legally relevant matters undergo a dichotomisation into facts and norms which in terms of social structure is a characteristic feature and bases itself on socially generalising (factual/normative) expectations[54]. It is their social function to induce the addressees of the law to act in the way they (*i.e.* the normative networks) prescribe, that is, to make sure they adhere to the norms. This occurs when the latter fulfil the prescribed behavioural expectations which have been fixed and generalised by means of the language of law, *e.g.*, when their behaviour conforms with or deviates from the norms. Thorough research is needed, however, to establish *exactly how* legal communication *occurs* in reality, *i.e.* how normative obligation *and* social impact of law are actually brought about.

6. Shifting Paradigms in Contemporary Legal and Social Theory

Understanding and explaining law, legal order and legal systems in this situation involves a grasp of the very sources from which the communicative structures of modern law have emerged. Law emanates from the societal system as well as from the legal system itself. The legal system is able to qualify its own operations as *law/non-law, legally valid/legally invalid, legal/illegal, lawful/ unlawful, right/wrong, just/unjust* and so on. The coding is what gives communications their legal meaning. When viewed as a dynamic, functional, legal system valid law continuously produces valid law through its communicative operations[55]. Through self-reflection the system constructs a legal world that mirrors or duplicates its environment (including other social systems in its environment), but only legally relevant operations are operative.

---

the contrary, they continue to deserve the greatest respect.

[54] For the dichotomic development of legal thinking see J. Llompart, *Dichotomisierung in der Theorie und Philosophie des Rechts*, Berlin, 1993, 17 ff. and 66 ff.

[55] W. Krawietz, "Recht und moderne Systemtheorie" in *Reason and Experience in Contemporary Legal Thought*, T. Eckhoff, L. M. Friedman e.a. (eds.), Berlin, 1986, 281-309; T. Eckhoff and N. K. Sundby, *Rechtssysteme. Eine systemtheoretische Einführung in die Rechtstheorie*, Berlin, 1988.

In this internal world, what is correct (or permitted) or forbidden is only that which is *legally* correct, *legally* permitted, *legally* forbidden. Thus, an order of *legal* meaning is created, and we can identify the various forms of normative expectations, institutional patterns and social structures in a legal perspective. From the point of view of legal theory the legal order is not, in my opinion, primarily a matter of words or norm sentences and their meaning but a set of forms, norms and ways of living and doing, *i.e.* a matter of institutions and different social systems.

Changes in the contemporary legal order are hard to identify precisely because they operate at the level of general background assumptions of the past which are usually taken for granted. The most important problem here is the lack of a socially adequate theory and sociology of law, represented by a well-integrated theoretical framework which is conceptually well-structured, empirically extensively tested and generally accepted by jurists and sociologists. What we actually have at our disposal are a number of contradictory and partial theories within different frameworks and various schools of legal thinking. It is against this background of tensions between rival concepts of law that we can best understand the debates of contemporary legal theory. The conventional perspectives of the longstanding orthodoxy are no longer adequate, in my view. Instead of indulging in self-defeating controversies legal theory should make it its task to link a wide variety of legal ideas and conceptions within a broader framework and locate and interpret the law and legal principles within the social context.

From a scientific point of view law should be studied from the perspective of social interaction and social organisation. The legal and social order is a man-made order. The laws governing it are man-made. There is no reason to believe that this order and these laws are founded upon extra-human, invariable and universal natural laws or laws of reason. But if they are not, the only way forward may well be to leave the realm of legal science and legal theory in its narrow traditional sense behind and to turn to the social sciences for a broader vision. Such a decision then raises the questions what a theory of law and society has to offer from this perspective and how legal theory as a social science can describe and explain the communicative structures and functions of law and legal systems more adequately than a conventional legal theory has been able to.

Traditional legal and social science paradigms have contributed significantly to our understanding of how man is produced by society and how he produces society. However, it may now be time to dethrone some of these orthodox paradigms of legal and social theory. A change of paradigm may be about to take place as new approaches and perspectives are being consolidated.

In the course of the 1980s institutionalist and systems-theoretical approaches to law began to come increasingly to the fore even in the hermeneutics of law.

These introduced a wide-ranging theory-substitution, *i.e.* previous, exclusively hermeneutic approaches were partly replaced, partly supplemented and brought up to date.

What this process achieved above all was that it rendered possible the renewal of analytical hermeneutics. Because of its many analytical-conceptual exaggerations the latter was denounced as early as the late nineteenth century – in Germany, at least, – as failed "conceptual analysis", "conceptual jurisprudence" (*"Begriffsjurisprudenz"*) or pure conceptualism, seen as mere constructivism which was not covered by politico-legal decisions[56]. From a methodological and theoretical point of view diverse varieties of a *New Interpretivism* (see fig. 3) then evolved. Where do I place myself in theoretical and philosophical legal thinking?

In respect of legal communication and norm-orientated legal action within the framework of a new kind of analytical-constructivist hermeneutics[57] - particularly on *levels 1-4* of legal argumentation and legal thinking – I am concerned, above all, with understanding by observing or observing by understanding[58].

Today two approaches may be regarded as already operating *beyond* the limitations of conventional legal hermeneutics: (i) the *institutional legal positivism* of Austrian and British provenance (Ota Weinberger, Neil MacCormick) and (ii) an *institutional and systems theory of law* concerned with the relations between *norms and action* which is politically functional, *i.e.* oriented on social norms, interests, goals and values (Max Weber, Schelsky, Torstein Eckhoff, Krawietz et al.).

---

[56] Cf. W. Krawietz, "Juristische Konstruktion, Kritik und Krise dogmatischer Rechtswissenschaft" in *Theorie und Technik der Begriffjurisprudenz*, W. Krawietz (ed.), Darmstadt, 1976, 1–10.

[57] Id., "Sprachphilosophie in der Jurisprudenz", 1484 ff.

[58] For this and the following see G. Kneer and A. Nassehi, "Verstehen des Verstehens. Eine systemtheoretische Revision der Hermeneutik", *Zeitschrift für Soziologie*, 1991, 341-356; A. Nassehi, "Kommunikation verstehen. Einige Überlegungen zur empirischen Anwendbarkeit einer systemtheoretisch informierten Hermeneutik" in *Beobachtung verstehen, Verstehen beobachten. Perspektiven einer konstruktivistischen Hermeneutik*, T. Sutter (ed.), Opladen, 1997, 134–163; W. L. Schneider, *Die Beobachtung von Kommunikation. Zur kommunikativen Konstruktion sozialen Handelns*, Opladen, 1994.

New Interpretivism in Legal and Social Theory

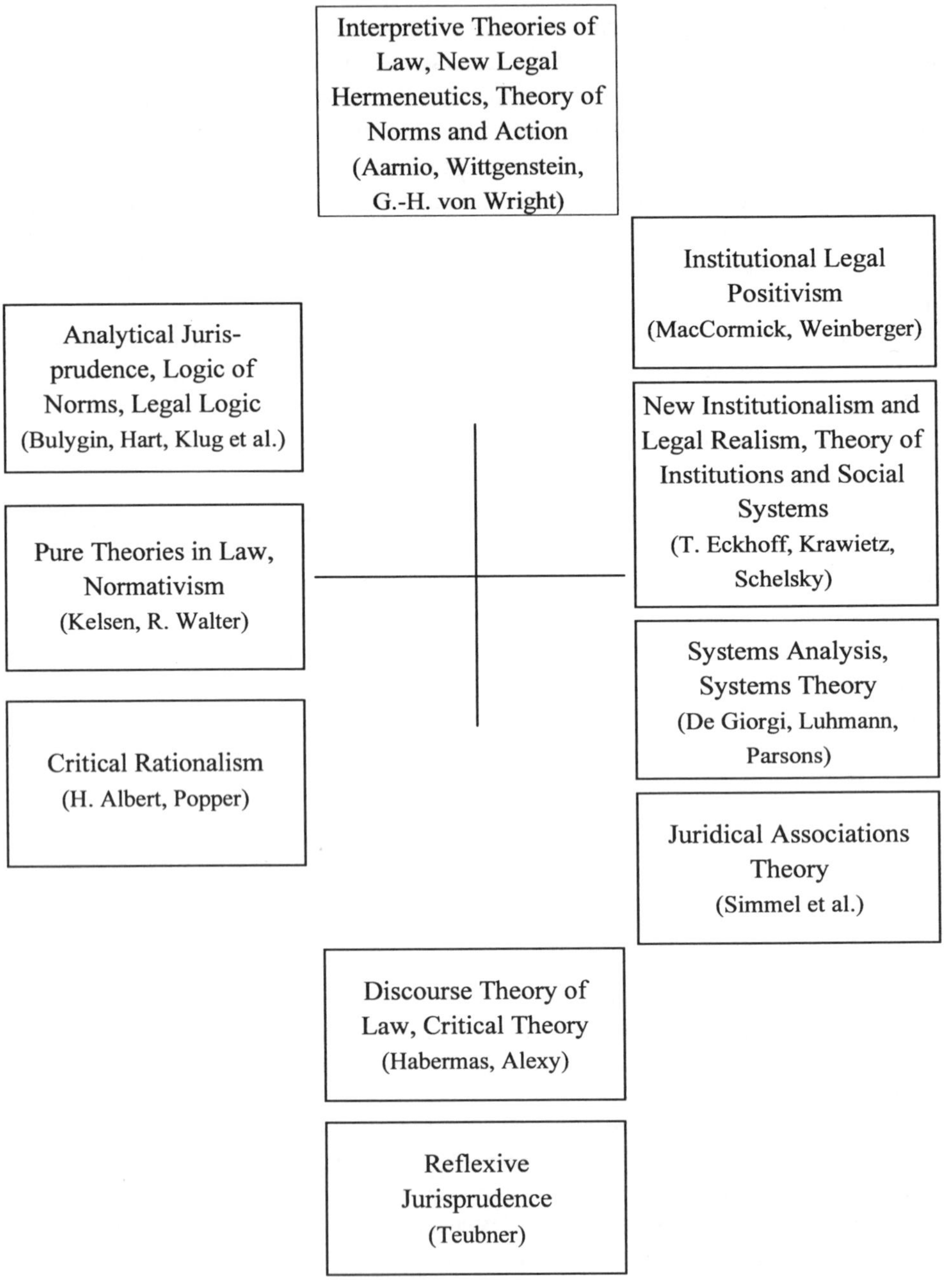

Fig. 3

The difference between the two orientations in this modern institutional theory of law, as I understand it, is this: the first one restricts itself to the widely shared *interpretive institutionalism* giving the normative view of an "ideal legal order" and "ideal theory" of decision making its due[59] while the latter is seeking to understand and explain law and to find its foundation with the help of the social sciences and by basing itself on a theory and sociology of law from the outset. In addition, the latter is also already located beyond the conventional legal positivism with its too one-sided orientation on the state and on inter-state-relations[60]. It would be most appropriate, therefore, – and even with reference to the self-conception of dogmatic legal science and its legal methodology – to regard it from the point of view of a *New Institutionalism* drawing in turn on the modern institutions- and systems theory[61]. What is new, above all, in this *New Institutionalism* is the fact that the theory of social institutions and systems in its cognitive interests concentrates strictly on observable, relatively well-defined, or, at least, definable social relations and references in order to be properly able to control normatively steered legal actions and not to lose sight of them.

In the realm of general systems theory (Parsons, Luhmann, De Giorgi) as well as that of the theory and sociology of law *systems analysis* and *juridical systems theory* (Eckhoff/Sundby, Krawietz, Gromitsaris, Chanos, Petra Werner, Schemann, Schröder, Veddeler e.a.) correspond to *New Institutionalism*. Central to both are efforts to renew the theories of norms and action in law and to develop them in the direction of a communications-theory of law. The representatives of this position understand the theory of law and state as well as social theory as theories of normative communications and legal actions (interaction, transactions) which – in every day life – are structured and steered to a significant extent by social institutions and systems. I am referring here specifically to the research undertaken by the above mentioned authors.

---

[59] See N. MacCormick, "Universal and Particular: The Problem with Precedent" in *Justice, Morality and Society*, 263–265 and 271.

[60] See D. Wyduckel, "Recht und Rechtswissenschaft im nachpositivistischen Rechtsrealismus" in *Sociological Jurisprudence and Realist Theories of Law*, E. Kamenka e.a. (eds.), Berlin, 1986, 349-365; M. Schulte, "Recht, Staat und Gesellschaft rechtsrealistisch betrachtet" in *Rechtsnorm und Rechtswirklichkeit*, A. Aarnio e.a. (eds.), Berlin, 317-332.

[61] W. Krawietz, "Rechtssystem als Institution? Über die Grundlagen von Helmut Schelky's sinnkritischer Institutionstheorie", *Rechtstheorie*, 1984, 209–243; id., "Ansätze zu einem Neuen Institutionalismus in der modernen Rechtstheorie der Gegenwart", 706–714; id., "Die Normentheorie Helmut Schelky's als Form eines Neuen Institutionalismus im Rechtsdenken der Gegenwart", 114–148; id., "Toward a New Institutionalism in Modern Legal Thinking. Facets of Rationality" in *Reason in Law*, I, C. Faralli and E. Pattaro (eds.), Milan, 1987, 313–325.

To these have been added recently studies which, following Simmel, deal among other things with the various forms of man's socialisation ("*Vergesellschaftung*"). They want to examine society-wide and empirically provable forms of association and social relations which are to be found in the everyday legal life of society, in order to study their effects on the continuing formation of law. In the emerging outlines of a *theory of social associations*[62] law appears not only as a structure but also as a medium which serves to regulate social relations. This leads one to conclude that all normative communication and social control in the legal systems of modern society, especially communication in the realm of law, are dependent to a high degree on societal structures. Through their normative structural make-up they determine the social associations, institutions and systems which, for their part, contribute substantially to determining all human action – be it action by individuals or by collective agents or subjects – and steering it with the means of law.

The relationship between the issuing of norms and rules and the compliance with rules is always the core of legal communication[63]. Our view of the continual communicative *correlation of norms and facts* which takes place in this relationship *from case to case* must not any longer be narrowed down to a normativist perspective or even to that of legal positivism (Kelsen, R. Walter) – which still happens not infrequently in legal method and general jurisprudence. Instead, the legal systems of modern society must be understood as information- and communication systems serving as a means of normative structuring and orientation for human action and interaction.

In the study of such communication systems and their normative networks a thorough analysis of the knots of these networks of legal relations in society appears to be of particular importance. From an anthropological, sociological and normtheoretical point of view they are occupied by the respective agents of the normative communication or action or rather by the legal *subjects*. The normative communication must be distinguished at all events from the intentions of those "individuals" who are involved in the politico-legal selection processes as their authors/originators or as participants without being part of these networks. It may, therefore, be possible to say – with a degree of exaggeration – that *it is communication that communicates* – and *not* its authors, human beings, individuals, persons, subjects or even legal subjects[64].

---

[62] Cf. id., "Assoziationen versus Staat? Normative Strukturelemente föderaler politisch-rechtlicher Gemeinschaftsbildung", *Rechtstheorie*, 1997, 321–339.

[63] W. Krawietz, *Recht als Regelsystem*, XI ff. and 132 ff.

[64] Cf. W. Kargl, "Kommunikation kommuniziert? Kritik des rechtssoziologischen Autopoiesebegriffs", *Rechtstheorie*, 1990, 352-373. See also R. Dziewas, "Der Mensch – ein Konglomerat autopoietischer Systeme?" in *Kritik der Theorie sozialer Systeme*, 113-132.

If this conception of communication in law were to become generally accepted the consequences for the analysis and description of the structure and functioning of legal norms, of legal order and legal systems would *pro futuro* be considerable. The conventional understanding of law which regards legal norms as expressing the will of a specific legislator who is thought of as an individual (so-called "will" theory) and in doing so follows the traditional subject theory and the voluntarism associated with it could then no longer be maintained in this form, not on the level of legal theory, at least. Indeed, the growing criticism being levelled against the *subject- and will theory of law* today means that nowadays *no* structural analysis of a legal order can be based anymore on atomistically conceived "individuals", "persons" or "subjects" *without the social background of these legal relations* and of the juridical communication systems being clarified. This is not to say, of course, that social systems could exist without human beings. Social systems, like other systems, are dependent on their environments including the existence of human beings, the latter being parts of these environments.

The difficulties arising in the construction of an information- and communication theory of law are not infrequently misjudged by those who – arguing from a theoretical perspective based on natural law or law of reason – wish to attribute spurious universalistic or, at least, particularistic moral or ethical qualities as constituent parts to positive law or try to incorporate these. This misguided position deflects from the now imperative need of an understanding of all law which is both normative-realistic and shaped by the imprint of history and society[65]. But even those seeking an empirically based access to legal action and to the analysis of law which is supported by experience and observation are in danger of missing the real object of any approach to law, namely the *normative legal text in the social context* of man's legal actions and its socially constituted meaning.

A theory of normative communication must conceive of law as a normative structure and, at the same time, as a social product without reducing it in a behaviourist way to a mere fact[66] which happens often enough in the sociological systems theory. The continual self-production of law which occurs in the legal system through legal communication is never a merely factual but a genuinely *normative self-production and self-reproduction*. This we are taught by an institutions- and systems analysis, as I understand it. It is important, therefore, to avoid a purely behaviourist point of view which seeks to infer the norms only

[65] Cf. H. Weber-Grellet, *Rechtsphilosophie*, 49 ff. and 89 ff.

[66] Like the critique of systems theory expressed by O. Weinberger, "Soziologie und normative Institutionstheorie" in *Recht und Institution: Helmut Schelsky Gedächtnis-symposium Münster 1985*, Rechtswissenschaftliche Fakultät der Universität Münster (ed.), Berlin, 1985, 33–58.

from factual expectations or from behavioural regularities[67]. To do this appears as inappropriate as attempting to deduce the law purely cognitively from the norms.

When describing and analysing the normative self-production it is necessary, therefore, – from the perspective of a communicative system conceived as self-referential, self-maintaining and self-reproducing – to be aware of the fact that one is not dealing with the iterative, as it were, merely repetitive production and reproduction of variations of well-known and long-familiar norms/facts of the legal system. Instead, it is possible also for *new informations* to enter legal communication while the stock of existing norms remains technically speaking – according to formal law – the same. These new informations have to be interpreted and mastered with the help of the existing reservoir of knowledge of norms and facts, if necessary even by way of legal analogy. As a result of this the stock of legal rules – of individual but generalisable legal rules, at least – is modified and in that sense increased[68]. The question, what influence such changes exert over the legal order and whether these affect the identity of the entire legal system[69] must remain unanswered for the time being.

The communication-theoretical perspective followed here assumes that legal system and state are not the same thing. Law exhibits a relative autonomy from the state. Whereas the positivist theories of law regard the formation of law as a process by which a legal norm is deduced from a higher-ranking norm and so on going back ultimately to an original or basic norm, the self-referential production and reproduction of law and of the legal system rest on self-organisation in law and society. This usually takes place on the basis of a division of labour and the differentiation of the societal system (multi-referentiality of law)[70]. Rather than focussing only on the formal and substantive production of directives and legal norms we also ought to devote more attention to the informal, genuinely social differentiations in the formation of law.

---

[67] The misgivings expressed in id., *ibid.*, 56 ff. have to be understood in this sense, too, when he raises the reproach against the systems theory (of Luhmann) that "he is pursuing a theory of behaviour in the behaviourist sense, that is, without taking account of practical informations in the realm of human actions". It appears misguided, indeed, "to reduce norms, purposes, preferences and values to descriptions of states of behaviour".

[68] A. Chanos, *Begriff und Geltungsgrundlagen der Rechtsanalogie im heutigen juristischen Methodenstreit*, Cologne, 1994, 78 ff., 88 ff. and 99 ff.

[69] See C. E. Alchourrón and E. Bulygin, *Normative Systeme*, 157 ff.

[70] In detail on the need to be prepared from the outset for the poly-contextuality and multi-referentiality of diverse social systems in the process of constructing a socially adequate theory of norms and action, especially of a communication theory of all legal action from the perspective of a legal and social theory see W. Krawietz, "Neue Sequenzierung der Theoriebildung und Kritik der allgemeinen Theorie sozialer systeme" in *Kritik der Theorie sozialer Systeme*, 25–28.

One of the chief areas to be analysed and investigated by communication research in law is that of the *normative structural couplings* which connect different social systems with each other – be it temporarily or permanently[71]. In this context it is important to take into account that legal communication and legal production frequently does not, – or, at least, not only – take place on the lines preordained by the constitution- and lawgiver. Apart from *formal* legal communication broad areas of *informal* communication come about, establish themselves and gain increasing importance for the development of law.

Whereas it were hitherto the various legal communications and procedures in the *secondary* system of law, such as the legislature, government, administration and judiciary, that the research interest in the legal sciences concentrated on, a thorough communication-theoretical investigation and exploration of the *primary* system of law remains to this day a task yet to be accomplished[72]. It is to be expected that this situation is going to change soon and quickly. The beginnings of a re-formulation and re-construction of the non-formalised procedures and juridical proceedings are already to be found in the political-functional studies of the legal order undertaken by Helmut Schelsky and others in their conception of the theory of norms and action[73].

When analysing the information- and communication systems of modern law in terms of legal and social theory it appears vital to base this analysis on the difference between *regional* and *global* society (global system, "world society"). From the point of view of an intercultural comparison of law and legal systems the first elements and components linking up to form a global society may well exist, especially so in the world of technology. A runway is a runway no matter in which part of the world pilots approach it. We recognise it when we see it. The same situation may become true for the law and legal systems due to the emerging technological advances and possibilities in juridical communication which appear to allow a world-wide network of law to spread. At present, however, we have neither *one* global law nor *one* global state. There are also a number reasons why it is highly unlikely that either of them can or will ever exist. *Law* – seen here as a normatively structured communication system comprising all its interactions and organisations – *on the level of global society* is no more than a *system of legal systems* which integrates all the different national legal systems within it[74].

---

[71] Cf. A. Schemann, "Strukturelle Kopplung. Zur Festlegung und normativen Bindung offener Möglichkeiten sozialen Handelns" in *Kritik der Theorie sozialer Systeme*, 219 ff.

[72] A detailed account in W. Krawietz, *El Concepto Sociológico del Derecho y Otros Ensayos*, México, 1991, 15 ff., 25 ff. and 98 ff.

[73] On this and the following see P. Werner, *Die Normentheorie Helmut Schelskys als Form eines Neuen Institutionalismus*, Berlin, 1995, 46 ff., 60 ff. and 104 ff.

[74] Already extremely pertinent A. Malmström, "The System of Legal Systems",

7. Concluding Remarks

The law and the legal systems of the modern world demand not only authority but also the power to bind and to impose legal obligation. They are not content with the legality they have established for themselves but they wish to imbue these with rightness and legitimacy. All such claims must be viewed with respect and esteem, but also with substantial scepticism. As a scientific enterprise, modern legal and social theory is not in the position to pass judgement on the facts it uncovers. What legal and social theory can do is to invite modern jurisprudence to face reality, especially the social reality of law, in the sense outlined above.

Compared with the present state of research in communications it appears that the research trends of formal logic, analysis of language and analytical hermeneutics as well as their applicability to law and jurisprudence are developing satisfactorily, in their fundamental aspects, at least. In contrast to this it would seem that research concerning a theory of legal communication is lagging behind somewhat. In view of the special characteristics of legal communication which in the view advocated here is to be regarded essentially as practical legal action in a social context (and *not* as a merely *cognitive* act of thought and/or language or even as a merely hermeneutic intellectual activity!) legal research on the *various levels on which the construction of the theory is taking place* will have to respond much more than previously to the requirements and insights emerging from basic research in law (in its broadest sense). Important impulses are at present coming from a new cultural anthropology and legal ethology[75] as well as a new kind of ontology of norms, in particular a new ontology of law[76]. Their results have to be considered in the light of the insights gained by *a theory and sociology of law* which has been engaged in the construction of a theory of norms and action for a considerable time. It aims, above all, at penetrating the relations between normative expectations of behaviour and concrete legal action both empirically *and* analytically. The theory of normative communication, especially legal communication, which is my main concern here, is an empirical theory of law based on experience and observation as the foundations of all legal (re-)construction. A scientific observer can maintain detachment in the face of facts of every kind. He can follow those facts to whatever empirical conclusion they may lead, but not further.

In recent times it has been particularly Opalek, of course, who has repeatedly expressed his fundamental "opposition between the linguistic and non-

---

Scandinavian Studies in Law, 1969, 127–149. See also W. Krawietz, *Recht als Regelsystem*, 51 ff.

[75] See particularly H. Hof, *Rechtsethologie*, 75 ff., 145 ff. and 183 ff.

[76] O. Weinberger, *Alternative Handlungstheorie*, 87 ff. and 234 ff. ("normative ontology").

linguistic conception of the norm"[77]. From the perspective of a legal realism with its critical stance *vis-à-vis* the socially established norms and their meaning which I have always advocated – in contrast, that is, to a merely analytical-hermeneutic legal theory and legal philosophy – it is on the basis of a non-linguistic concept of law that all juridical communications, norms and actions are identified, defined more clearly, connected with each other and communicatively and analytically-conceptually interlinked in networks. A (re-)construction of such network structures can only be achieved in intra-, inter-, and multi-disciplinary co-operation. Further, the fact that the debate about a socially adequate concept of legal realism is being blurred to this day by a number of controversies within legal theory and philosophy must not be disregarded in this context[78]. Only American legal realism and Scandinavian realism are regularly mentioned – with reference to the natural law and metaphysics critique[79]. German legal realism is hardly ever referred to despite being historically older and having decisively determined and influenced the two others, although it distinguishes itself significantly from these[80]. It alone, standing in the tradition of Ihering's and Heck's studies[81], on the one hand, and those by Kantorowicz, Max Weber, Theodor Geiger, Helmut Schelsky and others[82], on the other, provides me here with a basis for further studies of these problems.

Access to a socially adequate understanding of legal realism – seen here as a research orientation of sociological jurisprudence and legal theory[83] – is

---

[77] K. Opalek, "Unterschiedliche Normbegriffe: Theodor Geiger und analytische Normentheorie" in *Theodor Geiger*, 211 ff. and 216 f. Cf. further W. Krawietz, "Kazimierz Opaleks Rechtstheorie in internationaler Perspektive betrachtet" in *Sprache, Performanz und Ontologie des Rechts*, W. Krawietz and J. Wróblewski (eds.), Berlin, 1993, V–XX.

[78] Elucidating this L. J. Wintgens, "Realism and Nominalism: Is There any Space Left for the Subject?", *Associations*, 1998, 79–99. In the following I am, however, concerned with the empirical *and* analytical-conceptual foundations of sociological jurisprudence, *e.g.* the theory and sociology of law rather than the metaphysics of argumentation and justification of philosophical provenance.

[79] See for example C. E. Alchourrón and E. Bulygin, *Normative Systeme*, 102 ff. and 124.

[80] Cf. H. Weber-Grellet, *Rechtsphilosophie*, 55 and 89 ff.; P. Werner, *Die Normentheorie Helmut Schelskys*, 125 and 172, who – unlike Luhmann – have not failed to recognise the relevance of German legal realism and of sociological jurisprudence for the development of modern legal and social theory.

[81] Compare E. Dorndorf, "Zu den theoretischen Grundlagen der Interessenjurisprudenz", *A.R.S.P.*, 1995, 542–562.

[82] P. Werner, *Die Normentheorie Helmut Schelskys*, 26 ff. and 58 ff.

[83] T. Geiger, *Vorstudien zu einer Soziologie des Rechts*, Berlin, 1987[4], 1 ff. and 329, on the other hand, describes his position in respect of a sociology of law as "sociological legal realism".

frequently obstructed because some authors erroneously interpret and explain it on the background of the contrast between idealism and realism. This philosophical dualism was never relevant for the development of a (self-)critical normative legal realism which had already occurred – in its earliest and most consistent form in German legal realism – at the end of the last century. The latter having already moved *beyond* the positions of natural law and the law of reason and the appertaining metaphysics of argumentation and justification as well as beyond those of state-organised legal positivism understands law and the entire legal system of modern society as a normatively structured, institutionalised system of communications and action which has an actual existence in the real social world.

Every modern *legal system*, understood as a *societal subsystem consisting of both the primary and secondary system of law*, can be observed, described and explained in socially adequate terms with the tools of a theory of normative legal communication. Other than the more pragmatic American legal realism and also other than its Scandinavian form, the legal realism advocated by me is founded on a sociologically based concept of law (critically) reflected by a theory of norms and action. Such a conception does, however, have to be reconstructed and complemented by a theory of institutions and social systems, as I have pointed out elsewhere[84].

A socially adequate empirical access to a theory of normative communication in the field of law will, consequently, not to be achieved until law is conceived – entirely in the sense of Max Weber and Ludwig Wittgenstein – as something that can only be interpreted, understood and explained as embedded in human behaviour and in the diverse forms of societal life. To this extent the regulation of life by law is to be perceived as the result of directives and their associated activities which establish norms and with the help of which the legal order continually (re-) produces itself. It is, however, in the *deep structure of society* as a whole that the normative premises and hidden underpinnings of legal communication are to be found.

From these presuppositions spring distinctions with historical traditions, usually differentiated in terms of regional societies, but no more than conventional, which we know and deal with on the level of practical and dogmatic legal argumentation such as, for instance, those between civil law, criminal law and public law. The regulations on which these distinctions are based vary from one legal system to another. From the point of view of regional societies they are to be regarded as contingent and may even not exist at all. This

---

[84] It should be noted that what is meant here, are, – irrespective of the normativity of all law – *social systems*, *i.e.* systems of communication and action structured in accordance with normative meanings. See W. Krawietz, *Recht als Regelsystem*, 153 ff.; id., "Staatliches oder gesellschaftliches Recht?", 259 ff.

may be a painful realisation for some exponents of legal dogmatics who ascribe central importance to them. It is, nevertheless, a normative-institutional fact.

It follows that the complex problem of the norms and their application in the realm of law must not – as Kazimierz Opalek has shown in his studies in legal theory – simply be addressed either only on the logical-linguistic level, or only on the psychological or only on the sociological one[85]. This is the only way of preventing one or the other individual dimension of law from overshadowing the others[86]. As Opalek's research in the ontology/deontology of law demonstrates it is only possible to grasp, understand and explain normative legal communication sufficiently conceptually – by way of sustaining and justifying the norms with the help of methods employed by the analysis and philosophy of language – if and only if – this is done on the basis of a non-linguistic conception of the norm. He rightly refers contemporary legal theory, therefore, to the fact that the relations between legal norms and man's legal actions in the legal system have been successfully clarified.

Central to the research in the theory of an information- and communication theory in law which must set in at this point is the question *what it means to comply with a norm, especially, a legal norm* which has, for the time being, institutionally been established in everyday life. This does not refer to a merely factual accumulation of actual ways of behaving, *i.e.* mere regularities of behaviour[87]. The – presumably unavoidable – paradox of the problem is this: each legal norm to be applied which is meant to be structured by the standards of legal communication in each individual case must first of all be constituted on the basis of the existing valid law in this very same legal communication. If we understand it in this way the *legal rule* is – to formulate it paradoxically – the legal norm in the social form which it receives when it is complied with. In this view of the problem the conceptual interests pursued by Opalek in his theory of directives and norms coincide with those followed nowadays by the theory of norms based on the late philosophy of Wittgenstein. These were, however, already present in the theory and sociology of Max Weber and others, as they are in the *New Institutionalism* (of Helmut Schelsky) and in the theory of social systems (of Niklas Luhmann).

The nature of the communicative influence that legal norms as directives exert on human behaviour, especially on legal behaviour, thanks to their "directive meaning", is a different problem. It cannot be treated without having

---

[85] Expressly so K. Opalek, "Unterschiedliche Normbegriffe: Theodor Geiger und analytische Normentheorie", 211, 215 ff. and 225 ff. Also id., "Der Dualismus der Auffassung der Norm in der Rechtswissenschaft", *Rechtstheorie*, 1989, 433–447.

[86] W. Krawietz, "Sprachphilosophie in der Jurisprudenz", 1487 ff.

[87] W. Krawietz, "What Does it Mean 'To Follow an Institutionalised Legal Rule'? On Rereading Wittgenstein and Max Weber", *A.R.S.P.*, 1991, 7–14.

recourse to a theory and sociology of law and thereby to a sociological concept of law[88]. Clearly this aspect has hitherto been neglected in legal *and* social theory. It may concern here to demonstrate the requirement and the advantages of a conception of law which – with the help of the multi-level approach – is fully *integrated* since it is only within these parameters that a coherent *legal theory of information and communication* can be worked out and ultimately achieved. This is the desideratum of an intra-, inter- and multi-disciplinary approach to basic research in legal and social theory which in turn requires philosophical clarification.

[88] Id., "Legal Norms as Expectations? On Redefining the Concept of Law" in *Law, Morality and Discursive Rationality*, A. Aarnio and K. Tuori (eds.), Helsinki, 1989, 109-140; id., "The Concept of Law Re-visited. A New Approach to Theory and Sociology of Law" in *Law and Rights*, V. Ferrari (ed.), Milan, 1991, 155–170; id., "Dual Concept of the Legal System? The Formal Character of Law from the Perspective of Institutional and Systems Theory" in *Presciptive Formality and Normative Rationality in Modern Legal Systems*, W. Krawietz, N. MacCormick and G.-H. von Wright (eds.), Berlin, 1994, 43-52.

Bibliographical information[*]

I. Books

(as author)

1. *Das positive Recht und seine Funktion. Kategoriale und methodologische Überlegungen zu einer funktionalen Rechtstheorie*, Berlin, 1967.
2. *Juristische Entscheidung und wissenschaftliche Erkenntnis. Eine Untersuchung zum Verhältnis von dogmatischer Rechtswissenschaft und rechtswissenschaftlicher Grundlagenforschung*, Vienna/New York, 1978.
3. *Recht als Regelsystem*, Wiesbaden, 1984.
4. *El Concepto Sociológico del Derecho y Otros Ensayos*, México, 1991.
5. *Theorie und Technik der Begriffsjurisprudenz*, Darmstadt, 1976.

(as editor or co-editor)

6. (with T. Mayer-Maly and O. Weinberger) *Objektivierung des Rechtsdenkens*, Berlin, 1984.
7. (with H. Schelsky and G. Winkler) *Theorie der Normen*, Berlin, 1984.
8. (with H. Schelsky) *Rechtssystem und gesellschaftliche Basis bei Hans Kelsen*, Berlin, 1984.
9. (with W. Ott) *Formalismus und Phänomenologie im Rechtsdenken der Gegenwart*, Berlin, 1987.
10. (with A. Martino and K. I. Winston) *Technischer Imperativ und Legitimationskrise des Rechts*, Berlin, 1991.
11. (with G.-H. von Wright) *Öffentliche oder private Moral? Vom Geltungsgrunde und der Legitimität des Rechts*, Berlin, 1992.
12. (with M. Welker) *Kritik der Theorie sozialer Systeme. Auseinandersetzungen mit Luhmanns Hauptwerk*, Frankfort-on-Main, 1992.
13. (with L. Pospišil e.a.) *Sprache, Symbole und Symbolverwendungen in Ethnologie, Kulturanthropologie, Religion und Recht*, Berlin, 1993.
14. (with J. Wróblewski) *Sprache, Performanz und Ontologie des Rechts*, Berlin, 1993.
15. (with N. MacCormick and G.-H. von Wright) *Prescriptive Formality and Normative Rationality in Modern Legal Systems*, Berlin, 1994.
16. (with G. Preyer) *System der Rechte, demokratischer Rechtsstaat und Diskurstheorie des Rechts nach Jürgen Habermas*, Berlin, 1996.
17. (with E. Pattaro A. E.-S. Tay) *Rule of Law. Political and Legal Systems in Transition*, Berlin, 1997.

---

[*] Cf. complete bibliography until 1993 in *Rechtsnorm und Rechtswirklichkeit*, A. Aarnio, S. Paulson, O. Weinberger, G.-H. von Wright, and D. Wyduckel, (eds.), Berin, 1993, 797-831.

18. (with R. S. Summers, O. Weinberger and G.-H. von Wright) *The Reasonable as Rational? On Legal Argumentation and Justification*, Berlin, 1998.
19. (with E. Garzón Valdés and A. Sqella) *Neuer Konstitutionalismus und politische Herrschaftsstrukturen in vergleichender Perspektive - Iberoamerika und Europa im Dialog*, Berlin, 1998.

II. Articles

1. "Juristische Methodik und ihre rechtstheoretischen Implikationen" in *Rechtstheorie als Grundlagenwissenschaft der Rechtswissenschaft*, H. Albert, N. Luhmann e. a. (eds.), Düsseldorf, 1972, 12–42.
2. "Juristische Konstruktion, Kritik und Krise dogmatischer Rechtswissenschaft" in *Theorie und Technik der Begriffsjurisprudenz*, W. Krawietz (ed.), Darmstadt, 1976, 1–10.
3. "Begründung des Rechts - anthropologisch betrachtet. Zur Institutionentheorie von Weinberger und Schelsky" in *Theorie der Normen*, W. Krawietz, H. Schelsky, G. Winkler e.a. (eds.), Berlin, 1984, 541–556.
4. "Rechtssystem als Institution? Über die Grundlagen von Helmut Schelskys sinnkritischer Institutionentheorie", *Rechtstheorie*, 1984, 209–243.
5. "Ansätze zu einem Neuen Institutionalismus in der modernen Rechtstheorie der Gegenwart", *Juristenzeitung*, 1985, 706–714.
6. "Die Normentheorie Helmut Schelskys als Form eines Neuen Institutionalismus im Rechtsdenken der Gegenwart" in *Helmut Schelsky - ein Soziologe in der Bundesrepublik*, H. Baier (ed.), Stuttgart, 1986, 114–148.
7. "Paradigms, Positions and Prospects of Rationality. The Changing Foundations of Law in Institutional and Systems Theory" in *Samfunn, Rett, Rettferdighet. Festskrift til Torstein Eckhoffs 70-Årsdag*, A. Bratholm e.a. (eds.), Oslo, 1986, 452-469.
8. "Recht und moderne Systemtheorie" in *Reason and Experience in Contemporary Legal Thought*, T. Eckhoff, L. M. Friedman e.a. (eds.), Berlin, 1986, 281–309.
9. "Zur Korrelation von Rechtsfrage und Tatfrage in der Rechtsanwendung" in *Rechtsprechungslehre*, N. Achterberg (ed.), Cologne, 1986, 517–553.
10. "Normativismus oder Skeptizismus? Zum Verhältnis von Regelsetzung und Regelbefolgung in der kritischen Rechtstheorie Kants" in *Formalismus und Phänomologie im Rechtsdenken der Gegenwart*, W. Krawietz and W. Ott (eds.), Berlin, 1987, 321–342.
11. "Towards a New Institutionalism in Modern Legal Thinking. Facets of Rationality" in *Reason in Law*, I, C. Faralli and E. Pattaro (eds.), Milan, 1987, 313-325.
12. "Legal Norms As Expectations? On Redefining the Concept of Law" in *Law, Morality, and Discursive Rationality*, A. Aarnio and K. Tuori (eds.), Helsinki, 1989, 109–140.

13. "What Does it Mean 'To Follow An Institutionalized Legal Rule'? On Re-reading Wittgenstein and Max Weber", *A.R.S.P.*, 1991, 7–14.
14. "The Concept of Law Re-visited. A New Approach to Theory and Sociology of Law" in *Laws and Rights*, V. Ferrari (ed.), Milan, 1991, 155–170.
15. "Moral versus Legal Responsibility? Different Motives and Models for Attributing Rights and Duties" in *Öffentliche oder private Moral? Vom Geltungsgrunde und der Legitimität des Rechts*, W. Krawietz and G.-H. von Wright (eds.), Berlin, 1992, 43–55.
16. "Neue Sequenzierung der Theoriebildung und Kritik der allgemeinen Theorie sozialer Systeme" in *Kritik der Theorie sozialer Systeme. Auseinandersetzungen mit Luhmanns Hauptwerk*, W. Krawietz and M. Welker (eds.), Frankfort-on-Main, 1992, 14-42.
17. "Staatliches oder gesellschaftliches Recht? Systemabhängigkeiten normativer Strukturbildung im Funktionssystem Recht" in *ibid.*, 247–301.
18. "Kazimierz Opaleks Rechtstheorie in internationaler Perspektive betrachtet" in *Sprache, Performanz und Ontologie des Rechts*, W. Krawietz and J. Wróblewski (eds.), Berlin, 1993, V–XX.
19. "Recht ohne Staat? Spielregeln des Rechts und Rechtssystem in normen- und systemtheoretischer Perspektive", *Rechtstheorie*, 1993, 81–133.
20. "Taking Legal Systems Seriously: Legal Norms and Principles as Expectations" in *Sprache, Symbole und Symbolverwendungen in Ethnologie, Kulturanthropologie, Religion und Recht*, W. Krawietz, L. Pospišil e.a. (eds.), Berlin, 1993, 361–384.
21. "Dual Concept of the Legal System? The Formal Character of Law from the Perspective of Institutional and Systems Theory" in *Prescriptive Formality and Normative Rationality in Modern Legal Systems*, W. Krawietz, N. MacCormick and G.-H. von Wright (eds.), Berlin, 1994, 43–52.
22. "Theorie der Verantwortung - neu oder alt? Zur normativen Verantwortungsattribution mit Mitteln des Rechts" in *Verantwortung*, K. Bayertz (ed.), Darmstadt, 1995, 184–216.
23. "Ulrich Klugs Theorie und Philosophie des Rechts im Umriß" in *Ulrich Klug zum Gedächtnis*, Verein zur Förderung der Rechtswissenschaft (ed.), Cologne, 1995, 11–28.
24. "Sprachphilosophie in der Jurisprudenz" in *Philosophy of Language. An International Handbook of Contemporary Research*, II, M. Dascal, D. Gerhardus, K. Lorenz and G. Meggle (eds.), Berlin/ New York, 1996, 1470–1489.
25. "Professor Helmut Schelsky (1912-1984)" in *Rechtswissenschaftliche Fakultät der Universität Münster - Ein Porträt*, Münster, 1997, 42–48.
26. "Recht als normatives Kommunikat in normen- und handlungstheoretischer Perspektive" in *Normative Systems in Legal and Moral Theory,* E. Garzón Valdés, W. Krawietz e.a. (eds.), Berlin, 1997, 369 – 390.

27. "Reasonableness versus Rationality of Law? On the Evolution of Theories in Jurisprudence" in *Justice, Morality and Society. A Tribute to Aleksander Peczenik*, A. Aarnio e.a. (eds.), Lund, 1997, 221–245.
28. "Assoziationen versus Staat? Normative Strukturelemente föderaler politisch-rechtlicher Gemeinschaftsbildung", *Rechtstheorie*, 1997, 321–339.
29. "Theory and Research Programme of Legal Experience" in *New Approaches and Ways of Legal Thinking Revised*, A. Aarnio e.a. (eds.), Berlin, 1997, 167–209.

My Philosophy of Law[1]

NEIL MACCORMICK

EDINBURGH

1. Introduction

I believe in law. That is, I believe that there is a distinct sphere of human experience which we can construct as a specific domain of understanding and activity, to which the name "law" is appropriate and hallowed by usage. I further believe in law in the stronger sense that I think human life, the life of human beings in social relations with each other, is enhanced by having for its framework (or a part of its framework) some body or bodies of law that stabilise our mutual expectations. Simply: there is such a thing as law, and where it exists it tends to improve the lives of those who live by it. Law exists, and law has *prima facie* positive value.

It does not follow that law is identical with morality, or that the existence of a legal norm gives any guarantee of the moral correctness or legitimacy of the prescription, proscription, or empowerment (or whatever) that the legal norm embodies. The distinction between them is conceptual, in a way that I will describe below. Meantime let me say that the ground of the conceptual difference is the quality of autonomy that essentially characterises moral deliberation and decision making as such. The fully-developed moral agent is in a profound sense autonomous. He or she is the ultimate authority for and ground of the moral law that binds in conscience. But "the law of the land", positive law, is an institutional order, having ultimate legal authority in a self-referential way internal to a whole corpus of institutional norms, and having full moral authority only to the extent that it is worthy of assent from the point of view of the

---

[1] This paper is a substantially re-worked version of a paper which first took shape as my Otto Brusiin Lecture "Law as Institutional Normative Order" presented before the Finnish Academy of Science and Letters in September 1994; and which secondly became a paper "Institutional Normative Order: A Conception of Law" presented to a symposium in Cornell Law School on March 1-2 1997, which paper now awaits publication in *Cornell Law Review*. The opening and closing sections are entirely new, and there have been some revisions of other parts since the Cornell version.

autonomous agent. In this sense, law is a heteronomous order, and by that very feature differentiated in its very concept from morality in the sense proposed here.

I want also to differentiate law from politics and law from the state. I believe that politics ought to be conducted within a framework of law, and I believe that the state is most to be trusted when it succeeds in being a "state-under-law", a "*Rechtsstaat*", a "law-state". But it is not inevitable that either politics or the state will be effectively subordinated to law. In the context of the politics of a state or of some other institutionalised political order it is always possible that those who have control of legal institutions can bring into being undesirable or even evil bodies of law and modes of law-enforcement. That is, the law can be systematically diverted from what would be justifiable in terms of the autonomous agent devising common principles for coercive social ordering in free discourse with other such agents.

In all this, I am perhaps running ahead of myself. My hitherto undeclared assumptions are that I can make sense of something that I call "normative order", and that there are indeed different forms of normative order. My first task is to account for normative order. Thereafter, I will explain institutional normative order, then I will give a better and more articulated account of the two distinctions asserted in the opening paragraph of this essay: that between positive law and moral order; and that between law and politics.

2. The Normative and the "Ought"

At any given time, any one of us has an idea of how the world is, but only a broad and vague idea. Television, radio, newspapers and other media keep us broadly informed about what is going on, though our attention is confined to particular subjects that interest us. Our awareness of history and geography let us locate ourselves somewhere terrestrially in the context of some narrative awareness of our present time in its continuity with past events, either directly recalled or spoken to in some memories or texts or reports available to us. Our own idiosyncratic understanding of the natural and social sciences give us a broad idea of how things go along, and we have a common sense grasp of how other people are likely to act and how our social situation is likely to change over time. We have some cosmological view of the earth in relation to the rest of the Universe, and either do or do not have an awareness of or faith in a divine being that underpins it all and in some sense guarantees it. With or without that, we have an actual perceptual consciousness of our immediate surroundings, and can to some extent give an account of what is going on here now, though by the time any such account is given, things have already moved on into some new state of being. Even the most learned and perceptive and well-placed of us has only partial information in consciousness at any moment, always in a context of imperfect memory, possibly inaccurate scientific foundations, and conjecture concerning probabilities.

Since Hume, we have been used to contrasting the "is" and the "ought"[2] and in this I think we have mainly tended to contrast the straightforward factuality of the "is" with the somehow slippery character of the normative "ought". By drawing attention to the rather vague quality of our grasp of the "is", I seek to administer a modest corrective to this tendency. After all, I can usually be somewhat more certain about how things ought to be than about how they actually are. To hold or perhaps even to know that murder is wrong, or thus that people ought not to be killed wilfully and of malice aforethought, is to hold or know something that holds good everywhere and all the time (or, if I am thinking legally, everywhere within the jurisdiction by which my thought is bounded). Indeed, I can be a lot more confident that nobody ought to be murdered than I can be sure that nobody is being, has been, or is about to be murdered, even in my quite near vicinity. I can be certain that murder is wrong, but not that it won't happen. And the same goes for jumping the red traffic light, or for acts of housebreaking, or for lying or breaking promises.

To think about the world, certainly to think of it beyond one's immediate perceptual field, is to have some kind of picture or narrative account of it. This frames how I think it is, has been, has come to pass, and will probably go on. The meaning of such thoughts is clear enough, for they either match the world or they do not, and if they do, that is how it really is. (The trouble is that we cannot check it all by direct immediate inspection – that is indeed the very trouble from which I started.)

The "ought" is of course different. The picture or narrative as I hold it ought to be is not one that is confirmed by how events are or turn out. It is an ideal picture or narrative, one to which I envisage the world being made to conform, as it does on all the occasions when no one murders a neighbour, breaks into another person's house or jumps a traffic light, tells a lie or breaks a promise.

If, however, I have some practical commitments concerning the way the world ought to be, or the way it ought to go on, I can be fairly certain what these commitments add up to. In this way, I can have greater certainty about the ought than about the is. I can know better how the world ought to be (assuming my commitments are valid ones, and leaving the question of what, if anything, validates such commitments entirely aside for the moment) than I can know how it actually is. Personal commitment apart, the universality of legal norms entails that, assuming I have a correct grasp of valid norms of some system of positive law, I can know with considerable certainty how things ought

---

[2] D. Hume, *A Treatise of Human Nature*, P. H. Nidditch (ed.), Oxford, 1978, III.1.1, last paragraph.

to be according to that system of law even when I can never be so certain how they are or have been in the territory for which the law is valid. (This, I suppose, is a generalised version of Jerome Frank's "fact scepticism".)

Let us therefore acknowledge that the "ought", however puzzling we may sometimes find it at the deepest ontological level, has at least the possibility of a degree of clarity and certainty that the "is" often lacks. Nevertheless, all is not entirely simple. For in a concrete situation I may wonder what I or someone else ought to do or to have done, and may with some confidence conclude that the case is covered by a relevant norm like "thou shalt not kill" or "promises ought to be kept, and here a promise was made". Or I may take a single simple norm of that kind and reflect on it as in some way clearly valid for some context or jurisdiction. But it also seems to be the case that no such single normative judgement or proposition really makes sense on its own or in isolation. It is in its fitting together with a whole congeries of other norms that it makes sense. Especially in the context of the particular judgement – "what ought to be done or to have been done?" – or deliberation – "what to do now?" – there may be many normatively salient aspects of the situation, so that one's judgement or conclusion all things considered has taken account of more than one norm in its bearing on the situation. In this sense, normative judgements and deliberations do not relate to or presuppose or derive from single isolated norms, but rather some conception of normative order, about the way things ought to be and ought to go on taking the whole range of events things and possibilities as they appear to us at any particular time and place. This prompts an inquiry into the idea of "normative order".

3. Normative Order

Normative order is a kind of ideal order. At any given time we may form a view of the world as we think it is, including the set of ongoing human actions and intentions for action; we may set against that a view of the world as it could be or could become, leaving out certain of the actions, leaving some actual intentions abandoned or unfulfilled, while other actions take place instead of those left out, and other intentions are fostered and brought to fulfilment. A view of the world as it could be or could become is an ideal view of it. An ideal view may be constructed in terms that rule out or imperatively exclude certain ways of acting on all occasions on which such action might otherwise be contemplated, and that insist on or imperatively include certain other ways of acting as always called for despite any contrary temptation[3].

[3] Compare G.-H. von Wright, "Is and Ought" in *Man, Law, and Modern Forms of Life*, E. Bulygin e.a. (eds.), Dordrecht/Boston/Lancaster, 1985, 263-281.

There is a notorious ambiguity in the term "ideal" and most of its cognates in the various European languages. Sometimes we mean by it that which exists merely in idea, that is, within ideas held by some person or persons, whether for good or ill or in a neutral way. Sometimes, however, "ideal" conveys the notion of a favoured or even highly favoured idea. Normative order, of course, is ideal in the sense of the favoured or preferred idea, not merely the neutral idea. Yet it falls short of any "best of all possible worlds" perfectionism. Normative order is practical, both in the sense that it guides praxis, guides what we do, and also therefore practical in the sense of practicable. It is an order that is envisaged as a practically realisable state of the world given things as they are and persons as they are here and now. To the extent that it is realised, the world is a better, more satisfactory, world than if no such guideline were envisaged or followed.

The interaction of the practical and the normative is, of course, vital. We are not mere passive spectators in the processes or narratives of the world. We are ourselves the story-tellers in the narrative and the persons whose actings constitute the human part of the story. Our self-perception of ourselves as persons endowed with choice, so that the story takes the turnings it does because of the decisions we make and the things we make happen or prevent from happening, is crucial to the very idea of normative order. The story need not just unfold at random, though many of its vital facts and events lie outside of our control. It unfolds through our choices, and these choices are subject to critique and appraisal by reference to other possibilities that could have been chosen, and particularly by reference to those pre-envisaged possibilities that can be acknowledged as delimiting the sphere of minimally acceptable conduct. To work out what these acceptable minima are is to exercise practical reasoning and deliberation, to engage in practical discourse with oneself alone or with others. The output of such discourse is a conception of normative order defining the practically possible and reasonable, particularly in terms of that which constitutes the minimally acceptable.

"Norms" are propositions that we formulate with reference to, and as singled-out elements of, normative order. In primary form, they are either exclusionary provisions (negative duties, prohibitions) that rule out certain ways of acting on all occasions on which such action might otherwise be contemplated, or provisions of the converse type (positive duties, obligations) that call for or insist upon certain ways of acting as required of a person despite any contrary temptation, or countervailing reason for action.

This is not an attempt to explain norms or values in terms of value-free facts, of course. The notion of the "better" or "more satisfactory" built into the account of normative order as ideal order shows normative order to belong within, not independently of, values as fundamental elements in all human practical reasoning.

Also essential to making sense of these concepts is the way in which the practical concerns that which engages a person's will. Merely to envisage a possible world extrapolated from the actual one, even to think of it in some purely contemplative way as better than the actual is not to cross over into the realm of the normative. A steady commitment of the will to realisation of some ideal order as a coherent and realisable state of the world is what is required for that transition. The will directed towards realising a practicable, rationally coherent and minimally acceptable ideal order constitutes it as normative order. Only by reference to such an order is it possible to establish the difference of right and wrong in action. Those actions are right that are not excluded from the conceived order, those that it excludes as actions and to which it denies fulfilment in intention are wrong. The dichotomy between wrong and not-wrong (or between wrong and right-in-the-sense-of-not-wrong) is the fundamental differentiation of actions or of intended or planned acts in a normative order. What a person engages upon when aiming to make normative order actual is the task of, or commitment to, avoiding wrongdoing.

The world as already-in-part-ideal order is that upon which we base our conceptions of normative order, the ideal order that would exist were practically removable imperfections purged from the way things go on now. Most promises that are made are in due course kept. Truthfulness and honesty are more frequent for most of us than lying and cheating. To formulate the principles that promises ought to be kept, that lies ought not to be told nor frauds perpetrated, is to set terms for an ideal order, but not one that stands absolutely apart from actuality, neither in terms of what is commonly done, nor in terms of what are commonly asserted as principles for ideal order by others in our communities.

Thus normative order does not stand in absolute contrast with actuality. Quite a lot of what goes on is perfectly compatible with what is right from the point of view of any reasonable moral attitude. Moreover, this is the case, at least in part, because people share legal systems and moral attitudes or converge in the moral demands and conceptions of moral order they endorse. The world as it is does not unfold independently of human wills. On the contrary, the human world-as-it-is goes on as it goes on through human choices and decisions. However imperfectly, these choices and decisions reflect and conform to the conceptions of legal and moral rectitude held by the choosing and deciding agents. So normative order as ideal order does not by its envisaged contents or substance stand in any absolute contrast with the world as it is. Indeed, our normative commitments come out of our response to the world as it is, our satisfaction or dissatisfaction with it as it is and as it goes on, and our sense of the practicable alternatives to what does or might happen.

There are, it seems to me, three ways in which human beings come to an awareness and understanding of normative order. Through nurture, socialisation and education, we are exposed to and socialised into some common views of the right and the wrong, and gradually led to an ability to be at least partly self-regulating against the standing norms implicit, and partly explicit, in this common view. Then, in modern conditions, we fall into a series of rather institutionalised settings in which rules are made even more explicit than in the general familial and social milieu. For everyone nowadays this includes the experience of school, with compulsory attendance; for many, still, even in a secularising society, participation to some extent in a church, mosque, synagogue, or other structured religious observance plays an important part. Nearly everybody participates in sports and games actively or as spectator or as both, and expertise about rules of play and rules of national and international competitions organised by officials and representative bodies is at least as widespread as knowledge and understanding of state-law. Thirdly, though, state agencies such as police and courts and in a more remote way other official organs up to and including parliaments and international agencies define one particularly authoritative, explicit and highly regulated normative order for us.

At the very least, our picture of normative order emerges out of heteronomous orders, where others communicate norms to us and we learn to follow them, usually under some external incentive. The idea that any of us could invent a whole moral order for her- or himself is absurd; it is inevitable that we start from some learned or acquired framework of practical thought, and gradually develop our own critical awareness of it as something for which we take responsibility, and can adjust in the light of what seems to us reasonable. Our learning experience is one geared to developing an at least partial autonomy[4]. What we learn is to monitor and guide our own conduct against criteria of right and wrong that are conventional norms in some cases and formally enacted rules in others.

In a fundamental way, though, the possibility of developing fully autonomous judgement at the end of one's learning experience is that which makes intelligible the very concept of normative order. The telos of moral development is the fully responsible moral agent who takes responsibility for his or her judgements at all levels, and whose volitional commitment to some ideal of order is categorical, not conditional. Only a being that can act in a self-regulating way, judging between possible courses of action through voluntary commitment to some rationally willed order, and seeking to realise the willed order in action, can fully grasp the concept of "wrong" action, or therefore the concept of right-as-not-wrong action. Only such a being can make full sense of auxiliary

---

[4] See J. Nedelsky, "Reconceiving Autonomy", 1 *Yale Journal of Law and Feminism*, 7-36 (1989).

verbs such as "ought" or "should". As Thomas Reid[5] observed in controversy with David Hume[6], these are terms that every moral agent understands, but that are not definable in any terms simpler than themselves.

This account both presupposes and points toward reasons for believing the thesis that autonomy is fundamental to morality. Conceptually, I would suggest, the idea of autonomy that was sketched above is fundamental to any idea of normative order. For in the last resort only an autonomous being can respond through acts of volition to the requirements of normative order. Normative order guides choices, but does not cause them. Choices are voluntary responses to an idea of order, not conditioned reflexes. On the other hand, the concept of a rationally coherent order in which universalisable principles find their place presupposes the agent's exposure to some conventional or institutional social ordering initially heteronomous in character from the agent's point of view. In the development of moral agency, heteronomy precedes autonomy.

4. Institutional Normative Order

Necessarily, normative order involves judgement. Being subject to a norm is being liable to judgement by oneself and by others in case one's conduct does not match up to what is required. Particular norms are to be envisaged as fragments drawn from a presupposed ideal order in the sense indicated, or as propositions formulated to capture the sense of that order in relation to a given type of situation. They are exclusionary or mandatory prescriptions that posit some course of conduct as wrong, or as obligatory. To engage with a norm as an acting subject is to judge what must be done in a given context; to reflect in normative terms upon one's own or another's conduct in a given setting is to judge, against some envisaged norm, whether what was done ought to have been done or ought not to have been done. The judgement that an act ought not to have been done normally entails a consequential judgement of the measure of penitence or restitution, or of censure, that is apt to the case. All in all, to think normatively is to think judgementally. This is a general and significant truth about all forms of normative order.

Judgement is sometimes purely personal and autonomous; sometimes it is conventional and heteronomous, without being institutionalised. It can also, however, be institutionalised, or, if you will, organised. The first step towards this can be seen wherever in a question involving two parties, a third is asked to help. Such a third party can be a relatively impartial judge between two persons on whom some norm impinges differentially. Reference to such an impartial third party can become a standing practice

---

[5] T. Reid, *Essays on the Active Powers of the Human Mind*, Edinburgh, 1819, III, Essay 5, chapter 7, 578.

[6] D. Hume, *A Treatise on Human Nature*, III.1.1.

in a variety of situations. Thus over some range of topics, some persons may acquire a standing role as judges, to whom reference may be made; it can come about that the judgement of such persons acquires mandatory force within some normative order, in the sense that a person who wishes action taken in virtue of some normative judgement must either handle the matter in a purely voluntary way, or resort to compulsory action only under judgement of such a judge. Then appeals may or may not be allowed; but once judgement is institutionalised, there has to be some rule about the finality of judgement; a rule that it is obligatory to accept and carry out the judgement of the ultimate court, and that it is forbidden to take any further action beyond that ultimately authorised under the final judgement[7].

Norms involve judgement, and judgement, as we noted, is either personal and autonomous or in some measure institutionalised. Institutionalisation of judgement is a fundamental feature of the organisation of normative orders. In one form or another, it occurs in a wide variety of settings, through churches, sporting organisations, commercial guilds and leagues, international organisations and agencies; and also, of course, paradigmatically in the state.

An inevitable effect of institutionalisation of judgement, especially where there comes into being a group or a corps of judges acting in a co-ordinated way under a common structure of appeals, is that normative order must come to be conceived as systemic in character; and the system in question necessarily possesses, as Teubner[8] and Luhmann[9] point out, a self-referential quality. For it has to be a question in any dispute what the governing norm is and how it is to be interpreted. Finality of judgement entails final authority on the question what counts as a binding norm, and how it bears on the case. What makes the judgement final is a norm of the normative order that makes respect for judgements obligatory in every case; but the judgement that such a norm, or any other norm, belongs to the order, is itself one which can only be pronounced with final effect by an appropriate judge or court. And the same postulated normative order is that which makes a given judge or court appropriate, or (in the more technical term) "competent" to judge on the question.

Whenever this is so, it follows that, relative to any institutional normative system, there is a way, conclusive within the system, for determining what counts as an authoritative norm of the system, or a definitely established right or duty of some person

---

[7] Compare N. MacCormick, *H. L. A. Hart*, London, 1981, 103 ff.

[8] G. Teubner, *Law as an Autopoietic System*, A. Bankowska and R. Adler (transl.), Z. Bankowski (ed.), Oxford, 1993.

[9] N. Luhmann, "Law as a Social System", 83 *Northwestern University Law Review*, 136-150 (1989).

under the system. There is even a way of determining what counts as a person under the system, and what kinds of practical social and business arrangements can be set up with binding effect in the system[10]. The way is, of course, that of recourse to the judgement of those competent to judge. Otto Brusiin has remarked that, although questions about sales or marriages matter to us in quite diverse ways in the ordinary social milieu, what counts in law as a "sale" or a "marriage" is a question which the law-courts necessarily have ultimate authority to determine[11]. And they have associated authority to say what ulterior legal rights, duties, powers and the like follow consequentially upon the existence of a sale or a marriage according to law. But which law-courts? Could there be merchants' tribunals deciding about sales? Or sporting tribunals deciding about the valid transfer through "sale" of a footballer's contract? Or Church Courts deciding about marriages?

As we know, each of these is possible. There can be tribunals of many kinds, and these can deal with similar questions affecting the same human individuals. But the characteristic of an institutional normative order is that competent judgement in it is conclusive within its own order, except to the extent that there is co-ordinated cross-recognition of different orders, as obtained between Pope and Emperor in the middle ages, or between European Communities and member-state legal orders today. Where a plurality of judgements each conclusive within a particular order can be passed, the question is: Which ought to prevail? As a question within a self-referential system, such a question is of course self-answering, for the system's agencies can never say other than that the system's norm ought to prevail. As a question for a person confronted by competing judgements of substantially the same question in practically different senses, the issue is which to respect, on grounds external to the self-referential answer provided by rival normative orders. Shall a state-court decree of divorce, or a church-court prohibition or nullification of the state's decree be taken as final? Shall the judgement of the state tribunal or the Trade Union tribunal be observed? And so on.

The answer to the question "Which to respect?" has both moral and prudential aspects. Which ought one to respect all things considered? Which is it least disadvantageous, all things considered, to ignore? In cases of conflict the answer to the latter question, the prudential answer, will be considerably affected both by the weight and balance of conventional opinions and by power-relations, and these will also be relevant, though with different scales of weighting, to the former, the moral question. But in so far as power-relations enter the question, the issue is, as I shall shortly try to

---

[10] N. MacCormick, "Institutions, Arrangements, and Practical Information", *Ratio Juris*, 1988, 73-82.

[11] O. Brusiin, *Der Mensch und sein Recht*, U. Kangas (ed.), Berlin, 1990, 182.

show, one of politics. Whoever can make a judgement prevail in the last resort, in the sense of its being carried through by main force if necessary, and can reliably and predictably enforce such judgements in the general run, has political power; and that political power backs and to a degree reinforces the authority and prestige of the tribunal whose judgement is enforced and that of the normative order to which the tribunal self-referentially belongs.

In the world as it has been, and still to a very large extent is, power of the relevant kind has been territorially concentrated, and each relevant territory has been that of a state. The coercively predominant normative orders have been those of states, though they have rarely if ever succeeded in absolutely eliminating rival orders of one kind or another. This is why there has been such a tendency to take for granted the equation of "law" with "state-law", though this has had serious distorting effects for legal theory.

Two obviously significant aspects of the interrelation of coercive power with normative order (thus also the interrelation of state with law) are of course that of executive power and that of legislative power. The executive possesses the direct command of the agencies of organised physical coercion that can back up the power of judgement – or, in cases of serious breakdown, disown and overthrow it. The legislature possesses, normally, the kind of democratic or quasi-democratic (or other ideological) legitimation that contributes significantly to the acceptability and durability over time of the coercive power that is organised under the executive. A delicate and shifting balance of power-relations normally obtains here. But always there is a question whether the due exercise of either legislative or executive power is a matter subjected to judicial judgement, and hence itself incorporated into the normative order which it so crucially supports. Where it is so incorporated, the state is a "*Rechtsstaat*", a state-under-law, a "law-state", as Åke Frändberg tells us to call it[12].

In a law-state, the question what exercises of executive power are valid is a question of law; the political power of the executive is restrained under the authority of law. Likewise, it is for the courts to say what resolutions of the legislature constitute validly enacted norms of law, and how they are to be interpreted. The authority of the legislature is not a matter of democratic or ideological or hereditary legitimacy extraneous to law, but is itself conferred by law, or at least confirmed by it on terms that effectively limit the power of law making. Self-referentiality here shades over into "autopoiesis". In such a state there can also be an independent profession of legal science, analysing the valid law, discussing the limits of its validity, offering interpretations that display some overall coherence and systematicity in the legal

---

[12] A. Frändberg, *The Law-State*, Uppsala, 1994 (unpublished manuscript). I am grateful to have had sight of it, and to have the opportunity to follow the terminology proposed.

(normative) order conceived as an ideal unity. This scientific construction of order and system is itself an act of rational reconstruction extrapolating from the given material[13]. But in turn it is a reconstruction that reinforces the conception of law as a "system", and which posits the systematicity of law as a guiding ideal for judges in particular, and also to a degree for legislators and officials of executive government[14].

Law conceived as institutional normative order can thus come to be constitutive of a law-state. However, as Kelsen pointed out, there are two possible ways to conceive and represent the order as a working system. The first is a dynamic way[15]. Here, the process of change through time is central, including the way in which legal provisions themselves set the terms for valid change. This produces a representation of the order with a special focus on the processes of norm-creation, and on the processes of establishing institutional arrangements (contracts, trusts, and the like) within private and lower-level public law. When we represent a normative order in this dynamic way, we represent it in terms of the norms that regulate change, individuated as norms of competence, power-conferring rules, institutive rules of legal institutions.

The second is what Kelsen called a "static" representation[16]. Here, we represent the order by individuating rules or norms prescribing duties, or conferring rights either permissive or beneficial. Sometimes, in an even more microscopic way, we simply individuate particular duties and rights, depending on the current focus of attention. But this "static" conception proves to be misnamed; it concerns not *stasis*, but rather momentary normative judgement, whether the judgement envisaged is that of a court seeking to determine a litigated question, or that of a citizen engaged in practical judgement what to do or demand in a given setting, or indeed that of a scholar trying to produce a coherent representation of some branch of the law. The recognition of rights and duties in this practical-judgemental setting is in any event an intellectual procedure different from that of seeking guidance about the valid exercise of normative power within a normative order dynamically conceived; the two interact and overlap, but are not the same. Law as normative order has two aspects, the dynamic and the momentary. H. L. A. Hart sought to draw these together into a single structure of "primary and secondary rules", but there is a notorious difficulty about the interconnection of his "rule of recognition" with "rules of change" and "rules of adjudication"[17]. A proper

---

[13] N. MacCormick, "Four Quadrants of Jurisprudence" in *Prescriptive Formality and Normative Rationality in Modern Legal Systems*, W. Krawietz e.a. (eds.), Berlin, 1994, 53-70.

[14] J. Bengoetxea, "Legal System as a Regulative Ideal", *A.R.S.P.*, 1994, 66-80.

[15] H. Kelsen, *The Pure Theory of Law*, Berkeley, 1967, chapter 5.

[16] Id., *ibid.*, chapter 4.

[17] See N. MacCormick, *H. L. A. Hart*, 103 ff..

representation of a legal system may reasonably take one or other of several forms, depending on one's practical concerns of the time. Material which is characterised in one way in a dynamic perspective takes a different shape when viewed in a momentary-judgemental perspective. There is no single uniquely correct reconstruction of the raw material of law into a single canonical form of "legal system".

5. Law and Politics, Law and Morality

The penultimate task of the day is to sharpen our sense of the distinction between positive law and the two other realms of thought and action with which it is most intimately interrelated, and yet interrelated as something conceptually distinct, a genuine third term, not simply an amalgam of the first two. Politics is concerned with law – law making and law reform, appointments to key legal offices, maintenance of the forces of law and order, supporting the rulings of the courts. Yet politics is not law, nor law politics, despite occasional assertions to the contrary from the ramparts of Critical Legal Studies. Morality is concerned with law, with the criticism of legal decisions and legal rules, with the issue of obligation to respect the law, with the question of law's claim to be genuinely normative, genuinely engaged with the world of the "ought". Yet morality is not law, nor is law morality, nor a sub-department of morality, for all that this has sometimes been claimed by thinkers in the tradition of "natural law". I want to re-apply here ideas developed in some recent papers concerning these distinctions[18]. The key ideas are those of power, which seems to me especially focal for politics, and autonomy, which seems to me definitive for morality. Let us see how these ideas help with the distinctions sought.

Politics is a matter of power, of the actual exercise of power within human societies or communities, and of elaborating principles for the proper exercise of power. Political power is the power to direct social agencies and individuals to certain defined ends presumptively for the common good, to dispose of available goods (economic and non-economic) among persons and groups, and to protect the group against interference from agencies external to it. The power that we have in mind here is power-in-fact, not simply normative power; that is, power to make sure that somebody in fact acts in a certain way, rather than power to bring it about that somebody ought to act in a certain way. Political power is power-in-fact; but what is sometimes termed "legal power" is power of the other sort, normative power, power confined to the realm of the "ought".

---

[18] Id., "Beyond the Sovereign State", 56 *Modern Law Review*, 1-18 (1993); id., "The Concept of Law and *The Concept of Law*" 14 *Oxford Journal of Legal Studies*, 1-22 (1994); id., "The Relative Heteronomy of Law", *European Journal of Philosophy*, 1995, 69-85.

Law interacts with politics in many ways; sometimes as an object over and through which political power is exercised; sometimes as a control upon the use and abuse of power. But law is not itself constituted by the power-in-fact to effect social change. Law is a form of normative order, setting patterns of right and wrong conduct and conferring powers which are normative rather than coercive in their intrinsic character. Nobody doubts that the United States Constitution conferred and still confers the normative power to ban the manufacture, sale, and consumption of alcohol for beverage purposes. If exercised, this entails that according to law alcohol ought not to be manufactured, sold, or consumed for those purposes. The experiment of the nineteen twenties, however, proved that this legal normative power was not conjoined with sufficient power-in-fact to change the drinking practices of Americans. This sufficiently exemplifies the distinction I have here in mind – politics about power, law about normative order.

Certainly, one might want to add that not every exercise of brute power is itself a matter of politics. We are often inclined to contrast political with military approaches to the solution of civil conflicts (*e.g.*, in Northern Ireland or in Chechnya). The difference is in the element of persuasion, negotiation, discourse. Politics concerns the exercise of power through mainly peaceful discussion, persuasion, negotiation, within forms of government which at least purport to be directed towards a pursuit of the common good in a way that could in principle win general consent among the population governed. Still, however discursive politics may be, the discourse remains one of power in the sense defined.

In its discursive aspect, politics has essential connections with morality. Morality in its most fundamental sense has to be grasped in terms akin to those of Kant's *Groundwork of the Metaphysic of Morals*, and with some regard to Jürgen Habermas' ideas on a "procedural" account of the foundations of moral reasoning[19]. Morality concerns a normative order that is conceived to be valid independently of power and yet to be universal in scope, addressing every moral agent as such. Since it is independent of power, it is necessarily autonomous in its force – for each agent, its binding force or normative validity lies in that agent's own rational will. It is therefore discursive and controversial as well as autonomous. Moral principles are those we can argue out in conditions of free and uncoercive discourse, accepting that they must be universal in application and must take account of the interests and ideals of all persons capable of participating in the discourse or capable of being affected by its outcome. Each person is as fully entitled to enter into moral discourse as every other, and the ultimate

---

[19] J. Habermas, *Faktizität und Geltung. Beiträge zur Diskurstheorie des Rechts und des demokratisches Rechtsstaats*, Frankfort-on-Main, 1992.

judgement of right and wrong in moral matters is for each agent a matter of the conclusions one draws from the commitments on which one determines after engagement in actual or imagined discourse with others. The drawing of conclusions characteristic of a rational will depends upon arguments from a sense of overall coherence of the positions that we commit ourselves to in essentially discursive, uncoercive, contexts.

Morality in a less fundamental sense is located in the common or conventional principles and rules held by persons in communities, often in connection with religious observances and traditions. To show why this sense is less fundamental, one need only ponder the question why these principles and rules have authority over a moral agent. One or other of only two answers is possible. Either their authority derives from the agent's own willing commitment to them, or it derives from the power, however crude or subtle, of community opinion and persuasion or disapproval that keeps the individual in line. In the former case, they are incorporated in the agent's morality through autonomous choice, hence conventional morality is subordinated to individual autonomy. In the latter case, individuals are subjected to the exercise of power, however diffuse and ill-defined, and the rules of conventional morality are an element in the politics of community. If we are to understand morality as a distinct realm of thought and judgement, it can only be through giving conceptual primacy to the discursive-autonomous conception of morality.

Law has positivity. We look to law for answers to questions about what is obligatory or not, permissible or not, within some sphere of decision making. Inside that sphere of decision making, that is what "ought" to be done to satisfy the institutionalised system. Relative to a presupposed system, law lays down what is obligatory or permissible, not what from some ideal point of view ought to be obligatory or permissible. A properly taken decision that a certain rule shall be enacted into law does confer on that rule the character of being an actual rule of law. A properly taken decision about some disputed point of right between two persons settles conclusively the legal rights of each upon that point, just as a properly taken decision upon an accusation of crime settles conclusively the legal guilt or innocence of the accused person.

Law resembles morality in that it is normative; it resembles conventional morality in being a normative order commonly observed in some community or society, and backed by strong pressures of opinion, and by the regularly confirmed belief that others apply norms that are regarded as common standards for the group in question. States being territorial political communities organised under governments capable of wielding coercive power over individuals and groups and in response to external forces, the law of states is backed not only by opinion but also by the coercive force of political power. But it is important to remember that the law of the state is not the only law that human beings have, and that the "*Rechtsstaat*" is, as was argued already, that particular form of state in which the law provides decisive and actually operative criteria for the rightful use of power. Such states have empirically a greater durability than police-states or party-states. In law-states, the felt legitimacy of the exercise of governmental power is guaranteed by law, and this is not something that simply follows from the existence of a sovereign state as such. This further indicates that the legal and the political are not to be treated as identical however closely they interact in fortunate circumstances.

One manifestation of law's positivity lies in the way in which, on questions of law, there frequently seems to be a fact of the matter, checkable by reference to publicly accessible sources. If a person wants to find out whether there is a maximum speed limit on the roads of a country, or a maximum permitted level of blood alcohol for drivers, there are sources to which one can quite easily look for an answer. Explicit rules on such matters are to be found in pieces of legislation, frequently supplemented by pieces of subordinate legislation; and secondary sources such as legal text-books or government publications about road traffic assist in identifying them.

On the moral question how fast it is right to drive, or how much if any alcohol it is morally acceptable to drink before driving, there is no interpersonally checkable source establishing a quantitative limit; such questions are settlable only through moral discourse, weighing relevant arguments, and establishing considerations relevant to the issue in hand. Their settlement from time to time depends on the conscientious judgement of a moral agent, whether or not in conformity with the conscientious judgement of other agents actually or potentially participating in the relevant discourse. Of course, it would be difficult to comprehend a claim that the norms of positive law in the state regulating alcohol consumption by drivers are irrelevant or weightless in a moral deliberation on the topic in question. But it would be even harder to comprehend, far less accept, a claim that morally the enacted rules could have the conclusive character they have within legal deliberation.

The settled, positive, character of law is jurisdiction-relative[20]. How fast one may drive is a question differently answered in different places governed by different legal systems under the jurisdiction of different organs or agencies. The fact of the legal matter is a fact about some discrete legal system, and, where the law in question is state-law, the answer normally holds good only in respect of the territory of the given state. Sixty miles per hour is the maximum permitted speed on roads in the United Kingdom other than designated "Motorways", on which the maximum is seventy miles per hour. That holds good, of course, only for roads in the United Kingdom regulated by the Road

[20] N. MacCormick, "Comment" in *Issues in Contemporary Legal Philosophy: the Influence of H. L. A. Hart*, R. Gavison (ed.), Oxford, 1987, 105-113.

Traffic Acts. If I visit another country, such as Canada, I expect the rules to be different, and even expressed in different units of measurement. There, I have to check on maxima in terms of kilometres per hour; and so on. In each jurisdiction, I look for some distinct piece of legislation (or other authoritative law-text) that settles the matter within that jurisdiction.

Moral judgements, however personal and controversial, are not in this way relativistic. If I hold that driving above a certain speed is inherently dangerous to life and limb, or wasteful of natural resources, and if I hold that humans ought not to endanger each others' bodily safety, or make excessive demands on non-renewable resources, then I must hold that speeding is wrong wherever it may cause danger or use too much fuel. These judgements apply universally. No doubt they are susceptible only to being supported with arguments in a moral discourse, without any interpersonally authoritative source to check against; but in their own character they are universalisable claims, not restricted by jurisdiction or territoriality. Certainly, circumstances alter cases morally; but they do so in a universalisable way. The truth of moral matters is not checkable by reference to established, public and institutional sources. But their truth is an unrestricted and universal truth to the extent we can establish it at all.

Here may rest the argument on the dual contrast of law with politics and with morality. Law is both a normative and an institutional order, and this connects it with the two poles of the contrast. As a normative order, it replicates certain features of morality, and connects necessarily to morality in certain ways. As an institutional order, it connects necessarily to politics and is in part constitutive of the political, while well-conducted politics is necessary to the maintenance of systems of positive law, and especially state-law.

6. Finally: A Personal Agenda for the Philosophy of Law

The view I have stated here, appropriately to the genre of the work to which I am contributing, is both sketchy and programmatic. It is at least as much assertive as argumentative. In trying to settle basic issues for legal philosophy, it leaves out much that remains for argument and discussion. But where does it point, where will it lead as we try to unravel it all? As I see it, there are in this picture four principal domains for systematic further inquiry, and this should lead to a coherent and synoptic contribution to the philosophy of law. Having recently received the great boon of the award of a Leverhulme Personal Research Chair, for five years research starting in October 1997, I intend to spend the coming years working systematically on each of these four domains. They are as follows:

6.1. Institutional Theory of Law

The ideas I have suggested above about the "institutional" character of law are in part shared with Ota Weinberger of Graz, Austria, together with whom I have put forward what we have called an "institutional theory of law", or "institutional legal positivism". The ideas we put forward were originally developed independently, and our work emerged from different philosophical traditions. Perhaps our most important shared tenet is that, although law is normative, belonging to the realm of the ought, there nevertheless are highly significant "institutional facts" that constitute in large part the world of legal order. This factual-as-well-as-normative character of law is found wherever a normative order is in existence in a stable and established way, especially where it is supported by institutional agencies empowered by the normative order to act in executive, legislative or judicial capacities in relation to it. So far as concerns the normative character, I am conscious of a need to come to terms with a considerable body of recent work by such scholars as Joseph Raz, Frederick Schauer, Roger Shiner, Tom Campbell, Robert Alexy and Aulis Aarnio, as well as by Ota Weinberger himself. This will be of help in refining the ideas sketched above about normative order. Dick Ruiter and Eerik Lagerspetz in turn have made significant advances in relation to institutional theory which bears in an important way on the issues about institutional facts. Over and above this, there is an urgent task to try to develop a coherent and theoretically well-grounded account of the main institutions of law and there place within an account of institutional normative order. The themes of a project aimed at carrying this out would be: 1) ideal and actual in social (including legal) theory; 2) an understanding of "norms" and "the normative"; 3) normative orders: institutional and non-institutional; 4) wrongs, duties and obligations; crimes and civil wrongs; 5) rights and liberties; 6) powers; 7) persons and personality; 8) contract and property; 9) welfare rights and institutions; 10) general principles and values in legal order.

6.2. Legal and Moral Order

As stated, the institutional character of law differentiates it from morality, given the conception of morality that places at its centre the autonomy of moral agents and their personal responsibility for moral judgement and the achievement of moral order. This conception of autonomous morality requires thorough consideration and elaboration, in the light of a very large body of contemporary work, crucial in it being the more recent work of Jürgen Habermas, and particularly *Faktizität und Geltung*. It also requires careful consideration of Joseph Raz's work on moral freedom, and connected aspects of the moral realism proposed by John Finnis and other contemporary exponents of natural law. What is needed is a sensitive account of the differences and yet similarities and interactions between law and morality developed through an elucidation of autonomous morality set in juxtaposition with the "institutional" account of law. The same moral theory then leads into the development of certain theses about critical morality in relation to legal institutions and the "enforcement of morals" debate. Strictly, that which is in its essence autonomous cannot be "enforced" through a form of heteronomous order; but the issue of the proper scope for moral disestablishment remains a difficult one. To handle that issue properly leads into a general treatment of that part of a theory of justice, both corrective and distributive, that is relevant to and required for a complete legal theory.

More detailed headings for this study might be the following: 1) procedural ethics: autonomy and morality; 2) the right and the good; 3) reason and sentiment in ethical judgement; 4) foundations of justice; 5) moral realism and natural law; 6) state neutrality and "moral disestablishment"; 7) corrective justice: crime and punishment; 8) corrective justice: civil remedies; 9) distributive justice; 10) the inter-actions of law and morality

6.3. The Rule of Law and the "Post-Sovereign" State

Since Hans Kelsen's *General Theory of Law and State* there has been remarkably little work on the concept of the state and its interaction with that of law in the English-speaking traditions; there has, however, been important work by scholars such as Paul Craig, Trevor Allan, and Ronald Dworkin on some of the theoretical concepts of public law, and a large body of European work on the "*Rechtsstaat*" and related ideas needs to be assimilated. At the same time, the development in the European Union of a new form of legal order and with it a new form of polity or commonwealth has posed challenges for legal theory that we have barely begun to meet. The most original part of my own recent work has been given to some of the questions in this field, including those of sovereignty, the "post-sovereign state", the "*Rechtsstaat*", and democracy and subsidiarity in the setting of a pluralistic view of legal order. The time is now more than ripe for a re-statement of the interrelations and differences between legal and political order. This should make it possible to establish a new theory of states as political organisations that both show a capacity to be (imperfectly) disciplined through a framework of public law and yet also uphold what is the most significant, though by no means the only, form of law in the contemporary world, namely state-law. The main headings to be followed out here are the following: 1) law and politics: normative order and the discourse of power; 2) the state as polity, the state as legal entity; 3) *Grundnorm* and constitution; 4) the "*Rechtsstaat*" and the rule of law; 5) sovereignty in the state: legal and political conceptions; 6) beyond the sovereign state; legal order in the European Union; 7) democracy and subsidiarity in post-sovereign Europe;

8) constitutionalism and civic nationalism; 9) self-determination and other collective and individual rights.

6.4. Practical Reason and Legal Argumentation

In 1994, I added a substantially new Foreword for a second impression of my *Legal Reasoning and Legal Theory* (1978) drawing attention to a series of papers which have reconsidered and restated or revised earlier positions about legal reasoning in response to critical discussions and to new work by other authors in the field, most notably Robert Alexy but also Manuel Atienza, Ulfrid Neumann, Klaus Gunther, Richard Susskind and Bernard Jackson. At the same time, I have been involved in intensive collaboration with Robert S. Summers and others through the *"Bielefelder Kreis"* on an ambitious twelve-year project for a series of comparative studies of approaches to legal interpretation, first in relation to statutes, second, in relation to precedents[21]. This, together with reflection on ideas about interpretation proposed by Ronald Dworkin, Joseph Raz, Aleksander Peczenik, Aulis Aarnio, Andrei Marmor, and Jeremy Waldron, to say nothing of work in the Critical Legal Studies tradition, forms the basis for a new statement on the foundations of legal reasoning as a form of practical reason.

The basic idea of an institutional normative order, or at any rate one of its most salient virtues, is its capacity to establish common norms of conduct in reasonably clear-cut terms, open to a shared interpersonal understanding albeit also subject perennially to interpretation and re-interpretation. This suggests that a form of deductive-subsumptive reasoning will always have a central part to play in the processes of argumentation involved in the application of abstract law to concrete cases. This in turn suggests that the multifarious efforts of scholars and scientists to find suitable ways of formalising parts of legal reasoning and harnessing the resources of informatics to the establishment of practical systems of an intelligent knowledge-based kind have real prospects of success. But there are other, interpretative and substantive modes of reasoning that must always be involved in any complete piece of legal argumentation, and the prospects for applying machine intelligence to these are still remote if not, indeed, fanciful.

To form a rounded view of the full potentialities of human practical reasoning without a thorough study of the mixture of deductive with interpretative and substantive reasoning that is legal argumentation would be impossible. To develop such a view would be to make fully comprehensible the practical aspects of the idea of institutional

---

[21] N. MacCormick and R. S. Summers (eds.), *Interpreting Statutes. A Comparative Study*, Aldershot, 1991 and id., *Interpreting Precedents. A Comparative Study*, Aldershot, 1997.

normative order. The topics that such a rounded account must include are at least: 1) practical reason and "general practical discourse"; 2) reasoning and argumentation in law: discovery and justification; 3) deductive argumentation and its practical relevance; 4) universalisation and induction in practical reasoning; 5) argumentation and interpretation: working with statutes; 6) universal and particular: problems of precedent; 7) arguments from analogy; 8) arguments of principle; 9) time, narratives and legal argument; 10) the uses of coherence in legal thought; 11) argument and the proof of facts.

My original philosophical training was in Glasgow University, where the ideas of Kant and those of the intuitionist moral philosophers played a great part, along with a close regard to the history of philosophy and particularly to some of the great thinkers of the Scottish enlightenment. Afterwards, I went to Oxford and made contact both with R. M. Hare and with H. L. A. Hart, being very strongly influenced by the latter during the period when I was a junior colleague of his in the Oxford law faculty. Since my appointment to the Regius Chair in Edinburgh in 1972, without weakening my connections in the English-speaking traditions, I have greatly strengthened my links to philosophy and jurisprudence in the mainland of Europe and in Scandinavia. In recent years I have become ever more convinced of the necessity for legal theory to take serious account of the emergence of a "new legal order" in the form of the European Community.

We have to approach law now in a pluralistic way, not with the monolithic state always taken for granted as the foundation stone of any real legal order. We must be thoroughly comparativistic in our outlook as we grapple with the problems of understanding law in the context of globalisation. We cannot afford to reject the resources of any substantial philosophical tradition in developing our ideas to cope with the problems of the philosophy of law at the end of the twentieth century. This is not to advocate a facile eclecticism of approach, but even more is it to reject a hide-bound traditionalism or parochialism of view either in philosophical or in legal terms. I hope that I have been able to work in a spirit of intelligent openness to other philosophical traditions even while my own approach to method remains broadly within an analytical tradition. I have in particular tried to maintain active intellectual associations both in the world of britanno-american analytical philosophy and legal theory and in the world of continental scholarship in its critical and hermeneutic lines, and I have collaborated closely with several colleagues in these and other traditions. Moreover, especially in the context of growing attention to theoretical underpinnings for European Community law, it seems to me that we need to put considerable effort into transcending the mutual misperceptions of common lawyers and civil lawyers, and must construct our legal theories with a due regard to a sensible plurality of approaches to legal order even within the European Union, but also with due regard to a yet wider world of law.

Bibliographical Information

I. Books

(as author or co-author)

1. *Civil Liberties and the Law*, Edinburgh, 1977.
2. *Legal Reasoning and Legal Theory*, Oxford, 1994[2] (with new foreword).
3. *H. L. A. Hart*, London, 1981.
4. *Legal Right and Social Democracy*, Oxford, 1982.
5. (with O. Weinberger), *Grundlagen des Institutionalistischen Rechtspositivismus*, Berlin, 1985.

An Institutional Theory of Law. New Approaches to Legal Positivism, Dordrecht, 1986.

Il Diritto Come Instituzione, M. La Torre (transl.), Milan, 1990.

Pour une théorie institutionelle du droit, O. Nerhot and P. Coppens (transl.), Brussels, 1992.

6. *Derecho legal y socialdemocracia: ensayos sobre filosofia juridica y politica*, L. Gonzalez Soler (transl.), Madrid, 1990.

(as editor or co-editor)

7. *The Scottish Debate*, London, 1970.
8. *Lawyers in their Social Setting*, Edinburgh, 1977.
9. (with S. Panou and L. Vallauri) *Conditions of Validity and Cognition in Modern Legal Thought*, *A.R.S.P.*, 1985.
10. (with P. Birks) *The Legal Mind: Essays for Tony Honore*, Oxford, 1986.
11. (with Z. Bankowski) *Enlightenment, Rights and Revolution. Essays in Legal and Social Philosophy*, Aberdeen, 1989.
12. (with R. S. Summers) *Interpreting Statutes. A Comparative Study*, Aldershot, 1991.
13. (with P. Amselek) *Controversies About Law's Ontology*, Edinburgh, 1991.
14. (with A. Aarnio) *Legal Reasoning*, Aldershot, 1991, 2 vol.
15. (with Z. Bankowski and J. Wroblewski) *The Judicial Application of Law*, Dordrecht/London/Lancaster, 1992.
16. (with R. S. Summers) *Interpreting Precedents. A Comparative Study*, Aldershot, 1997.

(as translator or co-translator)

17. (with R. Adler) R. Alexy, *A Theory of Legal Argumentation*, Oxford, 1989.
18. *The Digest of Justinian: Book One* in *The disgest of Justinian*, T. Mommsen and J. Krueger (eds.), Philadelphia, 1995.

II. Articles

1. "Rights in Legislation" in *Law, Morality and Society. Essays in Honour of H. L. A. Hart*, P. M. Z. Hacker and J. Raz (eds.), Oxford, 1977, 189-209.
2. "To Motivation of the Judgement in the Common Law" in *La motivation des décisions de justice*, C. Perelman and P. Foriers (eds.), Brussels, 1978, 167-194.
3. "Spontaneous Order and Rule of Law. Some Problems" in *Jahrbuch des Öffentlichen Rechts der Gegenwart*, 1986, 1-13.
4. "Universalisation and Induction in Law" in *Reason in Law*, C. Faralli and E. Pattaro (eds.), Milan, 1987, 91-106.
5. "Smashing the Two-way Mirrow" in *Anti-foundationalism and Practical Reason*, E. Simpson (ed.), Edmonton/Alberta, 1987, 201-216.
6. "Why Cases have Rationes and What These Are" in *Precedent in Law*, L. Goldstein (ed.), Oxford, 1987, 155-182.
7. "Persons as Institutional Facts" in *Reine Rechtslehre im Spiegel Ihrer Fortsetzer und Kritiker*, O. Weinberger and W. Krawietz (eds.), New York/Vienna, 1988, 371-379.
8. "Is Nationalism Philosophically Credible?" in *Issues of Self-Determination*, W. Twining (ed.), Aberdeen, 1991, 8-19.
9. "Natural Law and the Separation of Law and Morals" in *Natural Law Theory*, R. P. George (ed.), Oxford, 1992, 105-133.
10. "Law" in *Scotland: a Concise Cultural History*, P. H. Scott (ed.), Edinburgh, 1993, 343-355.
11. "Constitutionalism and Democracy" in *Theories and Concepts of Politics*, R. Bellamy (ed.), Manchester, 1993, 124-147.
12. "Four Quadrants of Jurisprudence" in *Prescriptive Formality and Normative Rationality in Modern Legal Systems*, W. Krawietz e.a. (eds.), Berlin, 1994, 53-70.
13. "Legal Concepts" in *Encyclopedia of Language and Linguistics*, R. Asher and W. Simpson (eds.), Oxford, 1994, 2069-2074.
14. "Defeasibility in Law and Logic" in *Informatics and the Foundations of Legal Reasoning*, Z. Bankowski, I. White e.a. (eds.), Dordrecht/ London/Lancaster, 1995, 99-117.
15. "Children's Rights: A Test Case for Theories of Right", *A.R.S.P.*, 1976, 305-317.
16. "Formal Justice and the Form of Legal Arguments" in *Etudes de logique juridique*, VI, C. Perelman (ed.), Brussels, 1976, 103-118.
17. "Law, Morality and Positivism", 1 *Legal Studies*, 131-145 (1981).
18. "Der Rechtsstaat und die 'Rule of Law' ", *Juristenzeitung*, 1984, 65-70.
19. "A Moralistic Case for A-Moralistic Law", 20 *Valparaiso University Law Review*, 1-41 (1985).
20. "Reglas Sociales", *Revista de Ciencias Sociales*, 1986, 297-319.

21. "Institutions, Arrangements and Practical Reason", *Ratio Juris*, 1988, 73-82.
22. "Reconstruction after Deconstruction: A Response to C.L.S.M.", 10 *Oxford Journal of Legal Studies*, 539-558 (1990).
23. "Legal Deduction, Legal Predicates, and Expert Systems", *International Journal for the Semiotics of Law*, 1992, 181-202.
24. "Beyond the Sovereign State" 56 *Modern Law Review*, 1-18 (1993).
25. "What Place for Nationalism in the Modern World?" in *In Search of New Constitutions*, H. MacQueen (ed.), Edinburgh, 1994, 79-95.
26. "Sovereignty: Myth and Reality" in *De Lege*, Uppsala, 1995, 227-248.
27. "The Maastricht-Urteil: Sovereignty now", *European Law Journal*, 1995, 259-266.
28. "Time, Narratives, and Law" in *Time, Law, and Society*, J. Bjarup and M. Blegvad (eds.), *A.R.S.P.,* 1995, 111-125.
29. "The Relative Heteronomy of Law", *European Journal of Philosophy*, 1995, 69-85.
30. "Liberalism, Nationalism and the Post-sovereign State", 44 *Political Studies*, 553-567 (1996).

CONSTRUCTING THE COMPLEXITY OF THE LAW: TOWARDS A DIALECTIC THEORY

FRANÇOIS OST AND MICHEL VAN DE KERCHOVE

FACULTÉS UNIVERSITAIRES SAINT-LOUIS

BRUSSELS

There is no doubt that the law has always been complicated. It is a frequently heard complaint these days that we suffer from legislative inflation and that legal procedures are interminable and uncertain. But Leibniz wrote as early as 1678 that "it is not possible to know the law without a very large library"[1], while Bentham in an open letter to the American citizens said: "Everywhere the common law has set foot, security has disappeared"[2].

At that time, we may say that the law was only complicated, while today we are obliged to talk about its complexity. Complication arises from the accumulation of simple sequences. It is the repetition of the same code or the same logic that produces the effect known as complication, in the sense that clockwork or 18th-century automata were complicated, while relying simply on a limited number of mechanical gears. Complexity is something else entirely, arising from a multiplicity of interacting codes and different types of logic working together. Movements here are linear but also recursive, causal relations are multiple and circular. The actions of an automaton are always predictable, while those of a complex organism, because it is creative and interactive, are much less so.

However, the law has indeed become complex and we are therefore obliged to think in terms of this complexity. In her work, *Pour un droit commun*[3], Mireille Delmas-Marty makes the following observation: "Whether concerned to prescribe a norm, to interpret it or to justify it by reference to meta-judicial values, our patterns of thinking are still strongly influenced by the age of enlightenment. Precise rules, syllogistic reasoning and homogeneous values – in short, a 'monological' order – are vastly preferred by the legal profession. But it is also true that the law does not belong to lawyers and that it has evolved without them, sometimes in spite of them, towards a complexity that cannot be merely deplored and with which we are obliged to get to grips."

---

[1] G. W. Leibniz, "Trois textes sur le droit et la codification", *Archives de philosophie du droit*, 1986, 361.

[2] J. Bentham, "Lettre de J. Bentham, un Anglais, aux citoyens des divers Etats des Etats-Unis d'Amérique" in *Papers Relative to Codification. The works of J. Bentham*, IV, J. Bowring (ed.), Edinburgh, 1838-1843, 479.

[3] M. Delmas-Marty, *Pour un droit commun*, Paris, 1994, 193-194.

We are in fact witnessing a thorough shaking-up of judicial thinking, a general shift in the categories involved. M. Delmas-Marty mentions "precise rules"? These must now accommodate supranational law, subnational law and even transnational law. The rules now have vague limits, a variable area of application and debatable enforceability. Rules now are subject to the censure of constitutional and European courts.

"Syllogistic reasoning"? If, as is undoubtedly the case, lawyers have not yet taken leave of formal logic, they are at the same time obliged to take into account the logical systems relating to whatever is probable, reasonable or commensurate: a gradualist and comparative logic that no longer limits itself to bipartite divisions, but which explores the frontiers of the law so as to arrive at a finer adjustment of the scales of justice.

As for the "homogeneous values", what is left of these now that laws everywhere must answer to the rights of individuals and of groups, rights which themselves have been overrun by the rising power of recognised interests in our societies, which are both individualist and pluralist?

But complexity is perhaps even more radical than is suggested by this patchwork of sources and concepts. It takes on something of a paradox as soon as we realise that the law does not have complete control over the code of legality and illegality which it nonetheless administers (what, then, is the source of legality?), that it has no direct access to the facts that it nonetheless controls, that its boundaries, leaky and reversible, are both internal and external, that the rules which it sets up to reduce conflict and influence behaviour are themselves the subject of permanent conflict, that the actors in the judicial drama are both partners and opponents, that knowledge of the law implies a position both inside and outside of it, and that law's legitimacy depends both on the consensus in its favour and on the possibility of dissension to which it accommodates itself.

All these facts certainly constitute so many anomalies, paradoxes and logical affronts from the viewpoint of the classic theories which continue to preclude any third term. Based soundly on the principles of identity and of non-contradiction, classical thinking excludes any third term. It is therefore locked up in systems of irreducible opposition, condemned either to monism or to dualism or to unending oscillation between one pole and the other. Gaston Bachelard has described this reality well in arguing that scientific thought was characterised by the law of the "bipolarity of errors"[4]. It is in fact as if the mind can only escape from one error by falling immediately into its opposite, in a sort of pendulum movement of which the history of science provides many examples. As a theoretician of the exact sciences, Bachelard was attacking more particularly the

---

[4] G. Bachelard, *La formation de l'esprit scientifique*, Paris, 1977, 20.

permanent oscillation between empiricism and rationalism, while calling personally for a "rational materialism" or an "applied rationalism"[5].

It seems to us that legal thinking is no exception to this bipolarity of errors. Whether it is looked at from the point of view of existing theories or from that of the problems that it deals with, only irreducible dualisms appear. Everything is patterned on a binary structure, after the fashion of the scholastic *disputationes pro et contra*. And we are required to take sides, to declare our allegiance immediately and to rally round the one or the other flag. In the merciless struggle in which the different theoretical "*isms*" are locked, everything is soon simplified and fixed according to the logic of identity and exclusion: one either joins or is banished. And the same game is played again and again. The moment, however, that a novel point of view is taken and the straitjacket removed, the first thing to be noticed is not the correctness of one side's argument and the apparent error of the other, but the structure of the controversy as a whole: this implies a plurality of points of view, of a relative nature one to the other (none of them being able any longer to lay a claim to the whole truth), and, finally, in close solidarity: each one appealing to the other and being supported by it, on the pretext of refuting it.

At this point the following question arises: what if the truth were to reside precisely in the tension between the two poles, in their conflictual interdependence and the way in which they fit together – as if, by means of their very opposition, they were both trying to express something of the complexity of a reality that cannot be reduced to the one or the other? As if what was trying to gain expression in this way were precisely the excluded third term, which, like repressed feelings in psychoanalysis, persists in the form of a symptom. Here, then, the first intimations of the dialectic appear, in the following form: each of the poles, in spite of its claims to the contrary, contains at least partially and in a virtual sense its own counterpart (consider, for example, the highly debatable and yet, in France, nonetheless lively distinction between public and private law, or, again, the antagonism, as old as the law itself, between the letter and the spirit), or, another intimation: from the interplay between the two poles a resulting quality emerges, a third term that will transform the two others.

We have opted unequivocally to look carefully for this persistent third term. This will be our route; literally, our method. We shall systematically take up the opposing pairs inherent in legal thinking and, opening up the dialectical interplay of their reciprocal transformations, learn to look at the complexity of the legal reality revealed in the process.

The route itself has been marked out by some prodigious guides. Perelman, for example, who wrote in his *Traité de l'argumentation*, co-written with Lucie Olbrechts-Tyteca, "We set ourselves up against clear and irreducible philosophical oppositions presented to us by all types of absolutisms: the dualities

---

[5] Id., *Le matérialisme rationnel*, Paris, 1953.

of reason and imagination, science and opinion, hard evidence and wishful thinking, a universally recognised objectivity and idiosyncratic subjectivity"[6].

Or again, more recently, Pierre Bourdieu: "A rigorous science of the law is to be distinguished from what is usually called 'legal science' in that it takes the latter as its subject matter. In doing this it breaks free immediately from the alternative that dominates scientific thinking with regard to the law, of either formalism, claiming absolute autonomy for the judicial form with regard to society at large, or instrumentalism, which regards the law as a reflection or instrument of dominant social forces"[7]. And Bourdieu goes on to plead for a sort of "relative autonomy" of the law, which both results from and yet is ignored by these two conflicting points of view, the internal and external.

In the light of the above, let us look at some of the more recurrent juridicial dichotomies: natural law doctrine and legal positivism, subjectivity and objectivity, rationality and irrationality, prescriptive and descriptive, hierarchy and circularity, monism and pluralism.

Natural law doctrine and legal positivism first of all. On the one hand, we are taught that there is a radical distinction between the "law as it is" and the "law as it should be", and that scientific study – "pure" science in Kelsen's terms – is limited to the former, while the latter involves political and ethical judgements beyond the reach of science. The former involves a plea for the formal completeness of written legislation, which bases itself on its derivation from a higher norm, and the role of the judge is reduced to either a purely deductive capacity or a discretionary latitude. On the other hand, we adopt a cautionary approach to the study of the law, imbuing it with the aim of discovering the necessary "just relations" and "precepts for action", in such a way that positive law should no longer be separate from the ideal law (natural, rational, religious or sociological, whatever) on which it is based. Legislation therefore in no way represents the last word on what is law, since the law is based on higher principles of legitimacy, whose authorised interpreter the judge can, if necessary, claim to be.

What, however, do we see in practice? A legal doctrine that never stops moving from the analysis *de lege lata* to the plea *de lege ferenda*. A judicial line of argument that increasingly reflects basic rights, the requirements of democracy and the principles of the constitutional state – exponents of rational law within the field of positive law which, at the same time, themselves tend to become more and more positive in both texts and legal practice. We also see developing in the margin of the law new sources of general legal principles, such as the principle of

---

[6] C. Perelman and L. Olbrechts-Tyteca, *Traité de l'argumentation. La nouvelle rhétorique*, Brussels, 1970^2, 670.

[7] P. Bourdieu, "La force du droit. Eléments pour une sociologie du champ juridique", *Actes de la recherche en sciences sociales*, 1986, 4.

respect for another's legitimate expectations, which has already been shown to be necessary in both private and public law as an expression of certain aspirations based on common sense or social justice. As regards the philosophy of law, it has also been shown how the school of modern natural law gave rise to judicial positivism, while, conversely, almost all the positivists, including Kelsen, finally came round to a natural law position in that they were no longer content to describe, but also wished to establish, and even "justify" the compulsory nature of the law. It is therefore in no way incongruous to speak, as did Paul Foriers, of "positive natural law"[8], a clearly paradoxical notion, but a welcome expression of the interweaving, in the reality of judicial discourse, of text and ideal, letter and spirit, of the legal and the just.

The opposition between objectivity and subjectivity is not unique to the law. It is found throughout the social sciences. Bourdieu has gone so far as to say that, "of all the oppositions that divide social science artificially, this was the most basic and most harmful"[9]. In our field, it colours such diverse questions as the theory of the sources of law, the problem of the creation of rights and duties, the nature of responsibility, the scope of rights and the role of the legal subject, and the problem of interpretation. Here too, opposing positions have been taken up. Jean Dabin, supported by Paul Roubier, states that "the existence of rights is a necessity which is both logical and ontological"[10]. On the other side, Léon Duguit would like to see rights – a substantialist metaphysical concept – removed from the scientific study of the law as having no more value as a hypothesis than the phlogiston theory in outdated physics or the vital principle in physiology[11]. And Kelsen echoes him in considering the concepts of rights and of the legal subject as ideological left-overs from doctrines of natural law that "are now superfluous from the point of view of a scientific description of judicial data"[12]. It may be considered however, along with François Rigaux, that this legal objectivity involves an unjustifiable shift from an objective approach to law over to the idea that the law itself is necessarily of an objective nature[13]. If it is our legal system itself which is imbued with a subjective philosophy, it is enough to bear this interweaving of subjective and objective in mind. For the rest, as will be seen, the interplay of the actor and the system, in sociology in general, or of persons and things, in environmental law, constitute new expressions of the hybrid third term for which we are here making a case.

---

[8] P. Foriers, "Le juriste et le droit naturel. Essai de définition d'un droit naturel positif" in *La pensée juridique de Paul Foriers*, I, Brussels, 1982, 425.

[9] P. Bourdieu, *Le sens pratique*, Paris, 1980, 43.

[10] J. Dabin, *Le droit subjectif*, Paris, 1952, 29.

[11] L. Duguit, *Traité de droit constitutionnel*, I, Paris,1927[3], 297.

[12] H. Kelsen, *Théorie pure du droit*, Ch. Eisenmann (transl.), Paris, 1962, 175.

[13] F. Rigaux, *Introduction à la science du droit*, Brussels, 1974, 21, 24 and 122.

The opposition between rationality and irrationality provides a third area of conflict in legal thinking. For some, law is to be regarded as by nature rational, either in the strict sense of formal reasoning or in the wider sense of being prudent. For others, such as the German 19th-century school of historical law, on the other hand, the law is irrational. In the words of one the school's major figures, Grimm: "Law and poetry are brother and sister. (...). The origins of both are to be found in something that is doubly essential: of the order of the wondrous and of faith"[14]. Marxists, for their part, will support the idea that the law is no more than mystification and ideology: an instrument serving the interests of the ruling classes.

What if, here again, truth were dialectical? If legal discourse did indeed involve myth and faith, but then a "logical imagining": a passionate desire for logic, coherence and stability? Like the need to anchor the argument to an incontestable and infallible point of reference: a "mythologic", in fact, some effects of which one of us has described together with Jacques Lenoble and following on from Pierre Legendre[15], and whose current version in the grounds cited for legal decisions is that of the "rational legislator".

The opposition between "prescriptive" and "descriptive" opens up a new area of conflict, this time at the heart of legal positivism itself. On the one hand, legal order is taken to be a prescriptive order, in which any legal phenomenon is to be linked to a norm and it is a norm that ensures the legal and prescriptive nature of all the norms in the system. On the other hand – or, rather, on the other side of the Atlantic, since we are here referring to "American" realism – the law is taken to consist of a range of human behaviour, *i.e.* that of the judicial authorities who make the law by means of the decisions they take. Jerome Frank has referred in this respect to a "Copernican revolution". Whereas traditional thinking puts the rules at the centre of the system and considers it possible to deduce specific decisions from these, Holmes and the realist movement now put the decisions at the centre of the arrangement. Here, the rules derive from the decisions and not the other way round.

But revolutions, as we know, frequently bring us back to where we started. In turning Kelsen's pyramid upside-down, the realist movement does not lead us out of a linear logic: validity now derives from the base rather than the summit, but still nothing is being said about the way in which all the actors work together at the collective and recursive process of validating legal norms. We would do better to follow Hart here, of whom it has been said that he stood for a "normative

---

[14] J. Grimm, "Von der Poeie im Recht", *Zeitschrift für geschichtliche Rechtswissenschaft*, 1816, 27.

[15] J. Lenoble and F. Ost, *Droit, mythe et raison. Essai sur la dérive mytho-logique de la rationalité juridique*, Brussels, 1980.

realism"[16]. His position is indeed dialectical, since he considers that if complex legal systems effectively consist of primary and secondary norms, it is still possible for these to lose their validity if they fail to be accepted by officials and private persons ("internal viewpoint"). It is still possible, in any hypothesis, for the most fundamental norm in the system, which he calls the "rules of recognition", to be based in the final analysis on "practice" (usage, in other words, to which, as with customs, a sense of obligation is attached). And still possible, in certain circumstances, for judges themselves, working in the "shadow zone" involved in any rule, to help in defining the criteria for inclusion and validity that predominate in the system. In thus providing a balance, in line with reality in our opinion, between the prerogatives of the legislators and those of the judges, between norms and facts, between the top and the bottom, Hart frees himself from the military or Jovian idea of the pyramid. He does not, however, go so far as to subscribe to the opposite thesis, as represented by Luhmann, for example, which now claims that the validating relationships of different legal norms are symmetrical or circular, and in no sense hierarchical[17]. We should also speak, in current system-theory parlance, of an "tangled hierarchy" or "strange loop" in order to take into account the interactive and recursive processes of validation which do not in themselves remove the idea that, "normally", the higher norm constitutes the basis for the validity of the lower norm[18]. Similarly, as regards those theories that continue to believe in a narrow state monism and those that, following Gurvitch in particular, claim to see an absolutely horizontal pluralism, with no pre-eminence whatsoever for the state legal order, we think it possible to come down, as does Jacques Chevallier for example, on the side of a "stratified and hierarchic legal pluralism"[19].

"Normative realism", "tangled hierarchy", "stratified pluralism": these are three more hybrids, three dialectical products of the dichotomies in the study of the law, three properties generated by virtue of their own interaction; all three represent ways of extracting legal thinking from the two-dimensional plane in which it is too frequently imprisoned and of endowing it with relief and movement, the third dimension granted to the complexity of legal phenomena.

What is the precise nature of these "fields of tension" that we have been able to discern in the dichotomous field of judicial thinking? Most frequently, as we have seen, the "field of tension" is represented as a simple binary opposition

---

[16] E. Pattaro, *Lineamenti per una teoria del diritto*, Bologna, 1965, 191-210.

[17] N. Luhmann, "L'unité du système juridique", *Archives de philosophie du droit*, 1986, 174.

[18] For more details, see F. Ost and M. van de Kerchove, "De la 'bipolarité des erreurs' ou de quelques paradigmes de la science du droit", *Archives de philosophie du droit*, 1988, 177 ff.

[19] J. Chevallier, "Droit et État", *Revue interdisciplinaire d'études juridiques*, 1986, 24.

insistently demanding a choice between the one or the other camp involved. Reality is then neither complex nor paradoxical. It is simply divided and appears only to be waiting for the final victory of one thesis over the other.

Another way to deal with the "field of tension" is to reject the two theses involved and to replace them with a third theory. Perelman, for example, seems to have adopted this strategy of the "third road" fairly often, in particular in rejecting both deductive and inductive reasoning in favour of an argumentative reasoning. However, this may simply entail the creation of a new pair of contradictory concepts: in this case, argument now opposes demonstration (inductive or deductive), and the logic of controverse opposes formal logic[20].

Choosing one of two opposed terms or lumping them both together to be able to choose a third are two ways, as we have seen, of either covering up or claiming to go beyond paradox: either way is an attempt to get rid of it. It is obviously not the course we have taken, but it is admittedly an extremely common attitude of minds unhappy about coping with paradoxes or being immersed in complexity. As if the logical enigma posed by the former and the uncertainty generated by the latter threaten our usual ways of thinking and should be removed, hidden or overcome as soon as possible.

How, then, should we do justice to the paradox and think in terms of complexity, as Mireille Delmas-Marty invites us to do? A first approach might be that of a tranquil, or static, dialectic, aiming for a synthesis at equal distances from the two opposite poles. This is the strategy of the "golden mean", balance, conciliation and compromise. The merit of this approach is that it makes no secret of the tension between the two poles. Its weakness lies in the assumption that this can be held in check long enough to be able to arrive at a conciliatory synthesis. Life and history, however, are by definition forms of movement. It therefore follows that, apart from a brief "freeze-frame", any dialectic claiming to put an end to history would necessarily revert to a logic of simplification, which we know in certain circumstances can also be a totalitarian logic. Merleau-Ponty, a specialist in "dialectical adventures", and more particularly in the types claiming to be able to announce the end of history, has rightly concluded that the only good dialectic is one "without synthesis"[21].

This dialectic without synthesis is dynamic: its driving force is the recursive movement, or interaction if you prefer, which develops between two live poles. Only this can guarantee the "return of the third term", the third term excluded from the logic of simplicity: not a third option "*ex machina*" opposed to

---

[20] For more details, see F. Ost and M. van de Kerchove, "De la théorie de l'argumentation au paradigme du jeu. Quel entre-deux pour la pensée juridique?" in *Chaïm Perelman et la pensée contemporaine,* G. Haarscher (ed.), Brussels, 1993, 127 ff.

[21] M. Merleau-Ponty, "Interrogation et dialectique" in *Le visible et l'invisible*, Paris, 1964, 129-130.

the other two lumped together, but an internal third term analogous to a third dimension rising from the dialectical plane itself.

To our way of thinking, this dialectic without synthesis can claim to constitute the paradigm for a critical science of the law. This is, hypothetically, the function we allocate it in our work and some of whose capacities we shall try to set out in what follows.

For Thomas Kuhn, who popularised the use of the term "paradigm" in epistemology, a framework of thinking may warrant the term if it appears to provide an ontology, a methodology and an ethic. This appears to us to be the case with dialectics[22].

An ontology? In this respect we can repeat what Heraclitus has already said: dialectics teaches the negativeness of every object (which is, and is not, what it is) and the developmental nature of being (which becomes what it is).

A method? The systematic setting up of tension between complementary yet antagonistic elements. Demonstrating, in this process, that each term virtually includes its "other" and that these are therefore linked; following the patterns of their intertwinings and of, literally, their transformations; identifying in the common ground (in the general sense of "field" and not in the arithmetical sense of "average") of their relations the emergent and tertiary qualities which go on to contribute to their similar yet differentiated further reproduction; taking up the risk of uncertainty involved in the unprogrammed genesis so characteristic of complexity, life and history; liberating in this way the unheard-of heuristic power of the paradoxes that never cease to "make you think".

An ethic? As opposed to the fundamentalist claims to "the whole" – the whole truth, power, message or wealth – a dialectic reveals that identities are only relative and differences are never absolute. In so doing, it invites reasoned dialogue between different points of view. It opens up the way to a co-operative search for truth, on the basis of a diversity of opinions and assuming uncertainty in the result.

Between nihilist scepticism and dogmatic absolutism, it attempts to find a way – a "northwest passage", in Michael Serres' words – the way of the "informed third party" and of Hermes, towards an "open society" in which the law, certainly, has a part to play.

The development of a dialectical theory does not only allow us, as suggested above, to progress beyond a certain number of traditional dichotomies by which the history of general legal theory is divided into as many apparently inflexible schools of thought. It also allows us to surmount a multitude of binary oppositions throughout legal thinking which prevent it from grasping the

---

[22] F. Ost and M. van de Kerchove, "L'idée de jeu peut-elle prétendre au titre de paradigme de la science du droit?", *Revue interdisciplinaire d'études juridiques*, 1993, 191 ff.

complexity of the majority of practical legal phenomena. A number of examples should suffice to demonstrate the point.

A first type of opposition to divide legal thinking is that which isolates and gives pride of place exclusively to either the *strategic* or instrumental aspect of the law or its *representative* or symbolic aspect.

As illustrated particularly by classic utilitarian theories as well as more recent approaches of the economic variety, certain authors have no qualms, in the first place, about relying on only the strategic or instrumental aspect of the workings of the law, regarding every legal entity as a calculator aiming exclusively at maximising a vested personal interest[23] or regarding every court case as a "weighing-up of opposing interests"[24] or as a balance-sheet setting out the costs and benefits to be derived from the situation in question.

At the opposite extreme, however, other authors have taken to emphasising only the theatrical and spectacular side of the law. Some replace the idea of the calculating subject with the idea of the subject as actor, thus reducing the concept of the legal person to an individual aptitude for "playing a part in the legal drama"[25]. From the same viewpoint, court cases have been analysed not in strategic terms, but in symbolic terms, as a theatrical spectacle in which "the conflict can only be represented, enacted or rather re-enacted". Finally, the law's instrumental function has had its symbolic function set up in opposition to it, the assumption being that in many cases the legislator's intention has been not so much to ensure that the approved rules are obeyed and their related purpose achieved as to draw attention to the enactment of the rules itself, the drama and symbolic impact of which constitute the main purpose[26].

It is difficult, however, to avoid the idea that each of these approaches reveals the same radical flaw: reducing everything to an oversimplification. The complexity of the legal phenomenon in fact requires attention to be drawn to the

---

[23] See in particular R. Posner, *Economic Analysis of Law*, Boston/Toronto, 1986[3], 3-4. For a critical study of this type of approach, see A. Strowel, "Utilitarisme et approche économique dans la théorie du droit. Autour de Bentham et de Posner", *Revue interdisciplinaire d'études juridiques*, 1987, 1 ff.; id., "A la recherche de l'intérêt en économie. De l'utilitarisme à la science économique néo-classique" in *Droit et intérêt*, I, P. Gérard, F. Ost and M. van de Kerchove (eds.), Brussels, 1990, 37 ff.

[24] See in particular P. Heck, "Das Problem der Rechtsgewinnung" in *Das Problem der Rechtsgewinnung. Gesetzesauslegung und Interessenjurisprudenz*, R. Dubischar (ed.), Bad Homburg, 1968, 35. In this respect, see in particular M. Bürgisser and J.-F. Perrin, "Interessenjurisprudenz. Statut et interprétation de la loi dans l'histoire du mouvement" in *Droit et intérêt*, I, 327 ff.

[25] L. Raucent, *Pour une théorie critique du droit*, Gembloux, 1975, 272.

[26] See in particular G. Burdeau, *La politique au pays des merveilles*, Paris, 1979, 50; J.-P. Henry, "Vers la fin de l'État de droit?", *Revue de droit public et de science politique en France et à l'étranger*, 1977, 122-1227.

tensions which are continually being set up between these two poles and which help explain both the frequency of shifts and the diversity of combinations which reality requires us to face up to.

By way of illustration, we shall follow this viewpoint through to a consideration of its implications for the judicial process.

In taking account of the type of case to be considered, the traditional distinction between criminal trials and civil actions appears significant. Appealing much more directly and more openly to "society's moral interests than a civil case does, criminal trials are indeed "more theatrical by nature"[27]. The result is that "in a criminal trial, every effort is made for the spectator to identify negatively with the criminal by virtue of the way in which the crime and the criminal are represented" and of the "work of symbolic degradation by which the accused is presented as someone of a different type"[28]. In a civil case, on the other hand, it has been stated that "determining prices, assessing value, thinking up equivalents, these constitute the main preoccupation of the law"[29]. It must, however, be admitted that this sort of opposition is only relative. In fact, the presence in a criminal trial of "the physical person who is risking his neck" lends a "hybrid" air to the theatrical structure of the trial. It is a play into which an intruder enters (...). The presence of the protagonists shifts the trial irredeemably into theatre, but the physical presence of the accused pulls it up short of pure theatre and provides a counteracting force"[30]. On the other hand, it is clear that in a civil case, "the judicial ritual does not simply have an instrumental function", but "also proclaims in a symbolic way a certain order of justice characterised by the impartiality of the judge, equality of the contending parties and so on"[31].

To this it may be added that the relative importance of the instrumental and symbolic aspects of the court proceedings are likely to vary according to its different phases. With regard to criminal cases, for example, the investigative phase, like the prosecution phase, appears traditionally to be dominated by an instrumentalist logic. The basically "inquisitorial" nature of the pre-trial investigation, as it has been understood for several centuries now in the judicial systems with a Latin tradition in particular, has obviously reinforced this utilitarian aspect. We also know, however, that the intervention of the media has contributed to an increasing public interest in successive stages in the investigation, whose symbolic aspect has been considerably increased. As regards the prosecutor's role, his or her discretionary power also reinforces the idea that the prosecutor's job is primarily to carry out, after weighing up the interests

---

[27] A. Garapon, *L'âne portant des reliques. Essai sur le rituel judiciaire*, Paris, 1985, 20.
[28] Id., *ibid.*, 143.
[29] Id., *ibid.*, 25-26.
[30] Id., *ibid.*, 141.
[31] Id., *ibid.*, 165.

involved, a selection of those cases in which punishment appears to be more useful – more opportune – than letting things pass. Who would dare in this respect to deny that every act of prosecution is also a symbolic reinforcement of the value of the law that has been broken, or even, in certain extreme cases, that this is the essential function that it fulfils? The judgement phase, on the other hand, seems from its "accusatory" nature to transform the trial into a theatrical production whose aim is to present a certain picture of both the law and its transgression[32]. Who, however, would dare to claim that trials as we know them come up to the ideal cherished by such as Jeremy Bentham, in which the whole proceeding takes place "in effigy", *i.e.* as a form of pure representation, and in which the strategic defence of the real interests of the defendant, and even of society, would lose all purpose?

A second pair of opposite poles to provide a starting point from which to understand the phenomenon of the law is that of *co-operation* and *conflict*, of consensus and dissent.

Considered exclusively in turn as the expression of a uniform social conscience, or of an indefatigable class struggle, as a guarantor of harmonious industrial relations or, on the contrary, as the ultimate source of social conflict, the law should appear, it seems to us, in its basically "ambivalent" stature and be recognised as having an aspect which is both peace-orientated ("irénologique") and conflict-inducing ("polémogène")[33], to take up Julien Freund's terms. These aspects may be emphasised equally well as regards both the adoption of a rule of law and its enforcement.

The adoption of a rule of law, in the first place, involves this double aspect in varying degrees[34]. On the one hand it appears as a "determining principle of social consensus", inasmuch as it subjects all or some of the citizens to a general rule and constitutes, by virtue of this fact, a privileged instrument for the prevention and resolution of conflicts. On the other hand, however, this function will never be able to fully eradicate the importance of the conflicts, or at least the divergences, from which it has generally derived. Indeed, even if the rules relative to the production of norms are able to formalise and reduce the expression of

---

[32] Id., *ibid.* 145: "c'est une catharsis du délit et de la loi, de la transgression et de la répression".

[33] J. Freund, "Le droit comme motif et solution de conflits" in *Die Funktionen des Rechts*, L. Legaz y Lacambra (ed.), *A.R.S.P.*, 1974, 50.

[34] See in this respect P. Lascoumes, "Pluralité d'acteurs, pluralité d'actions dans la création contemporaine des lois" in *Acteur social et délinquance. Une grille de lecture du système de justice pénale. En hommage au Professeur Christian Debuyst*, F. Digneffe (ed.), Brussels/Liège, 1990, 145 ff.; Fr. Tulkens, "Les coups et blessures volontaires: approche historique et critique" in *ibid.*, 165 ff.; P. Landreville, "Acteur social et création de la loi" in *ibid.*, 215 ff. See also *La création de la loi et ses acteurs. L'exemple du droit pénal*, P. Robert (ed.), *Oñati proceedings*, Oñati, 1991.

these divergences to a certain extent, it remains true that such formalisation has its limits. Firstly, it is never wholly free from omissions and contradictions whose solution is likely to shift the conflict to another level. Secondly, the institution of a formal procedure does not exclude the possibility of its being outflanked and preceded in practice either by spontaneous use of more informal procedures, like direct negotiations between different interest groups, or by the uncontrolled expression of social antagonisms. Finally, it appears that, whatever the degree of consensus surrounding a judicial norm at the time when it was adopted, this situation is likely not to continue. In certain cases even, "in putting obstacles in the way of the constantly developing life of society by means of too strict a set of rules, (...) the law becomes in its turn a source of conflict (...), it disrupts social consensus and leads to revolts or explosions of violence"[35].

If we approach the problem of the application of the rule of law, and in particular its judicial application, a similar tension may be revealed.

If we consider the paradigmatic case of the jurisdictional act in a constitutional state, it is important to realise how much these two poles maintain extensive dialectic links with each other. As Julien Freund has very rightly suggested, it is even possible to state that "it is because the law is a source of conflict that it is also able to put an end to it"[36]. It is indeed because the parties are prepared to situate their conflict exclusively in the area of the law that they are led, on the one hand, to express more extremely the opposition between their respective claims rather than to look for an amicable way of settling them and, on the other hand, to reduce the scope of their conflict to its legal aspects alone, rather than to maintain it in all its psychological and social complexity. The "judicialisation" of conflicts therefore appears to be fundamentally ambivalent: far from being simply a "cooling-off" process for conflicts, it involves first the transformation from a problematical situation into a lawsuit whose form is both legal and conflictual, as the necessary prerequesite to any legal settlement. Although no longer considered to be "enemies" facing up to each other in a total and unregulated conflict, the litigants do not go so far as to become "partners", but are now "adversaries" involved in "winning" or "losing" the case *against* each other. The judicial "solution" to the court case therefore appears, as in any "zero-sum game" situation and despite any co-operative aspects involved, to bear the stamp of the antagonism that is present throughout the legal process. It is this ambivalence in the judicial resolution of lawsuits which in fact explains the periodical resurgence of so-called "alternative" ways of resolving conflicts, such as settlements[37] and mediation[38], which give more weight to negotiation than to

[35] J. Freund, "Le droit comme motif et solution de conflits", 55.

[36] J. Freund, *Sociologie du conflit*, Paris, 1983, 328.

[37] E. Serverin, P. Lascoumes and Th. Lambert, *Transactions et pratiques transactionnelles. Sujets et objets des transactions dans les relations conflictuelles de*

contention or more to conciliation and compromise than to a decision in favour of one side or the other. However, far from appearing to be a game from which all conflictual aspects have been excluded, played only between "partners" and in which everyone ends up a "winner"[39], it may reasonably be assumed that these processes aim, as in any "non-constant-sum game", at setting up paradoxical "partner/adversary" relations between the parties involved and at providing solutions in which, as implied in any form of compromise, these parties end up both "winners and losers".

The categories of reality and fiction have also traditionally represented a radical break in the theoretical approach to the phenomenon of the law. For some authors, the law belongs to the world of pure fact, as suggested in the teaching in various "realisms": Scandinavian realism, in which someone like Olivecrona studies "the law as fact"[40] and denounces the "magical" nature of legal constructions, or American realism, like that of Llewellyn, who is prepared to retain, as "real rules", only the practice of the courts, as opposed to the laws, which are relegated to the rank of "paper rules"[41].

For others, on the contrary, the law is pure discourse or text, whose function is to maintain the illusion or mystification of a basic fiction – that of the good authority or the good law, deserving of our love. As Pierre Legendre, for example writes: "Authority's grand aim is to be loved. The achievement of this prodigy has always entailed a specific branch of knowledge (that of the law), to set up this form of adoration while using its textual form as a pattern to cover up the conjuring trick, which is based on training pure and simple"[42].

Between the platitude of behaviourist realism and the systematic suspicion of radicalised depth psychology, between too much reality on the one hand and too little on the other, there must surely be room for a more subtle approach to the workings of the law. Like a game, the law insinuates its own possibilities into, and sometimes imposes them on, reality. It launches new meanings, it sets up

---

droit privé et de droit public, Paris, 1987.

[38] In this respect, see in particular *Les paradoxes de la médiation, Annales de Vaucresson*, 1988; J.-P. Bonafé-Schmitt, *La médiation: l'autre justice*, Lyon, 1992; *La médiation: un mode alternatif de résolution des conflits? (Lausanne 14 and 15 November 1991)*, Zürich, 1992.

[39] Such at least is the idealised picture painted by a certain number of the advocates of mediation. In this respect, see in particular J. Folberg and A. Taylor, *Mediation. A comprehensive guide to resolving conflicts without litigation*, San Francisco/ Washington/London, 1984, 10.

[40] K. Olivecrona, *Law as Fact*, London, 1971[2].

[41] K. W. Llewellyn, "A Realistic Jurisprudence, the Next Step" (1930) in *Jurisprudence. Texts and Readings on the Philosophy of Law*, G. Christie (ed.), Saint-Paul, 1973, 1099-1100.

[42] P. Legendre, *L'amour du censeur. Essai sur l'ordre dogmatique*, Paris, 1974, 5.

institutions and specific rules. "Everything, in legal rules, is a construct", wrote Jean Dabin. This legal surreality does not just extend to the re-construction of a prior natural or social fact. It also implies the "production of an object". In order to render things conform and reduce them to its own prescription, the law imbues them with content and form: sometimes this involves giving form to what is as yet formless, sometimes (undoubtedly more often) it involves de-forming what already has form and content in a different context.

Such is undoubtedly the essential function of legal order: more important than its coercive function (prohibition – punishment) to which it has often been reduced, or its regulatory-organisational function with which it is willingly identified today, it is this denominating function that typifies the law. This denomination entails both regulation and institutionalisation in the sense that here, in real terms, "things are done with words". The law recognises persons and things. Literally, it imbues them with legal existence. As it denominates, orders and ranks, the law allocates legal roles to the various actors in the life of society. To each particular status it attaches rights and duties, responsibilities and privileges. A status may be seen as the extension of factual reality, as in the case of parenthood attributed to the biological progenitors of a child. Sometimes, however, it may constitute a break in this respect, as in the case of adoption ("fictitious" parenthood). In all cases, however, this legal status is in turn bound to reflect on the different levels of real life.

In setting up this legal "surreality" different techniques are involved, including the numerous resources of legal conceptualism and the adoption of what Searle calls "constitutive rules".

It is the legal fictions, however, that reveal the artificiality of the law most clearly. Classical legal scholars pretend to believe that fictions are a misunderstood or perverted form of reality, and that it should be possible to ignore them and arrive directly and without contrivance at reality as it is. But, since this reality is bound to get away, because it can only ever be the product of a conventional denomination, fictions appear less of a flaw in, than indicators of the nature of legal discourse. In a sense backing up the fiction, turning it against itself (in the form of a fiction of a fiction), it reveals its essential performativity: both the impossibility of expressing the (natural) fact and the ability to produce the (legal) fact. Such is the paradox of legal language, which, as it expresses its incongruence with regard to the facts, endows itself with a certain power over them. Such too is the virtue of a dialectical theory in that it provides, between the opacity of a silent reality and the inconsistency of a deceitful unreality, a view of the richness of the surreal, narrative and performative universe created by the law.

The dialectic of *regulation* and *indeterminateness*, as well as that of stability and change, is also largely apparent in the judicial field. One of its most significant instances involves the classic but central question in legal thinking of the interpretation of prescriptive texts. We have steadfastly attempted to think of this question in terms of linking dialectically the aspects that many schools oppose to each other in a Manichaean way: as long as reasoning rests on the opposing myths of the judge as "pronouncer of the law" or of the "government of judges", there will be no understanding of the real process of interpretation[43]. Like language itself, whose meaningful activity it shares, interpretation *combines* constraint and liberty, at the level both of the rules to be interpreted (since no text, however authoritative or clear it may claim to be, is free of the need for interpretation) and of the dictates governing the process of interpretation (since, being rules themselves, there is no reason for thinking that they escape interpretation).

The very etymology of the terms "hermeneutics" and "interpretation" points up this bipolar status and evokes mediation and communication in the space governed by the two poles. Interpretation links together the author and the reader, technical language and everyday language, past drafting and present application, the subjectivity of the author and the objectivity of the message he produces, the abstract nature of a rule and the concrete nature of a single situation. Interpretation itself is a linking of the parts to the whole (the word and the sentence, the sentence and the chapter, the chapter and the complete book). Even more fundamentally, interpretation sets up a mediation between a primary, explicit but not entirely satisfactory meaning and a secondary meaning more in line with a given expectation, such as the justice of the solution.

In all these cases, the process is never one of a pure and simple decoding, of a strict matching of equivalents. In the course of the process there is transformation and therefore production of meaning – deconstruction and reconstruction. It therefore constitutes neither the simple reproduction of an already stated meaning nor the free invention of an as yet unformulated meaning: the meaning cannot be assigned to any particular point in the chain of communication, to which in fact no one (be it the constituant assembly or the supreme court) has the key and on which no one has the last word. Legal meaning is simply the chain itself, the uninterrupted and recursive pursuit of the interpretative process. This means that each interpreter is both free and constrained: free by virtue of the various openings in the language, constrained by the structure, both discursive and legal, of the field concerned[44].

A final pair of opposite poles remains for our attention here: the inside and the outside, the *internal* and the *external*. To illustrate the value of a dialectical

---

[43] On this question, see in particular F. Ost and M. van de Kerchove, *Entre la lettre et l'esprit. Les directives d'interprétation en droit*, Brussels, 1989; id., *Jalons pour une théorie critique du droit*, Brussels, 1987, 355-456; *L'interprétation en droit. Approche pluridisciplinaire*, M. van de Kerchove (ed.), Brussels, 1978.

[44] On these discursive and legal constraints, see F. Ost and M. van de Kerchove, *Jalons pour une théorie critique du droit*, 361-398.

approach to these, a reference to the question of the foundation of legal systems should suffice.

Two diametrically opposed answers have been given to this question, which has sometimes been represented as the "ABC" of legal thinking. Either it is claimed, on the side of natural law doctrine, that this foundation must necessarily be external to the law itself, as the only way of escaping from the paradoxes involved in self-reference and to endow the law with a true criterion of legitimacy. The law is then justified meta-legally: in divine will, natural order, reason, the national interest or any other hypostatised keyword. Others, on the contrary, will try to show that the power of the law derives from its own authority. The Kelsenian basic norm, the final point of legal positivism, constitutes the most complete, if not the most convincing example of this attempt.

But, to tell the truth, neither of these positions appears fully satisfactory. Invoking an external foundation means opening the door to a *regressio ad infinitum* (what is the basis of this basis, the origin behind this origin?) and leaving unexplained the principle of the operational closure specific to the legal order with such a "foundation". Conversely, claiming an internal foundation for the law means opening the door to all the *aporiae* of a *causa sui.*

The eternal swinging back and forth of legal thinking between natural law doctrine and legal positivism bears adequate witness to the fact that it is equally pointless to claim to base the law on the law as on non-law. It surely follows from this that it is the search for a foundation itself, the attempt to locate the final bedrock, that should be questioned, insofar as this constitutes the common assumption, albeit implicit, shared by the two opposing philosophies of legal positivism and natural law doctrine. The 20th century, as Jean Ladrière has recalled, has put an end to the idea of a search for basics, whether in the fields of speculative philosophy or of formal and empirical sciences. The aim of uncovering an ultimate origin has everywhere given way to progressive awareness of the paradox of the basis that can only be understood by means of its subtraction[45]. It is the radical dichotomy between founder and founded which then appears inadmissible, the absolute difference in character between two instances that no game, no bipolarity, no third term can bring closer together. The concept of complexity, on the contrary, leads to acceptance of the idea that a system is always both itself and something other than itself, itself and its own alternative. Instead of radical exteriorisation or an absolute beginning, it is rather a continuum which is revealed. Instead of a binary and inflexible opposition of terms, it is the interweaving of opposites which suggests itself. Authority, in a certain sense, founds itself, but this is conceivable only because authority, the governor, contains its own alternative: the individual, the governed. But if the governors

---

[45] J. Ladrière, "L'abîme" in *Savoir, faire, espérer. Les limites de la raison*, I, Brussels, 1976, 171 ff.

encompass the governed, the converse is also true: the individual is always part of the social structure and exists only to the extent of identifying him/herself with those in authority. Such in any case is the paradoxical lesson to be learned from the democratic concept of authority.

Undoubtedly, traditional legal thinking has tried, in a dogmatic way, to cover up such a paradox, in drawing clear boundaries between the interior and the exterior (legal and extra-legal), in adopting a reassuring chronology (pre-legal, legal and post-legal), in imposing a linear hierarchy (supra-legal, legal, infra-legal) and modelling itself on the rules of a logic of identity (legal is legal; legal is not non-legal).

As opposed to this kind of perspective, however, a dialectical idea of foundation leads to a bottomless condition, the winding-up into a coil of a game that continues to play itself, of a law that continues to regulate itself, in that it is always both itself and other than itself.

Bibliographical Information[1]

I. Publications setting out the general approach

1. *Jalons pour une théorie critique du droit*, Brussels, 1987.
2. *Le système juridique entre ordre et désordre*, Paris, 1988.
Legal System Between Order and Disorder, I. Stewart (transl.), Oxford, 1994.
4. *Le droit ou les paradoxes du jeu*, Paris, 1992.
Il diritto o vero i paradossi del gioco, S. Andrini and G. Lucidi (transl.), Milan, 1995.

II. Legal science

5. "Possibilités et limites d'une science du droit", *Revue interdisciplinaire d'études juridiques*, 1978, 1-39.
6. M. van de Kerchove, "Der Einfluss der reinen Rechtslehre auf die Rechtstheorie in Frankreich und Belgien" in *Die Einfluss der reinen Rechtslehre auf die Rechtstheorie in verschiedenen Ländern*, Vienna, 1978, 113-136.
7. "Défense et illustration d'une distinction", *Droit et société. Revue internationale de théorie du droit et de sociologie juridique*, 1986, 137-139.
8. "Comment concevoir aujourd'hui la science du droit?", *Déviance et société*, 1987, 183-193.
9. M. van de Kerchove, "L'influence de Kelsen sur les théories du droit dans l'Europe francophone" in H. Kelsen, *Théorie pure du droit*, H. Thévenaz (transl.), Neuchâtel, 1988², 225-288.
10. "De la scène au balcon. D'où vient la science du droit?" in *Normes juridiques et régulation sociale*, F. Chazel and J. Commaille (eds.), Paris, 1991, 67-80.
11. F. Ost, "Sobre la ciencia del derecho", *Revista de ciencias juridicas*, 1992, 125-147.
12. F. Ost, "Science du droit" in *Dictionnaire encyclopédique de théorie et de sociologie du droit*, A.-J. Arnaud e.a. (eds.), Paris, 1993², 540-544.
13. F. Ost and M. Van Hoecke, "Epistemological perspectives in legal theory", *Ratio Juris*, 1993, 30-47.

III. Interdisciplinary research in law

14. F. Ost, "Questions méthodologiques à propos de la recherche interdisciplinaire en droit", *Revue interdisciplinaire d'études juridiques*, 1981, 1-29.
15. "Pour une épistémologie de la recherche interdisciplinaire en droit. Avant-propos", *Revue interdisciplinaire d'études juridiques*, 1982, 1-7.

---

[1] Unless indicated otherwise, all publications are written together by F. Ost and M. van de Kerchove.

16. "Toward an Interdisciplinary Theory of Law" in *Theory of Legal Science*, A. Peczenik, L. Lindahl and B. van Roermund (eds.), Dordrecht/Lancaster/ London, 1984, 497-508.
17. F. Ost, "Dogmatique juridique et science interdisciplinaire du droit", *Rechtstheorie*, 1986, 89-110.

IV. The paradigms of legal science

18. "Rationalité et souveraineté du législateur, 'paradigmes' de la dogmatique juridique?", *Rivista internazionale di filosofia del diritto*, 1985, 227-251
19. "De la 'bipolarité des erreurs' ou de quelques paradigmes de la science du droit", *Archives de philosophie du droit*, 1988, 177-206.
20. "Le jeu: un paradigme fécond pour la théorie du droit?" in *Le jeu: un paradigme fécond pour le droit*, F. Ost and M. van de Kerchove (eds.), Paris, 1992, 239-276.
21. F. Ost, "Pour une théorie ludique du droit", *Droit et société. Revue internationale de théorie du droit et de sociologie juridique*, 1992, 89-98.
22. "De la théorie de l'argumentation au paradigme du jeu. Quel entre-deux pour la pensée juridique?", *Revue interdisciplinaire d'études juridiques*, 1991, 77-98.
23. "L'idée de jeu peut-elle prétendre au titre de paradigme de la science juridique?" in *Law at the Turn of the 20th Century*, L. E. Kotsiris (ed.), Thessaloniki, 1994, 115-142.

V. The definition of law and the different forms of legality

24. "Juris-dictio et définition du droit", *Droits. Revue française de théorie juridique*, 1989, 53-57.
25. M. van de Kerchove, "Les différentes formes de baisse de la pression juridique et leurs principaux enjeux", *Cahiers de recherche sociologique*, 1989, 11-28.
26. F. Ost, "Jupiter, Hercule ou Hermès. Quel modèle pour un droit postmoderne?", *Journal des procès*, 1990, no. 179, 14 ff. and no. 180, 19 ff.

VI. Legal rationality

27. J. Lenoble and F. Ost, *Le droit occidental contemporain et ses présupposés épistémologiques*, Paris, 1977.
28. J. Lenoble and F. Ost, "Prolégomènes à une lecture épistémologique des modèles juridiques" in *Domination ou partage? Développement endogène et transfert des connaissances*, B. Ribes (ed.), Paris, 1980, 79-91.
29. J. Lenoble and F. Ost, *Droit, mythe et raison. Essai sur la dérive mythologique de la rationalité juridique*, Brussels, 1980.
30. J. Lenoble and F. Ost, "Rationalité juridique et mythes fondateurs" in *Conceptions contemporaines du droit. Actes du 9ième Congrès mondial de l'I.V.R. (Basel 1979)*, P. Trappe (ed.), *A.R.S.P.*, supplementa, I, 1, 519-535.

31. F. Ost, *Bonnes moeurs, discours pénal et rationalité juridique. Essai d'analyse critique*, Brussels, 1981.
32. M. van de Kerchove, "Jurisprudence et rationalité juridique", *Archives de philosophie du droit*, 1985, 207-242.
33. "La référence à Dieu dans la théorie pure du droit de Hans Kelsen" in *Qu'est-ce que Dieu? Philosophie/théologie. Hommage à l'abbé Daniel Coppieters de Gibson (1929-1983)*, Brussels, 1985, 285-324.
34. "La referencia a Dios en la teoria pura del derecho de Hans Kelsen" in *Materiales para una teoria critica del derecho*, E. Mari e.a. (eds.), Buenos Aires, 1991, 73-116.
35. "L'outrage aux bonnes moeurs: révélateur d'une rationalité juridique de moins en moins assurée" in *Les bonnes moeurs*, J. Chevallier (ed.), Paris, 1994, 105-124.

VII. Interpreting the law

36. M. van de Kerchove, "La doctrine du sens clair des textes et la jurisprudence de la Cour de cassation de Belgique" in *L'interprétation en droit. Approche pluridisciplinaire*, M. van de Kerchove (ed.), Brussels, 1978, 13-50.
37. F. Ost, "L'interprétation logique et systématique et le postulat de rationalité du législateur" in *L'interprétation en droit. Approche pluridisciplinaire*, M. van de Kerchove (ed.), Brussels, 1978, 97-184.
38."Le 'jeu' de l'interprétation en droit. Contribution à l'étude du langage juridique", *Archives de philosophie du droit*, 1982, 395-409.
39. M. van de Kerchove, "Le sens clair d'un texte: argument de raison ou d'autorité?" in *Arguments d'autorité et arguments de raison en droit*, G. Haarscher, L. Ingber and R. Vander Elst (eds.), Brussels, 1988, 291-315.
40. F. Ost, "Originalité des méthodes d'interprétation de la Cour européenne des droits de l'homme" in *Raisonner la raison d'Etat. Vers une Europe des droits de l'homme*, M. Delmas-Marty (ed.), Paris, 1989, 405-463.
41. M. van de Kerchove, "La théorie des actes de langage et la théorie de l'interprétation juridique" in *Théorie des actes de langage, éthique et droit*, P. Amselek (ed.), Paris, 1986, 211-248.
42. *Entre la lettre et l'esprit. Les directives d'interprétation en droit*, Brussels, 1989.
43. "La lettre et l'esprit. Un siècle de doctrine belge relative à l'interprétation de la loi" in *Liber memorialis François Laurent 1810-1887*, J. Erauw e.a. (eds.), Brussels, 1989, 395-421.
44. "Interprétation", *Archives de philosophie du droit*, 1990, 165-190.
45. "L'interprétation téléologique: un objectif clair et distinct?" in *Le recours aux objectifs de la loi dans son application,* II, P. Orianne (ed.), Brussels, 1990, 303-324.

46. F. Ost, "L'herméneutique juridique entre hermétisme et dogmatisme. Le jeu de l'interprétation en droit", *Revue internationale de sémiotique juridique*, 1993, 227-247.
47. "Les colonnes d'Hermès: à propos des directives d'interprétation en droit" in *Interprétation et droit*, P. Amselek (ed.), Brussels/Aix-Marseille, 1995, 135-153.

VIII. Validity in law

48. F. Ost, "Le code et le dictionnaire. Acceptabilité linguistique et validité juridique", *Sociologie et sociétés*, 1986, 59-75.
49. F. Ost, "Essai de définition et de caractérisation de la validité juridique" in *Droit et Pouvoir*, I, *La validité*, A. Berten e.a. (eds.), Brussels, 1987, 97-132.
50. M. van de Kerchove, "Les lois pénales sont-elles appliquées? Réflexions sur les phénomènes de dissociation entre la validité formelle et l'effectivité des normes juridiques" in *Droit et Pouvoir*, I, *La validité*, A. Berten e.a. (eds.), Brussels, 1987, 327-346.
51. M. van de Kerchove, "Las leyes penales estan hechas para ser aplicadas? Reflexiones sobre los fenomenos de la separacion entre validez formal y eficacia de las normas juridicas", *Nuevo foro penal*, 1990, 181-198.
52. F. Ost, "Validité" in *Dictionnaire encyclopédique de théorie et de sociologie du droit*, A.-J. Arnaud e.a. (eds.), Paris, 1993^2, 635-639.

IX. The function of judging and the different methods of resolving conflicts

53. F. OST, "Juge-pacificateur, juge-arbitre, juge-entraîneur. Trois modèles de justice" in *Fonction de juger et pouvoir judiciaire. Transformations et déplacements*, P. Gérard, F. Ost and M. van de Kerchove (eds.), Brussels, 1983, 1-70.
54. F. Ost, "Entre jeu et providence: le juge des relations économiques" in *La magistrature économique et la crise*, A. Jacquemin and B. Remiche (eds.), Brussels, 1984, 37-89.
55. F. Ost, "Quelle jurisprudence, pour quelle société?", *Archives de Philosophie du Droit*, 1985, 9-34.
56. F. Ost, "Rapport général de synthèse" in *Les conflits collectifs du travail. Solutions négociées ou interventions judiciaires?*, J. Gillardin and P. Van der Vorst (eds.), Brussels, 1989, 109-131.
57. "Les rôles du judiciaire et le jeu du droit" in *Acteur social et délinquance. Une grille de lecture du système de justice pénale. En hommage au Professeur Christian Debuyst,* F. Digneffe (ed.), Brussels/Liège, 1990, 271-293.
58. F. Ost, "Jupiter, Hercule, Hermès: trois modèles du juge" in *La force du droit. Panorama des débats contemporains*, P. Bouretz (ed.), Paris, 1991, 241-272.
59. F. Ost, "Jupiter, Hercules y Hermes: tres modelos de juez", *Doxa*, 1993, 169-194.

60. F. Ost, "La jurisprudence de la Cour européenne des droits de l'homme: amorce d'un nouveau 'ius commune'?" in *Le droit commun de l'Europe et l'avenir de l'enseignement juridique*, B. De Witte and C. Forder (eds.), Deventer, 1992, 683-720.
61. M. van de Kerchove, "Médiation et législation" in *La médiation: un mode alternatif de résolution des conflits? (Lausanne, 14 and 15 November 1991)*, Zürich, 1992, 331-349.
62. F. Ost, "Justice aveugle, medias voyeurs", *Juger*, 1995, 101-114.
63. M. van de Kerchove, "Médiation et conciliation en droit pénal" in *Le contentieux interdisciplinaire*, G. De Leval, P. Lewalle and M. Storme, Brussels, 1996, 30-43.
64. M. van de Kerchove and F. Tulkens, "La justice pénale: justice imposée, justice participative, justice consensuelle ou justice négociée", *Revue de droit pénal et de criminologie*, 1996, 445-494.

X. The legal system

65."Creation and Application of Law: a Circular Structure?" in *The Structure of Law. Proceedings of the 2nd Benelux-Scandinavian Symposium in Legal Theory, Uppsala, 11-13 December 1986*, Å. Frändberg and M. Van Hoecke (eds.), Uppsala, 1987, 179-187.
66. F. Ost, "Entre ordre et désordre: le jeu du droit. Discussion du paradigme autopoiétique appliqué au droit", *Archives de philosophie du droit*, 1986, 133-162.
67. F. Ost, "Between Order and Disorder: the Game of Law" in *Autopoietic Law: a New Approach to Law and Society*, G. Teubner (ed.), Berlin/New York, 1988, 70-96.
68. "Auto-organisation des systèmes juridiques et hiérarchie des normes" in *Technologies et symboliques de la communication*, L. Sfez and G. Coutlée (eds.), Grenoble, 1990, 335-354.
69. F. Ost, "Le droit comme pur système" in *La force du droit. Panorama des débats contemporains*, P. Bouretz (ed.), Paris, 1991, 139-162.
70. "En quel sens les systèmes juridiques sont-ils autonomes?" in *Laws and Rights. Proceedings of the International Congress of Sociology of Law for the Ninth Centenary of the University of Bologna, May 30 - June 3, 1988*), II, V. Ferrari and C. Faralli (eds.), Milan, 1993, 355-369.

XI. Human rights

71. M. van de Kerchove, "Les droits de l'homme devant la violence instituée. Réflexions sur la 'douce violence'" in *La violence sociale*, H. Declève e.a. (eds.), Louvain-la-Neuve, 1983, 89-115.

72. F. Ost, “Actualité des droits de l'homme dans la crise de l'Etat-providence. Questions pour introduire un débat”, *Revue interdisciplinaire d'études juridiques*, 1984, 3-9.
73. F. Ost, “La conciliation des libertés”, *Journal des tribunaux*, 1985, 361-366.
74. F. Ost, “Théorie de la justice et droit à l'aide sociale” in *Individu et justice sociale. Autour de John Rawls*, F. Terré (ed.), Paris, 1988, 245-275.
75. F. Ost, “Le concept de 'démocratie' dans la jurisprudence de la Cour européenne des droits de l'homme”, *Journal des procès*, 1988, no. 124, 13-19.
76. F. Ost, “Ecologie et droits de l'homme”, *Journal des procès*, 1992, no. 226, 12-15.

XII. Ethics and the law

77. M. van de Kerchove, “Le problème des fondements éthiques de la norme juridique et le déclin du principe de légalité” in *La loi dans l'éthique chrétienne*, M. Kleiber e.a. (eds.), Brussels, 1981, 39-85.
78. F. Ost, “La légitimité dans le discours juridique: cohérence, performance, consensus ou dissensus?”, *A.R.S.P*, 1984, 191-204.
79. M. van de Kerchove, “L'Etat et la morale. Pour une éthique de l'intervention pénale” in *La souveraineté en question. Etat-Nation-Etat de droit*”, J. Etienne and P. Watté (eds.), Louvain-la-Neuve, 1988, 105-125.
80. M. van de Kerchove, “Pour une éthique de l'intervention du droit pénal, entre moralisme et instrumentalisme” in *Variations sur l'éthique. En hommage à Jacques Dabin*, Brussels, 1994, 449-467.
81. F. Ost, “Après nous le déluge? Réflexions sur la responsabilité écologique à l'égard des générations suivantes” in *Variations sur l'éthique. En hommage à Jacques Dabin*, Brussels, 1994, 389-411.
82. M. van de Kerchove, “Ethique pénale” in *Dictionnaire d'éthique et de philosophie morale*, M. Canto-Sperber (ed.), Paris, 1996, 1108-1114.

XIII. Law and temporality

83. F. Ost, “Les multiples temps du droit” in *Le droit et le futur*, F. Terré (ed.), Paris, 1985, 115-153.
84. F. Ost, “Temporal Pluralism and Legal Relativism. Contribution to the Study of De-legalisation” in *Law as an Instrument of Economic Policy: Comparative and Critical Approaches*, T. Daintith (ed.), Berlin/New York, 1988, 322-356.
85. F. Ost, “Temporalité juridique” in *Dictionnaire encyclopédique de théorie et de sociologie du droit*, A.-J. Arnaud e.a. (eds.), Paris, 1993[2], 607-609.
86. “Pluralisme temporel et changement. Les jeux du droit” in *Nouveaux itinéraires en droit. Hommage à François Rigaux*, Brussels, 1993, 387-411.
87. M. van de Kerchove, “Accélération de la justice pénale et traitement en 'temps réel'”, *Journal des procès,* 1996, no. 311, 10-13 and no. 312, 14-16.

88. F. Ost, "Mémoire et pardon, promesse et remise en question. La déclinaison éthique des temps juridiques" in *Le temps et le droit. Actes du 4e Congrès international de l'Association internationale de méthodologie juridique*, P.-A. Côté and J. Frémont (eds.), Cowansville, 1996, 15-31.

XIV. Codification

89. F. Ost, "Codification et temporalité dans la pensée de J. Bentham" in *Actualité de la pensée juridique de Jeremy Bentham*, P. Gérard, F. Ost and M. van de Kerchove (eds.), Brussels, 1987, 163-230.

90. M. van de Kerchove and F. Tulkens, "Un nouveau code pénal? Conclusions", *Journal des procès,* 1987, no. 116, 1987, 56-64.

91. F. Ost, "La codification, une technique juridique pour aujourd'hui?" in *L'Etat propulsif. Contribution à l'étude des instruments d'action de l'Etat*, Ch.-A. Morand (ed.), Paris, 1991, 237-252.

XV. Law and interest

92. F. Ost, *Entre droit et non-droit: l'intérêt* in *Droit et intérêt*, II, F. Ost and P. Gérard (eds.), Brussels, 1990.

93. M. van de Kerchove, "L'intérêt à la répression et l'intérêt à la réparation dans le procès pénal" in *Droit et intérêt*, III, P. Gérard, F. Ost and M. van de Kerchove, Brussels, 1990, 271-293.

THE PASSION FOR REASON

ALEKSANDER PECZENIK

UNVERSITY OF LUND/SWEDEN

1. The Background

1.1. Law, Power and Morality

Moral values play a great role in legal argumentation and decision making. To be sure, both are based on such institutional sources as statutes, precedents, legislative history etc. Yet, even justice is obviously relevant in legal reasoning. This has been the case since times immemorial, *e.g.* in Rome (where the common law, *ius gentium* was supposed to express justice), England (law and equity) and also Scandinavia ("*lov*" and "*dom*"). In modern law, the statutes are sometimes "read" in the way alien to a layman, in order to obtain reasonable decisions.

To be sure, no moral evaluation is necessary to solve routine cases. A decision in such a case follows from an established legal rule together with the description of the case. A "hard case" requires, however, a moral deliberation, which can justify a deviation from the wording of the law. The decision follows from a set of statements consisting of the legal rule in question, interpreted literally or adjusted, the description of the case and a reasonable (though not indubitable) additional premise. Such an addition can consist of a norm- or value-statement. Another interesting fact is the existence of the so-called legal dogmatics ("*Rechtswissenschaft*", "*Rechtsdogmatik*", "science of law", legal doctrine), consisting of professional legal writing, whose task is to systematise and interpret valid law.

The interpretation is almost always value-laden. To be sure, the jurists make a distinction between a cognitive inquiry into the law as it is (*de lege lata*), and justified recommendations for the lawgiver, *de lege ferenda*. But as every legal scholar knows, the distinction between *de lege lata* and *de lege ferenda* is not clear-cut. The legal doctrine is a good example of a practice of argumentation, pursuing knowledge of the law, yet in many cases leading to a change of the law.

1.2. Legal Realism

No wonder that generations of legal realists repeatedly "deconstructed" legal argumentation, both in legal practice and in legal dogmatics, as a mere facade, concealing the fact that the lawyers exercise power. From the beginning of the 20th century, legal realism presented itself in many countries, not the least in the United States and Scandinavia.

An important version of a psychological legal realism exerted a great influence upon Polish legal theory. Leon Petrazycki[1] an original theoretical system covering moral and legal philosophy, theory of science, psychology and sociology. Petrazycki's ontology was materialist in a broad sense: values did not exist. A materialist and, at the same time, adequate theory of law must be psychological.

The law is the same as legal impulsions ("emotions"). Legal rules are mere "impulsive phantasms", *i.e.* projections of shared legal impulsions. Legal dogmatics makes the law more uniform and better adapted to its social function to create peace. It uses analogy, induction, conceptual analysis and deduction in an as precise way as possible. But it is not an adequate scientific theory. Petrazycki was able to explain nearly all facts known about the evolution of law since the Roman times. Yet, legal institutions cannot be fully described in an individually psychological manner.

Petrazycki influenced works of two grand men of Polish legal theory, Kazimierz Opalek and Jerzy Wróblewski. It would lead us too far to attempt an analysis of their contribution to jurisprudence. Let it be enough to say that they both participated in a seminar in Cracow, led in the fifties by Jerzy Lande, for whom Petrazycki was the prophet. Via Opalek and Wróblewski, the atmosphere was created in Poland, in which it would be impossible to do legal theory without taking position for or against legal realism. Opalek was also a personal friend of Alf Ross.

Here, we go to another chapter of the Realist story, the Scandinavian one. Let me deal briefly with its evolution, from Hägerström to Olivecrona and Alf Ross[2]. The founder of the so-called Uppsala School, Axel Hägerström, built up his theory around the following theses concerning reality. All knowledge concerns something real. Only one reality exists and it includes objects located in time and space. A human being is thus real, since she exists during a certain time, and always occupies some position in space. Mental processes exist because they are indirectly related to time and space: people experience them as existing in time and space.

Time and space are objective. What cannot be placed in time and space does not exist. The reason why some concepts cannot be thus placed is their self-contradictory character. According to Hägerström, value concepts like "good", "beautiful" etc. are self-contradictory, if interpreted in an objectivist manner. They apparently tell something about the objects (*e.g.*, "this picture is beautiful")

---

[1] For references, see A. Peceznik, "Review: J. Wróblewski, *Sadowe stosowanie prawa & Wartosci a decyzja sadowa*", *Rechtstheorie*, 1975, 247-251.

[2] For references, see id, *On Law and Reason*, Dordrecht/Boston/London, 1989, 258.

but in fact they do not do it at all, and merely express feelings (such as one's admiration of the picture). Moreover, value statements lack truth-values, since they "describe" something outside of time and space. The value "existing" in an object, *e.g.*, goodness "existing" in it, does not exist in any definite sense at all.

All this sounds quite convincing. However, legal realism left some unsolved problems. Firstly, its philosophical foundations are controversial. Legal realism shows a skeptical attitude towards many concepts used in the everyday life, such as "valid law", "rights" and "values". But the ultimate basis for this form of skepticism is another concept, the concept of reality, solely composed of facts extant in time and space.

From the analysis of this concept, the legal realists derive their criticism of fundamental concepts of law. But what makes the concept of reality better established than the legal concepts[3]? Second, the consequences of legal realism are fatal. Any theory that regards valid law as a product of fantasy creates an unbridgeable gap between ordinary beliefs of the lawyers and legal philosophy. A lawyer has to use such concepts as "valid law" and "rights". A legal philosopher, meanwhile, tells him that their use was objectionable. This gap may easily cause professional frustration, leading to a retardation of legal dogmatics. A great American legal realist thus concluded with resignation: "A right man cannot be a man and feel himself a trickster or a charlatan"[4].

When I started my work in jurisprudence in the early sixties, legal realism had already seen its best days. The majority of the present-day philosophers of law do not bother about the Realists. Legal scholars, not the least in Sweden, use a language, which vaguely echoes Hägerström (talking about "evaluations", never about "values", using the word "natural law" as a contempt, etc.) but, as much as possible, avoid philosophical problems. Judges and legal practitioners regard legal scholars as moderately useful informers, but do not want to read grand theories. In the meantime, the ontological, epistemological and methodological questions posed by legal realism remain unsolved and almost forgotten. The ostrich has its head firmly in the sand.

This is a challenge: must we forget what is difficult to solve? Cannot we answer these questions in a better way than the legal realists themselves did?

1.3. Post-Realist Dilemmas

Many law theorists respond to this situation by adopting an external point of view. Instead of approaching philosophical problems involved in the law, they merely identify the problems and list various philosophical positions. Jerzy Wróblewski was perhaps the most important example. Wróblewski was one of

---

[3] See section 7.5 below.

[4] K. N. Llewellyn, *The Common Law Tradition. Deciding Appeals*, Boston/Toronto, 1960, 4.

my teachers, perhaps the most important one. My review of his works[5] was a respectful rebellion against the views of the master.

Others prefer not to speak about moral and legal knowledge. For example, Ronald Dworkin advocates a "constructive model", not a "natural model". Whereas the natural model deals with moral and legal knowledge, the constructive model focuses on responsibility. "The constructive model (...) demands that we act of principle rather than on faith. Its engine is a doctrine of responsibility that requires men to integrate their intuitions and subordinate some of these, when necessary, to that responsibility"[6]. Indeed, cannot one regard the ultimate basis of moral and legal justification as political rather than epistemological? Yet, if one discovers what responsibility requires of us, then one surely obtains knowledge about what responsibility requires of us. Dworkin wants to have a model without ontology, and perhaps even without epistemology. But, in my opinion, such a model must hover in the air.

If this is the case, a serious doubt occurs as regards the recent trend to let political theory colonise legal theory. In the continental tradition, much of legal theory dealt with epistemological questions concerning legal knowledge. The presently dominating philosophers of law – not only Dworkin but also such thinkers as Rawls, Habermas, Raz etc. – focus rather on political legitimacy. But they cannot escape epistemological questions concerning their own theories of political legitimacy.

2. The Problem

2.1. Meaning of Norm- and Value-Statements

A serious criticism of legal realism must start with recalling the strong side of this movement. Namely, the legal realists (and moral emotivists) have made an important point: norm-expressive statements and value statements statements have, first of all, a practical meaning, related to emotions and actions. One of formal properties of practical meaning of norm-expressive statements can be grasped in terms of qualification. Thus, these statements qualify human actions, events etc. as prescribed, permitted, forbidden etc. I disregard here more complex types of normative qualification.

"Forbidden", "prescribed" and "permitted" are words expressing a qualification (albeit that this is not their whole meaning). One can regard normative qualification as, so to say, inverted truth. For "true" and "false" are also qualifying words. A theoretical proposition, p, is qualified as true if the facts

[5] A. Peczenik, "Review: J. Wróblewski, *Sadowe stosowanie prawa & Wartosci a decyzja sadowa*", 247-251.

[6] R. Dworkin, *Taking Rights Seriously*, Cambridge (Mass.), 1977, 162.

are such as p describes them[7]. Later on, Svein Eng has expressed a similar view when discussing what happens in the case an utterance and reality do not fit each other. When the speaker then modifies the utterance, it indicates that what he intended was to utter a descriptive statement. When he tries to correct the reality, it indicates that he intended to utter a normative statement[8]. The practical meaning makes norm- and value-statements reasons for action. Even if one opposes legal realism, one should treat this insight seriously.

At the same time, however, norm-expressive statements and value statements have a theoretical meaning: they may be justified. Emphasising justifiability is more or less a revolution against legal realism. Justifiability implies that a person confronted with a norm-expressive statement or a value statement can ask "why?" and thus demand reasons, which support the statement. The reasons are of various kinds, but ultimately there is recourse to some values recognised in the society in question. The circumstance that the action in question is good or such that it ought to be performed is thus a sufficient condition for the thesis that this action fulfils at least one established criterion of evaluation[9].

The point is that the theory of the meaning of norm- and value-statements must be dualistic in this sense. Otherwise, it is easy to criticise. Yet, the problem remains, how the practical and the theoretical meaning are connected with each other. The easiest way to establish such a connection is to say that Reason motivates. In other words, once an agent states that an action would fulfil the established criterion for moral worth, she would also be motivated to perform the action. A battery of constraints may be useful here, one may for instance say that a morally sensitive agent would feel motivated, or that an agent being in the moral mood would be thus motivated and so on[10]. But let me leave out this subject as too psychological and speculative.

2.2. Is Knowledge of the Morally Justified Interpretation of Law Possible?

Now, cannot one claim – contrary to the legal realists – that norm-expressive statements and value-statements in legal argumentation can be well grounded and thus are not a mere expression of feelings? Consequently, cannot one argue that legal dogmatics, evaluative and yet presenting itself as a kind of science, gives us knowledge of the morally justified interpretation of law? To

---

[7] Cf., *e.g*, A. Peczenik, "Doctrinal Study of Law and Science", *Österreichische Zeitschrift für öffentliches Recht*, 1967, 133 and id., "Norms and Reality", *Theoria*, 1968, 119.

[8] S. Eng, "Noen synspunkter på en teori om etikk, rett og erkjennelse" (Some comments on theory of ethics, law and knowledge), *Tidsskrift for Rettsvitenskap*, 1991, 364.

[9] A. Peczenik and H. Spector, "A Theory of Moral Ought-Sentences", *A.R.S.P.*, 1987, 467 ff.

[10] Cf. S. Darwell, A. Gibbard, and P. Railton, "Towards Fin de Siècle Ethics", 101 *Philosophical Review*, 115-189 (1992) on "sensibility theory" advocated, *inter alia,* by John McDowell and David Wiggins.

argue along these lines has been the my life program. In this program, emphasis has been on epistemological questions: ontology, methodology and political philosophy have played secondary roles. The key topic has been weighing and balancing. For legal value judgements are almost always products of weighing.

3. Weighing in the Law

3.1. Weighing of Principles and Values

Later on, I realised that this way of thinking has some resemblance to the modern non-positivist theory of law. Many present-day legal-theorists no longer reduce the law to enacted rules. An influential school of legal theory follows such philosophers of law as Ronald Dworkin and Robert Alexy and incorporates general moral principles into the law. And they assume that these principles are both reasons for action and justifiable statements. According to Alexy, reasonable legal argumentation answers practical questions, *i.e.*, it decides what one shall or may do. Moreover, it claims to be right. In hard cases, this means weighing and balancing of general principles[11]. Furthermore, if one intends to say what ought to be done – without exclusive reliance upon authority – one must pay attention to all relevant moral principles[12]. The principles make the law coherent[13]. The word "principle" is vague, perhaps ambiguous. In any case, there are many kinds of principles[14]. In the present context, only one kind is relevant. Each principle of this kind, let me call it a value-principle, establishes an ideal, *i.e.*, it expresses a single value. One can express the same content in two different ways, *i.e.*, employing principles and values[15]. The ideal can be carried into effect to a certain degree, more or less. The higher the degree of realisation of the ideal, the better from the point of view of the principle. Chapter 1, section 2 of the Swedish Constitution ("*Regeringsformen*") thus stipulates, what follows: "The public power shall be exercised with the respect for equal value of all human beings and for each individual person's freedom and dignity." The greater respect for

---

[11] R. Alexy, *Begriff und Geltung des Rechts*, Freiburg/Munich, 1992, 125.

[12] Id., *ibid.*, 128.

[13] Cf., *e.g.*, N. MacCormick, "Coherence in Legal Justification" in *Theory of Legal Science*, A. Peczenik, L. Lindahl and R. van Roermund (eds.), Dordrecht/Boston/Lancaster, 1984, 235 ff.

[14] Cf., *e.g.*, R. Alexy, *Theorie der Grundrechte*, Baden-Baden, 1985, 71 ff.; R. Dworkin, *Taking Rights Seriously*, 14 ff.; P. O. Ekelöf, *Processuella grundbegrepp och allmänna processprinciper* (Fundamental concepts of legal process and general principles of law of procedure), Stockholm, 1956, 207; T. Eckhoff, "Retningslinjer og 'tumregler'" (Guidelines and "rules of thumb"), *Tidskrift for Rettsvitenskap*, 1980, 145 ff. with references to Scandinavian literature; J. Esser, *Grundsatz und Norm in der richterlichen Fortbildung des Privatrechts*, Tübingen, 1964^2, 39 ff.

[15] R. Alexy, *Theorie der Grundrechte*, 133.

equality, freedom and dignity, the better from the point of view of the provision. The provision expresses three principles: the equality principle, the freedom principle and the principle of human dignity.

The reasons to be weighed are mostly values and principles. But I think – contrary to Dworkin and Alexy – that any rule can be weighed[16] against other reasons. To be sure, one may say that what is weighed is not the rule itself, but a principle behind it. This way of putting it, however, is complicated, perhaps too complicated. Moreover, I find it easier to speak about weighing values than about weighing principles. This shift of emphasis from principles to values is not particularly important in itself, since any principle expresses a value[17]. However, Dworkin's theory of weighing principles is connected with his view that principles necessarily express individual rights[18]. On the other hand, not all values are linked to individual rights.

3.2. Prima Facie

When speaking about weighing of principles and values (and other reasons, too, see below), I thus assume that these have the *prima facie* character. A *prima facie* norm in this sense does not determine definitive duties. The latter must result from weighing and balancing of all morally and legally relevant values, principles and rules in the particular case[19]. The definitive (moral as well as legal), "all-things-considered" duty results from a weighing and balancing of many values and principles. Priority orders among them vary from case to case. The weighing is contextual, *i.e.*, depending on the total context of the discussed (actual or hypothetical) case, including all applicable moral considerations.

This approach to the *prima facie* duties is to some extent inspired by William D. Ross[20]. However, in my opinion, *prima facie* principles (and values) play the central role in justifying moral duties proper. Ross, on the other hand, played down the role of *prima facie* principles[21]. When speaking about *prima facie* norms (*inter alia* principles) and values, one may imply defeasibility or outweighability or both.

---

[16] A. Peczenik, *On Law and Reason*, 80 ff.; B. Verheij, *Rules, Reasons, Arguments. Formal Studies of Argumentation and Defeat*, Amsterdam, 1996, 48 ff.

[17] R. Alexy, *Theorie der Grundrechte*, 130 ff.

[18] R. Dworkin, *Taking Rights Seriously*, 82 ff.

[19] Cf. A. Peczenik, *Vad är rätt?* (What is law?), Stockholm, 1995, 444 ff. and 484 ff.

[20] W. D. Ross, *The Right and the Good*, Oxford, 1930, 27 ff.

[21] J. Dancy, "An Ethic of Prima Facie Duties" in *A Companion to Ethics*, P. Singer (ed.), Oxford, 1991, 225 ff.

3.3. Weighing, Defeasibility and Outweighability

All legal norms are defeasible in the sense of being changeable. But only the legislator, not the courts, can put most statutory norms out of the legal system. In other words, most statutory norms cannot be derogated by *desuetudo*. They are not irreversibly defeasible relatively to judicial practice, though irreversibly defeasible relatively to legislation. The legislator can justify the change of the statute by means of political argumentation, ideally assuming a weighing. But this weighing is not controllable by means of juristic argumentation *de lege lata*. For a court and a jurist, the defeat of the norm is justifiable by authority of the legislator, not by the force of his political argumentation.

Reversible defeat is another matter. In some cases, the courts can perform statutory interpretation *contra legem*. This means that they defeat the literal wording of the norm and put a new sense of the norm – perhaps a new norm – instead of it. Yet the literal wording of the norm stays in the text of the statute. Later on, the courts can change the interpretation and perhaps return to the literal reading of it. This kind of reversible defeat is justifiable by means of weighing. In this sense, the norm in question is (reversibly) outweighable. In extremely hard cases, weighing and balancing leads to the removal of the norm from the legal system (*desuetudo derogatoria*).

The so-called non-monotonic logic is a logical reconstruction of defeasibility[22]. "Non-monotonicity, or defeasibility, arises from the fact that arguments can be defeated by stronger counter-arguments"[23]. The "non-monotonicity of a logic means that the addition of a new information to a theory can make sentences underivable which used to be derivable on the basis of the smaller theory"[24]. The new ones defeat some old ones. Notice that the old information is not removed, it stays in the theory.

Less problematic is an addition of a new premise that converts a non-deductive reasoning step into a logically correct inference. Generally speaking, weighing in the law is a jump[25] *i.e.*, an enthymeme or a defeasible reasoning.

3.4. Weighing between Various Ways to Interpret the Statute

Thus, statutory interpretation is an important field of legal argumentation where weighing of reasons, including moral ones, is inevitable. The central part of this field is reasoning by analogy. Statutory analogy (*analogia legis*) consists in application of a statutory rule to a case which, viewed from the ordinary

---

[22] A. Peczenik, "Jumps and Logic in the Law. What Can One Expect of Logical Models of Legal Argumentation?", *Artificial Intelligence and Law*, 1996, 297-329.

[23] H. Prakken and G. Sartor, "A Dialectic Model of Assessing Conflicting Arguments in Legal Reasoning", *ibid.*, 331-368.

[24] J. Hage, "A Theory of Legal Reasoning and a Logic to Match", *ibid.*, 199.

[25] A. Peczenik, *On Law and Reason*, 114 ff.

linguistic angle, is included in neither the core nor the periphery of the application area of the statute in question, but resembles the cases covered by this statute in essential respects. When deciding not to reason by analogy, one can use the so-called *argumentum e contrario*. Statutory analogy and *argumentum e contrario* are no complete reasons but mere argument forms[26] each supported by a different set of reasons to be weighed and balanced[27]. Only important similarities between cases constitute a sufficient reason for conclusion by analogy. Judgements of importance are justifiable by weighing and balancing of various reasons, often principles. To be sure, some legal rules constraint the weighing. For example, the so-called principle of legality in penal law demands that no action should be regarded as a crime without statutory support and no penalty may be imposed without a statutory provision (*nullum crimen sine lege, nulla poena sine lege*). The precise meaning of these restrictions is, however, debatable in many countries. Moreover, they leave a lot of space for the weighing.

Another important problem in statutory interpretation that involves weighing concerns the purpose of the statute. The weighing and balancing of all circumstances of the case decides which data have priority in deciding what the goal of the statute is[28]. Indeed, the choice of goals is a complex matter, involving reasoning on many levels of abstraction. In Sweden, the goals are often found in *travaux préparatoires*. The use of *travaux préparatoires* reflects the fact that statutory interpretation issues are ordinarily viewed in Sweden as a problem of harmonisation of the statute and other authoritative materials. The harmonisation obviously requires weighing and balancing of the "sources". This weighing is seldom open, often tacit, but in any case inevitable. Yet, an influential minority of Swedish lawyers, led by Per Olof Ekelöf[29] protest against the great role of the preparatory materials. In Ekelöf's opinion, a judge should rely on his own judgement and see to it that the consequences of the application of the statute should be the same in hard cases as in the routine cases. Or should the goal of the statute be established in the light of everything the interpreter knows about the institutional history of the statute and the moral values of the society? Each method of establishing the goal requires weighing and balancing of reasons, and the choice between the competing methods does it as well.

In general, various reasons and methods, such as literal interpretation, analogy, systemic interpretation, historical interpretation and goal interpretation

---

[26] R. Alexy, *A Theory of Legal Argumentation*, Oxford, 1989, 279 ff.

[27] A. Peczenik, *Vad är rätt?*, 351.

[28] Id., *ibid.*, 375.

[29] P. O. Ekelöf, "Teleological Construction of Statutes", *Scandinavian Studies in Law*, 1958, 79 ff.

support statutory interpretation in hard cases. The choice between the alternatives depends on weighing and balancing of various legal arguments[30].

3.5. Weighing of Priority Orders Between Rules

Sometimes, one may avoid weighing and apply fixed priority orders between legal rules or between legal arguments. This is a well-known technique, applied in all the legal systems. As all lawyers know, statutory rules may be incompatible with each other, and all the legal systems contain some "collision rules" for choice between the incompatible norms. For example: when a higher norm is incompatible with a norm of a lower standing, one must apply the higher one. Where an earlier norm is incompatible with a later one, one must apply the later one. One may apply a more general norm only in cases not covered by an incompatible less general norm. It is not my intention to deny the importance of priority orders. However, the legal system is open in the sense that priority orders themselves are outweighable. They ought to be followed in principle, unless contrary reasons weigh more.

3.6. Weighing of the Sources of the Law

This is abundantly clear when one enters discussion about the so-called sources of the law[31]. According to the naive view of many lawyers, only statutes are binding law in the continental legal systems, whereas precedents and legislative preparatory materials (*travaux préparatoires*) are mere materials used to interpret the statutes. Yet, this naive view does not reflect the practice. An influential Swedish jurist, Folke Schmidt[32] expressed the opinion that *travaux préparatoires* and precedents are directives to be followed by the courts. Later on, Schmidt stated that "the text of the statute received more and more a function of a headline" whereas the *travaux préparatoires* "govern the administration of justice"[33].

Obviously, there are different degrees of legal normativity and bindingness. Statutes are so to say "more binding" that precedents and *travaux préparatoires*. Statutes are binding *de iure* in the sense that they *must* be regarded as authority reasons in legal argumentation. Precedents and *travaux préparatoires* merely *should* be thus regarded. The works of legal researchers *may* be thus regarded. These distinctions can be explicated without any recourse to weighing[34]. But the point of the distinctions is very much related to weighing. The legal

---

[30] A. Peczenik, *Vad är rätt?*, 376.

[31] A. Peczenik., "The Binding Force of Precedent" in *Interpreting Precedents. A Comparative Study*, N. MacCormick and R. S. Summers (eds.), Aldershot, 1997, 461-480.

[32] F. Schmidt, "Domaren som lagtolkare" (The judge as interpreter of statutes) in *Festskrift till Herlitz*, Stockholm, 1955, 263 ff.

[33] Id., *Facklig arbetsrätt* (Labor law), Stockholm, 1976,

[34] A. Peczenik, V*ad är rätt*, 218 ff.

sources that *must* be regarded as authority reasons are more important than those which merely *should* be thus regarded. The concept "more important" presupposes weighing. In particular, the following may be stated. If a collision occurs between a more important source and a less important one, the former has priority, if no overweighing reasons exist which reverse the priority order. If one assigns priority to a less important legal source before a more important one, one has the burden of argumentation for this priority. Overweighing reasons are thus required to follow a precedent contrary to the plain meaning of a statute. A *prima facie* more important legal source can, however, have a smaller weight than a number of less important ones, in cumulation. A number of precedents can thus jointly weigh more than a literal meaning of a statute. A counter-argument which "wins" against a stronger source of law must be stronger than a counter-argument which is sufficient to win against a weaker one.

3.7. Weighing-Dependent Legal and Political Concepts

Consequently, such concepts as "statutory analogy", "the purpose of the statute", "the (legal) meaning of the statute", "binding sources of the law" and so on, are weighing-dependent. The same can be said about more abstract, legal and political, concepts, such as "the rule-of-law state", "legal certainty" and "democracy"[35]. The main principle of the Law-State ("*Rechtsstaat*") demands that citizens enjoy a high degree of legal certainty ("*Rechtssicherheit*"), *i.e.*, that the exercise of public power is restricted by legal rules, and thus highly predictable. *Ceteris paribus*, the higher degree of predictability of the exercise of public power on the basis of legal rules, the better the Law-State. This "formal" principle of legal certainty must, however, be weighed and balanced against other principles (or values). Among these, one can mention justice[36], equality before the law, public accessibility of legal norms and legal decisions, independence of the courts, responsibility of power-holders and a minimum of human and political rights. The result of this balancing is legal certainty in the material sense.

The modern concept of democracy has doubtless a hard core. The organisation of public power is not democratic, unless "the social institutions provide means by which the rulers may be dismissed by the ruled"[37]. Neither is the organisation of public power democratic, if anybody can give himself a government position or exercise unconditional and unlimited power[38]. But some criteria (and thus democratic values), weighed and balanced against each other, must be included in the sufficient condition and in the measure of various degrees of democracy. Among these, one may mention free elections according to the

[35] Id., *ibid.*, 50-100.

[36] A. Peczenik, "Doctrinal Study of Law and Science", 138.

[37] K. R. Popper, *The Open Society and Its Enemies*, I, London, 1966^5, 124.

[38] G. Sartori, *Demokratietheorie*, Darmstadt, 1992, 210.

principle "one man one vote"; majority decisions within the elected political bodies; political representation of interests of the people; participation of citizens in political life; free formation of public opinion; free access to politically relevant information; division of power; responsibility of power-holders; predictability and moral acceptability of public decision making; and some other human and political rights.

The balance of values, which characterise the Law-State and the democracy-values, determines the degree of legitimacy of the law.

4. An Analysis of Weighing

4.1. Optimisation

The lawyers perform a weighing and balancing of reasons, in spite of not having a precise theory as to how much they do "weigh"[39]. Yet, some possibilities of explicating weighing are attractive, because they open a "window" to basic philosophical problems. Weighing can be conceptualised in different ways, *inter alia* as optimisation, cost-and-benefits calculus, aggregation of arguments and construction of chains of arguments. The choice between different approaches to weighing depends on philosophical considerations.

Some concepts borrowed from engineering and economics, *e.g.*, "Pareto-optimality", "diminishing utility" and "indifference curves" may serve as patterns for legal and moral weighing[40]. An important idea is that the more a principle is "pressed down" in the decision making, the greater "resistance" it makes. Thus, the freedom of speech of a journalist may be justifiedly limited to protect the interview "victim", but not entirely abolished.

On the other hand, the applicability of the technological and economic models to legal decision making may be contested at least for two reasons. First, there are no unambiguous yardsticks for moral and legal values[41]. Second, the problem to solve here is not to weigh two factors in isolation from everything else, but to weigh them against the background of "all things" to be considered. The function of juristic weighing is to find which of the *prima facie* applicable rules best fits in the given situation. The situation must be described "from all relevant points of view" and "as exhaustively as possible", whereby one must pay attention to "coherence of the system of rules as a whole"[42].

Optimisation is a general idea without criteria telling us how to optimise. It would be an adequate method for weighing, if the pair of factors to be weighed

---

[39] A. Peczenik, *On Law and Reason*, 284 ff.

[40] R. Alexy, *Theorie der Grundrechte*, 100 ff. and 145 ff.

[41] J. Habermas, *Faktizität und Geltung. Beiträge zur Diskurstheorie des Rechts und des demokratischen Rechtsstaats*, Frankfort-on-Main, 1992, 316, no. 33.

[42] Id., *ibid.*, 317.

could be isolated from all the other relevant "things" and if unambiguous yardsticks for weighing had existed. Hence, it helps us to understand the vague idea of weighing even in the situation where these conditions are not fulfilled. (The question how the word "understand" should be understood in this context must be left aside here.)

4.2. Costs and Benefits. Preference Utilitarianism

Another version of a contextual weighing can be regarded as a kind of a calculus of costs and benefits. (I am grateful to Wlodek Rabinowicz for this idea.) In one situation, one gains more when giving priority to a given value, in another situation, one gains more when preferring another. In one situation, "one" gains, *e.g.*, more by allowing the journalist to write freely, in another situation, "one" gains more by protecting the interview victim. But this formulation of the problem is vague. Who is "one"? It is by no means decisive that, *e.g.*, the journalist gains more money than the "victim" loses. A scandal journalist can gain millions, but it is not a good argument to leave the "victim" unprotected. Instead, the calculus must pay attention to two important things. First, the journalist's and the "victim's" gains and losses must be measured not only in money but also in non-monetary preferences, such as the pursue of self-respect, dignity etc. Second, the calculus must take into consideration gains and losses of "everybody" (all the members of the society in the long run).

Instead of speaking about gains, one can speak about fulfilment of preferences. This is an attractive approach and I endorse a kind of preference utilitarianism: morality is about maximising human preferences. *Nota bene*, I do not make any constraint ruling out altruist preferences. Mother Teresa's preference to help other people was as real as my preference for making money. Narrow interpretation of preferences as only egoist one's is a mistake[43]. The main reason to join preference utilitarianism is ontological. Preference utilitarianism liberates a philosopher from urge to talk about objective values, more or less hovering in the air.

The leading preference utilitarianist, R. M. Hare, has elaborated the following theory of two levels of moral thinking. The critical level includes a complete knowledge of other people's preferences in all thinkable cases, together with weighing and balancing of these preferences. On the basis of this knowledge, one can compute what action maximises the aggregate of preferences, according to the formula number of preferences (regardless whose) multiplied by strength of respective preferences. Only an "archangel" could perform such a task. One ought to follow a rule that thus maximises the fulfilment of preferences.

---

[43] A. Sen, "Rational Fools: A Critique of the Behavioural Foundations of Economic Theory" in *Philosophy and Economic Theory*, F. Hahn and M. Hollis (eds.), Oxford, 1979, 95-96.

The opposite of the "archangel", a "prole", lacks ability to think "critically". He must stay at the intuitive level, that is, merely follow his own moral intuitions and some established moral principles. The archangel could show that some intuitions and principles more or less correspond to the calculus of preferences. The prole does not know it but still acts rightly. Ordinary people are neither archangels nor proles but rather a mixture of both. They have some moral intuitions, follow some principles and have some ability to check whether these correspond to what other people wish[44]. Since we are no archangels, we cannot effectively make the preference calculus. This means that the preference calculus is another general idea without applicability criteria. It does not effectively determine our weighings. Yet, it does promote understanding. Indeed, weighing in morality and in the law must in some sense mirror a calculus of preferences.

4.3. Interlude – From Preferences to Values

Let me add what follows. Since there is a fairly well established consensus about principles and values, whereas the archangelic calculus remains an abstract ideal, the applied moral theory must be based on history, not only on the direct study of preferences. An important part of morality and, indeed, a part of the law consist of principles and values to be weighed and balanced in particular cases. A hypothesis is plausible that the language of principles and values together with the views about the content of these evolved by processes similar to natural selection in Darwin's sense[45]. In this process, they adapted to a great number of preferences of many persons during a long time. To follow principles and to respect values established in the society thus leads to approximately the same consequences as to follow the archangelic preference calculus. Preferences are always preferences of individual human beings. On the other hand, I do not assume that all values are individual. It is plausible to speak about many kinds of values, individual values, collective values and product-values. There exists a considerable consensus – at least in the Western culture – that there are many values, among other things many moral values of very different character: human life, liberty, personal integrity, property, justice, helpfulness, truth, keeping promises, working efficiently, taking care of one's children, executing public office loyally to the law, good environment, order, progress and other common goods, knowledge, art, technology, state, law and other cultural products. All these values can be called "moral" in a broad sense. And all of them, rather than merely the principles that express individual values, actually are and ought to be weighed and balanced in the law.

Yet, ontological problems remain unsolved. Values supervene on human preferences. "Values are not part of the mind-independent world but something

---

[44] R. M. Hare, *Moral Thinking*, Oxford, 1981, 44 ff.

[45] See section 5.6 below with references to Petrazycki and Popper.

that we project upon the word, or – more precisely – upon the whole set of possible words"[46]. The idea that values are projections of preferences upon the world resembles strongly Petrazycki's approach[47]. But he found it untenable to regard the mind-dependent values as existing. For him values were "emotional phantasms"[48]. Leaving the ontological problems open, I regard values and norms, constituted by preferences, as "data" that the agent is supposed to consider, evaluate and weigh in his process of deliberation. The talk about "data" abstracts deliberately from the motivational force of moral beliefs. What is left is only the intellectual aspect of the rational agent, calmly deliberating the values. This does not imply that real people are so calm. Just the opposite, they are (at least often, if not always) emotionally motivated by the deliberation. But this motivation is personal and thus uninteresting in the context of justification.

By the way, this is not Hare's way to see the matter. Instead, Hare treats preferences as causal factors that determine decision and action. Hare's own theory is, however, open to criticism[49]. Not even amalgamation of heterogeneous preferences of one single person is always possible[50]. For own preferences (desires) are not what an agent computes in the process of deliberation. Instead, the agent computes the value (established by means of preferences) of the objects he prefers (desires).

4.4. Aggregation of Arguments

Let me repeat. I take values and norms, constituted by preferences, to be "data" that the agent considers, evaluates and weighs in his process of deliberation. A Swedish case[51] may serve as an example. A foreigner A, who had considerable ties to both Sweden and the Federal Republic of Germany, owned a car, registered in the latter country. He borrowed a sum of money, giving the property right to the car as security (a so-called "security transfer"). Later, a person rented the car and visited Sweden. The Swedish authorities sequestered

---

[46] W. Rabinowicz and J. Österberg, "Value Based on Preferences. On Two Interpretations of Preference Utilitarianism" in *Preference and Value. Preferentialism in Ethics*, Dept. Philosophy Univ. of Lund (ed.), Lund, 1996.

[47] L. Petrazycki, *Teoria prawa i panstwa w zwiazku z teoria moralnosci* (Theory of law and state in connection with theory of morality), I, Warsaw, 1959 (Russian edition *Teorija prava i gosudarstva v svyazi s teoriey nravstvennosti*, St. Petersburg, 1907), 55 ff. and 266 ff.; id., *Teoria prawa i panstwa w zwiazku z teoria moralnosci* (Theory of law and state in connection with theory of morality), II, Warsaw, 1960, 97 ff.

[48] Id., *ibid.*, I, 56, 62, 122, 272 and 276 and id., *ibid.*, II, 21.

[49] W. Rabinowicz and B. Strömberg, "What if I Were in His Shoes. On Hare's Argument for Preference Utilitarianism" in *Preference and Value. Preferentialism in Ethics*, 176 ff.

[50] W. Rabinowicz and J. Österberg, "Value Based on Preferences. On Two Interpretations of Preference Utilitarianism", 224.

[51] NJA 1984, 693.

the car as security for A's unpaid taxes. The dispute concerned the question whether the German security transfer should prevent sequestration in Sweden. The Supreme Court overruled the sequestration and stated: "The demand for order and simplicity of the system together with difficulties for the creditors in Sweden to judge the credit risks otherwise than according to Swedish rules constitute the main reason against ascribing security transfer according to foreign law an effect against the transferor's creditors here in Sweden (...). The interest of the creditors in Sweden to be able to assess their credit risks according to Swedish law competes with the interest of the foreign transferee/creditor not to risk a loss of his right because the property without his participation has been moved to Sweden (...). One should weigh the proffered reasons against each other and one must then pay attention to the development of the international trade and to more and more intense commercial co-operation between various countries". In this case, the Supreme Court assigned the decisive importance to "development of the international trade" and to "more and more intense commercial co-operation between various countries". But obviously, these values are not the only ones that should decide about the application of foreign law in Sweden. One must consider other values, as well, *e.g.*, the wealth of the nation, the dominant public opinion in Sweden, etc. As soon as one states that one thing weighs more than another, the question occurs "Why?". Then, one needs another argument and another act of weighing. Briefly: x may weigh more than y in isolation but, in a certain situation, z can occur, and reverse the order: x weighs less than y+z. Then, x+q weigh perhaps more that y+z. In this way, the weights can be aggregated[52].

In such a weighing, the weight of any considered reason is affected by all the other reasons. All of them are components of a single complex relation. Assume, *e.g.*, that the lawgiver considers introducing a certain economic regulation. The regulation is justifiable by means of weighing and balancing of economic freedom and some demands of equality. But how great is the weight of equality? The answer can depend on the fact that restricting liberty for the sake of equality can reduce economic efficiency. The weight of efficiency is in its turn affected by its relation to such collective values as environment, culture and progress. And so on. Upon this approach, one does not weigh isolated arguments but, precisely as Habermas demanded, all arguments to be considered "as exhaustively as possible", whereby one must pay attention to "coherence of the system of rules as a whole"[53].

But important problems are still unsolved.

---

[52] A. Peczenik, "Juridiska avvägningar" (Legal weighings) in *Festskrift till Strömholm*, Uppsala, 1997, 697-708.

[53] J. Habermas, *Faktizität und Geltung*, 317.

First, one must repeat that there are no unambiguous yardsticks for moral and legal values[54]. Thus, this approach to weighing is, again, merely a general idea without criteria telling us how to weigh. Second, some authors criticise the very idea of cumulating (aggregating, accruing) of arguments[55]. Verheij considers the following example. Assume that you want to go out and walk. Hot weather is a reason for not walking. Rain is another reason for not walking. Yet, hot weather and rain jointly may be a pleasant combination, no longer a reason for not walking. Hence, two reasons for not walking neutralise each other, instead of constituting a stronger reason for not walking. Verheij tries to solve this problem in a rather formalistic manner, by treating the putative accrual of reasons "hot-and-rain" as another reason, not as a cumulation of "hot" and "rain". But the real problem is still unsolved. In some cases, reasons cumulate into a stronger reason, in other cases they do not. One needs here a complex vectorial analysis of reasons that I am neither capable nor willing to perform. Let it suffice to say that reasons proffered in legal argumentation cumulate often enough to make cumulation an interesting rule of thumb: *ceteris paribus*, two reasons pulling at the same direction are stronger than each of them alone. This is another idea without precise application criteria.

4.5. Chains of Arguments

However, aggregation is not the only thing that matters in this context. A chain of arguments is something more than a cumulation. It is a structured cumulation. Intuitively, a chain of arguments gives us more information than a mere cumulating would. The chain "x because of q because of r" is stronger than cumulating "x and q and r". This idea of cumulating-and-chain must not be confused with chain-without-cumulating. A well-known example of the latter is hearsay evidence in legal process. Charles says that p because John told him that p and John told him so because he has heard it from Peter. If Charles knows nothing more but merely what he has heard from John, and John nothing more but what he heard from Peter, the weight of Charles's assertion is obviously much lesser than that of Peter's. Such a chain weakens – not strengthens – evidence. But the justificatory chains are different. Each reason in the chain has already a weight, and this weight is increased when the reasons that support it are added. *Ceteris paribus*, the longer the chain of thus cumulated arguments support a statement, the stronger the weight of the statement[56].

But this theory should not be misunderstood. The assertion "each reason has already a weight" does not mean that the weight is a kind of foundation that

---

[54] Id., *ibid.*, 316, no. 33.

[55] B. Verheij, *Rules, Reasons, Arguments*, 57 and 161 with references to, *inter alia*, Pollock and Prakken.

[56] A. Peczenik, "Jumps and Logic in the Law", 297 ff.

would be impossible to doubt. Each reason has already a weight due to another chain, for example "x because of a because of b".

5. Coherence

5.1. Enter Coherence

Such a chain of arguments has no obvious end. Weighing of such chains can easily result in a complex system of priorities between the arguments. *Ceteris paribus*, the more coherent such a system is, the more reasonable the result of weighing. In general, defeasibility of legal justification, *inter alia* the idea of *prima facie*, makes the problem of coherence interesting. Coherentists regard all reasons in general as defeasible. This applies even to observational data. Indeed, the data that allegedly falsify a hypothesis are theory-laden. There are no unshakable foundations of science. To be sure, foundationalists claim that all knowledge ultimately rests on evident foundations, such as empirical data[57]. However, foundationalism has been rebutted by coherentism: the alleged foundations are not certain. Roughly speaking, whatever is justifiable, is justifiable on the basis of the background system of beliefs. In Keith Lehrer's terminology – whatever is justifiable, is justifiable on the basis of the background system of acceptances and preferences. Lehrer justifies the step from beliefs and desires to acceptances and preferences, as follows: "Beliefs and desires often are capriciously and sometimes perversely within me and contrary to my better judgement. I am not in a position to say that all my beliefs and desires are worthy of my trust. But what makes me worthy of my trust is my capacity to evaluate my beliefs and desires (...). The positive evaluation of belief, I have called *acceptance* and the positive evaluation of desire, I have called *preference*"[58].

5.2. The Concept of Coherence

What is coherence, then? Coherence is related to the well-known theory of reflective equilibrium. One aims at mutual adaptation of the general principles and individual moral convictions[59]. However, coherence of a total belief system is much more complex than reflective equilibrium. Metaphorically speaking, a coherent belief system is like a network of argumentative circles, mostly quite big ones.

---

[57] Cf., *e.g.*, R. M. Chisholm, *Theory of Knowledge*, Englewood Cliffs, 1966, 30 ff.

[58] K. Lehrer, *Self-Trust. A Study of Reason, Knowledge, and Autonomy*, Oxford, 1997, 3.

[59] J. Rawls, *A Theory of Justice*, Oxford, 1971, 20; D. Prawitz, "Om moraliska och logiska satsers sanning" (On truth of moral and logical sentences) in *En filosofibok tillägnad Anders Wedberg*, L. Bergström, H. Ofstad and D. Prawitz (eds.), Stockholm, 1978, 153.

The network is like this:

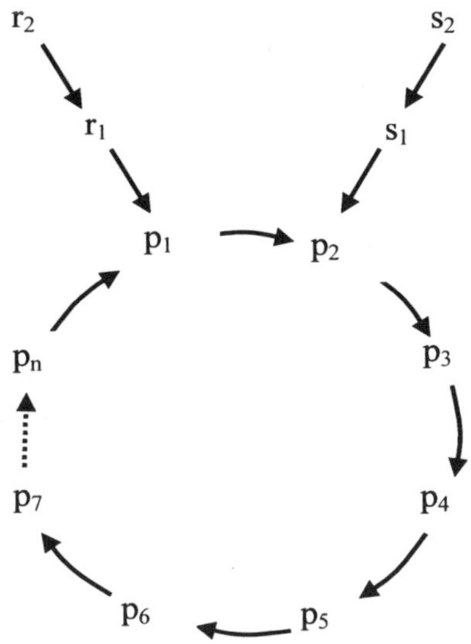

A single chain of arguments, p_1-p_n, may be represented as a circle. In such a chain, p_1 supports p_2, p_2 supports p_3, etc. But "supports" does not always mean "deductively entail". Often the step from p_1 to p_2, etc. is only explicable as a reasonable support: p_2 follows from p_1 together with another premise, say r_1. This premise is reasonable, which simply means that it is a member of another such circle.

The following restatement of Laurence BonJour's theory is a good (though not entirely unproblematic) answer to this question.

"A system of beliefs is a justification-conferring, coherent system if:

(i) It is logically consistent,
(ii) It has a high degree of probabilistic consistency,
(iii) It has a significant number of relatively strong inferential connections among component beliefs,
(iv) It is relatively unified, *i.e.*, does not divide into relatively unconnected subsystems,
(v) It contains few unexplained anomalies,
(vi) It provides a relatively stable conception of the word and remains coherent (*i.e.* satisfies (i) – (v) in the long run) and
(vii) It satisfies the *observation requirement*, *i.e.*, it must contain laws attributing a high degree of reliability to a reasonable variety of cognitively spontaneous beliefs, including introspective beliefs"[60].

[60] Cf. J. W. Bender, "Coherence, Justification and Knowledge" in *The Current State of Coherence Theory. Critical Essays on the Epistemic Theories of Keith Lehrer and*

Whereas BonJour discusses coherence *of* a belief system, Keith Lehrer focuses on coherence of acceptances and preferences *relatively to* a belief system. In the following part of this contribution, I will apply some of Lehrer's ideas. It is not my intention to deliver a study of Lehrer's theory. The point is rather to take it as a starting point of my own considerations. Let me merely state that Lehrer's theory seems perfectly capable to deal with several objections many authors[61] raise against "epistemic coherence theory".

One of Lehrer's key concepts is "justification game". For example, Lehrer lets a skeptic play various hypothetical "justification games" against the "claimant" (who holds some beliefs on the basis of the background system of acceptances and preferences). The concept of winning the justification game is this: "If what the claimant accepts is something that is more reasonable for her to accept than the (…) objection (...) then the claimant wins"[62]. If what he accepts is less reasonable than the objection, he loses. The loss means that the acceptance in question is defeated. Lehrer has taken reasonableness as a primitive concept[63]. He defines both "justified acceptance" of a belief and "justified preference"[64] in terms of "more reasonable to accept/prefer than… ."

The latter concept, albeit primitive, is related to the idea of truthworthiness. "Reasonable acceptance and preference may be inductively inferred from truthworthiness in what one accepts and prefers"[65]. "My trustworthiness is a capacity to accept and prefer what is worth accepting and preferring"[66].

It is my contention that the expression "weighs more than" in juristic contexts seems to work analogously to Lehrer's expression "is more reasonable than". Moreover, I assume that truthworthiness is a capacity to evaluate as more weighty what is worth evaluating as more weighty. Thus, one may reformulate the concept of winning the justification game in terms of "weighing more". If what a person accepts/prefers weighs more for her than the skeptical objection, then the person wins the justification game against the skeptic.

It must be noted here that Lehrer's theory is open for some logical problems. Erik Olsson[67] has elaborated a formal proof (inspired by Wlodek Rabinowicz) of the following. If p is less probable (and thus less reasonable) than

---

Laurence BonJour, with Replies, Dordrecht/Boston/London, 1989, 5, referring to L. BonJour, *The Structure of Empirical Knowledge*, Cambridge (Mass.), 1985, 9, 10, 92, 102-3, 106, 116, 123-4, 141, 151-4, 170, 191.

[61] *Inter alia* J. Raz, *Ethics in the Public Domain. Essays in the Morality of Law and Politics*, Oxford, 1994, 279-286.

[62] K. Lehrer, *Theory of Knowledge*, London, 1990, 119.

[63] Id., *ibid.*, 127.

[64] Id., *Self-Trust*, 36 ff.

[65] Id., *ibid.*, 56.

[66] Id., *ibid.*, 57.

[67] E. Olsson, *Coherence. Studies in Epistemology and Belief Revision*, Uppsala, 1997, 3:7.

q and q is justified, then p is a competitor that loses the justification game and is to be removed. This is the case even if p is entirely independent from q. This is devastating for Lehrer's theory. Almost all justifiable beliefs are less probable than something else, for example than the belief that the world is not going to implode tomorrow. Yet, they must be kept in the system of beliefs. Yet, Olsson's criticism is less terrible than it appears to be. First, Lehrer's theory can be adjusted to avoid the criticism, for example Lehrer himself made some steps in this direction[68]. Second, the reconstruction of reasonability in terms of probability can be given up without serious consequences for Lehrer's epistemology. (After all, comparative reasonableness is a primitive concept Lehrer refuses to define).

5.3. Correcting Errors: The Role of Time in Lehrer's Theory

Back to the Lehrer's theory of coherence. One cannot "objectively" determine at time t_1, whether justification is "really" undefeated. Only later on, at t_2, when one's acceptance system changes, one is in a position to judge whether one's earlier justification was defeated or not. "How can a person ascertain that she is completely justified in accepting that p or that her justification is undefeated (...)? At a given point in time, a person can only evaluate such a claim in terms of her acceptance system (...). It is the only epistemic court for synchronic adjudication, judgement at a time (...). We are, however, diachronic creatures (...). As a result, an individual remembers that (...) some of the things that he accepted were false (...). (W)hen the time for evaluation of various claims to truth arrives, the basis for evaluation must be the system he has then (...). Others (...) may disagree, and I may come to agree, and I may come to agree with them at some later date when further information has won my acceptance"[69].

Assume, now, that one has succeeded to eliminate at the time t_2 all the false acceptances the person in question made at the earlier time t_1. At this way, one arrives at the "verific system", that is, that part of a person's (coherent) acceptance system which contains all her true acceptances but has been purged of all her false acceptances. Assume, furthermore, that this verific system has been strengthened even more, namely that one has succeeded to eliminate all true but unfounded beliefs. For example, true but unfounded beliefs do not suffice in a court. To win a case, it is not enough that the party in question tells the truth, if the truth is not supported by evidence. Assume, finally, that the system has been weakened to allow for some "harmless" errors. For example, if ten witnesses independently say that x committed a murder, it is not important that one of the witnesses happens to lie. The other nine are quite enough[70]. Lehrer thus arrives at a solution – the theory of an "ultrasystem". The definition of the ultrasystem is

---

[68] K. Lehrer, *Knowledge*, Oxford, 1970, 193 ff., loyally noticed by Olsson.

[69] Id., *Theory of Knowledge*, 151.

[70] Id., *ibid.*, 132 ff.

complex[71]. The following informal description must suffice here. The personal system of acceptances/preferences can be thus improved by adding some reasons for true beliefs and by eliminating the false beliefs, except the "harmless" ones. Lehrer insists that it can be done in many alternative ways. What is completely justified must cohere with all such alternative systems. Lehrer calls all of them members of the "ultrasystem".

5.4. Epistemological Conservatism

Lehrer does not say much about how the errors are corrected, in order to make personal justification to convert into knowledge. One can approach this problem by appealing to epistemological conservatism[72]. Conservatism is easy to understand when we enter the discussion about coherence in time. (By the way, Lehrer's theory of a verific system in which all the errors have been corrected, as was explained above, is easy to understand only if the time component is considered). When time passes new data flow in and have to be accommodated in the system. Some of these new data when combined with our old beliefs introduce incoherence that must be removed. This process is the subject of theories of belief revision (in the light of new information about the static world) and theories of belief updating (in the light of new information about the world that is supposed to be changing). Conservatism comes into play in these theories as the principle of minimal change. Modifications made in a person's belief system in order to provide space for the new information should be as small as possible. From this perspective, one can make a distinction between synchronic and diachronic coherence: the first abstracts from time, the second involves time[73]. This idea can be illustrated by BonJour's requirement that a system of beliefs is coherent enough to justify knowledge only if it is stable, that is "converges on and eventually presents a relatively stable long-run picture of the world"[74]. When considering time in this context, we almost leave an individual perspective, and approach a social one. The time relevant here neither begins nor ends with the span of life of an individual.

5.5. Social Dimension of Diachronic Coherence. Discourse Theories

Now, is the recourse to stability of the belief system in the society a more efficient criterion of truth than a recourse to the background system of acceptances and preferences of an individual? In one respect, it seems to be an even less suitable tool for the search for knowledge. For surely, various members of the society have different beliefs about a lot of things, not to speak about

---

[71] Id., *ibid.*, 194.

[72] Cf., *e.g.*, L. Bergström, *Värdeteori* (Value theory), Stockholm, 1990, 102.

[73] A. Peczenik, *Vad är rätt?*, 603 ff.

[74] L. BonJour, *The Structure of Empirical Knowledge*, 170.

different desires. Pressure towards incoherence is thus greater in the collective system than in an individual system. It is not obvious that all (or almost all) members of the society could agree on one single coherent system of acceptances and preferences, regardless how much they work on belief revision and belief updating.

Yet, from another point of view, the social perspective brings us a hope. For there is no doubt that the members of the society communicate with each other and thus make it possible for any single person to correct errors in her system of acceptances and preferences. In other word, asking what other persons think is a good method to pass from a personally justified belief system to "verific system", that is, that part of a person's (coherent) acceptance system which contains all her true acceptances but has been purged of all her false acceptances (see above).

One may refine this idea by only taking into account what others *rationally* think. Discourse theories provide an idealised procedure for admitting rational opinions only. Thus, according to Habermas[75] a proposition is true, if the validity claim with which we utter it is justifiable. This claim is justifiable if and only if people participating in the rational discourse would agree that p[76]. The perfectly rational discourse would exist in the ideal speech situation in which intellectual communication of people would not be impeded by violence and everybody would have the same chance to ask and answer questions, interpret others' views, recommend actions, etc.[77] Robert Alexy has elaborated a well-known theory of rational practical discourse[78]. Some among Alexy's rationality rules express the idea of coherence. For example: every speaker must give reasons for what he or she asserts when asked to do so, unless he or she can cite reasons, which justify a refusal to provide a justification. Other rules introduce the relation between persons participating in the discourse. For example: everyone who can speak may take part in discourse. These rules flow from the idea that neither discrimination between persons nor violence is a reason. An optimally rational debate, by definition governed by reasons alone, must thus be free of both discrimination and violence.

5.6. Correcting Errors: Natural Selection

One can also learn something of Popper and Petrazycki. Popper's answer is in terms of "natural selection of hypotheses: our knowledge consists, at every moment, of those hypotheses which have shown their (comparative) fitness by

---

[75] J. Habermas, "Wahrheitstheorien" in *Wirklichkeit und Reflexion. Walter Schultz zum 60. Geburtstag*, Pfüllingen, 1973, 218.

[76] Id., *ibid.*, 240.

[77] Id., *ibid.*, 252 ff.

[78] R. Alexy, *A Theory of Legal Argumentation*, passim.

surviving so far in their struggle for existence; a competitive struggle which eliminates those hypotheses which are unfit"[79]. Let me also recall Petrazycki's observation: "By processes which, in a way, are similar to natural selection in Darwin's sense (...) the linguistic terms become brilliantly although unconsciously adapted to the proper orientation among phenomena"[80].

Here again, we leave an individual perspective and approach the social one. For the selection neither begins nor ends within the span of life of an individual. Yet, the individual who pursues knowledge has always the last word. My knowledge is knowledge in view of my standards of knowledge. Both paying attention to what others think and following the discourse rules are good (albeit highly idealised) standards in constructing one's coherent system of acceptances and preferences. Nothing more than that, but nothing less either.

5.7. Criteria for Coherence

Let me now change the perspective. The question to deal with here is no longer: "Can an individual achieve knowledge (and thus access to truth) by recourse to reasonability in the light of the background system of acceptances and preferences?" but: "What circumstances indicate that this test of reasonability has been passed?"

Alexy and Peczenik[81] have developed some criteria of coherence of a theory. The word "theory" is used here in a broad sense, covering both descriptive, for example empirical theories, and normative or evaluative theories (norm systems or value systems). The more the statements belonging to a given theory approximate a perfect supportive structure, the more coherent the theory.

Ceteris paribus, the degree of coherence of a theory depends on such circumstances as how great a number of supported statements belong to it, how long chains of reasons belong to it, how many chains of reasons support one and the same conclusion, how great number of general concepts belong to it, how high the degree of generality of these concepts is, how great number of cases it covers, and how great number of fields of life it covers. The degree of coherence is determined by weighing and balancing of the criteria. For example, the supportive chain of reasons may be particularly long when one uses less general concepts, and shrink substantially when the concepts applied become more general. In such a case, one must perform a complicated act of weighing in order

---

[79] K. R. Popper, *Objective Knowledge*, Oxford, 1972, 261.

[80] L. Petrazycki, *Teoria prawa i panstwa w zwiazku z teoria moralnosci*, I, 104 (my translation).

[81] R. Alexy and A. Peczenik, "The Concept of Coherence and its Significance for Discursive Rationality", *Ratio Juris*, 1990, 130-147. See also, with some additions, A. Peczenik, *On Law and Reason*, 158 ff.

to answer the question which theory is more coherent, the more general one, or the one containing the longer chain of reasons.

These criteria are nothing more than rules of thumb[82]. *Ceteris paribus*, the more coherent a theory the more reasonable it is in the light of the background system.

An obvious circle involved here is that weighing and balancing of criteria of coherence must be as coherent as possible, which invokes the same criteria of coherence. There is no way out from this circle. But the theory as a whole is self-confirming, not self-destroying. It is all you can require from a theory of coherence.

5.8. An Objection: Coherent Prejudice?

The main point of theories of coherence is epistemological. What is the relation between the coherent system of beliefs and truth? We must deal with the "isolation objection": cannot a coherent system of beliefs be false, isolated from the world?

This objection has two versions. Let me call them local and total. The local version is a simple misunderstanding. It feeds on highly coherent but false fiction novels and moral prejudices. Cannot one, for instance, agree with Joseph Raz[83] that the "racist's belief in the untruthworthiness of members of a certain race, bred on prejudice, is not justified even if it coheres best with all the racist's other (mostly racist) beliefs"? No, one cannot. For all the other racist's beliefs cannot be mostly racist. Views concerning human races are only a small part of the total belief system of any person, including Adolf Hitler. In order to function in this world, any person must have beliefs about physical phenomena, geographic locations, animals, plants, food, language and so on. Even if a racist is a paranoid anti-Semitist, he cannot coherently say "all Jews are worthless" without explaining how it was possible that "worthless" Jews, including Albert Einstein, elaborated a great part of modern physics. Some Nazis tried to speak coherently, and they rejected Einstein's theory of relativity. Yet in vain: the Nazi regime was not as stupid as to give up an effort to build atomic weapon, thus assuming a lot of Jewish work as the theoretical foundation. In brief: prejudice can be internally coherent, but it does not matter if it does not cohere with other parts of a person's total worldview[84].

[82] See sections 4.4 and 4.5 above.

[83] J. Raz, *Ethics in the Public Domain*, 284.

[84] By the way, Raz himself writes that "coherence theory (...) must relate to the totality of one's views", see id. *ibid.*, 286.

5.9. A More Profound Objection: Circularity

In this way we arrive at the total version. Here we approach the most profound problem of coherentist justification, that is, its circularity. "The coherentist response (...) begs the question, since it simply assumes that a person has a reason to think that a belief is true if it coheres with the rest of her beliefs. This is a depressing but perhaps not surprising conclusion"[85].

However, Lehrer sees clearly that this circularity makes it impossible to logically prove that coherence renders truth. "My claim that justification depends on coherence is not intended as an argument to prove to a skeptic that we are truthworthy. It is the claim that our justification for what we accept depends on a system of acceptance containing general claims about our competence and truthworthiness. When there is an adequate match between acceptance and reality, coherence converts to knowledge"[86]. "Knowledge" is an epistemic concept. It is not logically equivalent to any combination of natural (non-epistemic) concepts. "Coherence is the glue which bonds the natural world, as we conceive of it, to the world of epistemic value, as we conceive of that. The glue of coherence requires matching surfaces of acceptance and truth to hold fast, but it does not bond across possible words"[87].

Lehrer's theory is also applicable to preferences: "Reasonable acceptance and preference may be inductively inferred from truthworthiness in what one accepts and prefers"[88]. Moreover, autonomous preferences are in the center of our system of acceptances and preferences. "Autonomous preference (…) enables us to be trustworthy in what we accept and prefer and, ultimately, to obtain knowledge and wisdom from undefeated justification based on autonomous evaluation"[89]. Simply speaking: we assume (autonomously) that we have knowledge and wisdom. Once this is assumed, Lehrer shows that both knowledge and wisdom is linked to coherence.

This fits neatly into Searle's ontology: "I have not demonstrated that external realism is true. I have tried to show that it is presupposed by the use of very large sections of a public language"[90].

---

[85] F. Tersman, *Reflective Equilibrium. An Essay in Moral Epistemology*, Stockholm, 1993, 102.

[86] K. Lehrer, "Coherence and the Truth Connection: A Reply to My Critics" in *The Current State of Coherence Theory*, 275.

[87] Id., *Self-Trust*, 76.

[88] Id., *ibid.*, 56.

[89] Id., *ibid.*, 103.

[90] J. R. Searle, *The Construction of Social Reality*, London, 1995, 194.

5.10. No Privileged Position for a Skeptic

To understand this kind of coherentism, one must keep in mind that neither skepticism in general nor the isolation objection in particular has a privileged status, compared with other beliefs. It is merely a competitor of other beliefs. If someone says that my personally justified, coherent system of beliefs is not "objectively" justified, he has to win the competition with my system[91]. Consequently, if I want to argue that I am justified in accepting or preferring x, I must appeal to my system of acceptances and preferences at that time. And if the skeptic wants to convince me that I am wrong, the appeal to my acceptance system at that time is again all he can make.

Now, this kind of coherentism is applicable to legal argumentation that justifies norm-statements and value-statements. If a lawyer argues in favor of a norm-statement and value-statement, he must appeal to his system of acceptances and preferences at that time. If the skeptic wants to convince him that the argumentation is wrong, the appeal to this system at that time is again all he can make. And it is more reasonable that the widespread practice of legal argumentation is justifiable than that it is a mere collection of phantasms.

6. Law and Morality

6.1. Legal Argumentation as a Special Case of Moral Argumentation

Back to the law. It is plausible to say that a reasonable legal argumentation is a special case of a reasonable moral argumentation[92]. Both moral substantive reasons and legal authority reasons, based on such sources of the law as statutes, precedents, preparatory legislative materials etc., are relevant in both moral and legal reasoning. Various sources of the law have, however, a privileged position in legal reasoning:

- Their weight in the law is so great that only particularly strong substantive reasons are sufficient to override them.
- They are apt to explain legal decisions. It is thus quite natural to say, "*A* was sentenced to prison because the statute required it".
- They are also necessary from the legal point of view. Without sources of the law, a conclusion has no legal support.

Notice that this theory does imply that a good lawyer weighs and balances his "purely" moral convictions (resulting from a moral deliberation and which do not take the law into account) and the law. This, however, does not make him a morally bad man. Since what a good man is, is possible to tell only when one

[91] K. Lehrer, *Theory of Knowledge*, 176 ff.

[92] This thesis is stronger than Alexy's view that legal argumentation is a special case of *practical* argumentation, cf. R. Alexy, *A Theory of Legal Argumentation*, 212 ff.

takes into account the role in which the "good man" acts. If he acts as a lawyer, the law morally binds him.

6.2. Prima Facie Law and Prima Facie Morality

Established legal norms have a *prima facie* moral relevance[93]. Reasonable morality does not only express general principles, it also allows for reliance on traditions, at least at the "prole" level. Thus, valid legal rules are morally relevant, *i.e.*, constitute moral *prima facie* (and thus defeasible) reasons that must be weighed and balanced against moral principles. This implies a theory which relativises the difference between moral principles and legal rules. Namely, both moral principles and legal rules have a moral (!) *prima facie* force. In this way, we arrive at a synthesis of legal and moral theory, avoiding both the separation of law from morality and the natural law dogmatism. In this context, one can distinguish between two kinds of moral considerations and thus between "morality 1" and "morality 2". Morality 1 expresses general principles but ignores valid law. Morality 2 requires a weighing and balancing between these principles and the enacted law. Morality 2 thus assumes that valid laws are morally relevant, *i.e.*, constitute moral *prima facie* reasons. Only morality 2, not morality 1, determines all-things-considered (not merely *prima facie*) duties and values. Thus, the established law has a *prima facie* moral relevance.

The theory pays due attention to both authoritative rules and moral weighings. The first component has been emphasised by many versions of legal positivism, together with several theories of formalism of the law[94]. Robert S. Summers has in many works[95] dealt with the importance of the formal character of the law. He has identified "formal attributes" in legal rules, interpretive methods, legal reasons and legal system viewed as a whole. Indeed, there is no doubt that an important function of legal institutions (*inter alia* legislation, judicial practice and legal dogmatics, as well) is to always attempt replacing contextual weighing and balancing with a fixed priority order between legal rules. On the other hand, all such orders have been so far open for corrections in hard cases, by means of weighing in the particular context. This component has been emphasised by innumerable versions of the natural law theory, together with several theories of the role of morality in the law[96]. A political theorist, and perhaps even a legal methodologist, may say: weighing in a particular context is merely a last resort, to be employed by a lawyer only if no general and stable

---

[93] A. Peczenik, *On Law and Reason*, 250 ff.

[94] Cf., *e.g.*, J. Raz, *Ethics in the Public Domain*, 330 with the reference to F. Schauer and E. Weinrib.

[95] R. S. Summers, "The Juristic Study of Law's Formal Character", *Ratio Juris*, 1995, 237 ff. See also id., "My Philosophy of Law" in this volume.

[96] Cf., *e.g.*, Dworkin's and Alexy's theories, mentioned above.

priority order is in sight. An epistemologist may say: but, as a last resort, weighing is inevitable. And the epistemological question to answer is whether the weighing is justifiable or not. There is no contradiction between the view of the methodologist and the view of the epistemologist. They simply have different jobs. The present author certainly does not advocate a legal system heavily loaded with hard cases. But he wants to know in what sense a solution of such cases is justifiable.

6.3. Why to Obey the Law?

In other words, there exists a moral *prima facie* duty to obey the law. It can be justified by the following consequentialist argument. The purely moral argumentation is relatively uncertain, in consequence of its ultimate dependence upon personal preferences and feelings of various individuals. On the other hand, the law is more "fixed". A morally evil chaos would thus follow if a society no longer possessed a legal order. This observation is similar to Hobbes'[97] who characterised an individual's life in a stateless environment as "solitary, poor, nasty, brutish, and short". (This does not mean that one must accept Hobbes' contractarian theory of law). Most people agree intuitively that the lawless life would be "brutish and short". For others, one can argue that we need the law because we are not indestructible angels[98]. Thus, we *prima facie* ought to follow the law because the law introduces order and order is *prima facie* better than chaos.

A critic may now object that only some, not all, legal provisions create *prima facie* moral duties, while others are *prima facie* morally neutral, or even *prima facie* immoral. For example, she may claim that no one has a *prima facie* moral duty to obey a Nazi rule, forbidding Jews to marry "Arians". But this is a misunderstanding of the concept of "*prima facie*". *Prima facie*, one ought to obey this rule because all order (even a Nazi order) is *prima facie* better than chaos. At the same time, one has the *prima facie* duty not to obey the Nazi rule because it collides with many moral values. An act of weighing and balancing is necessary to determine that the second duty prevails: all-things-considered, one ought not to follow the Nazi rule.

Weighing may also be necessary to determine whether a certain normative order as a whole is or is not valid law. It thus would not be valid law, if it is so extremely immoral that the order it creates is worse than chaos. But an act of weighing is not necessary to establish a *prima facie* moral duty to follow provisions that already have been recognised as legally valid. Such a provision may be bad. But one still has a *prima facie* moral duty to follow it, since it

---

97 Hobbes, T., *Leviathan* (1651), Harmondsworth, 1968, chapter 13.

98 Another human being whose nature is far from angelic can kill me tonight if there were no police, cf., *e.g.*, H. L. A. Hart, *The Concept of Law*, Oxford, 1961, 189 ff.

belongs to a system that totally, as a whole, produces order and this order is *prima facie* better than chaos.

This duty is justifiable in the light of the evaluation of the legal system as a whole. And the evaluation is justifiable in the light of the background system of acceptances and preferences. Two coherentist points go hand in hand.

6.4. Why is Order Prima Facie Better than Chaos? A Utilitarian Answer

But why is order *prima facie* better than chaos? The most convincing answer (in my opinion) is, what follows. Order is *prima facie* morally better than chaos because it, on average, facilitates fulfilment of preferences of people (according to the formula, number of preferences multiplied by strength of respective preferences). As a consequence of it, each of us has a *prima facie* moral obligation to obey the law, because more and stronger preferences of human beings would remain unfulfilled, had many people violated the law.

This argument is contestable on the same ground as rule utilitarianism in general. For example, Joseph Raz[99] has pointed out that "law breaking is liable to undermine the effectiveness of the government in many cases. In others, violations of law have no such effect. Offences never known to anyone or violating the interests of one private individual only, (...) generally do not diminish the government's effectiveness". Raz is right in one important point: the utilitarian argument for the conclusion that order is *prima facie* better than chaos must be supplemented with a kind of universalisation maxim. Paraphrasing (and weakening) Kant's categorical imperative, one may assume something like the following norm: *Prima facie*, act only according to the maxim about which one could rationally wish that it be a general law. The hypothesis is plausible that general obedience to this weak norm in the long run promotes fulfilment of human preferences. However, "plausible" does not mean "irresistible". As the (non-Kantian) *prima facie* clause indicates, one may proffer counter-arguments to be weighed and balanced against this hypothesis and against the utilitarian justification of the duty to obey the law in general. Weighing means here an estimate of reasonableness in the light of a coherent system of acceptances and preferences.

By the way, there is an affinity between utilitarianism and coherentism. A utilitarianist must (coherently) argue for all principles that some non-utilitarianists regard as unshakable foundations of moral argumentation. When thus arguing, he must pay attention to all members of the society, and balance their preferences (or their happiness etc.). Indeed, Hare[100] considers his theory as utilitarianist, holistic and coherentist (but, at the same time, Kantian).

---

[99] J. Raz, *Ethics in the Public Domain*, 349.

[100] R. M. Hare, "Foundationalism and Coherentism in Ethics" in *Moral Knowledge? New Readings in Moral Epistemology,* W. Sinnott-Armstrong and M. Timmons (eds.), New

The utilitarian argument can be supplemented with recourse to tradition. Any tradition comprises some basic values and patterns of rationality, which are taken for granted within the tradition and may almost never be criticised. "Like all traditions law is comprised of beliefs [and] practices which are, or are believed to be, transmitted from the past and which retain authoritative significance in people's current beliefs, practices, etc."[101]. Utilitarianism and traditionalism can be combined much along Hare's pattern: utilitarianism at the Archangel's level, traditionalism at the prole's level. One needs here a hypothesis about the survival of the fittest among the preferences[102]. Since the tradition of the society develops in the process of continual contest in which different preferences fight for recognition, it is plausible that following the tradition leads to approximately the same consequences as following the preference calculus. Thus, we have a general *prima facie* obligation to obey the legal order, because it expresses our tradition. But, needless to say, this hypothesis is open to counter-arguments to be weighed and balanced against it.

6.5. Why is Order Prima Facie Better than Chaos? Some Other Answers

No doubt, one can try to support the general *prima facie* duty to obey the law with any other moral theory, as well.

Thus traditionalist justification may be made more profound by putting it into a communitarian and Wittgensteinian contexts. As a background, mention must be made here of Hegel and Bradley[103]. Modern communitarian philosophers have emphasised that a person is social and thus inevitably must rely on values of her society[104]. If so, only the tradition of the society can ultimately determine what is right and good. Wittgensteinian inspiration is similar. He links knowledge to "language-games"[105] and these are social in an important sense. Private language is impossible, because no one would correct mistakes committed by the lone speaker whose language no one else can understand[106]. Only the tradition of the

York/Oxford, 1996, 194 ff.

[101] M. Krygier, "Thinking Like a Lawyer" in *Ethical Dimensions of Legal Theory*, W. Sadurski (ed.), Amsterdam/Atlanta, 1991, 68; id., "Law as Tradition", 5 *Law and Philosophy*, 237 ff. (1986); M. Polanyi, *Personal Knowledge. Towards a Post-Critical Philosophy*, Chicago, 1962, 54.

[102] See section 5.4 above.

[103] Cf. R. Norman, *The Moral Philosophers. An Introduction to Ethics*, Oxford, 1983, 145 ff.

[104] M. J. Sandel, *Liberalism and the Limits of Justice*, Cambridge (Mass.), 1982, 147 ff., 173 ff.; cf. A. Peczenik, *Vad är rätt?*, 430-439.

[105] L. Wittgenstein, *On Certainty*, Oxford, 1979, no. 204; cf. no. 344.

[106] Id., *Philosophical Investigations*, Oxford, 1953, no. 256 ff. (notice the word "can"); cf. A. Aarnio, *Reason and Authority. A Treatise on the Dynamic Paradigm of Legal Dogmatics*, Aldershot, 1997, 114 ff.

society, not a lone individual, can determine what is justified, right and good[107]. Since the law is an important part of the tradition of our society, one might conclude that, *ceteris paribus*, we have the obligation to follow the law.

A classical answer to the question "Why ought we to obey the law?" is that people unanimously consent and thus promise to obey the law. This is a classical moral and political theory[108]. But the promise argument must be supplemented with a reasonable answer to the question "Why ought one to obey promises?"[109] One must also state precisely, what kind of promise creates the duty, an actual (explicit or implicit) or a hypothetical one. Actual is rather rare. If asked, the citizen "would certainly reply, that the affair depended not on their consent but that they were born to such obedience"[110]. Implicit is difficult to identify[111].

Hypothetical would perhaps be given behind the "veil of ignorance" where rational egoists must make impartial choices, because they know almost nothing about their place in the society, their talents or their views about the good and the evil[112].

6.6. Reasonability of the Prima Facie-Clause

At the end of the day, all such theories are contestable and in the need of further support. This makes it reasonable to add the *prima facie*-clause. Instead of "Why is order better than chaos?" one should ask "Why is order *prima facie* better than chaos?" Instead of "Why ought we to obey the order-creating law?" one should ask "Why ought we *prima facie* to obey the order-creating law?" The *prima facie*-clause indicates that whatever one says to justify the obligation to follow the law is open to counter-arguments. These must be dealt with on the ground of other reasons, and these are defeasible, as well. In other words: none of them is the sole foundation of legal philosophy. All are only reasonable ideas, competing with other arguments in the light of the background system of preferences and acceptances.

---

[107] Cf. id., *ibid.*, 101 ff. and id., *The Rational as Reasonable*, Dordrecht/ Boston/London, 1987, 213 ff.

[108] See, *e.g.*, W. Kymlicka, "The Social Contract Tradition" in *A Companion to Ethics*, P. Singer (ed.), Cambridge, 1991, 186 ff.; J. Hampton, "Contract and Consent" in *A Companion to Contemporary Political Philosophy*, R. E. Gooding and P. Pettit (eds.), Cambridge, 1993, 379 ff.; C. W. Morris, "A Contractarian Account of Moral Justification" in *Moral Knowledge?*, 215 ff.

[109] Cf. W. Kymlicka, "The Social Contract Tradition", 188, with a reference to Hume.

[110] Hume's famous words, see J. Hampton, "Contract and Consent", 380.

[111] Id., *ibid.*, 381.

[112] J. Rawls, *A Theory of Justice*, 136 ff.

7. Knowledge of Morally Justified Interpretation of Law

7.1. The Bad Luck of Moral and Legal Theorists

Coherentism is applicable to all knowledge, even in natural sciences. Yet, in natural sciences, it is profitable in terms of pragmatic success to forget the profound and necessarily coherentist questions concerning justification in the light of the background system as a whole. Instead, strict theories evolve (in the process resembling natural selection) based on some assumptions, philosophically speaking uncertain but assumed within the paradigm in question. When pursuing moral and legal knowledge, we are less lucky.

To be sure, one can find analogies between matrices (and paradigms) in 0natural science and legal research. According to Aulis Aarnio[113] the matrix of legal dogmatics, in a modified Kuhnian sense, consists of the following four components. 1) a set of philosophical background presuppositions, *inter alia* the assumption that legal reasoning is based on valid law; 2) pre-suppositions concerning the sources of the law; 3) presuppositions concerning legal method; 4) a set of values, first of all concerning legal certainty and justice. Each legal paradigm contains a particular interpretation of the matrix[114]. Legal reasoning of different times and societies is underpinned by different sets of assumptions concerning valid law, legal sources, legal method, legal certainty etc. But all legal reasoning is based on some presuppositions of these kinds.

Yet, the disciplinary matrix of lawyers does not allow them to proceed as precisely and uncontroversially as the natural scientists do. It rather compels them to allow for hard cases and the moral reasoning they require. And there is no disciplinary matrix for moral reasoning.

Both scientific knowledge and nontrivial knowledge of legal and moral norms progress by trial and error, and one must resort to a certain convention to define what "error" means[115]. Yet, the situation of moral and legal knowledge is much worse than that of knowledge in general. In morality and in the law, defeasibility is more radical. In natural science, a cluster of sophisticated, precise, complex, relatively uncontroversial and useful theories has already evolved. No matter that the theories provoke epistemological problems. It is a fact that such a cluster of theories exists. It is also a good luck of mankind that it exists. In the humanities, we are somewhat less lucky, as for example the history of sociology amply shows. In practical contexts, among other things those concerning the

[113] *E.g.*, A. Aarnio, "Paradigms in Legal Dogmatics" in *Theory of Legal Science*, 25 ff.

[114] Concerning description of various paradigms of legal research, see J. Dalberg-Larsen, *Retsvidenskaben som samfundsvidenskab* (Legal science as social science), Copenhagen, 1977, 513 ff.

[115] K. R. Popper, *The Logic of Scientific Discovery*, 40 ff. and id., *Objective Knowledge*, 261 ff. See also A. Peczenik, *On Law and Reason*, 138 ff.

question of what ought to be (as opposed to what actually is), we are even less lucky. Consequently, determination of "error" in legal science is often holistic and circular.

Is this just a historical coincidence, or can these differences be explained?

A possible explanation of the "bad luck" of moral and legal theorists is that human systems of preferences, perhaps for biological reasons, are vague and subject to irrational (emotional) change. Thus, human beings are unable to develop sophisticated, relatively stable and commonly accepted moral theories. An individual's personal preferences and feelings, within the flexible and ever-changing framework of the cultural heritage determine the ultimate step of moral argumentation.

This is a descriptive, contingent explanation. What theory of legal and moral knowledge fits into it?

7.2. Knowledge of the Morally Justified Interpretation of Law?

Legal argumentation is a practice pursuing knowledge of the law, yet relying upon weighing and balancing of values. This is a serious problem. The following diagram illustrates the problem:

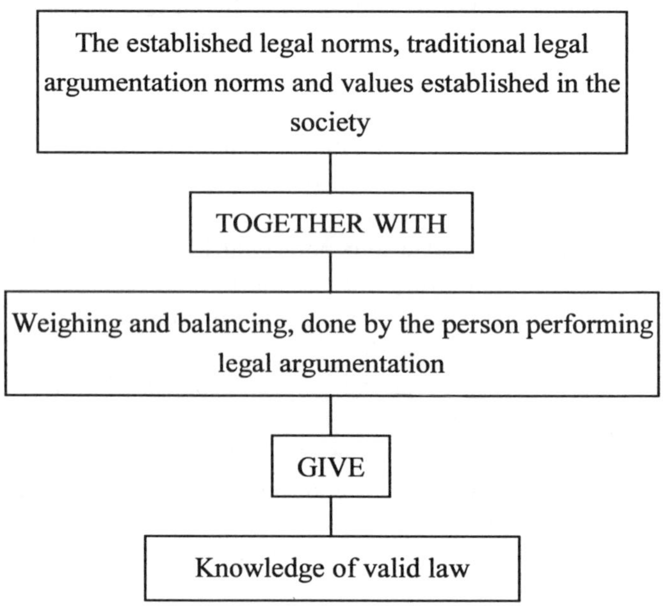

More precisely, there are at least two problems involved here. First, one must explicate the expression "knowledge of valid law". Without additional argument, let me state that this expression refers here to knowledge of the morally justified interpretation of law.

Second, in what sense, if any, can evaluations give us knowledge? To say that a theoretical proposition gives us knowledge may be thought about as the same as to say that it is true. Can a legal interpretative statement then be true, even if justifiable by a set of premises containing evaluations?

7.3. Prima Facie Noncognitivism as Regards All-Things-Considered Moral and Legal Statements. Prima Facie Revisionism as Regards Prima Facie Moral and Legal Statements

One way of answering our question involves a theory, which is cognitivist as regards *prima facie* norm- and value statements and, at the same time, noncognitivist as regards all-things-considered norm- and value statements. The former are true if they correspond to the cultural heritage of the society. The latter may be more or less reasonable in the light of the acceptance- and preference-system of an individual, but they are not true in the ontological sense.

By the way, this is also applicable to the lawyers' utterances *de lege lata* even if Svein Eng is right that they have a peculiar, fused modality, neither purely descriptive nor purely normative. According to Eng, to press them into this dichotomy is the same as to suppress the peculiarity of the legal language[116]. There exists an extensive institutional practice of such fusion[117]. But the normative component makes the fused utterances as problematic – epistemologically speaking – as the normative and evaluative ones.

From the ontological point of view, such a theory would be realist as regards *prima facie* values. Such values exist in the culture of the society. Moreover, they are irresistible for an individual belonging to this culture. The communitarians are right that a person is social and thus inevitably must rely on basic values of her society. Wittgenstein is right that both the language an individual uses and the rules she follows are created by the society[118]. If so, no individual is in the position to consistently adopt an external point of view towards her own society. She must endorse the basic rules and values, or stop living. It does not suffice to accept some "spurious" moral and legal statements in Ingemar Hedenius' sense[119] about that others endorse them. All this can be stated here regardless of two obvious caveats. Firstly, this realism is rather not literal. It involves a great portion of revisionism. For surely, ordinary speakers put something more in their statements of basic moral and legal values or norms than a mere reference to cultural heritage. And secondly, the demarcation line between

---

[116] S. Eng, *Definisjoner, karakteristikker og interesser. Bidrag till u/enighetsanalyse; med saerlig sikte på jus og allmenn rettsteori* (Definitions, characteristics and interests), Oslo, 1996 (mimeographed), 378.

[117] Id., *ibid.*, 409-410.

[118] Cf. section 7.5 above.

[119] I. Hedenius, *Om rätt och moral* (On law and morality), Stockholm, 1963^2, 51.

basic and non-basic values is inevitably vague. No wonder that Svein Eng[120] has criticised our distinction between the culture-bound values and personal-coloured weighing. In his view, one must perform an act of weighing already in order to ascertain what values are relevant. Nonetheless, the point remains that one cannot jump out of one's own culture. The starting point of weighing consists always of some "old", already accepted, values. To start a weighing, one must have something to weigh. All this can be said regardless of the fact that, from the epistemological point of view, a moral person has a choice what to doubt and what to regard as certain. The moral person himself must make the choice. He could have done another way around. Any value can be doubted. But one cannot doubt all or almost all the socially established values simultaneously. The only constraint here is coherence (and epistemological conservatism).

At the same time, the theory would not be ontologically realist as regards all-things-considered values. These are not pre-existent, but continually created in the process of moral reasoning. In other words, moral reasoning does not discover them but merely creates, invents them.

In view of such a theory, knowledge of *prima facie* values is possible, whereas a well-argued belief concerning an all-things-considered value merely expresses something essentially similar to knowledge, not knowledge in the literal sense.

But how can I be sure that this theory is adequate? After all, many well-known arguments can be proffered both against non-cognitivism and against the grounding of *prima facie* values on cultural heritage. Of course, I cannot be sure. Rather, the theory appears to be more reasonable than its competitors. This estimate is defeasible. In other words, *prima facie* moral and legal statements are *prima facie* truth-evaluable in the light of cultural heritage whereas all-things-considered moral and legal statements are *prima facie* not truth-evaluable.

7.4. A Comparison with Ontological Relativism and Error Theory

This use of the idea of *prima facie* is rather similar to but not identical with the theory of ontological relativity. According to this theory, there are many justifiable views of reality, each corresponding to a different ontological or metaphysical system. The validity of any metaphysics is relative. A metaphysics presupposes a background theory which defines the concept "real"[121] and states what to regard as individual objects, their parts, their kinds etc.[122] There may be

---

[120] S. Eng, "Noen synspunkter på en teori om etikk, rett og erkjennelse", *Tidsskrift for Rettsvitenskap*, 1991, 283 ff.
[121] W. V. O. Quine, *Ontological Relativity and Other Essays*, New York, 1969, 53 ff.
[122] N. Goodman, *Ways of Worldmaking*, Sussex, 1978, 7 ff.

many metaphysical systems, “all such systems being wholly comprehensive and mutually incompatible, but all equally valid descriptions of one's reality”[123].

Yet, the theory of ontological relativity faces an important problem[124]. Can one make sense of the ontological opinion that p (for instance the meta-ethical thesis that value judgements are capable of being true) is true relatively to the background theory 1, yet false relatively to the background theory 2? The immediate question must be “Is p true all-things-considered?” The ontological relativist ignores this question. I think that the question is good, but all answers I can think about are defeasible.

John Mackie's error theory is an alternative view. “Indeed, ordinary moral judgements involve a claim to objectivity which both non-cognitive and naturalist analyses fail to capture. Moral scepticism must, therefore, take the form of an error theory, admitting that a belief in objective values is built into ordinary moral thought and language but holding that this ingrained belief is false”[125]. Once, I made an impression of accepting this[126].

I agree with Mackie[127] that there are important arguments against the common sense belief in objective values. Yet, there is no way to establish the non-defeasible conclusion that these arguments prevail and thus make the common sense belief an error.

The error theory may be weakened to become the theory that moral and legal statements are *prima facie* false. But this weaker theory is contestable, as well. For it is not even *prima facie* plausible to tell, *e.g.*, “It is not true that Hitler ought not have murdered Jews”, whereas it is more plausible to say, *e.g.*, “The conviction that Hitler ought not have murdered Jews is not a matter of truth but only a matter of strongly justified moral opinion”.

To be sure, one can plausibly insist that there be only one world, but we may see it in different ways, *inter alia* because of different understanding of certain utterances[128]. But this does not help much the value theorist who is supposed to make a justified choice between these different ways.

Both ontological relativism and error theory give us important insights into the nature of values. But, as most philosophical theories, they are defeasible. A philosopher is like Sisyphus – always attempting to give non-defeasible answers to questions that do not have such an answer.

---

[123] H.-N. Castañeda, *On Philosophical Method*, Indianapolis, 1980, 19.

[124] L. Bergström, *Värdeteori* (Theory of values), Stockholm, 1990, 125.

[125] J. Mackie, *Ethics. Inventing Right and Wrong*, Harmondsworth, 1977, 48-49.

[126] A. Peczenik, *The Basis of Legal Justification*, Lund, 1983, 78.

[127] J. Mackie, *Ethics*, 49.

[128] J. Searle, *The Construction of Social Reality*, 195.

7.5. The Passion for Reason

So is the humanist and, indeed, the jurist. The failure of so many attempts to construct moral and legal theories *more geometrico* has lead to the well-known talk about two cultures (the humanities as something very different from the natural science). It has also opened the door for many kinds of rather loose speculations in the spirit of post-modern and other poetry. This kind of frustration is psychologically explainable, yet premature. For even if moral and legal theory cannot be as precise as physics, it still can be deemed as more or less reasonable. We all pursue rationality, both in morality and in the law. Why? If this is not the problem of truth, I do not see any other answer than that we have a preference towards rationality. More precisely, a preference towards coherence. A passion for reason.

You think you do not have it? All right, go and shout at each other, and fight.

8. Coherence in the Law

8.1. The Postulate that the Law Should Be Coherent Does Not Necessarily Follow From Epistemological Coherentism

It is important to notice that the postulate that the law should be as coherent as possible does not follow logically from the epistemological coherence theory.

First of all, such a coherence theory deals with knowledge. Law, on the other hand, is an institutional phenomenon, categorically different from knowledge. This is what Raz[129] seems to have in mind when writing that "coherence is but one of at least two components in any theory of law. The other component provides the base to which the coherence account applies". This base must be the same for all "believers"[130].

Secondly, the theory is applicable to legal knowledge, but what is legal knowledge? The problem remains open whether the result of legal argumentation deserves the name of knowledge, as we will see later.

Thirdly, even if there is a legal knowledge, there are important constraints upon the postulate that such a knowledge shall be as coherent as possible. An increase of coherence may lead to an unacceptable complexity of knowledge. This phenomenon is known even in natural science. (Wave and particle theories of light are not coherent with each other, but an effort to press all data into a coherent theory would lead to excessive complexity).

---

[129] J. Raz, *Ethics in the Public Domain*, 289.

[130] Id., *ibid.*, 288.

8.2. Yet, the Postulate of Coherence of the Law is Reasonable

Yet, the postulate of coherence of the law is reasonable. It is obvious as regards the minimum of perfect coherence, *i.e.* logical consistency. For no one doubts that inconsistency is apt to create insecurity in the implementation of the law: neither the authorities would know what rules to apply, nor the citizens would be able to plan their lives in trust to the law. Consistency of the law is thus an important value, though it must be weighed and balanced against other values.

Less trivial is the role of the support component in the law. In general, the definitive moral obligations are all-things-considered ones. This means that all reasons for and against such an obligation must be considered before one knows whether one ought to follow the moral norm in question. It is a conceptual anomaly to tell that one has a moral obligation to do x, and yet to refuse to tell why[131]. It is even more anomalous to tell that one has a legal obligation to do x and to refuse to tell why. To be sure, the "why?" may be simply answered by quoting authorities. Yet, a legal argumentation, which is not, at least implicitly, based on a coherent system of norms and values, is an *ad hoc* argumentation. And its result may easily be unjust[132]. In the modern society, there are also some more particular reasons for coherent justification of legal decisions and opinions[133]. The parties of a litigation and the citizens in general do not blindly trust the lawgiver or the decision makers. They simply want to know why the decisions are as they are. Moreover, a coherent justification of legal norms and interpretations facilitates the social control over the law making and law-implementing institutions, and this is an important requirement of democracy.

All these considerations make the postulate of coherence in the legislation and in the implementation of the law reasonable. Indeed, coherence (sometimes called also "unity" or "integrity") of the legal system is a basic assumption of legal dogmatics and – to some extent – legal decision making, too. By the way, all segments of knowledge (among other things, all kinds of science) are based on assumptions. Such assumptions can be neither demonstrated nor falsified within the segment in question. They are taken for granted and to some extent determine what counts as belonging to this segment.

---

[131] L. L. Fuller, "Positivism and fidelity to law" in *Philosophy of Law*, J. Feinberg and H. Gross (eds.), 1986[3], 91: "Coherence and goodness have more affinity than coherence and evil".

[132] N. MacCormick, "Coherence in Legal Justification" in *Theory of Legal Science*, 243.

[133] G. Bergholtz, *Ratio et Auctoritas. Ett komparativrättsligt bidrag till frågan om domsmotiveringens betydelse främst i tvistemål*, Lund, 1987, 352 ff.

8.3. Coherence of Law Versus Other Values

But such assumptions are not absolute. They compete with other values. I thus agree with Joseph Raz[134] that perfection (and – let me add – coherence) should not be "purchased at the cost of losing contact with reality". For example, coherence of law should be an important goal of legal argumentation. But it must always be weighed and balanced against other things. One can, for instance, say that coherence of law competes with the value of subsidiarity (decision making at the lowest efficient level). Namely, if the decision making is decentralised, it may be more just, more informed and so on, but, at the same time – the coherence between the practice of decision making at one place will be incoherent with the practice at another place. Moreover, stability of law competes with the value of dynamic adaptation of the law to the so-called requirements of the life. In particular, some incoherence in the law may be justifiable if it promotes efficient working of market economy and conflict-free co-operation of people. Finally, Raz claims "that because the law is meant to be taken as a system based on authority its content is to determined by reference to the intention of legal authorities and their reasons, and, therefore, that, given the vagaries of politics, including (...) judicial involvement in politics, there is no reason to expect the law to be coherent"[135].

But authority, dynamism and subsidiarity can be justified only within a coherent moral/political theory. Within such a theory, one cannot regard the law as a product of politics only. Rather, the law is a product of an interplay between politics and – to paraphrase Ronald Dworkin's famous words – the sense of justice of the public and the legal profession. The politicians may indeed create a mess. One of important functions of the lawyers in general and legal scholars in particular is to bring order into it.

In their practice of argumentation, the lawyers often claim that their job is:

- to regard the law of a state as one legal system;
- to regard inconsistency and insufficient coherence as defects of this system; and
- to eliminate the defects by legal interpretation.

The fact that the lawyers often make this claim indicates that a social norm like "a state's law should be interpreted as one system" exists in the lawyer's argumentation practice.

This theory of the function of the lawyers reminds us of Kelsen's famous view that the lawyers presuppose the "*Grundnorm*". The laws inherit their validity from the legally valid Constitution. Then, the lawyers take for granted the "*Grundnorm*" that the Constitution is valid, that is, ought to be obeyed[136]. This

[134] J. Raz, *Ethics in the Public Domain*, 289.
[135] Id., *ibid.*, 300.
[136] H. Kelsen, *Reine Rechtslehre*, Vienna, 1960², 203 ff.

"*Grundnorm*" converts a variety of norms into unity, since it is the basis of validity of all norms that belong to this legal order[137]. The "*Grundnorm*" is open to many interpretations but the simple point to make here is that the postulate of coherence of the law is something important for lawyers.

8.4. The Unity Postulate in Spite of the Lack of Clear Criteria

Thus, I subscribe to the thesis Raz beautifully presents (and, unfortunately, refutes): "Given the law's settled rules and doctrines, a court ought to adopt that solution to the case before it which is favoured by the most coherent of the theories (*i.e.* set of propositions) which, were the settled rules of the system justified, would justify them"[138].

Raz's negative conclusion is: "Given multiplicity of criteria, it is possible that sometimes coherence has to be sacrificed for some other good" and "there is no way of deciding which mix of coherence and other values is best"[139], because "there is no general method of rationality"[140]. To this, I answer that coherence certainly is no method of rationality, yet it is a supreme postulate of rationality. Human beings have a propensity to ask "why?", and to search for reasons for any value or principle they assume. In this way, one may establish mutual support between the plurality of values.

Moreover, no living person is a Hercules who efficiently can put all her beliefs into a coherent system. This is only the goal of knowledge and a goal of morality, unreachable but irresistible. Once again, a human being is often like a Sisyphus, pursuing unreachable goals like reason, truth, justice and coherence.

8.5. Pockets of Coherence

Indeed, Raz mentions (but not discusses) the thesis that "morality is not a system or a coherent body of principles. It contains, to be sure, pockets of coherence, and it is consistent. But it contains of a large number of principles which neither derive from a common source not are capable of fitting into a uniform system or a system whose principles are mutually supportive and interdependent"[141]. I agree that neither values nor principles derive from a common source. But I insist that they are capable of fitting into a uniform system or a system whose principles are mutually supportive and interdependent. But unfortunately, the support will always be defeasible.

As regards the law, Raz is perfectly right when he states: "The coherence to which value pluralism is hostile is the felt need (...) to subsume the plurality of values under as few as possible supreme principles. While these attempts ought to

137 Id., *ibid.*, 197.
138 J. Raz, *Ethics in the Public Domain*, 302.
139 Id., *ibid.*, 303.
140 Id., *ibid.*, 305.
141 Id., *ibid.*, 298.

be resisted, we must recognise that the application of each of the distinct values ought to be consistently pursued, and this generates pockets of coherence"[142]. In brief, the postulate that the system of law of a state should be interpreted in the way making it as coherent as possible is only a *prima facie* social norm, to be weighed and balanced with other values.

8.6. Pockets of Coherence and Plurality of Legal Roles

Plurality of pockets of coherence is only to be expected. Hector-Neri Castañeda stated the following: "Knowledge and justified belief are multifarous in their species and types. The species or types of knowledge and justified belief are determined by the background takens-for-granted"[143]. Social conventions this person knows and social roles in which she acts *de facto* influence and – if the communitarians are right – must influence the "takens-for-granted" of each person.

Plurality of pockets of coherence corresponds to the plurality of social roles. As already stated, legal argumentation is a special case of moral argumentation. What is special is that a person performing legal argumentation enters a particular social role, the role of a lawyer. This role has social consequences. Reasoning like a lawyer strengthens legal order and order is *prima facie* better than chaos. Thus, the law is morally binding on the utilitarian ground.

However, legal argumentation is not uniform. There exist various legal roles and corresponding types of argumentation. Each role determines its own delimitation between routine cases in which the law ought to be followed without deliberation and hard cases requiring a weighing and balancing of the law against moral considerations. The delimitation of routine cases includes a valuation. This valuation is implicitly included in the assumed role. It is not justifiable inside this but it certainly is justifiable within another role, perhaps within the role of a philosopher. A lawyer performs this delimitation intuitively, and so he must and ought to do.

Justified argumentation of a judge is affected by the duty of the judge to make a binding decision, regardless whether the reasoning is conclusive or not. Moreover, the procedural framework binds the decider. The procedural framework deciding, *e.g.*, about the degrees of objectivity required from an attorney and a prosecutor also binds argumentation made by the parties.

Justified argumentation accessible for a public official depends on the nature of his job. For example, a chairman of a philosophical department may justify his decision to interpret library regulations very much contrary to their wording but in the best interests of the students.

---

[142] Id., *ibid.*, 315.
[143] H. N. Castañeda, *On Philosophical Method*, 232.

Justified doctrinal interpretation of the law (performed by legal scholars in the so-called legal dogmatics) is partly different from the one used in judicial practice. Certainly, the best argumentation in legal questions must consider all legally relevant *prima facie* reasons.

This applies to both legal dogmatics and legal practice. The differences are mainly the following. A legal scholar has no power to make binding decisions. The scholar chooses his subject matter freely. The judge, on the other hand, is bound by claims, demands and motions of the parties. The scholar searches for problems, whereas the judge restricts himself to the problems, which are necessary for the case in adjudication. The scholar may freely make recommendations *de lege ferenda*. The scholar may boldly propose new juristic methods whereas the judge must make a correct decision in the light of the prevailing legal method[144]. The scholar expresses himself in a more abstract manner and is less oriented towards actual cases and facts[145]. The scholar uses many examples of both actual and hypothetical situations. The most important difference is that the doctrinal argumentation often claims to be more rational, *i.e.*, more coherent than judicial argumentation. It is therefore "system-oriented". Among "all things" to be considered, systemic connections with other norms and values are especially important[146]. Increased coherence is thus an important goal of interpretation of the law both in legal dogmatics and in legal practice. In legal practice, however, the role of this goal is more limited. Only the norms applicable to the considered case are to be considered. Their coherent reworking can decrease their coherence with other legal norms. Moreover, the norms are made as coherent as the case requires, together with its possible role as a pattern-establishing precedent. The interpretation increasing mutual coherence of norms in the considered case may decrease their coherence in other cases.

The similarity between doctrinal and judicial interpretation is, however, even more important than all these differences. Both deal with the same subject matter (valid law), the same working materials (statutes, precedents etc.) and both must use weighing and balancing in order to interpret the law in a coherent and morally acceptable manner.

Consequently, unity of the law is assumed both in legal practice and in legal dogmatics, but in two different manners. In legal practice, it is assumed as much as the decided case and its possible precedent function requires. In legal dogmatics, it is assumed to the extent enabling the scholar to establish a total view of the legal system as a unity.

---

[144] R. Lavin, "Om förvaltningsrättslig forskning en replik" (On research in administrative law, an answer), *Förvaltningsrättslig Tidsskrift*, 1990, 72 ff.

[145] Id., "Är den förvaltningsrättsliga forskningen rättsdogmatisk?" (Is research in administrative law legal dogmatics?), *Förvaltningsrättslig Tidsskrift*, 1989, 118.

[146] See also id., *ibid.*, 123.

From another point of view, the unity assumption is, however, stronger in legal practice than in legal dogmatics. In practice, the decider must solve the case, and thus he must regard the law as unity to the extent demanded by this purpose. In legal dogmatics, a scholar must put the question whether the law can be regarded as a unity. He must even try to answer this question in the affirmative. But when all juristic attempts to interpret the law as a unity fail, he can peacefully give up. He did his best, and yet the chaos cannot be avoided.

9. A Reflective Question: Why Shall the Legal Theorist Rely on Coherentist Epistemology?

The reader may now ask "Why do we lawyers need all this talk about coherence, when the author himself admits that the best law is not always the most coherent one?" The answer to this question is surprisingly simple. Recourse to coherence is inevitable, if not at the lawyer's level, then at another, higher, level. For if anyone tells us that the best law in the particular situation is not the one which is the most coherent, she must coherently(!) argue that this is the case. Let us call such a view the Legal Anti-Coherentist Thesis (LACT). The LACT is precisely in the same position as Lehrer's skeptic. Paraphrasing Lehrer, let me state the following. The LACT has no privileged status compared with other beliefs. It is merely a competitor of other beliefs. It has to win the competition with the view that the best law is the most coherent one. If what the coherentist accepts is something that is more reasonable for her to accept than the LACT, then the coherentist wins.

The ultimate basis of all theories about blessings of incoherence must be composed of coherent argumentation. Coherentism is self-supporting. Anti-coherentism is self-destroying. One consequence of this observation is that the discussion of coherence is useful not only for the traditional legal dogmatics but also for more critical orientations of legal research. Whatever you criticise, you must criticise in a reasonable, that is, coherent manner. Thus, only coherence at a higher level of argumentation may justify incoherence at a lower level.

Bibliographical Information

I. Books

1. *Wartosc Naukowa dogmatyki prawa* (Scientific value of legal dogmatics), Kraków, 1966.
2. *Essays in Legal Theory*, Copenhagen, 1970.
3. *Causes and Damages*, Lund, 1979.
4. *Juridikens metodproblem* (Problems of method in legal research), Stockholm, 1980[2].
5. *The Basis of Legal Justification*, Lund, 1983.
6. *Grundlagen der juristischen Argumentation*, Vienna/New York, 1983.
7. *Rätten och förnuftet* (Law and reason), Stockholm, 1988[2].
8. *Rättsnormer* (Legal norms), Stockholm, 1987.
9. *On Law and Reason*, Dordrecht/Boston/London, 1989.
10. (with A. Aarnio and G. Bergholtz) *Juridisk Argumentation* (Legal argumentation), Stockholm, 1990.
11. Juridikens teori och metod (Theory and method in legal research), Stockholm, 1995.
12. *Vad är rätt?* (What is law?), Stockholm, 1995.

II. Articles

1. "Wykladnia a fortiori" (Interpretation a fortiori), *Zeszyty naukowe Uniwersytetu Jagiellonskiego,* 1962, 123-149.
2. "Uprawnienie i obowiazek" (Right and duty), *Panstwo i Prawo*, 1964, 225-233.
3. "Problemy prawoznawstwa a logika norm" (Jurisprudential problems and the logic of norms), *Panstwo i Prawo*, 1965, 47-55.
4. "O definicji sankcji prawnej" (On the definition of legal sanction), *Panstwo i Prawo*, 1965, 450-454.
5. "Normy planowe a nauka prawa" (Planning guidelines and legal dogmatics), *Panstwo i Prawo*, 1966, 694-704.
6. "Doctrinal Study of Law and Science", *Österreichische Zeitschrift für öffentliches Recht*, 1967, 128-141.
7. "Problem wynikania norm prawnych" (The problem of inference between legal norms), *Studia Filozoficzne*, 1967, 213-223.
8. "Norms and Reality, *Theoria*, 1968, 117-133.
9. "Plaszczyzny badania prawa" (Planes of legal research), *Panstwo i Prawo*, 1968, 232-243.
10. "Juristic Definition of Law", 78 *Ethics*, 255-268 (1968).
11. "Empirical Foundations of Legal Dogmatics", *Logique et Analyse*, 1969, 32-64.
12. "The Concept of Rights", *Archivum Iuridicum Cracoviense*, 1969, 47-60.

13. "Petrazycki o dogmatyce prawa – krytyka czy obrona?" (Petrazycki about legal dogmatics: criticism or defense?) in *Z zagadnien teorii prawa i teorii nauki Leona Petrazyckiego*, Warsaw, 1969, 137-149.
14. "Analogia legis. Analogy from Statutes in Continental Law" in *Legal Reasoning. Proceedings of the World Congress for Legal and Social Philosophy*, H. Hubien (ed.), Brussels, 1971, 329-336.
15. "Principles of Law. The Search for Legal Theory", *Rechtstheorie*, 1971, 17-36.
16. "Towards the Juristic Theory of Law", *Österreichische Zeitschrift für öffentliches Recht*, 1971, 167-182.
17. "Om rättvisa" (On justice), *Tidsskrift for Rettsvitenskap*, 1972, 520-531.
18. "The Concept 'Valid Law'", *Scandinavian Studies in Law*, 1972, 211-252.
19. "Rättsordningens struktur" (The structure of a legal order), *Svensk juristtidning*, 1974, 369-380.
20. "Leon Petrazycki and the Post-Realist Jurisprudence" in *Sociology and Jurisprudence of Leon Petrazycki*, J. Górecki (ed.), Urbana/Chicago/London, 1975, 83-107.
21. "The Structure of a Legal System", *Rechtstheorie*, 1975, 1-16.
22. "Forskning i allmän rättslära – finns den?" (Research in jurisprudence – does it exist?) in *Studier tillägnade Hilding Eek, Seve Ljungman och Folke Schmidt.* Stockholm, 1976, 357-376.
23. "Juridisk operationism" (Legal operationalism), J.F.T., 1977, 112-131.
24. "Juridisk operationism – huvudpunkter" (Legal operationalism – main points) in *Uppsalaskolan och efteråt*, S. Strömholm (ed.), Uppsala, 1978, 135-142.
25. "Causation and Fault in Torts" in *Festschrift für Helmut Schelsky*, Berlin, 1978, 371-390.
26. "Rätt och fel i juridisk argumentation" (Right and wrong in legal argumentation), *Lundaforskare föreläser*, 1979, 14-21.
27. "Beyond Realism", *Cornell Law Forum*, 1979, 12-17.
28. "Kan juristerna tänka rationellt?" (Can the lawyers think rationally?) in *Rationalitet i rättssystemet*, Ulla Bondeson (ed.), Stockholm, 1979, 200-215.
29. "Non-equivalent Transformations and the Law" in *Reasoning on Legal Reasoning*, A. Peczenik and J. Uusitalo (eds.), Vammala, 1979, 47-64.
30. "Non-equivalent Transformations and the Law", *Rechtstheorie,* 1979, Beiheft 1, 163-176.
31. "Cumulation and Compromise of Reasons in the Law" in *Nomos*, XXI, New York, 1979, 190-204.
32. "On the Nature and Function of the Grundnorm", *Rechtstheorie,* 1981, Beiheft 2, 1981, 279-298.
33. (with A. Aarnio and R. Alexy) "The Foundation of Legal Reasoning", *Rechtstheorie*, 1981, 133-158, 257-280 and 423-449.
34. "Legal Research and Growth of Science" in *Memoria del X Congreso Mundial de Filosofia del Derecho y Filosofia Social*, Mexico, 1981, 17-28.

35. "Two Sides of the Grundnorm" in *Die Reine Rechtslehre in wissenschaftlicher Diskussion*, Vienna, 1982, 58-63.
36. "Rationality of Legal Justification", *A.R.S.P.*, 1982, 137-163.
37. "Legal Errata" in *Deontic Logic, Computational Linguistics and Legal Information Systems*, II, A. Martino (ed.), Amsterdam/New York/Oxford, 1982, 103-125.
38. "Right and Wrong in Legal Reasoning", *A.R.S.P.*, Supplementa, I, 1, 1982, 37-75.
39. "Rätt och moral" (Law and morality), *Svensk juristtidning*, 1982, 609-620.
40. "Taking Laws Seriously", 68, *Cornell Law Review*, 660-684 (1983).
41. (with A. Aarnio and R. Alexy) "Grundlagen der juristischen Argumentation" in *Metatheorie juristischer Argumentation*, W. Krawietz and R. Alexy (eds.), Berlin, 1983, 9-87.
42. "Is There Always a Right Answer to a Legal Question?" in *Essays in Legal Theory in Honor of Kaarle Makkonen*, Helsinki, 1983, 239-258.
43. "Vad är den juridiska argumentationen?" (What is legal argumentation?) *Tidsskrift for Rettsvitenskap*, 1983, 49-76.
44. "Juridiska data. Ett bidrag till rättens ontologi" (Legal data. A remark on ontology of the law), *Tidskrift för Rätssociologi*, 1983, 253-262.
45. "The Rationality and Its Limits", *Rechtstheorie,* 1984, 415-422.
46. "Opraktiskt paradigmskifte i juridiken" (Impractical paradigm shift in legal research), *Svensk Juristtidning*, 1984, 453-461.
47. "Legal Data. An Essay About the Ontology of Law" in *Theory of Legal Science*, A. Peczenik, L. Lindahl and B. van Roermund (eds.), Dordrecht/Boston/Lancaster, 1984, 97-120.
48. "La racionalidad del razonamiento juridico: dialogo, logica y verdad", *Anuario de Filosofia Juridica y Social*, 1984, 223-234.
49. "Den juridiska argumentationens rationalitet" (Rationality of legal argumentation), *Festskrift till Jan Hellner*, Stockholm, 1984, 419-432.
50. "Creativity and Transformations in Legal Reasoning" in *Theorie der Normen. Festgabe für Ota Weinberger zum 65. Geburtstag,* W. Krawietz e.a. (eds.), Berlin, 1984, 277-298.
51. "Legal Research, Growth of Science and Moral Theory" in *Objektivierung des Rechtsdenkens. Gedächtnisschrift für Ilmar Tammelo.* W. Krawietz e.a. (eds.), Berlin, 1984, 137-154.
52. "Die Rationalität der Juristischen Argumentation: Dialog, Logik und Wahrheit" in *Rechtsprechungslehre*, N. Achterberg (ed.), Cologne, 1984, 293-310.
53. "Rationality of Legal Reasoning: Dialogue, Logic and Truth" in *Rotterdam Lectures in Jurisprudence*, Arnhem, 1984, 45-52.

54. (with A. Aarnio) "Más allá del Realismo: Una Crítica de la Reconstrucción de la Dogmática Jurídica por Alf Ross" in *Alf Ross. Estudios en su Homenaje*, Valparaiso, 1984, 127-152.
55. "Operational Approach to the Theory of Law" in *Estudios de Filosofia del Derecho y Ciencia Juridica. En Memoria y Homenaje al Catedrático Don Luis Legaz y Lacambra*, II, Madrid, 1985, 199-212.
56. "On the Rational and Moral Basis of Legal Justification", *A.R.S.P.*, 1985, 263-267.
57. "Moral and Ontological Justification of Legal Reasoning", 4 *Law and Philosophy*, 289-309 (1985).
58. "Varför skall juridiska värderingar vara rationella?" (Why shall legal evaluations be rational?) in *Rationalitet och empiri i rättsvetenskapen*. A. Peczenik, D. Prawitz, L. Lindahl and J. Hellner (eds.), Stockholm, 1985, 9-23.
59. (with Jerzy Wróblewski) "Fuzziness and Transformation. Towards Explaining Legal Reasoning", *Theoria*, 1985, 24-44.
60. "Den juridiska argumentationens rationalitet: dialog, logik och sanning" (Rationality of legal argumentation: dialogue, logic and the truth), *Filosofisk Tidskrift*, 1985, 24-35.
61. (with A. Aarnio) "Beyond the Reality. A Criticism of Alf Ross' Reconstruction of Legal Dogmatics" in *Meaning, Interpretation and the Law,* A. Peczenik (ed.), Tampere, 1986, 10-29.
62. "A Model of Legal Reasoning", *Rechtstheorie*, 1986, 67-87.
63. "Authority Reasons in Legal Interpretation and Moral Reasoning" in *Neue Zugänge zum Recht*, R. Voigt (ed.), Siegen, 1986, 75-104.
64. "Skäl och dom" (Reason and judicial decision) in *Festskrift til Torstein Eckhoff,* Oslo, 1986, 515-528.
65. "Om rättens förnuftiga vidareutveckling - ett bemötande" (On the reasonable development of the law), *Tidsskrift for Rettsvitenskap*, 1986, 677-693.
66. "Pufendorf, Karl Olivecrona und die Gegenwart" in *Samuel von Pufendorf* 1632-1982, K. Å. Modéer (ed.), Lund, 1986, 132-136.
67. "Valid Law and Moral Reasoning", *Acta Analytica*, 1986, 143-162.
68. "Vazece pravo i moralneo rasudinovanje" (Valid law and moral judgment), *Filozofska Istranivanja*, 1987, 195-204.
69. "Moral Thinking, the Law and Rationality" in *Festgabe für Alois Troller zum 80. Geburtstag*, W. Krawietz and W. Ott (eds.), Berlin, 1987, 465-476.
70. "Demokrati och rättstillämpning" (Democracy and application of law) in *Återupprätta rättsstaten*, P. Unckel (ed.), Falun, 1987, 31-63.
71. "Motståndsrätt mot förtryck" (Right to resist oppression) in *Vad kan medborgaren göra?,* Timbro Idé, 1987, 109-130.
72. (with H. Spector) "A Theory of Moral Ought-Sentences", *A.R.S.P.*, 1987, 441-475.

73. "Why Should Value-Statements be Rational?" in *Reason in the Law*, C. Farrali and E. Pattaro (eds.), Milan, 1987, 107-128.
74. "Authority Reasons in Legal Interpretation and Moral Reasoning", *A.R.S.P.*, 1988, 144-151.
75. "Legal Reasoning as a Special Case of Moral Reasoning", *Ratio Juris*, 1988, 123-136.
76. "Some Theses Concerning Legal Reasoning" in *Law and Argumentation*, B. Melkevik (ed.), Tromsö, 1989, 21-32.
77. "General Clauses and Legal Certainty" in *Limits of Legal Regulation*, R. Voigt (ed.), Pfaffenweiler, 1989, 99-128.
78. "Weighing Rights" in *Enlightenment, Rights and Revolution*, N. MacCormick and Z. Bankowski (eds.), Aberdeen, 1989, 175-198.
79. "Democracy, Judicial Decision Making and the Right to Resist Oppression", *Internationales Jahrbuch für Rechtsphilosophie und Gesetzgebung*, Vienna, 1989, 141-167.
80. "Om den förvaltningsrättsliga forskningen och rättsdogmatiken" (On research in administrative law and legal dogmatics), *Förvaltningsrättslig Tidsskrift*, 1989, 41-52.
81. "Dimensiones morales del derecho", *Doxa*, 1989, 89-109.
82. "Los principios juridicos según Manuel Atienza y Juan Ruiz Manero", *Doxa*, 1989, 325-327.
83. (with R. Alexy) "The Concept of Coherence and its Significance for Discursive Rationality", *Ratio Juris*, 1990, 130-148.
84. "Coherence, Truth and Rightness in the Law" in *Law, Interpretation and Reality*, P. Nerhot (ed.), Dordrecht/Boston/ London, 1990, 275-309.
85. "Rätten, etiken och den demokratiska rättsstaten" (Law, morality and the democratic Rechtsstaat), *Insikt och Handling*, 1991, 77-106.
86. "Rättspraxis och rättsdogmatik" (Legal practice and legal dogmatics), *Festskrift till Ulla Jacobsson*, Stockholm, 1991, 161-174.
87. "Prima-Facie Values and the Law" in *Ethical Dimensions of Legal Theory*, W. Sadurski (ed.), Amsterdam/Atlanta, 1991, 91-110.
88. "Legal Rules and Moral Principles", *Rechtstheorie*, 1991, 151-167.
89. (with G. Bergholtz) "Statutory Interpretation in Sweden" in *Interpreting Statutes. A Comparative Study*, N. MacCormick and R. S. Summers (eds.), Aldershot, 1991, 311-358.
90. "Juristens dilemma: rationalism eller nihilism" (The lawyer's dilemma: rationalism or nihilism), *Svensk Juristtidning*, 1991, 799-807.
91. "Den polska normaliseringen" (The Polish normalisation), *Svensk Juristtidning*, 1991, 394-403.
92. "En domares frihet att tolka lagen" (The judge's freedom to interpret the law), *Tidskrift för Sveriges domareförbund*, 1991, 21-29.

93. "Legal Collision Norms and Moral Considerations" in *Coherence and Conflict in Law*, P. W. Brouwer, T. Hol, A. Soeteman, W. G. van der Velden and A. H. de Wild (eds.), Deventer, 1992, 177-200.

94. "Weighing Values", *International Journal for the Semiotics of Law*, 1992, 137-152.

95. "En förståelsemodell för etik, rätt och argumentation" (Explanatory model for morality, law and argumentation), *Tidskrift for Rettsvitenskap*, 1992, 20-47.

96. "Sammanhängande domsmotivering" (Coherent justification of legal decisions), *Tidfskrift för Sveriges Domareförbund*, 1992, 11-20.

97. "Why Shall Legal Reasoning be Coherent?", *Indian Socio-Legal Journal*, 1992, 103-107.

98. "Sources of Law" in *Rechtsnorm und Rechtswirklichkeit. Festschrift für Werner Krawietz zum 60. Geburtstag*, A. Aarnio, S. S. Paulson, O. Weinberger, G.-H. von Wright and D. Wyduckel (eds.), Berlin, 1993, 75-85.

99. "Morality, Law and Rights" in *Sprache, Performanz und Ontologie des Rechts. Festgabe für Kazimierz Opalek zum 75. Geburtstag*, W. Krawietz and J. Wróblewski (eds.), Berlin, 1993, 141-157.

100. (with R. Schött) "Juridisk konservatism" (Legal conservatism), *Svensk Juristtidning*, 1993, 709-734.

101. "Svenska lagmotiv i Europeisk union" (Swedish legislative preparatory materials in the EU), *Juridisk Tidskrift*, 1994, 306-312.

102. "Legal Reasoning, Law and Truth", *Ratio Iuris*, 1994, 146-176.

103. "Why Shall Legal Reasoning be Coherent?", *A.R.S.P.*, 1994, 179-184.

104. "Unity of the Legal System" in *Prescriptive Formality and Normative Rationality in Modern Legal Systems. Festschrift for Robert S. Summers*, W. Krawietz, N. MacCormick and G.-H. von Wright (eds.), Berlin, 1994, 71-82.

105. (with A. Aarnio) "Suum Cuique Tribuere. Some Reflections on Law, Freedom and Justice", *Ratio Iuris*, 1995, 142-179.

106. (with S. Urbina) "Why Officials? On Legal Positivism Old and New", *Rechtstheorie*, 1995, 139-162.

107. "A Conception of Democracy", *A.R.S.P.*, 1995, 59-61.

108. "Law-State, Legal Certainty and Legitimacy of Law", *A.R.S.P.*, 1995, 118-123.

109. "Rätt och moral i olika juristroller" (Law and morality in different legal roles) in *Rättsstaten - rätt, politik och moral*, F. Sterzel (ed.), Uppsala, 1996.

110. "Jumps and Logic in the Law. What Can One Expect of Logical Models of Legal Argumentation?", *Artificial Intelligence and Law*, 1996, 297-329.

111. "The Ways of Legal Certainty" in *Rule of Law*, A. Bröstl (ed.), Kosice, 1996, 22-27.

112. "Legal Principles according to Manuel Atienza and Juan Ruiz Manero" in *Interests, Morality and the Law*, A. Aarnio, K. Pietilä and J. Uusitalo (eds.), Tampere, 1966, 84-88.

113. (with G. Bergholtz) "Precedent in Sweden" in *Interpreting Precedents. A Comparative Study*, N. MacCormick and R. S. Summers (eds.), Aldershot, 1997, 293-314.
114. "The Binding Force of Precedent" in *Interpreting Precedents. A Comparative Study*, N. MacCormick and R. S. Summers (eds.), Aldershot, 1997, 461-480.
115. "Juridiska avvägningar" (Legal weighings) in *Festskrift till Stig Strömholm*, Uppsala, 1997, 697-708.
116. "The Passion for Reason. Some Remarks on Coherence in the Law" in *Normative Systems in Legal and Moral Theory. Festschrift for Carlos E. Alchourrón and Eugenio Bulygin*, E. Garzón Valdes, W. Krawietz, G.-H. von Wright and R. Zimmerling (eds.), Berlin, 1997, 309-322.
117. "Discussion with Robert Walter on Jörgensen's dilemma", *Ratio Juris*, 1998, 392 ff.
118. "Serväss, nej dubbelfel! Rättsvetenskapen och rättens kris" (Service ace, no double mistake! The crisis of law and the crisis of legal research) in *Rätt i förändring*, H. Hydén (ed.), Lund, 1997, 41-47.
119. "Against Reductionism", *Associations*, 1998, 101-120.

MY PHILOSOPHY OF LAW

ROBERT S. SUMMERS

CORNELL UNIVERSITY, ITHACA, NEW YORK[1]

1. Introduction

I have not yet worked out a complete philosophy of law, and the partial philosophy I do have is addressed merely to law in developed western societies, especially in the United States and Great Britain. I am ultimately striving for an overall synthesis that takes due account of the major contributions of the four great branches of legal theory: natural law thought, positivism, instrumentalist theory, and historical jurisprudence. I do not classify the totality of my own work as representative of any one of these branches, though I have published books and articles in which I attempt to contribute to various aspects of the first three[2].

Most of my current thinking and my academic writings of a theoretical nature have, for about ten years now, been devoted to what I call the formal character of law[3]. (I also publish on American commercial law and contract law.) I do not offer my theoretical work on formality as itself a comprehensive general theory of law, let alone as an attempt to synthesise the major truths in all four of the great branches of legal theory. Rather, in my work I treat formality as only one of the major characteristics of law.

---

[1] The author wishes to record his indebtedness to his secretary, Mrs. Pamela Finnigan, and to his research assistants: Theodore McCutcheon, Cornell Law School Class of 1998, Shelley Detwiller, Cornell Law School Class of 1999; and Darian Ibrahim, Cornell Law School Class of 1999.

[2] Among the books, see *Instrumentalism and American Legal Theory*, Ithaca/London, 1982; *Lon L. Fuller*, London, 1984; *Form and Substance in Anglo-American Law*, Oxford, 1987 (with P. Atiya); *Essays on the Nature of Law and Legal Reasoning*, Berlin, 1992.

[3] My thought is in the course of evolution, and I now reject some of the views I earlier espoused. My major prior writings in article form on formality are, in reverse historical order: "How Law is Formal and Why it Matters", 82 *Cornell L. Rev.*, 101 ff. (1997); "The Juristic Study of Law's Formal Character", *Ratio Juris*, 1995, 237 ff.; "Der formale Charakter des Rechts II", *A.R.S.P.*, 1994, 66 ff.; "A Formal Theory of Law", *Ratio Juris*, 1993, 127 ff.; "The Formal Character of Law", 51 *Cambridge L.J.*, 242 (1992).

Among all such characteristics, I would not even rank this characteristic – the law's formality – as the single most important. I would reserve that status for the law's characteristic general purposes and essential content. Those purposes and that content include the humanistic values of liberty, dignity of the individual, justice, and other basic rights secured or securable through law.

An emphasis on the humanistic values to be realised through the law's content has traditionally been a primary focus of natural law theory, and of much instrumentalist thought. Positivists, too, from Bentham onward, have stressed humanistic values. At the same time, traditional positivists and even some instrumentalists have also focused to some extent on the nature and importance of appropriate form in the law. Even some natural law theorists have dwelled on the importance of form[4]. However, compared to the overall emphasis that natural law theorists and instrumentalist theorists have given to the value content of law, and compared to the overall emphasis that many positivists have given to such non-formal factors in law as state power, coercion and force, and direct official action, form itself has had rather less attention.

I also believe that the systematic study of the major varieties of form in law can be taken far beyond where all prior and contemporary theorists have left it[5]. Moreover, formality is one of law's most important characteristics. Indeed, it may be that form is law's most foundational characteristic, for without form there can be no law at all, even when such non-formal ingredients of law as trained personnel, required material resources, and knowledge of effective legal technique happen to be readily available in abundance.

What is a general theory of form in the law, as I conceive it, and what are its central topics? First, it is necessary to explain what I mean here by "law". I refer to (1) rules and other types of legal precepts or norms, (2) basic functional elements of a legal system that are institutional in character such as legislatures, courts and the processes for creating such private law as contract, wills, and property arrangements, and (3) the legal system as a whole. Second, in the general theory I offer here, I introduce various concepts of form already rooted in basic, English usage and I introduce what I hope is a perspicuous and stable terminology for designating these concepts. I then apply these to the foregoing types of legal phenomena[6]. Third, in the theory, I treat

---

[4] J. Finnis, *Natural Law and Natural Rights*, Oxford, 1982.

[5] For earlier works devoted in significant part to form in the law, see G. del Vecchio, *The Formal Basis of Law*, J. Lisle (transl.), New York, 1914; R. von Jehring, *Der Geist des römischen Rechts*, Darmstadt, 1993; id., *Law as a Means to an End*, I. Husik (transl.), Boston, 1913; M. Weber, *On Law in Economy and Society*, M. Reinstein e.a. (transl.), New York, 1978, 2 vol.

[6] I draw on the *Oxford English Dictionary*, 1989 here for the relevant general usage of "formal"

systematically how form in law and the formal features of law serve as means to ends. Finally, in the theory I seek in a preliminary and not yet fully developed fashion to give due credit to form. Here, I explore the general importance of form for traditional legal theory, and for practical affairs. These are topics and questions that have not yet been treated together in a systematic way in the history of legal philosophy. Thus, it is simply not possible to say how the treatment I offer here differs from standard answers in the subject. There is simply no such standard treatment that is at all systematic.

Before turning to the various ways in which the phenomena of law are "formal", and to how the formal in law contributes to its efficacy, I will explain how I became interested in this subject. There are two main origins of this interest. In the 1980's, I co-authored a book on the "form and substance" of Anglo-American law with Professor Patrick Atiya of Oxford University[7]. In that book, my co-author and I considered how a broad range of legal phenomena can be characterised as formal, defended the thesis that the English system is more formal than the American, and considered what differences it can make that one legal system is more formal than another.

While I no longer work within exactly the same conceptual framework of form and formality adopted for that book, that framework was useful for the purposes then at hand, and it has stimulated me to reflect further, as here, on how law is formal and why it matters.

One other major origin of my interest in form in the law should be stressed. This origin is at least equal in importance to the factor I have just identified. Over the past fifteen years, I have been re-reading the major classics of political and legal theory. In doing this I have kept the nature and role of form in the law at the forefront of my consciousness. In so doing, I have encountered numerous isolated remarks that I have found worthy of extended reflection. For example, Plato emphasised that a society should "proceed to legislate with a view to perfecting the form and outline of our state"[8].

Plato went on to stress the role of the rule of law – itself a largely formal concept[9]. He especially emphasised the importance of formal features of rules such as generality[10] and definiteness[11]. Plato also dwelled on the importance of the role of writing in formally

---

and "form", though not for definitions of basic legal phenomena such as "legislatures", "courts", "legal rule", etc.

7 R. S. Summers and P. S. Atiya, *Form and Substance in Anglo-American Law*, Oxford, 1987. It was republished in 1991 with minor revisions.

8 Plato, *Dialogues*, B. Jowett (transl.), New York, 1937, 504.

9 Id., *ibid.*, 487.

10 Id., *ibid.*, 486

11 Id., *ibid.*, 491.

expressed law[12]. Aristotle, too, emphasised formal features of law[13], and from Plato and Aristotle forward to modern times, one encounters in the works of classical theorists many profound and insightful remarks on the nature and significance of various types of form in the law. Yet such remarks are usually brief, *en passant*, and almost entirely undeveloped. Among more recent scholars, the most suggestive of all for me has been the great nineteenth century German jurist who was a professor at the University of Göttingen, Rudolf von Jhering.

While he, like his classical predecessors, did not work out anything like a general theory of the formal character of law, von Jhering, too, offered many brief and fruitful thoughts on the nature and place of form in the law. For example, he said that "form is rooted in the innermost essence of law", and that "form is the sworn enemy of the arbitrary and the twin sister of liberty"[14].

Upon reflecting on these classical writings, I concluded that the formal character of law is a major void in the history of western legal theory.

One of my own teachers and one of the two leading positivist theorists of the twentieth century, H. L. A. Hart of Oxford, did not give form in the law its due[15]. Nor did Kelsen, the other leading positivist[16]. Nor has any other theorist. It cannot even be said that the systematic study of legal form somehow came to a premature standstill. It really never began.

My motivations in pursuit of a general theory of form in the law have not, however, been confined to the solely intellectual and theoretical. The American legal culture, especially on the academic side, includes powerful anti-formal strains"[17]. Thus my own country has special needs for a theory that seeks to give due credit to form in the law. So, too, the English and German legal cultures, but for a very different reason. In England and Germany, form tends to be taken for granted, and so in those countries it has not been the subject of much systematic reflection.

Before turning to the rudiments of my own general theory of form in the law, I wish to enter two important disclaimers or qualifications. First, in offering my theory, I do not purport to present any discoveries or new facts about law. Rather, I attempt mainly to call attention to neglected aspects of the familiar. I do not apologise for this.

---

[12] Id., *ibid.*, 530, 576, 603 and 632.

[13] *The basic works of Aristotle*, R. McKeon (transl.), New York, 1941, 1326.

[14] R. von Jehring, *Der Geist des römischen Rechts*, 471 and 479.

[15] H. L. A. Hart, *The Concept of Law*, Oxford, 1961.

[16] See, *e.g.*, H. Kelsen, *General Theory of Law and State*, Cambridge (Mass.), 1945.

[17] R. A. Posner, *The Problems of Jurisprudence*, Cambridge (Mass.), 1990, passim and D. Kennedy, "Legal Formality", 2 *J. Legal Studies*, 351 ff. (1975).

As Wittgenstein said: "The aspects of things that are most important for us are hidden because of their simplicity and familiarity"[18]. Moreover, as the great American jurist and philosopher of law, Oliver Wendell Holmes, once said, what we often most need is not more "investigation of the obscure," but rather "education in the obvious"[19]. Though I do think that much of what I offer here is in the end obvious, it may not be, at the outset for most readers, all that obvious.

Thus the variety of recognised senses of the word formal that I present here may not be quite so obvious. at least at the outset. Precisely how one or more, of these senses applies to rules, institutions, and other legal phenomena may not be quite so obvious. Also, the overall cumulative application of these various senses of formal to the phenomena of law – the overall pervasiveness of form in law – may not be quite so obvious.

Further, the extent of credit to be given appropriate form in legal theory may not be quite so obvious. Just how each major variety of form can contribute to the realisation of ends through law may not be quite so obvious. Furthermore, the types of interplay – functional and conceptual – between the formal and the non-formal in law may not be quite so obvious.

At the outset, I will identify and isolate what is formal about law. To do this, I introduce conceptualisations of the varieties of form and formal features in legal phenomena, and then introduce for these varieties a terminology that I believe to be felicitous, that marks the relevant distinctions and connections, and that provides consistency of reference and economy of expression.

With these conceptualisations and terminology, it then becomes possible at least to see a whole set of related questions: "What in the law is formal?" "How pervasive is formality in the law?" "What are its main varieties?" "How are they related, if at all?" "What ends and values do these varieties serve?" "What is the overall practical importance of form, in all its varieties, in the law?" "What is relevant to the design of appropriate form in each variety?" "What are the major types of flaws of form?" "What would a comprehensive pathology of form in the law look like?" "How does the study of form cast light on traditional problems of legal theory and jurisprudence?"

Some of these questions have received relatively little or no treatment in the history of legal theory and jurisprudence. Nevertheless, I have a second disclaimer. I do not wish to claim that what I offer here is wholly novel. Others have emphasised and continue to emphasise form in the law in one or more major respects. What I do claim

[18] L. Wittgenstein, *Philosophical Investigations*, G. E. M. Anscombe (transl.), London, 1953, 129, at 50.

[19] O. W. Holmes, *Collected Legal Papers*, New York, 1921, 292.

here is that a general theory of law's formal character, as I conceive it, has yet to be developed at all systematically. Obviously, in the space of the pages that follow, I can merely suggest how this might be done, and I can do so only in relation to a few of the questions about form that I have just posed. The main questions in the theory I will sketch here, in necessarily abbreviated fashion, are these: "What is the nature and general importance of form and formal features in legal phenomena, and how does the formal character of law cast light on traditional problems of legal theory?"

2. How Form and Formal Features Serve Ends and Values

To serve ends and values, law must be validly created either by officials or by private citizens, and then implemented either through citizen action, through official action, or through some combination of these. In modern circumstances, these creative and implementive actions presuppose institutions such as legislatures, court systems, administrative officials and bodies, institutions of private law and more. These actions also presuppose accepted criteria for the identification of validly created law. And much more.

But let us concentrate, for now, merely on such institutions and on such criteria of validity. When these institutions and criteria exist and are operational, they can serve such important ends and values as the constitution of legitimate authority, rationality in law making and administration, procedural justice, the realisation of democratic self-governance, limited government, and the rule of law.

Now, what are some of the varieties of form and of formal features in such institutions that play roles at least as partial means to such ends and values? Such institutions are formal in the sense that they have minimal defining features that are formal. A court cannot be a court without, for example, the feature of judicial independence, a feature to be secured partly through rules prescribing a certain content.

This defining feature pertains to the minimal constitutive form of a court, and so is formal in perhaps the most fundamental sense of the word recognised in our language[20]. This formal feature also contributes to the legitimacy of judicial authority, and to the legitimacy of exercises of this authority. This is merely one major type of contribution of the formal in only one sense of that word, namely, that which pertains to the minimal constitutive form of one type of institution.

---

[20] The *Oxford English Dictionary* includes as its first standard meaning of "formal": pertaining to the form or constitutive essence of a thing. In using the expression "minimal constitutive form", I do not mean to take sides in the ancient nominalist-realist debate, nor do I mean to commit to any one model for the analysis of concepts.

Another major contribution of still another variety of formal feature in a court is this. A duly designed judicial procedure allows each side to the dispute a fair opportunity for a hearing and affords an opportunity for rational determination of relevant facts and applicable law. This feature is formal in the sense that it is procedural. "Of or pertaining to procedure" is simply another well established meaning of the word formal[21]. And here formality in this sense serves procedural justice and adjudicative rationality.

Similarly, an electoral process to constitute the membership of a legislature is procedurally formal. And when a democratically elected legislature, with an upper house and lower house, is duly constituted and in operation, it, too, is formal in its defining features and in its procedures. It is formal in its dual chambers, and in its committee system which brings division and specialisation of labour. The specified relations between chambers, and within the committee system are structural, in that they pertain to relations between parts within a whole.

"Of or pertaining to structural form" is another well recognised meaning of formal in our language[22]. Features of structural form contribute to the realisation of such important ends and values as democracy, legitimacy of authority, rationality in law making, and procedural justice, *e.g.*, through provisions for hearings on bills, through debate, and through requirements of passage in both houses.

At the same time, the nature of the generally accepted criteria for the identification of valid law within a system can also serve such values as legitimacy of authority and democracy. One such accepted criterion will be "duly enacted and promulgated" by the properly constituted, duly authorised, and procedurally licit legislature. Such criteria of validity as these are formal because one established meaning of formal in our language is: "that which pertains to the forms that assure validity"[23].

Moreover, such criteria are formal in the further sense that they are "source-oriented", another recognised meaning of formal. Without acceptance of such criteria, for example, statutes could not be valid, nor democracy served.

To this point, I have indicated how several major varieties of the formal in legal institutions and in criteria for identifying valid law in a system may operate to contribute to basic social ends and values. I have not yet even introduced the subject of the creation and implementation of the ordinary garden-variety types of social policies that may be thought of as the very *raison d'etre* of so many legal institutions. Here, too, it is similarly

---

[21] *Ibid.*, entry for "form": "A set, customary, or prescribed way of doing anything; a set method of procedure according to rule (*e.g.*, at law); formal procedure" (entries no. I.11.a. and b.).
[22] *Ibid.*, entry for "form" no. I.5.a.
[23] *Ibid.*, entry for "formal" no. A.5.

demonstrable that appropriately formal features of legal phenomena, features themselves of major significance, contribute to the realisation of important policy ends and values.

But here I can only consider one major example. Let us consider the problem-specific policy of securing safe and efficient highway travel. Here it will be fruitful to imagine a projected linear sequence that begins with a democratically adopted, legitimate, procedurally proper, and validly promulgated rule that, say, specifies a 70 mph speed limit on all major highways, and usually ends with all private citizens who are drivers learning of this rule, and voluntarily applying it to themselves out on the highways with success in almost all instances of its applicability. (In this example, I assume a high correlation between speeds above 70 and unsafe driving, an assumption that might not hold in respect to some highways, *e.g.*, German "*Autobahns*".)

I have already indicated how in the very existence and operation of institutions and of criteria of validity, major formal features, contribute to such fundamental ends and values as democracy, legitimacy, rationality, and procedural propriety and fairness. What about the valid rules of law that emerge from a law making process? Are these in any major ways formal, and how do these varieties of formality in the rules so created contribute to the realisation of the ends and values such as safety and efficiency of highway travel? Just what are the major choices of form?

One choice, albeit an easy one here, is whether to leave the form of the rule to customary practice, adopt it as a matter of common law, incorporate it in a statute, put it in a constitution, or something else. Certainly the subject of a highway speed limit does not rise to a constitutional level. Nor can it be left to the diversity and informality of customary practices. The best choice of what might be called "encapsulatory" form here is the fixed verbal form of a statute.

Among other things, this will represent an expression of popular will through votes of elected legislators, will then in turn be promulgated widely, will appear in fixed verbal form that can be readily learned, and will promise certainty. (The various types of encapsulatory form are likewise recognised in our language as formal)[24].

Another major choice at the outset will be whether the legislature should put such a policy in a rule at all. Other alternatives might include simply the adoption of a general principle, or a broad grant of discretion to traffic officials, or the like. The choice here is a choice between alternative types of "preceptive" form, another recognised variety of form in our language[25]. A general principle or a broad grant of discretion to officials simply could not provide enough guidance, here. The preceptive form of a rule would,

[24] *Ibid.*, entry for "formal", no. A.1.c.

[25] The preceptive is formal in that it always involves minimal constitutive forms of rules and the like.

however, promise more guidance to citizens out on the roadways (albeit less guidance than particular orders, which themselves would be inefficient). Let us assume that a choice of the preceptive form of a rule is adopted, and that it is made on the ground I have indicated, namely, its superior policy efficacy.

This, then, must be counted as another contribution of appropriate form to the ultimate realisation of the ends and values sought, namely safe and efficient highway travel.

But this is far from all that may be credited to appropriate form here. I have so far implicitly taken for granted an important, though obvious, choice of what may be called expressional form[26], namely that the relevant rule should be in writing, and should be cast in lay vocabulary. Statutes are always written, and having a rule prescribing a speed limit in such written form best serves the relevant policy ends, as well as legitimacy, certainty, and still other values. Many other types of choices of form arise in the course of creating the written statutory rule itself.

Thus, a rule has defining features that are formal: its degrees of prescriptiveness, generality, definiteness, completeness in its various parts, and its structure – its specification of relations between the parts of the rule. All of these features pertain to the minimal constitutive form of rules, and so are formal[27]. They also contribute to the ends and values to be served by the rule. Again, these ends and values are not confined to the problem-specific policy of the rule, here safety and efficiency on the highways.

Consider generality, for example. While this formal feature of the rule under consideration must be tailored to the policy objective of highway safety and efficiency, and so be of such generality as to apply to virtually all highway users, this is not all that is at stake in choosing degrees of generality. Also to be served is the immense social value of substituting general rules to be applied by citizens on their own to their own special circumstances in place of particular commands issued to particular individuals by particular officials on particular occasions. This social value is not to be measured solely in terms of cost savings and efficiency. It includes, as well, the dignity and the autonomy of citizen-self-direction under law (in contrast to being ordered around by officials).

That the formal feature of definiteness in a rule poses important choices of degree is also evident, and the appropriate resolution of such issues serves not merely the determinateness and guidance required for discrete levels of safety and efficiency in highway travel. It also serves "learnability" of the law, the efficacy and dignity of citizen self-direction, ease of determining the law's factual applicability, dispute avoidance, fair

---

[26] *Ibid.*, entry for "form", no. I.9.
[27] *Ibid.*, see note 19.

advance notice of the law's behavioural standards, delimitation of scope for police intervention and police arbitrariness, and more.

The specification of the relationships between parts of a rule is another major variety of form in rules, namely, structural form[28]. The appropriate design of structural form likewise poses major choices. For example, a speed limit rule may include a part that specifies a minimum fine for exceeding it. This is a choice of part in the name of completeness, a formal feature. But the further choice of whether to make the fine automatic, or to make it discretionary, is a structural choice in the sense that it is a choice about the relation within a rule between the part that specifies the speed limit and the part that provides for a fine for exceeding it.

Such a choice pertains to the relation between parts of a whole. What ends and values are at stake in such a structural choice? Not merely policy efficacy. Some further ends and values that may be served by an appropriate choice here are the minimisation of scope for official arbitrariness, equality before the law, fair notice of possible adverse legal consequences, dispute avoidance, and ease of administration.

We are still at the legislative stage in the linear projection of the sequences of events from law creation to law implementation. Of the further stages along any such projection, several major ones will be familiar. Beyond due enactment pursuant to appropriate powers and procedures to assure validity, other steps include due promulgation, a formal act, and official dissemination of rule content among the rule's addressees (also a formal act). Moreover, the principles of legality and the rule of law operative in many systems not only presumptively favour the adoption of general rules, themselves formal in the foregoing ways, but also generally require not only due promulgation, and official dissemination, but also prospectivity of rule. These principles of legality are broadly procedural and so in a straightforward and familiar sense formal[29].

Let us suppose that the legislature adopts, promulgates and disseminates a 70 mph speed limit (for general conditions on all major highways). It would be possible to imagine here a variety of "scope" and other interpretive issues that might arise with respect to such a statute. For example, does the rule apply to drivers of emergency vehicles? If the rule applies only in day time driving, with a slower speed for darkness, when does darkness occur? And so on. This introduces the relevance of an interpretive methodology.

How is such a rule to be interpreted? A general interpretive methodology might exist on which rule-interpretors could rely to determine answers to such questions. Indeed, such methodologies do exist in developed legal systems, and may, for judges at

---

[28] *Ibid.*, entry for "form", no. I.5.a.

[29] *Ibid.*, entry for "form", no. I.11.a. and b.

least, be more or less elaborate and refined[30]. Because these are methodological, they are formal, for this just is another important sense of the word formal in our language[31]. A formal methodology that accurately and efficiently yields determinate answers to interpretive questions serves important values, too. It generally (in regard to the usual statute) serves the policies of predictability, certainty, equality before the law, dispute avoidance, ease of administration, and other related values.

A written statutory rule, validly adopted, promulgated, and disseminated, when duly interpreted and applied to circumstances, may be said to generate, in particular sets of circumstances, what I will call a legal reason for action. Here, that reason would be a reason for the citizen to act on voluntarily, and would take the general form of: "Drive no faster than 70 mph." This very reason, through which various policy and other ends and values may be served, is itself formal in a number of ways. It is derivatively formal in that it derives from a formal lawmaking process in accord with authoritative forms assuring validity.

This reason is formal also in its degree of determinateness, which is also derivative, for the various formal features of the rule itself, such as generality and definiteness, contribute to this determinateness. So, too does the very preceptive form of the rule. So, too does its fixed verbal form in writing in a statute. Furthermore, such a reason is formal not only in its authoritativeness, and its determinateness, but also in its peremptoriness. The reason generally pre-empts competing substantive reasons emergent in the circumstances. For example, the driver is not free to drive above 70 mph merely to visit a mortally ill relative in a hospital. Such peremptoriness is formal in the sense that it generally operates independently of the variable content of competing reasons[32].

Thus, at the end of the various stages in our linear projections from rule creation to rule implementation through voluntary citizen self-application, we see how appropriate form in many varieties contributes specifically to the realisation of policies and other ends and values. And were we to subtract any of these varieties of form, or significantly reduce their degrees or levels, we could easily imagine how the ends and values at stake would be affected.

In the type of example I have posed, the rule so created would be effectively implemented without incident by citizen self-application on the front-lines of human interaction in, say, 99% of the cases. The life of such a rule of law, and of the many laws

---

[30] D. N. MacCormick and R. S. Summers (eds.), *Interpreting Statutes. A Comparative Study*, Aldershot, 1991.

[31] *Oxford English Dictionary*, entry for "form", no. I.10.

[32] On peremptoriness, see also H. L. A. Hart, *Essays on Bentham*, Oxford, 1982, chapter 10.

like it in many systems, is almost entirely a life led outside of court. There would, however, be some "trouble cases", only a few of which would end up in court. In one kind of trouble case, a non-judicial official responsible for administering or enforcing the law intervenes upon observing a failure of compliance. A simple illustration in the 70 mph speed limit example would involve a citizen who exceeded the limit by, say, 20 mph. By electronic means, an arresting police officer might determine the fact of non-compliance, arrest the speeder, and issue a summons directing that the speeder either pay a stipulated fine by mail or appear in court on an appointed day.

In some western countries, the speeder would in nearly all cases simply pay the fine by mail. In this type of example, the arrest itself terminates an instance of unsafe driving and so serves the policy of safety. The arrest and the fine also lend credibility to the entire enforcement process and thus contribute to general deterrence of speeding, thereby also serving the policy of safety. Similarly, the very presence of patrol cars on the highway deters speeding and so furthers the policy. Important formal features of the law itself here are that it is embodied in a written statutory rule which all drivers and police are taken to know, and which can be readily learned by virtue of its simplicity and definiteness, themselves formal features.

All these formal features converge to limit drastically the scope for disputes over non-compliance, and the availability of accurate electronic devices for determining non-compliance with precision delimits the scope for disputes over the fact of non-compliance even more drastically. Here, too, the appropriate formality of the law contributes in various ways to its policy efficacy.

Moreover, safety and efficiency of traffic flow in this example are not the only values to be served by such formality in cases of official intervention and coercive enforcement. The contribution of form to cases of administration and to avoidance of disputes is valuable too. So are the contributions of form to the realisation of still other values.

A determinate law is enforceable by an official in a highly objective fashion and lends legitimacy to the entire enforcement process. It also delimits scope for official arbitrariness in determining the existence of any violation in particular cases.

The contributions of appropriate formality are to be seen not only in the conditions for voluntary citizen-self-application and in the efficacy of coercive enforcement. Appropriate formality here contributes to securing the freedom and dignity of citizen self application of the law as well. For a highly determinate and readily applicable rule forbidding driving above 70 mph also at the same time limits the power of officials to arrest or otherwise interfere with the freedom of those who drive below

70 mph, too. Here, as the great Rudolph von Jhering might have put it, form is the "twin sister of liberty" and the "sworn enemy of the arbitrary"[33].

In some small proportion of cases, the alleged speeder will dispute that he or she was speeding, and will demand a judicial hearing in court to determine the fact of a violation if that be the fact, prior to imposition of penalty. Here, the minimal constitutive form of a court, its structural form, its procedural form, and its further formal features contribute to impartial, objective, rational, and fair determination of the fact of any violation, and to the similar resolution of any issue or issues of statutory interpretation that may have arisen. For example, a court just is formally organised to secure that the judge (and any jury) will be independent and so impartial.

Furthermore, the provision for, on the choice of the accused, of such a judicial proceeding implements a fundamental principle of legality and the rule of law that no person shall be subjected to penalty against his or her will without a fair opportunity to challenge the facts or the law on which such penalty is premised before an independent and impartial tribunal. This requirement of the rule of law is, like all such requirements, formal too, at least in the sense that it is broadly procedural.

In the foregoing linear progression from the creation of a speed limit law to its promulgation, its dissemination, its voluntary citizen self-application in over 99% of the instances, and its disposition of the relatively few trouble cases, we also see a relatively distinctive combination of formal and non-formal elements within an overall functional unit that we may call the penal technique. In this technique (which is only one of five major techniques or modalities whereby law creates and implements policy), it is typical that the legislature prohibits anti-social behaviour, officials promulgate and disseminate this prohibition, citizens self-administer it, police and prosecutorial officials also administer it, and penal and correctional officials stand ready to enforce sanctions as ordered.

It should be plain that any such overall *modus operandi* of the law – any such general operational technique – is formal both in the sense that it is broadly procedural and also in the sense that it is structural. It is structural precisely in the respect that it connects, integrates, and co-ordinates various parts within an operational whole[34]. It specifies general relations between parts consisting of institutions and other functional elements within the system, elements that function along a linear projection from creation of law to its ultimate implementation to serve policy and other goals.

At the same time, the penal technique is not the only basic modality for the effectuation of legal goals within a legal system. As I have suggested, there are other

---

[33] R. von Jhering, *Der Geist des römischen Rechts*, 471 and 479.

[34] *Oxford English Dictionary*, entry for "form", no. I.5.a.

major ones, including the private grievance-remedial technique, the administrative-regulatory technique, the public-benefit conferral technique, and the private-ordering technique (which includes the great socio-legal institution of contract). Moreover, even within these techniques there are important variations on the standard linear sequences from law creation to implementation, important variations in the roles of personnel, and important variations in the contributions of form to the realisation of the relevant ends and values through law. Indeed, in some typical linear sequences, officials have vast discretion at the point of application, and there is little or no scope for citizen- self-application. This is true, for example, of judicial awards of child custody as between divorced parents.

Again, it is important to stress that form and formal features hardly make up the whole of the law. Much in the effective functioning of law is not formal at all: rule content consisting of social policy or moral principle, various trained personnel, material resources, communicative devices, social acceptance, coercive capacity, and more. Perhaps the most important non formal social asset of all is simply an alert, informed, legally sensitive, and co-operative citizenry. The most successful legal systems seek to capitalise at every opportunity on this vital social asset.

3. Some Implications for Legal Theory

I have so far tried to demonstrate, in quite practical terms, which, and how many, major varieties of form and formal features pervade law and contribute in various ways as means to the realisation of ends and values through uses of law. I now turn to some illustrative implications of this that are somewhat more theoretical in nature.

3.1. Form and Formal Features in Law as Means to Ends

While there is much more to law than form and formal features, I hope to have demonstrated in the preceding section how form and formal features contribute to the capacity of law to serve as means to ends. This also bears on two staple topics of legal theory. One of these is the very nature of law itself. The other is the relation between law and morals. All agree that law is instrumental in nature. And all would also agree that the instrumental efficacy of law is traceable partly to non-formal factors such as the general social acceptance of law's content, the internal point of view of officials toward the law they apply, and also the law's general coercive capacity.

But I have tried to show in the preceding section that numerous varieties of form and of features of form contribute in their own ways to the law's instrumental efficacy and so to its very nature. I have sought to identify and isolate many of the numerous and specific types of contributions of a wide variety of forms and formal features of law to the ultimate efficacy of an illustrative authoritative policy as projected linearly from initial embodiment in a rule on through various implementive stages to citizen self-application of rule in the human interactions of daily life.

In my effort to demonstrate by way of example the general truth that form and formal features are indispensable to law's instrumental efficacy, and so cast light on the very nature of law, I did not stop to explore the many issues of alternative design of form and formal features, nor did I stop to explore the growing scholarship on how such issues may be best resolved (scholarship, incidentally, in which the relevant legal phenomena are often not seen to be formal in any respect). For my present purposes, such efforts are not necessary.

My present legal theoretic aim has been only to offer a perspicuous, albeit brief, representation of form and formal features as important elements of the law as social means, and thereby contribute in a modest way to our general understanding of the nature of law itself. It is possible to under-estimate the contributions of form and formal features of law to its instrumental efficacy, and many scholars in the social sciences and in philosophy have in fact, been guilty of this[35]. It is not merely that numerous varieties of formality figure importantly in the creation and implementation of numerous policies such as the safety and efficiency of highway travel.

It can be said with justification that law extends and enriches the general menu of possible ends and means of social life, and that the law's form and formal features are indispensable to this. For example, without law, and appropriate form in the law, we could not have contractual relationships that are as satisfactory as those we do have. Bargain consideration, or its equivalent, as required by the law of contract, is itself formal, and is applicable to highly varied content. It provides some evidence that the relevant promise was actually made.

It also tends to put negotiating parties in a cautionary and circumspective frame of mind, so that by their own lights, they make better choices. It is also partly through form that we have the very institution of money which itself greatly facilitates contractual agreements and exchanges. Indeed, it is through agreements and the exchanges pursuant thereto that, in developed liberal societies, we not only realise many of our personal ends but at the same time experience free, autonomous, self-direction and self-governance.

As further examples of how form in law contributes to the enrichment and extension of the means and ends of social life, consider the disposition of our property by will or through trusts. These devices, like contract and property, are creatures of the law, and without appropriate form defining and validating their very existence, we simply could not "leave property by will", or "transfer property in trust". Countless

[35] J. Searle, *The Constitution of Social Reality*, London, 1995.

further examples could be cited. I will cite merely one further, more collective, example. Without appropriate legal form we would not have the very social phenomenon of "electing legislators". This phenomenon, of course, requires actual elections, and elections are highly formal, not merely in terms of their minimal constitutive form, but also structurally, and procedurally. In these and in many other ways, then, form and formal features in law and legal phenomena are indispensable to the vast enrichment of the means and ends of social life that we today enjoy.

When theorists have treated the law as a means to ends, they have also often viewed themselves as addressing one or more facets of that other staple topic of legal theory that addresses the relations between law and morals. And in this, theorists have often emphasised only those ends that may be characterised as substantively moral. The protection of life and limb is an obvious illustration, as in my highway speed limit example. But the values at stake in a truly comprehensive general treatment of the relations between law and morals are not confined to the substantively moral, and only if we specifically address the end-serving contributions of the varieties of form and formal features in the law, especially relatively high degrees of certain formal features, can we see fully how this is so.

In my demonstration in the second part of this essay, I reminded the reader how, at various stages in a linear projection of the sequences involved in creating and implementing law, law's form and its formal features help to serve many important social values beyond those that, in ordinary terms, qualify as substantively moral. These values include political legitimacy, democracy, procedural justice, instrumental rationality (in designing means-end relations), certainty and predictability, objectivity in application of laws, the dignity of autonomous self-direction, equality before the law, minimisation of scope for official arbitrariness, dispute avoidance, ease of administration, and more. Many such values might be called fundamental political values, and others general legal values. Some of these values have been studied extensively in the history of legal theory, but others have not yet had their due[36].

Although such values, most of them, are not substantively moral, they are not without moral significance. Fundamental political values and general legal values may be served through law, including its appropriate forms and formal features, even when the social policy content or the substantive moral content is not appropriately

---

[36] Among the important questions that arise here, especially in regard to each general legal value, are these: (a) "How is it to be defined?", (b) "Why is it prizeable?", (c) "Is it intrinsically valuable or only instrumentally so?", (d) "Can it be served even when the social policy or moral principle embodied in the content of the rule is not?", (e) "Does its implementation generally require high degrees or levels of formality?", (f) "How is it to be weighed against other values?"

incorporated in the law or is otherwise not well served. Often, these various values require for their realisation relatively high degrees of formality in the features of implementive rules and other legal phenomena.

Moreover, even when policy or other substantive moral content is duly incorporated in the law and the law can be highly effective in implementing it, the law makers may sometimes make the further choice when drafting the law's final form and content to sacrifice some level of substantive value realisation in exchange for a higher level of realisation of fundamental political values or of such general legal values as predictability, objectivity in application of law, delimitation of scope for official arbitrariness, dispute avoidance, and the like, a matter to which I return later on in this essay.

Then, too, the law must cope with types of social problems wherein no social policies or other substantive moral ends strongly dictate the law's immediate content. Whether to require highway users generally to drive right or to drive left is one of the most familiar examples. Here, general legal values, many of which, again, cannot be served without high degrees of formal features in rules and other legal phenomena, can receive special emphasis.

Rules can be firm and determinate here, whatever their content. Yet, general legal values are, most of them, at one or two removes from substantive moral notions. General legal values are in one sense internal to law itself. This does not, of course, mean they are all devoid of moral significance. Among other things, many of these values implicate a variety of issues of fairness in the relationship between citizen and state, and such fairness is itself a matter of morality.

3.2. The Organisational Functions of Form and Formal Features in Law and Legal Phenomena

I return here to that staple of legal theory, the nature of law. Another fundamental facet of law's basic nature is that it is a distinctive and complex mode of social organisation. The institutions and processes of law in developed societies are highly organised.

Rules, principles, maxims, rulings, orders, etc. are similarly highly organised phenomena of law. The creations of private citizens as law makers are organised, often highly so: corporations, partnerships, contractual relations, bundles of property rights, wills, trusts, and other property arrangements, and still more. And, of course, the system as a whole is highly organised. The formal character of law is one important and neglected key to understanding law as a complex mode of social organisation.

There are several different senses in which such phenomena of law may be said to be organised. Each basic functional element of the system, *e.g.*, the legislature and the court system is itself internally organised, *i.e.*, internally constituted. Then, the relations between such elements are organised so to be functionally connected, integrated, and co-ordinated, as required. So, too, the system as a whole is organised so that it operates systematically, methodically, and in accord with the dictates and constraints of the principles of legality and the rule of law. Then the various bodies of law are also themselves organised to be generally coherent and free of contradictions. Bodies of law are organised so that their specific content is readily accessible, too.

Without concepts of the minimal constitutive forms of the institutions, rules, principles, and other precepts, and of the system as a whole, no phenomena of law and no system of law could exist. As a sagacious American judge once put matters: "Those who are impatient with the forms of law ought to reflect that it is through form that all organisation is reached. Matter without form is chaos; power without form is anarchy. The state, were it to disregard forms would not be a government, but a mob. Its action would not be administration but violence"[37].

Even if the prospective creators of a legal system had available to them in abundance all of the non-formal requisites of effective law ranging from the ready potential for social acceptance of law once created, to trained administrative and other personnel, to knowledge of desired policy, to knowledge of means-end relations, to all required material resources, and more, it still would not be possible to create a functional system of law.

Without conceptions of the minimal constitutive form of a legislature, of a court, of a rule, and so on, the creators of a system would simply not know where to begin. Those who would create the system must have concepts of form, including the very "formative principle which holds together the several elements" of each institution, of each type of legal phenomena, and of the system as a whole[38]. Of course, those various concepts of minimal constitutive forms are each themselves further analysable into various formal features, as we have seen.

Many of these concepts of minimal constitutive form are internally quite complex. It should now be plain that all such concepts of minimal constitutive form in institutions, rules, and so forth are essentially organisational in nature. These concepts specify how parts of the system are themselves to be constituted on their own, and also how the whole system is to be put together organisationally, *i.e.*, constituted.

Minimal constitutive form is not the only concept of form that is essentially organisational. All varieties of form are organisational or contribute to the organised character of law and its organised activities. Concepts of structure – of how parts are put

---

[37] Judge Bleckley in *Cochran v. State*, 62 Ga. 731, 732 (1879).

[38] This usage is recognised in the *Oxford English Dictionary*, entry for "form", no. I.4.d.

together – are concepts that are often elaborated beyond their constitutive minima and are independently significant to the extent that they are so elaborated.

Concepts of legislative structure and judicial structure are illustrative. For example, a legislature need not have more than one chamber to be a legislature, yet it often has two. A legislature need not even subdivide itself into a set of committees, yet this is typical. once these elaborate steps are taken, relations between parts must be specified, and this generates structure. Then, too, ideas of procedural design are formal. And so are ideas of accommodative form for institutions – ideas of how far the scope of operation of an institution is to apply to varied subject-matter content[39].

Concepts of appropriately definitive form in institutions are, likewise formal. For example, on one view of appropriate legislative definitiveness, the composition, structure, procedure and accommodative scope of the legislature are tightly organised and operate in highly regularised fashion. On another conception, the legislature is less tightly organised, and less regularised in operation. But whatever the degree of the governing concept of definitiveness, this idea is itself a formal organising idea[40].

So far, I have merely suggested (and without attempting to be comprehensive) how the creation of legal phenomena and of a system of law are necessarily dependent upon prior notions or concepts of form: at least minimal constitutive form, structural form, procedural form, accommodative form (applicability to variable content), and definitive form. But the concepts or ideas of appropriate form, in all their varieties, required for the design of an organised system of law is one thing, the availability of actual social means of organising and so implementing this design, something else. What are the functional phenomena of law including institutions, processes and the systems as a whole organised out of?

They are, as I have indicated, organised in light of relevant concepts of minimal constitutive form, and thus not only out of non-formal social means such as knowledge of social cause and effect, trained personnel, and material resources, but also out of other social resources including most importantly, but not exclusively, out of prescriptive rules, principles, orders, and other preceptive phenomena.

Here, let us briefly consider only rules. Form and the formal features of rules have a double role. At the very outset, we must at least have ideas of the minimal constitutive form of a rule, the elaborated structural form of a rule, the expressional form of a rule, and the encapsulatory form of a rule.

---

[39] See the special usage for "formal" in the *Oxford English Dictionary*, at A.1.d., "free from the descriptive content that would restrict it to any particular subject-matter." See also *ibid.*, entry for "form" at II.18.a. ("a mould").

[40] *Ibid.*, entry for "form", no. I.8.

All these forms are required for the internal organisation and existence of rules. And if valid legal rules are to exist, then they must conform as well to the criteria for the validity of such rules in the legal system, and I have already indicated the extent to which the criteria assuring validity are formal.

Valid formal phenomena, rules, are required for, and play large roles in, organising the creation of the institutions, the processes, the implementive devices, and the system of law as a whole. Such rules prescribe organisational content and so prescribe the form and formal features of institutions and of the system, all in accord with concepts of their minimal constitutive forms, concepts of structural form, concepts of procedural form, concepts of accommodative form (applicability to variable content), concepts of definitive form, and so on. Of course, in some systems, the rules prescribing some organisational features must be prescribed in constitutional encapsulatory form.

A valid legal rule prescribing some variety of form or formal feature of some incipient legal phenomenon such as a legislature, all in accord with an appropriate concept of minimal constitutive form may be said to be in the nature of an "atomic legal particle" – one of the small units out of which legal institutions and other phenomena of law are put together. But it does not follow that the basic legal phenomena, duly constituted, can be reduced to rules or even reduced to something essentially like rules. A legislature is an institution, not a rule or set of rules.

A court system is a complex institutional organisation, not a rule or set of rules. An administrative bureaucracy is just that, not a rule or a set of rules. Nor are these and other basic legal phenomena reducible to something like a union of primary and secondary rules. Rules, themselves formal in many ways, do, however figure prominently in the construction of legal phenomena and of the system as a whole. The content of many rules prescribes much of the organisation of these phenomena and of the system as a whole. (Of course, the content of other types of rules prescribes social policies and moral principles, too.)

And, important though they are, rules are not the only "atomic" particles out of which organised legal phenomena and legal systems as a whole are constructed. As I have stressed throughout, functional law requires the incorporation and integration of non-formal resources too. But the "atomic particles" out of which a functioning legal order is made also go well beyond non-formal resources, too. The constitutive form, the structural form, the procedural form, the accommodative form, and the overall definitive form of, say, a legislature is itself not merely a function of the precision of basic rules prescribing these forms.

Some of the rules themselves may even have large gaps in them. (For example, the organisationally prescriptive rules of the American constitution say nothing of political parties.) Other major factors besides prescriptive rules that may contribute to the definitiveness of institutions and other legal phenomena in their actual operation include social agreement on desired institutional features; public perception that the forms and formal features in place are fitting, right, and good; the stability and continuity of actual customary practices in conformity with those features; the readiness of officials, judges, and affected parties to criticise departures from prescribed or accepted organisational forms, and the readiness of affected persons to take remedial or other related action in the face of departures from prescribed or accepted organisational forms.

Law, then, is a complex mode of social organisation. Moreover, the very organisational contours of institutions and other legal phenomena, including the system as a whole, can be analysed in relatively comprehensive fashion in terms of the major varieties of form and formal features at work. Indeed, the very existence of law, as we know it, is dependent upon the creation and maintenance of legal phenomena in accord with concepts of organisational form appropriate to those very phenomena.

And the formal "atomic particles" out of which these phenomena are created include another highly formal type of phenomenon, namely, rules prescribing the form and formal features of such phenomena. Form, then is an essential key to understanding the highly organised character of law itself, and an essential key to understanding what figures in that highly organised character.

The formal character of law, then, may be said to be internally organisational. At the same time, the formal character of law also provides the "formative principle(s) (...) which hold together the several elements of functional law"[41]. That is, it is through form and features in all their varieties that the non-formal as well as the formal are integrated into working law. Thus, the formal in law provides stable channels and foci for the expression of social acceptance, acquiescence, and assent with respect to the law's content and its requirements. It is through the formal in law that institutional and other roles for trained personnel are defined. It is through the formal in law that the necessary deployment of material resources, and the mobilisation of coercive capacity is organised and authorised. Without due form, these and other non-formal social assets could not be appropriately brought into play.

It is also true that law, as a complex aggregation of organisational forms (in part) duly integrated and duly co-ordinated, is, in virtue of this very formal character, also relatively distinctive as a type of social phenomenon, a truth that casts further light on law's very nature. Here, law as a whole may be said to be "characterised by, or regarded according to its form"[42]. That is, law's formal character, itself an aggregation of minimal constitutive forms and of varied formal features, can, in virtue of such features (though

---

[41] *Ibid.*, entry for "form", no. I.4.d.

[42] *Ibid.*, entry for "formal", no. A.2.

not only in virtue of) be readily differentiated in illuminating ways from other social phenomena that, in the history of legal theory and the study of society, have been associated with law as cognate means of social control and social facilitation.

Consider, again, the relation between law and morality. The forms and formal features of law and of morality are really quite different. It is enough to cite two major examples. First, law is indisputably in major part an affair of rules, and rules are, in major respects, formal. But there is a persuasive body of thought to the effect that morality is not truly a matter of rules at all. Second, and on the institutional plane, it can be said that social morality lacks anything like a legislature, which, as we have seen, is formal in major respects. Moreover, social morality lacks anything like a judiciary, and a judicial system is highly formal, as we have seen.

3.3. Form, Formal Features and Legitimate Civic Authority

Without legitimate civic authority, nothing we now recognise as law could exist. I will now focus more narrowly and frontally, than I have heretofore, on the various types of appropriate form in the creation and functioning of legitimate civic authority as such. It is only through these that the conditions for the existence of authority, including the very sources of valid law that figure in source-oriented criteria of validity, can be realised.

Appropriate form, in several major varieties, is required to localise civic authority in determinate institutional roles. Thus, the relevant institutions must be brought into being in the first place. As I have explained, we must, therefore, have a conception of a legislature with power to make general written law – a conception of the relevant minimal constitutive form for a legislature. Compositional, structural, and procedural form, and form accommodating variable content, must all be specific, and this may be done initially through the preceptive form of rules prescribing these formal features. At the same time, the non-formal social assets required for the effective functioning of such a determinate locus of civic law making authority must be duly organised within the overall formal framework. These include elected legislators, other trained personnel, material resources, and more.

But far more is required for the existence of legitimate civic authority to create general written law than a determinate locus for personnel within institutional roles. Further formal organisation is required not only to secure quality in law making, but also to specify what is to count as the exercise of authority. In the case of a legislature, there must be some agreement, duly specified, on what is to count as the making of a law.

This calls for organisation with respect to what persons are legally qualified to participate as legislators, what powers they are to have, by what procedures they are to act, in what mode they are to express their legislation, how such action is to be promulgated, and how disseminated. Again, specification of these normally requires the use of rules having the requisite organisational content, itself formal in the major ways already specified: constitutively, structurally, procedurally, definitively, and so on.

Without a determinate locus of authority in determinate institutional roles, and without determinate specification of how this authority is to be exercised, legitimate civic authority could not exist, no matter how many persons around there may be who are willing to claim authority, and have access to required material resources, etc. For one thing, the institutional locus of authority could not be sufficiently identifiable and could not be sufficiently constant in time to enable it to become a social object of genuine acceptance, acquiescence, or assent.

Thus, at least for a liberal society, such a locus could not survive as legitimately authoritative. And appropriate form, in most of the major varieties I have just identified, would be required for this very identifiability and constancy. Indeed, even unanimous consent of all in the society to some presumed objective authority could not legitimise such a "locus" if devoid of the determinateness and constancy that only appropriate form can provide. There is, therefore, far more to the constitution of legitimate civic authority than merely the social acceptance of a rule that confers power to make or apply law. In this, all the major varieties of form and formal features ordinarily identifiable in institutional legal phenomena must figure in significant ways. This is not to say that functional and legitimate authority is merely formal. Nor is it to say that the only sources of legitimacy are acceptance, acquiescence, and assent over time.

Matters are still more complex than I have so far indicated, having limited my focus to a single illustrative type of civic authority, namely that of a legislative body with general power to make written law. In developed western systems of law, authority is divided, partly to take advantage of the values of specialisation of legal labour, and, in some systems, partly to provide internal checks and balances. Thus, a full analysis here would address not only the requirements of appropriate form in the constitution of legitimate legislative authority. The analysis would also address the requirements of appropriate form in the constitution of legitimate executive, judicial, and other authority, including the authority of private persons to create and implement law in the form of contracts, wills, property arrangements, and the like.

3.4. Some Priorities of Form and Formal Features in Rules and Rule Application

In the very course of creating law, many situations arise in which it may be justified to formulate the law so that it takes a form that more fully serves what I call general legal values even at the price of some sacrifice of the basic policy at stake. I will cite one example to render my meaning more concrete.

A legislature may choose to adopt a law retiring all police officers at age 60, even though this may not maximally serve the policy of having a fit police force, given that some officers are still quite fit at 60, and some no longer fit prior to 60.

Yet such a formally firm and definite rule secures a fit force to a considerable degree (let us assume), and would also be better than a vague rule (retire when no longer fit), given that the formally firm and definite rule better serves such general legal values as predictability, minimisation of scope for arbitrariness, dispute avoidance, the saving of the costs of case by case inquiries into fitness, and more. However, it is not correct to say merely that appropriate form in a rule has a special priority here. Instead, it is better to say that the form more appropriate to serving general legal values may take priority at some level over the form more appropriate to serving problem-specific policy. Thus, the priority is of one type of form over another.

I now turn to another type of priority of appropriate form. In general, officials, judges, and citizens are not free to depart from, or to rewrite, formal rules of law once validly created and still in force. In this, they are generally required to honour the form and the formal features of established rules, except insofar as the "rules of change" recognised in a system authorise such departures. If this were not so, society could hardly be said to be governed in accord with the rule of law.

A presidential or other high administrative official generally has no power to depart from or rewrite a statute or binding precedent, let alone a constitution.

Further, a highest appellate court is generally required to adhere to a constitutional provision, and also to a formal statute even if the constitution or statute might even be readily improved in its content or in its form, and by that very court, then and there.

It is true that in common law countries, the highest appellate courts do have some power to over-rule or modify valid precedent. Most such courts seldom do so, however, merely on the basis that the court would have decided the precedent differently if the case were now before it for the first time.

Nor can a citizen change the law or avoid its reach merely because of some truly exigent circumstance. A motorist is not allowed to exceed the speed limit merely to say farewell to a dying relative at a hospital, even if there is no evident risk to the safety of others.

Likewise, a judge is generally not free to rewrite a contract or a security agreement such as a mortgage, or indeed, any other privately created instrument. For example, a court is not free to block a mortgagee bank from foreclosing against a debtor no matter how inequitable or unjust this may be, as where, for example, the delinquent debtor is an unemployed widow with five children and no place to go.

In all the foregoing instances, the law is in part paying homage to appropriate form and the values this serves. The conflict is not a conflict between "the formalistic" or "mere form," on the one hand, and genuine values on the other. In all the foregoing instances, the claims of form are backed at least by general legal values and rule of law values. And commonly the claims of form are also backed by social policies, moral principles, and even justice itself, at least in what John Rawls would call a "tolerably" well ordered society[43]. It is true that sometimes it is, in an especially compelling case, necessary and even justified to disregard the claims of form and the values form serves in order to "do justice in the particular case."

This might be thought of as a reversal of the general priorities of form, and such rule departures comprise a general subject requiring fuller study than legal theorists have so far given it. But at least in a tolerably well ordered society, it remains generally true that it is adherence to, not departure from, antecedent law with all of its formality, that normally serves justice, even in particular cases.

Let us return to the our highway speed limit illustration. Here, form serves justice at almost every turn. When drivers self-administer a determinate speed limit, and conform to it, they thereby accord other drivers their due, and thus act justly toward them. These other drivers will have formed justified expectations of general compliance and will be seeking to co-ordinate their own behaviour accordingly. Every such instance may be thought of as a particular case in which, among other things, justice is done when drivers comply.

At the same time, when police fail to enforce the speed limit against serious violations, this is unjust to other drivers then and there abiding by the law. It frustrates their own justified expectations, and imposes an unfair burden on them. When police do arrest speeders, and they are duly penalised, the police and the judges thereby see to it that the speeders receive their own just deserts. That is, justice is done in these particular cases.

To the extent that fines or penalties are proportionate to the degree of the offence, such punishment itself is just. Also, to the extent that disputant speeders go on to receive a fair trial, they also realise procedural justice in the particular case. Now, in all of these ways in which justice may be done, appropriate form plays major roles. Form in the law is not fundamentally at war with justice in the particular case. On the contrary. The general priorities of appropriate form, in a tolerably well ordered society, normally secure justice in the particular case.

---

[43] J. Rawls, *A Theory of Justice*, Cambridge (Mass.), 1971.

Bibliographical Information

I. Books

1. (with D. N. MacCormick) *Interpreting Precedents. A Comparative Study*, Aldershot, 1997.
2. *Essays on the Nature of Law and Legal Reasoning*, Berlin, 1992.
3. *American Legal Theory*, New York, 1992.
4. (with P. Atiya) *Form and Substance in Anglo-American Law*, Oxford, 1991^2.
5. (with D. N. MacCormick), *Interpreting Statutes. A Comparative Study*. Aldershot, 1991.
6. (with K. Clermont) *Law: Its Nature, Functions and Limits*, St. Paul, 1986^3.
7. *Lon L. Fuller*, London, 1984.
8. *Pragmatischer Instrumentalismus,* Freiburg, 1983.
9. *Instrumentalism and American Legal Theory*, Ithaca/London, 1982.
10. *More Essays in Legal Philosophy*, Oxford, 1971 (as editor)
11. *Essays in Legal Philosophy*, Oxford, 1968 (as editor).

II. Articles

1. "How Law is Formal and Why It Matters?", 82 *Cornell L. Review*, 101 (1997).
2. "Rudolf von Jhering's Influence on American Legal Theory. A Selective Account" in *Jhering's Rechtsdenken*, O. Behrends (ed.), Göttingen, 1996, 61-76.
3. "H. L. A. Hart's *The Concept of Law*. Estimations, Reflections and a Personal Memorial", 45 *J. Legal Ed.*, 587 (1995).
4. "The Juristic Study of Law's Formal Character", *Ratio Juris*, 1995, 237-247.
5. "The Formal Character of Law. Criteria of Validity for Contracts", 9 *J. Contract Law*, 29 (1995).
6. "The Formal Character of Law", *Rechtstheorie*, 1994, 125-162.
7. "Der Formale Charakter des Rechts II", *A.R.S.P.,* 1994, 66-84.
8. "A Formal Theory of the Rule of Law", *Ratio Juris*, 1993, 127-142.
9. (with G. Marshall) "The Argument from Ordinary Meaning in Statutory Interpretation", 43 *No. Ireland Law Q.*, 213 (1992).
10. "The Formal Character of Law", 51 *Cambridge L.J.*, 242 (1992).
11. "On Analysing and Characterising the General Style of a Legal System as Formal or as Substantive", *Rechtstheorie*, 1992, 27-34.
12. "Statues and Contracts as Founts of Formal Reasoning" in *Essays for Patrick Atiya*, P. Cane, and S. Stapleton, (eds.), Oxford, 1991, 71-85.
13. "Theory, Formality and Practical Legal Criticism", 106 *Law Quarterly Rev.* 407 (1990).
14. "The Ideal Socio-Legal Order. Its Rule of Law Dimension", *Ratio Juris*, 1988, 154-161.

15. "Form and Substance in Legal Reasoning" in *Essays in Honour of Torstein Eckhoff*, S. Evju (ed.), 1986, 452-470.
16. "On Identifying and Reconstructing a General Legal Theory: Some Thoughts Prompted by Professor Moore's Critique", 69 *Cornell L. Rev.*, 1014 (1984).
17. "Pragmatic Instrumentalism and American Legal Theory. A Summary Statement", *Rechtstheorie*, 1982, 257-268.
18. "Pragmatic Instrumentalism in the Twentieth Century American Legal Thought. A Synthesis and Critique of Our Dominant Theory about Law and Its Use", 66 *Cornell L. Rev.*, 861 (1981).
19. "Professor Fuller's Jurisprudence and America's Dominant Philosophy of Law", 92 *Harvard L. Rev.*, 433 (1978).
20. "Two Types of Substantive Reasons. The Core of a Theory of Common Law Justification", 53 *Cornell L. Rev.*, 707 (1978).
21. "Naive Instrumentalism and the Law" in *Law, Morality and Society. Essays in Honour of H. L. A. Hart*, P. Hacker and J. Raz (eds.), Oxford, 1977, 119-131.
22. "Evaluating and Improving Legal Processes. A Plea for Process Values", 60 *Cornell L. Rev.*, 1, (1974).
23. "The Technique Element in Law", 59 *Calif. L. Rev.*, 733 (1971).
24. "The New Analytical Jurists", 41 *New York U.L.Rev.*, 861 (1966).
25. "Professor H. L. A. Hart's Concept of Law", *Duke L.J.*, 629 (1963).
26. "H. L. A. Hart on Justice", 59 *J. of Philosophy*, 497 (1962).

NEO-INSTITUTIONALISM: MY VIEWS ON THE PHILOSOPHY OF LAW

OTA WEINBERGER

GRAZ/AUSTRIA

1. Introduction

My philosophy of law is a result of two elements: the basic intention of my philosophical endeavour to develop logical analysis and rational argumentation in the field of practical philosophy, especially in jurisprudence, and the reaction on different influences on my philosophical deliberations.

I grew up in a tolerant and undogmatic family in a town with Czech and German population – Brno, in the former Czechoslovakia. I did not enjoy any religious education, and national feelings were always unknown to me.

My main teacher in jurisprudence was Weyr, a close friend of Kelsen and the head of the Brno school of the pure theory of law. He evoked my interest for the structure theory of law and for the logic of norm sentences. But my attitude towards the pure theory of law was from the beginning divided: I accepted the "is-ought" distinction as well as the distinction of analyses *de lege lata* and *de lege ferenda*, but I did not believe that legal validity were only a matter of a hypothetical assumption, and that legal politics lay outside jurisprudence.

I did not become a partisan of a specific philosophical school. The main influences came from Kant, Schopenhauer, from logical positivism (Carnap) and analytical philosophy, Wittgenstein (but not in the interpretation of ordinary language philosophy, yet more in the conception of reconstructivism), von Wright, Popper, and many others.

I fear that my work may give the impression that my interests are too widespread: logic of normative sentences, other systems of practical reasoning (formal teleology, formal axiology, logic of preference), structure theory of law, action theory, theory of institutions, general theory of argumentation, problems of justice and democracy. My personal impression is quite different. I feel that this diversity of philosophical investigations is more or less linked at least indirectly to my basic intention to make logical analysis more effective in the broad field of practical philosophy.

Reviewing the development of my work I see one essential breach. Since 1978 the notion of action – and of human capacity to act – takes a basic role in my philosophy. In the logic of norm sentences (and in deontic logic) the concept of action played always an important role as an element of the content of norm sentences. But now the understanding of the anthropological role of action as an essential feature of human life became the starting point for the construction of the framework for practical philosophy.

Norms as well as institutions were understood as tools for determining action, and they were explained as entities in this anthropological frame. This anthropological view provided the underpinning for my epistemological conception, and it is the reason for the dichotomous semantics appropriate for man as a being able to act and to create institutions.

In the first stage of my philosophical work I presented critical analyses of the first attempts to deal with the logic of norm sentences, and mainly with the mainstream of this endeavour, deontic logic. On the other side I argued in favour of the view that logic of norm sentences is an important topic of philosophical analysis. Step by step I tried to define the main principles of a genuine logical system of norm sentences[1].

Meanwhile I published several articles on different problems of general jurisprudence, especially on the structure theory of law. About 1978 I decided in favour of the action-theoretical approach and the respective theory of institutions as the appropriate basis for legal and social philosophy. Since this time I hold that it is justified to regard my conception as a specific theory which I call "neo-institutionalism" (to distinguish my teaching from the classical institutionalism of Maurice Houriou, Carl Schmitt and others)[2].

2. What serves Legal Philosophy for?

Law is an ideal entity, a product of social and cultural development. It is not an object to be grasped by help of sensuous experience, but must be understood in an hermeneutic process. Law and its understanding must be rationally justified in several respects. Legal rules are justified in a *de lege ferenda* perspective or as a matter of interpretation (*de lege lata*). The system of law has to be analysed and constructed as a realm of legal dogmatics. Every legal decision must be justified in a reasonable process of argumentation. And – last, but not least – general jurisprudence as the knowledge of the structure and the working of legal systems in general has to be underpinned by a philosophical argumentation. To elaborate the gnoseological and methodological basis of these kinds of reasoning in the field of law is the essential task of legal philosophy. We

---

[1] Cf. O. Weinberger, *Die Sollsatzproblematik in der modernen Logik, Prague, 1958; id., Alternative Handlungstheorie. Gleichzeitig eine Auseinandersetzung mit Georg-Henrik von Wrights praktischer Philosophie*, Vienna/Cologne/Weimar, 1996 and id., "Der normenlogische Skeptizismus", *Rechtstheorie*, 1986, 13–81.

[2] D. N. MacCormick worked out at the same time a conception that was very similar with mine. Therefore we decided to publish our views in one book. D. N. MacCormick and O. Weinberger, *Grundlagen des Institutionalistischen Rechtspositivismus,* Berlin, 1985.

may not speak about legal philosophy *expressis verbis*, but we must deal with at least some basic problems of legal philosophy if we want to pursue jurisprudence on a scientific level. We can follow the ideal of justice which is immanent in the theory and practice of law only on an appropriate philosophical basis.

In the following I shall try to explain the main theoretical pillars and some essential achievements of neo-institutionalism.

3. The Anthropological Basis of Neo-Institutionalism and its Semantic System

Human beings are characterised by a specific form of behaviour and activity which can be expressed by two connected anthropological theses: (i) we have the ability of acting on the basis of an information process of teleological character, and (ii) we are social beings.

Action is a kind of behaviour which is dependent on an information process by which the choice how to act is realised and by which the realisation of the activity is controlled. The description of the structure of the information process on which action is based provides the basis for practical philosophy. The deliberation how to act works in a field of cognitive information concerning the actual situation and causal laws. The realm of action is a class of trajectories (sequences of behaviour) which are possible continuations of the actual state of the system under consideration. Therefore practical consideration presupposes reasoning using modalities: the necessary, the possible, and the contingent. Action theory presupposes knowledge transcending the ascertainment of existing states of affairs. Descriptive knowledge – even if it includes the knowledge of necessities and possibilities – cannot yield and justify choices or practical decisions how to act. Only on the basis of another – additional – kind of information practical decision making is possible. For the realisation of action determining information processes we need practical informations which provide measures for selection: purposes, norms, values, and preferences.

Both basic features of man, the ability to act and the social character of man find their essential expression in our ability and actual practice of building institutions. The extreme elasticity of our inherited equipment is compensated by the fact that we are able to establish institutions. Institutions are – in my conception – frames for action and interpersonal co-operation. Types of behaviour as elements of the way of life are institutionalised, and in general followed by individuals as agents, and forms of co-operation with other persons are established. Institutions are not only habitual regularities, but they are defined and directed by a core of practical informations how we should act and how action should be judged as good or bad or indifferent.

The anthropological character of human beings, namely their ability to act, implies a complex conception of knowledge and a specific semantic system for practical philosophy.

The objects of our recognition are not restricted to states of affairs which can be experienced, but also the field of empirical laws and the finding of possibilities are topics of our recognition. Besides this the recognition of institutional facts and the understanding of empirical realities as objects in their institutionalised role are essential features of knowledge in the world view of acting persons.

We can conclude: human reality – the realm of facts – is not only the reality in the sense of systems of brute facts (including possibilities), but also classes of institutional facts. And therefore recognition in the human world view is not only the ascertainment of physical facts given by our experience, but also the realm of institutional facts which can be grasped only in a complex considerations embracing observation as well as understanding of practical information by which the institutional role of the objects is determined. For example, a coin can be described by its physical (brute) features, but we can understand it as a coin, *i.e.* in its institutional function, only if we also consider the use of this object in the normative frame of the monetary system. The consideration of the institutional function of objects in everyday life are in fact often understood in their institutional relation – thing of such current expressions as "my father" or "I have no debts". Their meaning is not purely descriptive, but the notions "father" and "debts" are understood in their institutional function defined by legal relations.

To describe the world as it is in the sense of brute facts, their relations and regularities, and possible lines of development of objects under consideration we need only a descriptive language completed by modal notions (possible, necessary, and contingent). But in order to be able to speak about institutional facts, and in order to be able to realise deliberations determining action we need also a language sphere of practical sentences by which we can express practical information, because only by practical informations selection processes can be determined.

Therefore in the whole field of practical philosophy we must use a semantic system of dichotomous character which is built on the categorial distinction of descriptive (cognitive) and practical sentences.

The structure of action determining information processes is the essential reason for the necessity to work in practical philosophy with a system of dichotomous semantics. This semantics leads to the conception that it is necessary to construct logical systems of practical reasoning. With this problems I shall deal in the next two paragraphs.

4. The Logic of Norm Sentences

The main steps towards the definition of the task how to build a logic of norm sentences were: Hume's and Kant's clarification of the semantic separation of ought sentences from descriptive ones, Poincaré's recognition that traditional logic which deals only with propositions does not provide any rule which would yield an ought conclusion following from descriptive premises only, Jörgensen's recognition of the dilemma between the traditional definition of inference based on truth-relations, the fact that ought sentences (imperatives) have no truth value, and the indubitable fact that in practice of everyday life as well as in our reasoning in the normative disciplines we draw inferences which are as evident as inferences based on descriptive premises only. Since this problem has been formulated by Jörgensen there exist three lines of thought in this field: (i) norm-logical scepticism: there is no valid normative inference (this view is always accompanied by some advice how to deal with normative inference by help of a substitute operation); (ii) simply ignoring this pressing philosophical problem (this was the case with the founders of deontic logic and other authors who conceived ought sentences as a special kind of descriptive sentences, *e.g.* Rödig); (iii) introducing a generalised notion of inference which allows to be applied also to normative sentences as premises and conclusions (Alchourròn, Martino and myself) and postulating the construction of a genuine logic of norm sentences (von Wright in his new development and myself).

The mainstream of logical systems which tried to deal with a logic applicable in normative disciplines, namely deontic logic, is burdened by serious difficulties (which in my opinion imply that these systems are not applicable in jurisprudence and ethics). Deontic logic uses deontic sentences as descriptive sentences: it takes deontic sentences as arguments of truth-functional connectors. It is not able to provide an appropriate expression for hypothetical norms. In analogy with alethic modal logic deontic logic recognises the following deontic inference schemes as valid: (a) "From '$O(p \& q)$' follows 'Op' and 'Oq'", and (b) "From 'Op' follows '$O\ (p \vee q)$'". The validity of such inferences is problematical, because of the fact that the assumption of a normative premise does not guarantee the fulfilment of the content of the premise. If p is not realised then the conclusion 'Oq' in (a) and of '$O(p \vee q)$' in (b) is not justified. Deontic logic presupposes the interdefiniability of deontic operators which is not justified in open systems.

To deny the existence of logical relations between norm sentences (*e.g.* logical incompatibility of the obligation p and the obligation non-p, or the obligation p and the permission non-p within the same normative system) or the validity of evident normological inferences (*e.g.* the rule of subsumption) is absurd.

The main principles on which a genuine logic of norm sentences should be build up are the following:

There are two categories of elementary sentences: descriptive sentences and normative ones. There is a rule defining the content of elementary ought sentences in relation to the content of elementary descriptive sentences: 'Op' is an ought norm which is fulfilled if and only if 'p' is the case.

Elementary normative sentences are formed by a normative operator (*O*, *P*, *F*) and a formula indicating the content. Only the ought operator (*O* or *F*) is basic; the other operators are introduced in a secondary function.

Normative incompatibility is not the same as incompatibility in propositional logic; it is defined as the opposition of *'Op'* and *'O ¬ p'*, and *'Op'* and *'P ¬ p'*.

The generalised notion of inference can be introduced by the following definition: a sentence c is a consequence of the propositional premises p_1, p_2, ... p_n and the normative premises n_1, n_2, ... n_m if and only if c by reason of logic cannot be false if c is a proposition or invalid if c is a normative sentence although all propositional premises are true and all normative premises are valid.

By deductive operations no duty can by derived that is not – at least implicitly – contained in the premises.

Connectors with normative arguments can be introduced, but they are not truth-functional.

The connector ">" forming normative conditional sentences is a two-place functor with one descriptive and one normative argument; it can be defined by the following rules:

(i) If *'Op'* then *'q > Op'* (rule of hypothetical extension)

(ii) If *'q > Op'* and *'q'* then *'Op'* (rule of detachment).

Normative consequences can be deduced only from classes of premises which contain at least one normative premise, and descriptive consequences follow only from classes of premises which contain at least one descriptive premise (non-derivability thesis).

In normative contexts we can introduce quantifiers, namely internal and external quantifiers. Normative rules are formed by external general quantification.

There are different types of deducing normative consequences; from ought sentences given as premises follow ought sentences which state a subclass of obligations stated by the premises; there are consequences based on the detachment rule; and there are consequences justified by the relations between the normative operators, *e.g.* "From *'Op'* follows *'Pp'*". From general norm sentences follow the respective individual norm sentences, and from general rules and appropriate individual descriptive sentences individual normative conclusions are deducible by subsumption.

In order to be able to deal with problems of legal dynamics it is useful to introduce a specific hypothetical norm sentence (empowering conditional). As a condition of this norm sentence a norm setting act is introduced whose content is identical with the normative consequent of the conditional sentence. If the respective act is realised then its normative content can be justified as a new content of the system containing the empowering normative rule.

5. Other Systems of Practical Reasoning

Argumentation in different fields of practical disciplines uses also other logical systems, namely formal teleology, formal axiology, and logic of preferences. It would exceed the frame of this essay if I would explain these systems and discuss the relations between them[3].

6. My Conception of Action Theory

Action cannot be defined in a behaviouristic way. It is not only the succession of states that characterises action, but the fact that the succession is determined by a specific information process. I conceive action as a behaviour induced by a determining information process of a specific structure, and the structure of this information process characterises what an action is. This method of defining the notion of action leads to a formal conception of action and to the effect that not only individual human beings but also collectives and institutions may be bearers (or subjects) of action if they can realise in some direct or indirect way the relevant information processes. Action is in principle based on teleological choice processes in a field of possible lines of action.

The action determining information process is bound to the existence of some preconditions: (i) the subject disposes of a field of possible lines of future behaviour, (ii) the subject has some descriptive information about the actual situation and of causal relations, and some practical informations (teleological intentions, preferences or norms. (iii) the subject is able to optimise the choice among the possible lines of behaviour following its practical orientation given by its system of practical informations, and to lead its activity in the chosen direction.

The basic structure of the determination of action is a teleological one, but in this frame also normative determination takes its place, mainly because of two reasons: in order to stabilise the forms of action and in order to co-ordinate the action of one subject with the behaviour and the expectations of other subjects. All forms of co-operation are bound to normative regulation.

There are two distinct problem situations in which we are dealing with action: (a) the deliberation searching for the optimisation of choices and of the decisions how to act, and (b) the task of understanding action (*i.e.* the behaviour of subjects) through the interpretation of their motives. Motive interpretation tries to reconstruct the information process which evoked the action (*i.e.* the behaviour understood as an action). Both considerations about action are based on the same

---

[3] Cf. O. Weinberger, *Rechtslogik*, Berlin, 1989[2] and id., *Alternative Handlungstheorie*, passim.

formal structure of the information process, only the use made of this structure in the analysis is quite different.

7. The Theory of Institutions

There is an important link between acting and human institutions. Institutions are frames for action. It is an essential feature of man that we are forming institutions, and that our lives take place in a field of institutions. Institutions stabilise the way of life in two respects: they establish types of behaviour and action, and they are indispensable bases for human interaction and co-operation. The fundamental idea of my concept of institution is expressed by the following thesis: institutions have a core of practical informations which provide the ideal basis of the institution by defining the aims, the values, preferences and, if needed, the structure of the organisation supporting the institution.

My conception of institutions stands neither in the tradition of sociological individualism which tries to explain social phenomena as effects of individual behaviour nor in the tradition of holism which looks at the individual's behaviour as determined mainly by social factors. Neo-institutionalism conceives the relation of individuals and social phenomena as a process of mutual interplay: human individuals are determining the mind of institutions and established institutions provide the frame for the behaviour and the expectations of the individuals and for all kinds of human interaction.

Institutions are the place where the individual and society meet. They are complex entities of ideal and real character. Therefore they can be recognised only by both, the understanding of their ideal side and by the observation of the respective social processes. Institutions are the most important determinants of our way of life.

Institutions are essential factors leading to stability of the individual behaviour and of social bodies. They also provide the basis for social development. Established institutions are factors of stability even in the flow of evolution, insofar as they have a tendency to adhere to their basic ideas – at least with the main tendency to preserve the basic ideas of the institution. But they underlie also an important evolution in two respects: firstly, through an inner evolution of the ideas and the life within the institution, and secondly, by the fact that institutions are social realities which provide the basis for the formation of new, so to say secondary, institutions.

The influence of institutions on our life becomes apparent in the fact that many terms of everyday life are not purely descriptive, but shaped by institutional relations (*e.g.* "my wife", "the university").

We can distinguish different kinds of institutions. A typology of institutions provides only a rough information about the broad field of different institutions. I divide them firstly in normative and real institutions. Normative institutions are pieces of a normative system forming an ideal and functional totality of normative relations ("*Rechtsinstitute*") and real institutions which are bound to a personal and/or material equipment. Legal institutions (such as marriage, agreement, offence) are, of course, indirectly related to the real institution of the state. Their being there as a social fact is bound to this reality.

In the view of neo-institutionalism the system of law is not composed of isolated rules, but legal rules form functional complexes.

The normative meaning of rules is to determine duties and rights, and to confer legal power to the effect of producing private autonomy or organisation structures.

The field of real institutions is rather differentiated. There are organised institutions with an equipment of persons in different roles and of material things serving the realisation of the tasks of the institution.

In social life there are institutionalised subjects which take specific roles in society besides persons as human individuals. The establishing of institutionalised persons – legal persons in the realm of law – are bearers of duties and rights, and it is normatively stated how these subjects can act by help of their organs. Institutionalised persons are actual realities of social life, *e.g.* co-operating collectives, but their function and role in society is based on normative regulation.

8. Legal Rules, Legal Dynamics, and the Notion of Valid Law

It is the fundamental aim of analytical jurisprudence to define linguistic tools for expressing all possible legal content, and to characterise or justify on this formal basis the rational operations which correspond to legal processes, especially to the creation of legal rules and to the application of them in processes of adjudication.

In the first stage the theory of the legal rule has been dominated by the aim to find a unique form for expressing all possible legal content. There are two traditional forms of this basic structure of the legal rule: (a) the general hypothetical normative sentence (the general normative conditional), and (b) Kelsen's general sanction rule.

There exist many objections against Kelsen's view that the law can give orders only by stating sanction for the opposite behaviour[4].

[4] I shall not repeat these objections against the sanction theory of legal rules which in Kelsen's teaching is linked with the thesis that the norm stating duties of citizens is superfluous because it follows logically from the sanction norm. (This view is not correct as Hart has shown, and evidently inconsistent with normological scepticism in the late teaching of Kelsen.) Cf. O. Weinberger, *Normentheorie als Grundlage der Jurisprudenz und Ethik. Eine Auseinandersetzung mit Hans Kelsens Theorie der Normen*, Berlin 1981.

Both traditional forms are conceived of as the universal formal structure of the whole legal content, and the rule of subsumption is defined as the universally valid form of applying these rules. From this conception follows: if we had a complete list of all valid rules which form the content of the legal system all obligations and all rights could be deduced if we would insert all actual findings of the relevant states of affairs as premises.

In analytical jurisprudence two "revolutions" took place: (i) more detailed analysis has proven that we must take into consideration also some kinds of rules which are not reducible to the presupposed universal standard form, and (ii) more attention was paid to the processes of argumentation by which the decision of actual cases in the light of legal rules are produced and justified.

The main forms of legal rules which are not formally reducible to generalised normative conditionals are: legal principles, teleological rules, and power conferring rules. Esser and especially Dworkin have discussed the role of principles as arguments for finding and justifying legal decisions, and the latter has shown convincingly, that the logical determination of decisions by legal principles is rather different from the application of rules of behaviour. Golunski has explained the role of teleological norms in opposition to normal rules of behaviour. I myself have proven that power conferring rules are formally not reducible to normative conditionals determining duties of behaviour. These findings led to the differentiated conception of neo-institutionalism concerning legal rules.

Neo-institutionalism is a conception of analytical jurisprudence which works with differentiated forms of legal rules and which takes care of the different types of rational operations applied in legal argumentation. This is important for this legal theory because it underlines the role of the ideal background by which the content of the law is justified and argues against the tendency for atomisation which characterises the old conception of the unifying theory of the legal rule. The main types of legal rules and the appropriate rational operations with them are the following:

(a) rules of behaviour which form the basis for subsumption;

(b) teleological rules which can be applied in relation to the recognition of appropriate means to fulfil the respective task;

(c) legal principles which have more abstract or teleological content and which are applied by weighing their relative importance[5];

[5] Legal principles are used as arguments in de lege ferenda justifications as well as in specifying legal decisions or solutions of so-called hard cases which are not determined by simple subsumption. Dworkin conceives principles as an element of natural law used to argue for decisions in hard cases, but I hold that they are at least an implicit content of the body of law of the system under consideration. The methodological difference in these two

(d) power conferring rules by which a subject gets the power to create valid norms of the legal system[6].

Neo-institutionalism regards the system of law as a dynamic system, but in a quite other sense then the pure theory of law (Kelsen, Merkl). In the mind of the idea of purity Kelsen conceives dynamic processes as movements only in the body of norms. In my conception of legal dynamics the interplay of normative rules with social processes and acts of will is essential. The justification of norm creation is based on both elements: given valid norms of behaviour and power conferring norms, and actual facts including acts of will.

The definition of valid law concerns two fields, namely the validity of a legal system as a whole and the question whether a certain normative content is valid in the frame of a system presupposed to be valid. The first question is answered in the conception of neo-institutionalism by the thesis that the legal system is really valid if and only if it is working as a normative basis of the system of institutions of the state. The problem of validity of distinct elements of a legal system is determined by processes of legal dynamics. This concerns the validity of legal rules as well as the validity of individual norms arising in legal life or in processes of adjudication.

Neo-institutionalism holds the view that to the realm of valid law belong not only rules of behaviour, power conferring rules, teleological rules and individual norms arising out of processes of norm creation dependent on these rules, but also the system of established legal principles. Valid law is not only what has been explicitly stated by norm creating act, but also what is *de facto* institutionalised implicitly.

Many theorists postulate additional criteria of moral character for valid law. Really valid – *i.e.* legitimate law – must fulfil at least minimal moral standards and/or criteria of democratic genesis of the rules. In normal situations the adoption of a moral filter for valid law gives the judge more moral competence then the legislator. Moral standards are not univocally determined, therefore morality as a filter against immoral law is not effective and may come into conflict with the idea of truthworthiness in legal life.

The demand for democratic norm creation is an interesting desideratum, but it seems to me not very realistic in view of the fact that even in democratic

---

conceptions of principles is that in my view the principles used are not given by nature or natural reason, but most be justified by arguments as elements embodied in the respective positive system.

[6] Power conferring rules are the basis of two kinds of norm creating processes: the power to form new normative situations by acts of private autonomy (agreements, will, etc.) or official power of legislation and adjudication.

systems broad fields of norm creation do not follow this principle (*e.g.* the creation of the law of the EU).

Modern legal theory is confronted with the phenomenon of "degenerated" legal systems of the type of Nazi law which followed evidently inhuman ends. To deny the institutionalised existence of such systems does not describe the sociological reality adequately. And to hold the theoretical view that it was not law cannot work as a tool for eliminating immoral law. In such degenerated systems judges mostly do not have the power to prevent the degeneration of the political system which causes the degeneration of the law. But judges have always the task to do the morally best out of their competence, yet on the basis of the power conferred to them, not against actual legal rules. But afterwards when the inhuman system is overcome we may decide that we will treat legal relations which arose during the period of degenerated law in such a way as supposing that these relations were not valid from the beginning (did not arise).

9. Positivism versus Jusnaturalism

This traditional dispute has to be judged form the point of view of juristic argumentation. Natural law can have a place in juristic thought if and only if it provides objectively valid arguments for legal argumentation.

The justification of value criteria which we accept as convincing must not be conceived of as objectively valid, everlasting and not subjected to further examination – as holds jusnaturalism – but they may be only historically and socially determined convictions which may be criticised in the course of time and on the basis of social and functional analysis. Therefore a position "beyond simplistic positivism and jusnaturalism" seems well founded: rational justification and not mere respect of power offers the basis for legislation and adjudication, but not arbitrariness as some positivists hold, and so-called natural law arguments are not valid as immanent absolute criteria, but even apparent value evidence should be a matter of critical deliberation.

10. Juristic Theory of Argumentation

The problems of argumentation have attained a central position in present-day legal philosophy. In the first place it is the debate about the role of logical relations and deduction in juristic thought. Logicism stands against two conceptions: normological scepticism and rhetoric argumentation. A famous philosopher and scholar in practical thought, G.-H. von Wright, has called it stubbornness to deny norm-logical relations and inferences, and I have presented many important arguments against normological scepticism[7]. Logical relations

---

[7] Cf. O. Weinberger, "Der normenlogische Skeptizismus", passim.

and norm-logical inference represent the core of juristic argumentation. But exact logical analysis proves that juristic argumentation is to a high degree so-called rhetoric argumentation which tries to achieve plausibility.

The theory of rhetoric argumentation has been developed as a theory in the field of pragmatics only: it has studied the problems of plausibility as a field of pragmatic relations between a rhetor and his audience. Good reasons were defined as arguments which were effective in evoking convictions of the audience. In opposition to this view I distinguish carefully between the real validity of plausibility arguments and their effectiveness in evoking convictions in a certain audience. In fact invalid reasons may in some situation evoke (false) convictions, and valid arguments (and even strict proofs) may fail to have convincing effects. Only the careful distinction of these two distinct perspectives in which we can analyse plausibility arguments allows to find an answer to the question whether an argument is well-founded in an objective sense, and this question is central for a scientific theory of plausibility argumentation.

The notion of good reason for plausibility is of course relative in respect to the field of theses argued for.

Theses and the conviction of their validity concern two distinct realms: facts (and laws governing their causal relations) and values (or other practical informations like norms or purposes).

It is evident that even in the pragmatic conception of argumentation we should distinguish two types of evoking convictions, the so-called rational argumentation and other methods of persuasion. Perelman used the idea of the universal audience as a criterion of rational argumentation, but as this idea is a cultural and historical criterion it fails in case of argumentation about new conceptions. Habermas' discourse philosophy has stated criteria for ideal discourses, in the first place independence of power, but I doubt whether "*Herrschaftsfreiheit*" is a working guarantee for the rationality of discourses and of a rational method of evoking convictions. In my opinion rational discourses of plausibility are multidimensional processes which are not subjected to a clear and general validity criterion, only the claim for critical scrutiny holds as a general, but vague directive.

Argumentation as a pragmatic process can take different forms: it is a searching endeavour if the participants are mainly interested to find the truth or to get an appropriate practical orientation. But in everyday practice, in legal and political discourses the argumentation is often governed by the intention to plead in favour of a certain interest. In this case argumentation changes fundamentally: the rhetor is looking for reasons supporting his theses which are in some way fixed in advance, but not searching for the objectively best conception.

In legal life different types of argumentation are used. I should mention interpretative argumentation which is a task of legal dogmatics as well as of officials applying the law. Legal science which has the task of interpreting and systematising the law is an institutionalised part of legal life which influences legal practice. But the official interpretation which is applied in the practice of adjudication is a strong reason for doctrinal understanding of the law, because it shows how the law works in fact.

11. Theory of Justice

The ideal of justice is immanent to all juristic activity, but we have no general knowledge what justice is. In my opinion it is not the task of the theory of justice to provide a picture of a just society which could function as a fundamental political program. Investigations of justice are more of a critical analysis then an advice how to define and organise a fair society.

Individual and political action is simultaneously directed by utility considerations and ideals of fair and just behaviour. It is a sound way of life to search for harmony of both aims.

The ideals of justice are determined by biological and cultural factors. Everybody has a kind of intuitive feeling of justice and follows some ideas as criteria of just behaviour and action. The same is true for social groups or institutionalised bodies. The theory of justice can presuppose the existence of an intuitive sense of justice, not as a fixed and absolutely valid standard, but as an actual basis for consideration. Value conviction has to be cultivated by theoretical analysis and deliberation. Justice is in principle orientated on relations to fellow beings, and it is the expression of a certain form of solidarity with them. The theory of justice tries to clarify and rationalise our sense of justice and deals with the evolution of criteria of justice in relation to social development. Therefore in our society we can speak of a mutual relation between criteria of justice and ideals of democracy.

Traditionally the ideas of equality, of freedom and solidarity are fundamental elements of the analysis of justice.

An important part of the approach in justice theory is dominated by formal conceptions in which two ideas are essential: the demand for formal equality and the principle of universalisability. I have tried to show that formal principles are not sufficient to define a working conception of justice[8].

The principle of formal justice (or formal equality) demands that under the same relevant conditions the same legal consequences should be established. This principle is equivalent to the postulate that legal judgement has to be determined by general rules. The principle of formal justice is an important tool for critical analysis – it is unjust to treat cases which are in relevant features similar in different way – but not sufficient for answering the question “what is just?”. It

[8] Cf. O. Weinberger, *Moral und Vernunft. Beiträge zu Ethik, Gerechtigkeitstheorie und Normenlogik*, Vienna/Cologne/Weimar,1992.

must be accompanied by a value decision about the relevant conditions and the appropriateness of stated legal consequences.

Universalisability has been conceived as a tool for deciding about the acceptability of moral and/or legal rules. This criterion can be applied for judging proposed rules as just only in combination with a value decision about the elements to be universalised. Universality is not valid in an absolute sense, but only in relation to the conditions defining duties and rights which are stated by norms of the given legal system[9].

Equality and freedom are often treated as ideals of justice which are both plausible, but in actual conflict: more equality means less freedom, and vice versa. I do not agree with this conception. In my opinion a discussion of these principles of justice should start with the analytical recognition that there is no equality as such, but that there are different types of equality. And the same is true concerning freedom. We should not postulate a maximisation neither of equality nor of freedom, but try to establish an acceptable system of measures to support social and civil equality and personal freedom as a basis for defining our way of life as individuals and as beings following ideals of solidarity.

From the institutional point of view two demands of justice are important: justice concerning the organisation of roles within institutions and the postulate of a just legal procedure. It is always an important question to find a moral equilibrium of roles established in institutions. The arrangement of roles has to be judged simultaneously from different angles: effectiveness of the organisation, a balanced determination of duties and rights, of work and reward. Procedural justice has to guarantee that true findings should be taken as a basis for adjudication, that equal concern of litigants is granted, and that the organisation of the process offers an optimal chance for the realisation of the legal ought.

12. My Conception of Democracy

The notion of democracy is vague in many respects. The cluster of ideas linked with this notion can be approximately defined by the famous Lincoln formula "Democracy is the rule of the people, by the people and for the people". This definition is so far away from a description of political reality that it is clear that it characterises only a basic tendency of the democratic world view. It expresses the idea of the people's sovereignty without specifying the methods how to achieve it. Different theories of democracy provide a theoretical framework explaining the function of democratic systems in political reality (*e.g.*

---

[9] The so-called principle of reciprocity is not a formal principle with universal validity. It can be applied only in relations of partnership, but it does not concern every interpersonal relation.

the well-known explanation of Schumpeter based on the competition of elites in the fight for gaining a majority in elections).

From several sides problems concerning the practice of democratic systems have been discussed. The following problems have determined my conception of democracy: (i) the fact that democratic systems can be destroyed by democratic vote (or more generally speaking: democratic forms can always be misused); (ii) majority decision can establish inhuman law (*e.g.* cancel minority rights); (iii) the recognition that the evolution of the modern information society has two opposite effects: it provides broad knowledge of actual political and social facts, but it makes manipulation of information possible and is the basis for political indoctrination in a more extended way than it was possible in classical democracy.

Democracy is not only a system of formal rules how to determine the collective will of society and how to elect empowered representatives, but it is also a specific world view which aims at establishing a specific way of life.

Therefore democracy is not only a formal system of formation of the collective will of the people by vote or by empowering representatives, but also the acceptance of an open system of material principles concerning the ideals of political and social life. History shows that formal rules for the organisation of the democratic system can be misused and do not suffice to guarantee democratic life really. They must be based on democratic habits and convictions in broad circles of the population. And there must be an extended system of institutions which are able to provide for an open democratic discussion.

The interpretation of the system of democratic ideas which form the democratic ideology can be given in neo-institutionalistic terms: the democratic system is a kind of political institution which contains rules defining the working of the institution, namely the form of ruling the respective state and society. The system of material ideas on which this institution is based has the role of leading ideas of the democracy as an institution. The democratic *idées directrices* are preconditions of a democratic life, namely such postulates that serve the realisation of the democratic rule: transparency, periodicity of voting, the possibility of free organisation of groups, freedom of opinion and of speech, protection of minorities, organised and public control, etc.

This class of leading ideas is the place where human rights are rooted, and – last but not least – where the preconditions of the working of an open society are postulated. This system of leading ideas of democracy cannot be cancelled by mere voting, but they are not petrified as such, because they are subjected to discussion so that their limits and concrete form can be developed, modified and transformed.

A consequence of this conception of democracy is the close relation between the democratic way of life and the establishment of a working open society.

In my conception of democracy the problems of effectiveness of ruling is an important aspect of shaping social institutions. Only if effectiveness of control is granted the democratic system will have chances to win the political struggles with opposite political systems. Institutional theory pleads for a differentiation of institutional structures dependent on the function of the respective institution.

Also monocratic methods of decision making are acceptable, if transparency and public checking is realised. Hierarchic organisation which is often necessary in order to reach effectiveness of ruling is acceptable if public control is granted and if democratic changes in power relations are institutionalised.

The neo-institutional conception of democracy is a kind of discursive democracy, because it is based on the conviction that social discourses are an effective means for testing social ideas and for their actual realisation and for social progress. But this discursive democracy stands more in the tradition of Popper then in the tradition of Habermas' discourse philosophy. (Discourses are not conceived as criteria of truth or as a guarantee for finding the best solutions.)

In our days the intrusion of marketing methods in political propaganda – sometimes also realised by central propaganda institutions of the state – imply an acute danger for the effectiveness of social discourses. The idea of the open society and of discourse democracy presuppose that there are rational processes of discussion, not a predominance of emotional indoctrination. I hold that this kind of indoctrination is an actual danger for democratic life. Democratic processes cease to be ruling from the social basis and becomes more and more a ruling of people representing the interest of economic leaders[10].

[10] Cf. O. Weinberger, *Alternative Handlungstheorie*, chapter X.

Bibliographical Information

I. Books

1. *Die Sollsatzproblematik in der modernen Logik*, Prague, 1958.

2. *Studie k logice normativních vět: Teorie* důsledkových *vztahů a hypothetická normativní věta, Dvě oblasti logiky normativních vět* (Essays in the logic of norm sentences: The theory of inference relations and normative conditional. Two fields of the logic of norm sentences), Prague, 1960.

3. *Philosophische Studien zur Logik. Einige Bemerkungen zum Begriff der Identität. Philosophische Bemerkungen zur Sollsatzlogik*, Prague, 1964.

4. *Rechtslogik*, Berlin, 1989^{2}.

5. *Logische Analyse in der Jurisprudenz*, Berlin, 1979.

6. *Normentheorie als Grundlage der Jurisprudenz und Ethik. Eine Auseinandersetzung mit Hans Kelsens Theorie der Normen*, Berlin 1981.

7. (with D. N. MacCormick) *An Institutional Theory of Law. New Approaches to Legal Positivism*, Dordrecht, 1986.

8. *Law, Institution and Legal Politics. Fundamental Problems of Legal Theory and Social Philosophy,* Dordrecht, 1991.

9. *Moral und Vernunft. Beiträge zu Ethik, Gerechtigkeitstheorie und Normenlogik,* Vienna/Cologne/Weimar, 1992.

10. *Die Brünner rechtstheoretische Schule (Normative Theorie),* Vienna, 1980.

11. *Alternative Handlungstheorie. Gleichzeitig eine Auseinandersetzung mit Georg-Henrik von Wright's praktischer Philosophie*, Vienna/Cologne/Weimar, 1996.

II. Articles

1. "Über die Negation von Sollsätzen", *Theoria*, 1957, 102-134.

2. "Théorie des propositions normatives. Quelques remarques au sujet de l'interprétation normative des systèmes K_1 et K_2 de G. Kalinowski", *Studia Logica*, 1960, 7-25.

3. "Die Norm als Gedanke und Realität", *Österreichische Zeitschrift für öffentliches Recht*, 1970, 203-216.

4. "Fundamental Problems of the Theory of Legal Reasoning", *A.R.S.P.*, 1972, 61-94.

5. "The Concept of Non-Satisfaction and Deontic Logic", *Ratio*, 1972, 16-35.

6. "Der Erlaubnisbegriff und der Aufbau der Normenlogik", *Logique et Analyse*, 1973, 113-142.

7. "Contrary-to-fact and Fact-Transcendent Conditionals and Contrary-to-fact Conditionals by Means of Truth-Functional Logic", *Ratio*, 1974, 15-32.

8. "Gleichheitspostulate. Eine strukturtheoretische und rechtspolitische Betrachtung", *Österreichische Zeitschrift für öffentliches Recht*, 1974, 23-38.

9. “Ex falso quodlibet in der deskriptiven und in der präskriptiven Sprache”, *Rechtstheorie*, 1975, 17-32.
10. “Wissensaussage und die Unmöglichkeit ihrer Objektivierung”, *Grazer Philosophische Studien*, 1975, 101-120.
11. “Begründung oder Illusion. Erkenntniskritische Gedanken zu John Rawls' Theorie der Gerechtigkeit”, *Zeitschrift für Philosophische Forschung*, 1977, 234-251.
12. “Der nomische Allsatz”, *Grazer Philosophische Studien*, 1977, 31-42.
13. “Rationales und irrationales Handeln” in *Recht und Gesellschaft. Festschrift für Helmut Schelsky zum 65. Geburtstag*, F. Kaulbach and W. Krawietz (eds.), Berlin 1978, 721-744.
14. “Tatsachen und Tatsachenbeschreibungen. Eine logisch-methodologische Überlegung zu einem Grundlagenproblem der Sozialwissenschaft” in *Sozialphilosophie als Aufklärung. Festschrift für Ernst Topitsch*, K. Salamun (ed.), Tübingen 1979, 173-187.
15. “Handeln und Schliessen. Überlegungen zum Begriff der praktischen Inferenz” in *The Law between Morality and Politics,* Van Dun, F. (ed.), *Philosophica*, 1979, 5-36.
16. “'Wissen' und 'Nicht-Wissen' in der praktischen Argumentation. Überlegungen zu einem Grundlagenproblem der Moraltheorie und Rechtspolitik”, *Rechtstheorie*, 1979, 391-408.
17. “Dialektik und philosophische Analyse” in *Logik der Sozialwissenschaften,* E. Topitsch (ed.), Königstein/Ts., 1980[10], 278-309.
18. “Jenseits von Positivismus und Naturrecht” in *Contemporary Conceptions of Law. Proceedings of the 9th IVR World Congress (Basel 1979)*, P. Trappe (ed.), *A.R.S.P.,* Supplementa, I, 1, 1982, 43-56
19. “Die Naturrechtskonzeption von Ronald Dworkin” in *Das Naturrechtsdenken heute und morgen. Gedächtnisschrift für René Marcic*, D. Mayer-Maly and P. M. Simons (eds.), Berlin, 1983, 497-515.
20. “Die formal-finalistische Handlungstheorie und das Strafrecht” in *Festschrift für Ulrich Klug zum 70. Geburtstag,* G. Kohlmann (ed.), Cologne, 1983, 199-213.
21. “Eine Semantik für die praktische Philosophie” in *Beiträge zur Philosophie von Stephan Körner,* R. Haller (ed.), *Grazer Philosophische Studien*, 1983, 219-239.
22. “'Is' and 'Ought' Reconsidered. Comment on G.-H. von Wright's Lecture 'Is and Ought'”, *A.R.S.P.*, 1984, 454-474.
23. “Objectivity and Rationality in Lawyer's Reasoning” in *Theory of Legal Science*, A. Peczenik e.a. (eds.), Dordrecht/Boston/ London, 1984, 217-234.
24. “On the Meaning of Norm Sentences, Normative Inconsistency, and Normative Entailment. A Reply to Carlos E. Alchourrón and Eugenio Bulygin”, *Rechtstheorie*, 1984, 465-475.

25. "Freedom, Range for Action, and the Ontology of Norms", *Synthese*, 1985, 307-324.

26. "The Expressive Conception of Norms - an Impasse for the Logic of Norms", 5 *Law and Philosophy*, 165-198 (1985).

27. "Logic and the Pure Theory of Law" in *Essays on Kelsen,* R. Tur and W. Twining (eds.), Oxford, 1986, 187-199.

28. "Der normenlogische Skeptizismus", *Rechtstheorie*, 1986, 13-81.

29. "Angst vor dem menschlichen Wahn" in *Fanatismus und Massenwahn,* A. Grabner-Haider e.a. (eds.), Graz, 1987, 4-34.

30. "The Role of Rules", *Ratio Juris*, 1988, 224-240.

31. "Verfassungstheorie vom Standpunkt des neuen Institutionalismus", *A.R.S.P.*, 1990, 100-118.

32. "The Logic of Norms Founded on Descriptive Language", *Ratio Juris*, 1991, 284-307.

33. "Neoinstitucionalismus a teorie politiky" (Neo-Institutionalism and the theory of politics) in *Pocta prof. Victoru Knappovi, Právník,* 1993, 985-990.

34. "Habermas on Democracy and Justice. Limits of a Sound Conception", *Ratio Juris*,1994, 239-253.

35. "Natural Constituents of Justice", 13 *Law and Philosophy*, 1-25 (1994).

36. "Zwei Hauptprobleme der modernen Demokratie", *Journal für Rechtspolitik*,1995, 1-9.

37. "Normological Inference and the Generation of Legal Norms", *Ratio Juris*, 1995, 261-270.

38. "Luhmann's Approach to Ethics, Jurisprudence, and Legal Sociology", *A.R.S.P.*, 1996, 543-552.

39. "Basic Puzzle of Discourse Philosophy", *Ratio Juris*, 1996, 172-181.

40. "Information and Human Liberty", *Ratio Juris*,1996, 248-257.

41. "Handlungsentscheidung als Optimierungsprozess" in *Normative Systems in Legal and Moral Theory. Festschrift für Eugenio Bulygin and Gedächtnisschrift für Carlos E. Alchourrón*, W. Krawietz, e. a. (eds.), Berlin, 1997, 153-161.

Law and Philosophy Library

1. E. Bulygin, J.-L. Gardies and I. Niiniluoto (eds.): *Man, Law and Modern Forms of Life*. With an Introduction by M.D. Bayles. 1985 ISBN 90-277-1869-5
2. W. Sadurski: *Giving Desert Its Due*. Social Justice and Legal Theory. 1985 ISBN 90-277-1941-1
3. N. MacCormick and O. Weinberger: *An Institutional Theory of Law*. New Approaches to Legal Positivism. 1986 ISBN 90-277-2079-7
4. A. Aarnio: *The Rational as Reasonable*. A Treatise on Legal Justification. 1987 ISBN 90-277-2276-5
5. M.D. Bayles: *Principles of Law*. A Normative Analysis. 1987 ISBN 90-277-2412-1; Pb: 90-277-2413-X
6. A. Soeteman: *Logic in Law*. Remarks on Logic and Rationality in Normative Reasoning, Especially in Law. 1989 ISBN 0-7923-0042-4
7. C.T. Sistare: *Responsibility and Criminal Liability*. 1989 ISBN 0-7923-0396-2
8. A. Peczenik: *On Law and Reason*. 1989 ISBN 0-7923-0444-6
9. W. Sadurski: *Moral Pluralism and Legal Neutrality*. 1990 ISBN 0-7923-0565-5
10. M.D. Bayles: *Procedural Justice*. Allocating to Individuals. 1990 ISBN 0-7923-0567-1
11. P. Nerhot (ed.): *Law, Interpretation and Reality*. Essays in Epistemology, Hermeneutics and Jurisprudence. 1990 ISBN 0-7923-0593-0
12. A.W. Norrie: *Law, Ideology and Punishment*. Retrieval and Critique of the Liberal Ideal of Criminal Justice. 1991 ISBN 0-7923-1013-6
13. P. Nerhot (ed.): *Legal Knowledge and Analogy*. Fragments of Legal Epistemology, Hermeneutics and Linguistics. 1991 ISBN 0-7923-1065-9
14. O. Weinberger: *Law, Institution and Legal Politics*. Fundamental Problems of Legal Theory and Social Philosophy. 1991 ISBN 0-7923-1143-4
15. J. Wróblewski: *The Judicial Application of Law*. Edited by Z. Bańkowski and N. MacCormick. 1992 ISBN 0-7923-1569-3
16. T. Wilhelmsson: *Critical Studies in Private Law*. A Treatise on Need-Rational Principles in Modern Law. 1992 ISBN 0-7923-1659-2
17. M.D. Bayles: *Hart's Legal Philosophy*. An Examination. 1992 ISBN 0-7923-1981-8
18. D.W.P. Ruiter: *Institutional Legal Facts*. Legal Powers and their Effects. 1993 ISBN 0-7923-2441-2
19. J. Schonsheck: *On Criminalization*. An Essay in the Philosophy of the Criminal Law. 1994 ISBN 0-7923-2663-6
20. R.P. Malloy and J. Evensky (eds.): *Adam Smith and the Philosophy of Law and Economics*. 1994 ISBN 0-7923-2796-9
21. Z. Bańkowski, I. White and U. Hahn (eds.): *Informatics and the Foundations of Legal Reasoning*. 1995 ISBN 0-7923-3455-8

Law and Philosophy Library

22. E. Lagerspetz: *The Opposite Mirrors*. An Essay on the Conventionalist Theory of Institutions. 1995 ISBN 0-7923-3325-X
23. M. van Hees: *Rights and Decisions*. Formal Models of Law and Liberalism. 1995 ISBN 0-7923-3754-9
24. B. Anderson: *"Discovery" in Legal Decision-Making*. 1996 ISBN 0-7923-3981-9
25. S. Urbina: *Reason, Democracy, Society*. A Study on the Basis of Legal Thinking. 1996 ISBN 0-7923-4262-3
26. E. Attwooll: *The Tapestry of the Law*. Scotland, Legal Culture and Legal Theory. 1997 ISBN 0-7923-4310-7
27. J.C. Hage: *Reasoning with Rules*. An Essay on Legal Reasoning and Its Underlying Logic. 1997 ISBN 0-7923-4325-5
28. R.A. Hillman: *The Richness of Contract Law*. An Analysis and Critique of Contemporary Theories of Contract Law. 1997 ISBN 0-7923-4336-0; 0-7923-5063-4 (Pb)
29. C. Wellman: *An Approach to Rights*. Studies in the Philosophy of Law and Morals. 1997 ISBN 0-7923-4467-7
30. B. van Roermund: *Law, Narrative and Reality*. An Essay in Intercepting Politics. 1997 ISBN 0-7923-4621-1
31. I. Ward: *Kantianism, Postmodernism and Critical Legal Thought*. 1997 ISBN 0-7923-4745-5
32. H. Prakken: *Logical Tools for Modelling Legal Argument*. A Study of Defeasible Reasoning in Law. 1997 ISBN 0-7923-4776-5
33. T. May: *Autonomy, Authority and Moral Responsibility*. 1998 ISBN 0-7923-4851-6
34. M. Atienza and J.R. Manero: *A Theory of Legal Sentences*. 1998 ISBN 0-7923-4856-7
35. E.A. Christodoulidis: *Law and Reflexive Politics*. 1998 ISBN 0-7923-4954-7
36. L.M.M. Royakkers: *Extending Deontic Logic for the Formalisation of Legal Rules*. 1998 ISBN 0-7923-4982-2
37. J.J. Moreso: *Legal Indeterminacy and Constitutional Interpretation*. 1998 ISBN 0-7923-5156-8
38. W. Sadurski: *Freedom of Speech and Its Limits*. 1999 ISBN 0-7923-5523-7
39. A.R. Lodder: *DiaLaw*. On Legal Justification and Dialogical Models of Argumentation. 1999 ISBN 0-7923-5830-9

KLUWER ACADEMIC PUBLISHERS – DORDRECHT / BOSTON / LONDON